34·95

Therapeutic Processes for Communication Disorders

Why do many people with disorders of communication experience a sense of demoralization? Do these subjective experiences have any bearing on how such problems should be treated? How can professionals dealing with speech, language, hearing and other communication disorders analyze and respond to the subjective and relational needs of clients with such problems?

In this book, authors in the fields of communication disorders analyze the psychological, social, and linguistic processes and interactions that underpin clinical practice, from both client and clinician perspectives. The chapters demonstrate how it is possible to analyze and understand client–clinician discourse using qualitative research, and describe various challenges to establishing relationships such as cultural, gender, and age differences. The authors go on to describe self-care processes, the therapeutic use of the self, and various psychological factors that could be important for developing therapeutic relationships. Also covered are the rarely considered topics of spirituality and transpersonal issues, which may at times be relevant to clinicians working with clients who have debilitating, degenerative, and terminal illnesses associated with certain communication disorders.

While this book is geared toward the needs of practicing and training speech-language and hearing clinicians, other professional such as teachers of the deaf, psychotherapists, nurses, and occupational therapists will find the ideas relevant, interesting and easily translatable for use in their own clinical practice.

Robert J. Fourie is a qualified speech-language therapist, audiologist and psychologist working and living in Cork. He is currently a lecturer in speech and hearing sciences at University College Cork in Ireland.

Therapeutic Processes for Communication Disorders

A guide for clinicians and students

Edited by Robert J. Fourie

Ψ Psychology Press
Taylor & Francis Group

HOVE AND NEW YORK

First published 2011
by Psychology Press
27 Church Road, Hove, East Sussex BN3 2FA

Simultaneously published in the USA and Canada
by Psychology Press
270 Madison Avenue, New York, NY 10016

Psychology Press is an imprint of the Taylor & Francis Group, an Informa business

Copyright © 2011 Psychology Press

Typeset in Times by RefineCatch Limited, Bungay, Suffolk
Printed and bound in Great Britain by
TJ International Ltd, Padstow, Cornwall
Cover design by Lisa Dynan

British Library Cataloguing in Publication Data
A catalogue record for this book is available from the British Library

Library of Congress Cataloging-in-Publication Data
    Therapeutic processes for communication disorders : a guide for
    students and clinicians / edited by Robert J. Fourie.
      p; cm.
    Includes bibliographical references and index.
    ISBN: 978–1–84872–041–1 (hbk)
    1. Communicative disorders—Treatment. 2. Speech therapist and
    patient. 3. Speech therapy. I. Fourie, Robert J.
    [DNLM: 1. Communication Disorders—therapy. 2. Professional-
    Patient Relations. WL 340.2 T398 2010]
    RC423.T46 2010
    362.196′855—dc22
                                              2010017997

ISBN: 978–1–84872–041–1 (hbk)

Contents

List of figures and tables	ix
List of contributors	xi
Preface	xiii

PART I

Focussing on the client   1

1 **Ruminations of an old man: A 50-year perspective on clinical practice**   3
DAVID LUTERMAN

2 **From alienation to therapeutic dialogue**   9
ROBERT J. FOURIE

3 **Shaping practice: The benefits of really attending to the person's story**   21
ROZANNE BARROW

4 **Exploring clinical interaction in speech-language therapy: Narrative, discourse and relationships**   35
NINA SIMMONS-MACKIE AND JACK S. DAMICO

5 **Product and process depictions of rapport between clients and their speech-language pathologists during clinical interactions**   53
IRENE P. WALSH AND JUDITH FELSON DUCHAN

6 **Clinical linguistic proficiency: Managing multiparty interactions**   67
ALISON FERGUSON

7   Challenges to therapeutic processes: The cross-
    cultural context   79
    LINDA HAND

8   Exploring gender and power in clinical encounters   93
    MARY-PAT O'MALLEY

9   How audiologists and speech-language
    pathologists can foster and combat stigma in people with
    communication disorders   105
    DAVID DOWNS

10 Establishing relationships in speech-language
    therapy when working alongside people with mental
    health disorders   123
    IRENE P. WALSH AND DANA KOVARSKY

11 Constructivism and adaptive leadership: Framing an
    approach for clinicians to overcome barriers to counseling 139
    ANTHONY DILOLLO

12 The social construction of relationships in healing
    interactions from ancient times to the present   153
    JUDITH FELSON DUCHAN

PART II
Focussing on the clinician   167

13 The transference relationship in speech-language therapy   169
    KIRSTY MCDONALD

14 Self-reflection in clinical practice   183
    ELLEN-MARIE SILVERMAN

15 Using oneself as a vehicle for change in relational
    and reflective practice   195
    ELAINE GELLER

16 Burnout and self-care in the practice of speech
    pathology and audiology: An ecological perspective   213
    ELEANOR ROSS

17 Spiritual dimensions of the clinical relationship   229

CINDY S. SPILLERS

References   245
Appendix   273
Author index   275
Subject index   281

Figures and tables

Figures

3.1   Some of the oscillating processes that merge to form
      practice   25
3.2   Information from externalizing conversations with Eleanor   29
3.3   Information from externalizing conversations with Maeve   30
3.4   "Hearing the story" – the benefits of really attending   32
11.1 Iterative model for adaptive leadership for therapy   150
13.1 Transference   171
17.1 Alonso's picture of his stuttering   234

Tables

5.1   Differences between product and process views of rapport   64
7.1   Content of talk on language and culture   83
11.1 Similarities between aspects of constructivist counseling
      and adaptive leadership   149

Contributors

Rozanne Barrow is at the Department of Speech and Language Therapy, Beaumont Hospital, Dublin, Ireland.

Jack S. Damico is at the Department of Communicative Disorders, the University of Louisiana, Lafayette, LA, USA.

Anthony DiLollo is at the Department of Communication Sciences and Disorders, Wichita State University, Wichita, KS, USA.

David Downs is at the Department of Communication Sciences and Disorders, Wichita State University, Wichita, KS, USA.

Judith Felson Duchan is at the Department of Communicative Disorders and Sciences, State University of New York at Buffalo, Buffalo, NY, USA.

Alison Ferguson is at the School of Humanities and Social Sciences, University of Newcastle, NSW, Australia.

Robert J. Fourie is at the Department of Speech and Hearing Sciences, University College Cork, Ireland.

Elaine Geller is at the Department of Communication Sciences and Disorders, Long Island University, Brooklyn Campus, NY, USA.

Linda Hand is at the Division of Speech Science, Department of Psychology, University of Auckland, Tamaki, Auckland, New Zealand.

Dana Kovarsky is at Department of Communicative Disorders, University of Rhode Island, Kingston, RI, USA.

David Luterman is at the Department of Communication Sciences and Disorders, Emerson College, Boston, MA, USA.

Kirsty McDonald is at the Department of Speech and Language Therapy, Northern General Hospital, Sheffield, UK.

Mary-Pat O'Malley is at the Discipline of Speech and Language Therapy, National University of Ireland, Galway, Ireland.

Eleanor Ross is at the Department of Social Work, School of Human and Community Development, University of the Witwatersrand, Johannesburg, South Africa.

Ellen-Marie Silverman is a private practitioner, The Speech Source, Inc., Whitefish Bay, WI, USA.

Nina Simmons-Mackie is at the Department of Communication Sciences and Disorders, Southeastern Louisiana University, Louisiana, LA, USA.

Cindy S. Spillers is at the Department of Communication Sciences and Disorders, University of Minnesota, Duluth, MN, USA.

Irene P. Walsh is at the Department of Clinical Speech and Language Studies, Trinity College, Dublin, Ireland.

Preface

In ancient Greek dramas, a character would often step forward to explain the context of the upcoming play so that the audience might better interpret the meanings and significances of the play. In a similar way, it is necessary for me as the editor of this volume to step forward to explain the context, background, and reasons for choosing this topic as interesting, relevant, and important to the professions encompassing communication disorders and audiology.

As a practicing speech-language therapist and audiologist, I have worked in various settings including schools for the deaf, and universities; both as lecturer and as clinical supervisor. During my practice as a clinician, I often noticed how the relationships between myself and my clients, whether they were children, parents of children, or adults, played a key role in determining how well the therapy seemed to progress; how much clients committed to the process of therapy; and indeed my own commitment, well-being, and enjoyment of the work. Similarly, I reflected with my colleagues with regard to the differences between how teachers (or physicians) would deal with a clinical problem, and how speech and hearing therapists would deal with it.

I recall a conversation I had with my clinical manager in which we discussed these very things and asked each other: "What does it mean to be a therapist and therapeutic; what makes us different to other professions such as physicians and nurses? And what makes therapy *therapeutic*?" These intriguing questions return to me whenever I reflect on my practice as a clinician. For example, I noticed a qualitative difference in the way my child clients with hearing impairments related to me and the way I observed them relating to their teachers. Consequently, I wondered if this qualitative difference could be measured, described, or teased out in some way and made more explicit. At that time I suspected that without the agenda of a school curriculum, clinicians could focus on developmental goals and the well-being associated with improved communication. However, there is more to it than that. Clinicians generally work on a one-to-one level with individuals who have lost their ability to easily regulate their relationships through communication. Invariably, the special quality of a relationship evolves to provide a context for working together to restore this regulation of relationships and thus improve the client's quality of life. Such relationships typically involve a type of "flow" in which working together successfully becomes possible. On the other hand, I have had personal experiences of what it is like when such flow does not occur; and things do not work out so well. Such working relationships can be quite uncomfortable and uneasy, and do not aid the achievement of clinical goals.

I have also noticed how therapists in training, with high anxiety levels and a hyper-focus on the apparently curative psycholinguistic activities of therapy, can forget to establish a person-to-person relationship with their clients; and thus sabotage their attempts to achieve their psycholinguistic or medical goals. Specifically, I noticed how anxiety, due to inexperience, influenced the clinical interactions of some students; thus in turn resulting in anxiety in the client and an associated difficulty focussing on tasks. However, when I turned to the literature to better understand these issues I found there were few books and only a handful of published research papers covering these topics in communication disorders. I therefore invited authors to contribute to this book in order for them to provide a blend of personal opinions, common sense, clinical perspectives, philosophical stances, and research in progress.

Contributors to this book are from, Ireland, Britain, South Africa, the United States, Australia, and New Zealand and thus generally reflect ideas from the English-speaking world and they all have extensive experience working in the fields of communication disorders and audiology. As such this book is a unique collection covering a range of topics rarely covered in the literature. However, many of the data examples reported in these chapters are still in the process of being reworked for peer review; and in some cases represent provisional theoretical attempts at analysis. Therefore, the reader should understand that these data are illustrative rather than conclusive at this time. Furthermore, the chapters in this book are not homogeneous and do not necessarily agree in all respects with each other; in fact, some authors lay out quite different perspectives. Nevertheless, I believe that these differences create an authentic intellectual texture for thinking about therapeutic relationships in practice. While most of the chapters in this book have an inductive, qualitative focus, I believe that this focus provides a starting point for further research, both quantitative and qualitative.

The book is divided into two parts, with the first part focussing on the client and the second on the clinician. In Chapter 1, David Luterman looks back on 50 years of clinical practice and outlines 10 useful principles for clinical intervention based on his own clinical experiences. In Chapter 2, I examine how clients become demoralized and alienated by their experiences of losing their abilities to eat or communicate. In Chapter 3, Rozanne Barrow explains how hearing the perspective of the client makes intervention more meaningful. In Chapter 4, Nina Simmons-Mackie and Jack Damico explore narrative-based therapy with particular reference to how relationships arise in the context of clinical discourse. In Chapter 5, Irene Walsh and Judith Felson Duchan assess the assumptions underlying various conceptions of "rapport". In Chapter 6, Alison Ferguson discusses the management of clinical relationships in which the client is accompanied or in a group. In Chapter 7, Linda Hand discusses how cultural contexts shape and challenge therapeutic processes. In Chapter 8, Mary-Pat O'Malley explores power dynamics within speech-language therapy and how such dynamics can hinder the process of therapy. In Chapter 9, David Downs assesses the role of stigma in clinical dynamics and how clinicians might counteract it. In Chapter 10, Irene Walsh and Dana Kovarsky provide some guidance for understanding clinical dynamics when working with people who have mental health disorders. In Chapter 11, Anthony DiLollo examines barriers to counseling from a constructivist perspective and promotes the concept of adaptive leadership in therapy. In Chapter 12, Judith Felson Duchan provides a history of clinical interaction through the ages, which is relevant to informing current practices in speech-language therapy. In Chapter 13, Kirsty McDonald applies ideas from psychotherapy, such as transference and projective identification, to the area of clinical interaction in speech-language therapy. In Chapter 14, Ellen-Marie Silverman describes how clinicians can improve their practice by engaging in clinical reflection. In Chapter 15, Elaine Geller describes the idea of the clinical use of self in clinical relationships and how the clinician's own thoughts, feelings, and values can promote good practice in therapy. In Chapter 16, Eleanor Ross provides information and guidelines on how therapists can care for themselves and thereby prevent burnout. Finally, in Chapter 17, Cindy Spillers explores the existential and spiritual dimensions of clinical practice.

I hope you the reader will find each chapter as interesting as I did. I would like to thank each of the authors for their excellent contributions to this volume. Finally, I hope this book will inspire clinicians, old and new; and that it will lead to more research in this intriguing area of practice in communication disorders.

Robert Fourie, Editor
April, 2010

Part I
Focussing on the client

1 Ruminations of an old man

A 50-year perspective on clinical practice

David Luterman
Emerson College, Boston

INTRODUCTION

I have been blessed with 50 years of active clinical involvement. I began my professional life as a diagnostic audiologist and morphed into a rehabilitation audiologist, specializing in helping families of newly diagnosed hearing-impaired children make the transition to their new reality. I feel incredibly fortunate to have stumbled into my life work and have found a niche that nourishes me and at the same time benefits others. To participate in and facilitate the personal growth of clients provides moments of grace that makes our profession so worthwhile. Immersed in my life journey it seemed disjointed; from this vantage point it seems inevitable. At this stage in my life, I find myself more reflective with a strong desire to look back, distil my clinical experience and pass it on to current and future generations of clinicians. Here then is the "Luterman 10."

1 GRIEF IS NOT PATHOLOGY

At heart, we are grief workers. We are dealing with people undergoing transitions in their lives because they have lost the life they thought they were going to have; whether this is the parent of an autistic child or the spouse of a patient with aphasia or the adult child of a parent who is living in a nursing home and who has a swallowing disorder. Grief is not culture bound or disability specific: it is endemic to disability. While many things have changed in our profession, the human equation is unchanging; we are dealing with clients who are emotionally *upset not emotionally disturbed*. Grieving and the concomitant feelings are a normal response when a person is suddenly confronted with a life challenge for which there was no preparation; as a profession we need to give ourselves permission to do the necessary grief work. While technology may have altered the therapeutic landscape, it does not bypass the need to interact with our clients on an emotional plane.

2 IGNORING THE EMOTIONAL COMPONENT CAN BE PERILOUS

When people are emotionally upset they cannot process information well. I had to learn this the hard way as a practicing diagnostic audiologist. After making the diagnosis of hearing loss in a child, my notion of counseling at that time was to give information. I rapidly developed set speeches about the audiogram, hearing aid maintenance and educational options. I gave these mini-lectures without recourse to the parent's emotional state. What I learned on subsequent evaluations, much to my dismay, was that they retained almost nothing of what I had said. They were much too upset to retain much content and, in fact, I had overwhelmed them with information and contributed to their fear and anxiety. Especially in the early stages of diagnosis, people are helped best by being allowed to grieve.

I have found that people are seldom allowed to grieve as most people conspire to make them feel better. They do this by instilling hope ("they will find a cure") or by positive comparisons ("It could be worse he could have . . ."). All this serves to do is to emotionally isolate the person and deny them the freedom to grieve. What people in emotional pain often need the most is to be listened to and have their feelings validated. This is counterintuitive for most people as the tendency is to want to take the pain away by solving the problem or distracting them. I have learned that I cannot take the pain away; these disabilities represent a loss and that loss will always be there, despite anything I might say or do. What I can take away is "feeling bad about feeling bad."

Once as I was beginning to facilitate a support group for parents of newly diagnosed deaf children, one mother looked at me and said "you are going to make me cry" and I said to her "No. I am going to give you permission to cry," whereupon she started to cry. In the past I would have felt guilty that I caused that parent to cry; what I have come to understand is that I am not putting the feelings in but creating the conditions that enable the feelings to emerge. What I have also come to understand is that feelings just *are*; you do not have to be responsible for how you feel but always for how you behave. This notion has enabled me to enter the realm of feelings with clients to their benefit because embracing painful feelings is the first step in healing. The current emphasis on evidence-based practice I find worrisome because emotional growth does not readily lend itself to measurement, yet it is in the emotional realm where a great deal of the action takes place. Communications are best achieved when there is both content and affect components present. I hope we can learn, as a profession to balance our content counseling with our affect counseling and value both equally.

3 COUNSELING IS NOT ABOUT MAKING CLIENTS FEEL GOOD

The purpose of counseling is not necessarily to make people feel better, the entertainment industry does that. The goal of counseling should be to empower clients so that they can make self-enhancing decisions for themselves and their family members. In the course of the counseling experience, painful feelings will emerge including anger. I have always seen the emergence of the painful feelings as a positive sign because these clients are not in denial and if I am mindful of my role, they will take ownership of the communication disorder; there can be no meaningful change without ownership of the problem by the client. This ceding of responsibility to the client is often in itself painful for clients, as frequently they prefer a passive role in the habilitation process hoping and expecting the professional to "fix" it.

4 LISTENING IS OUR MOST IMPORTANT CLINICAL TOOL

As a beginning clinician I assumed my professional role was to give information and direction to the client; that I needed to be a very active participant in the therapeutic process. I had a "lesson plan" mentality with specific goals in mind and my scripted mini-lectures were designed to ensure that clients left our encounter with the information that I thought they needed. In retrospect, I can see that the set speeches and advice giving were a reflection of my own insecurities and need to limit the clinical interaction in predictable, content-based ways that I could manage. Listening to the client without a pre-conceived "lesson plan" enables the client to participate more fully in the therapeutic endeavor; it forces clients to be active in the relationship. Listening for client affect and reflecting it back enables the client to identify their feelings and express them in a safe relationship; this attenuates client isolation and validates their feelings. Listening deeply to our clients is a great gift we can give them.

As I have become more self-confident in my clinical skills I have been able to cede more and more control of the therapeutic process to the client. Learning proceeds best when the learner is an active participant in the process. Listening enables the clients to reveal themselves allowing me to find ways to be most helpful; the client will teach us if we listen. I had to learn to cultivate the art of not doing and at the same time being present for the client. The irony here is that often the less I do the more the client learns.

5 OVER-HELPING TEACHES HELPLESSNESS

In the early stages of diagnosis, clients are usually overwhelmed and feeling very inadequate to cope with the disability. This is a critical juncture for the clinician because the tendency is to want to rescue the client from their actual and felt inadequacy. If we rescue by advice giving and taking responsibility away from the client we can contribute to their fear and sense of inadequacy. It is very easy to teach helplessness and create the dependent client who then accepts a passive role, expecting the clinician to fix it. I have had to learn how to be responsible *to* my clients rather than being responsible *for* them. Finding the therapeutic equator of helping is not easy because it is constantly shifting with each client and at different times with a client. I have had to learn to trust clients to eventually make the best decision for them, and that wisdom resides within the client. My role is to judiciously share my information as the client needs it and asks for it. I avoid giving advice and assuming responsibility for the client at all costs. Enhancing the client's self-esteem is the premier goal of the therapeutic encounter, thereby creating the independent client who no longer needs us.

6 THE SUPPORT GROUP IS AN INVALUABLE CLINICAL VEHICLE

It is hard for me to conceive of a program that does not include a support group. Having a catastrophic event in your life becomes emotionally isolating because almost everyone in the client's everyday life is invalidating his or her painful feelings, while seldom understanding what the client is experiencing. The support group is usually the one place that individuals are understood; feelings can be validated and help can be given and received. Professionals, by nonjudgmental listening, can validate feelings, but lack the instant credibility that the members of a support group have. Support groups are not disability specific; I think they are especially helpful for the families of clients who are often on the periphery of clinical services. Mixed support groups, where there are clients and family members, are very challenging to facilitate but usually helpful in promoting family unity. My major clinical role in the past 45 years has been as a group facilitator for parents of young deaf children. I have found this to be an immensely rewarding activity; every group has presented unique challenges and has invariably taught me something valuable

7 A COLLABORATIVE FAMILY-CENTERED MODEL IS THE MOST EFFICIENT ONE

It is unfortunate that students in our training programs are seldom exposed to a family-centered model of service delivery; the individual pullout model seems to be one of choice. I think this is an easier model to select for the beginning therapist as he or she need only focus on the identified patient. Unfortunately, this is the least efficient way of working with clients. By working with the family unit, we can extend the goals of therapy to the home and create a milieu that is supportive of change. This model requires a greater skill set of a therapist because it mandates working with family members who do not have an overt communication disorder. Families also need to be broadly defined to include the milieu of the client whether this is a hospital setting or a classroom. Training programs need to see that the pullout model is a way to start the training but students need to be quickly exposed to and trained in the broader model of a family-centered approach to service delivery; family-centered therapy needs to be the gold standard.

8 AFFIRMATIONS ARE WORDS FOR EVERY OCCASION

Words spoken mechanically without feeling and/or out of context will never be helpful "This too shall pass" were the words the wise men came up with for the king who wanted something to say for all occasions. There are counseling words that are equally useful that I call affirmations. "It must be so hard" is an empathetic remark that validates the client's experience while "that's OK" gives sanction to the client's feelings. Probably the most useful words are "uh huh" that says to the client "I hear you. Tell me more." In a long counseling career, probably the most useful words to the clients are the ones I haven't said.

9 MISTAKES ARE NUGGETS OF GOLD

I have come to see that clinical mistakes are inevitable. Even after 50 years I still have my occasional gaffes. I have had to learn to be gentle with myself and accept the fact that errors are an inevitable consequence of clinical growth. I think any learning and growing clinician needs to be pushing at the boundaries of their comfort zone; however, in that boundary region reside errors. I have learned that the "mistake" is a useful marker for what I need to learn. I learn best from my blunders and it is only a mistake if I do it twice. Fortunately we are not brain surgeons, clients usually recover from the gaffes and there is often an opportunity to apologize and correct the error and move on; if the fundamental relationship is strong it can withstand errors.

10 SELF-CARE IS A CRITICAL COMPONENT OF CLINICAL WORK

On the surface, a counseling relationship looks conventional in that two people are in dialogue. The reality is that one person, the counselor, is helping the other by practicing selfless, deep listening. The mantra for the counselor needs to be "It's not about me." Deep listening requires that the counselor put aside all personal agendas and be there in the service of the other; this is

not an easy thing to do and rarely experienced outside of a counseling relationship. Being in service to the other is very demanding and while in many
cases technology has altered the clinical landscape, the most important clinical "tool" is still the clinician. Clinical tools need periodic care and much
like the audiologist sending the audiometer out to be recalibrated, clinicians
must take periodic timeouts to recalibrate themselves. To be a selfless listener
requires a personal centering that mandates clinicians have a fulfilling personal life; we need to be able to give to our clients from our abundance. Too
often one sees in the helping profession clinicians with strong needs to be
needed that they fulfill by creating dependent relationships. Clinical burnout
is a consequence of clinicians who do not practice good self-care and have
many dependent relationships.

Fifty years seems like a long time yet it has gone by bewilderingly fast;
it has been a marvelous ride – much better than I ever expected. I am often
asked how I have been able to remain clinically active for so long amidst
so much pain and suffering without burning out. For me it's a matter of
practicing good self-care, avoiding developing dependent relationships with
clients, and above all, understanding that personal growth is often forged in
the crucible of the pain of these disabilities. I do not see disabilities as traged-
ies but rather as powerful teachers that promote transcendence. We give to life
what life demands and the disabilities often force clients to develop capacities
that would otherwise lie latent. I love being able to participate in promoting
growth and when you love what you do it is not work; I have often been
amazed that they actually pay me to do it. I would love to be around for
another 50 years but the actuarial tables are against me.

ACKNOWLEDGMENT

Reprinted with permission from the American Academy of Audiology:
Luterman, D. (2001). Ruminations of an old man – A 50-year perspective on
clinical practice. *Audiology Today*, *22*(2), 32–37.

2 From alienation to therapeutic dialogue

Robert J. Fourie
University College Cork, Ireland

INTRODUCTION

If you listen to *People are strange*, a song by The Doors, you may hear in the lyrics allusion to the experience of being alienated. The Doors do this by creating in their song, images of a stranger in the rain, perhaps rejected, and certainly alone. The singer of this popular song is far away from home, where nobody knows his name. Perhaps the singer is a person with a communication disorder, experiencing the namelessness of aphasia, or the strangeness of stammering. Perhaps this stranger has acquired the communication disorder or maybe he has lived with it for a long time. Either way, this person seems demoralized, alienated, lost, and depressed; and is experiencing a loss of identity: perhaps not knowing who he is anymore. Perhaps his next song will be a song leading him to voice his demoralization and to seek help from one of us. Perhaps one of us will not be a strange face in the rain; and we will be able to help this strange singer to find his way home. The home of who he thought he was; who he had hoped he would become – but for the loss of his connection through communication.

Such experiences are probably most obvious, but not limited to the communication disorders following strokes, where damage can obliterate large portions of the individual's self (Brumfitt & Clarke, 1982); and could therefore evoke strong and negative emotions (Parr, Byng, Gilpin, & Ireland, 1997). According to Parr and her colleagues, thoughts of suicide are not uncommon in people who have had strokes that have interfered with their communication (Parr et al., 1997). Brumfitt and Clarke's description of the loss of communication resulting in a crisis of self-identity are illustrated as follows: "If I am no longer what I was, what on earth am I now? Perhaps I am now utterly different; just the opposite to what I was. If I was strong, am I now weak? If I felt constrained, am I now free? If I was always pushed to one side, can I now be a burden?" (Brumfitt & Clarke, 1982, p. 3). The individual asking these questions is asking questions that try to answer the universal question: Who am I? Who am I becoming? These questions seem fundamental to the life issues each of us must face in our existence (Yalom, 1980). The following poem by Walt Whitman (1860, p. 425) comes to mind:

I thought I was not alone, walking here by the shore,
But the one I thought was with me, as now I walk by the shore,
As I lean and look through the glimmering light – that one has utterly
   disappeared,
And those appear that perplex me.

Walt Whitman (1819–1892) Leaves of Grass

Is this one of whom Walt Whitman speaks, in fact, a lost aspect of his own self? Alienation is something few of us wish to contemplate because it is so negative, dark, and unappealing. Why focus on something we all hope to escape? However, as speech and hearing clinicians, we inevitably look into the shadows of other people's lives and are tasked with the job of trying to make possible something meaningful out of what we see. We are tasked with listening to our clients' stories (see Chapter 3), relating to them in an ongoing way (see Chapter 5) and accompanying our clients on a journey (Spillers, 2007; see also Chapter 17).

BEING AT HOME IN TOGETHERNESS AND THE LOSS OF CONNECTION

Being together, cooperating, and looking after each other are the love stories humans have being telling each other for millennia; and it is the plots of these stories that have guaranteed our survival in a harsh evolutionary environment. Perhaps we emulated wolves, and realized that to work together with others was more successful than being on our own (Schleidt, 1999). To be in relationship with others – to connect and to be part of something, is fundamental to human life and survival: We can be and do very little if we are not part of the lives of others.

Some of the ways in which we express this connectedness is through talking, gossiping, listening, eating together, singing together, and laughing. It is written into our genes that there is safety in numbers (Dunbar, 1996); and we all hope that if we are ever in trouble, that our friends, our family and our society will help us. We will not be alone in facing what existence has to offer. But what if, when we face the inevitabilities of suffering, loneliness, possible death, and difficult choices, we find ourselves looking at strange faces in the rain? What if the connectedness and the familiar world we knew and enjoyed when all was well, unexpectedly dissolves when troubles arrive? What if all our connectedness is gone and we are left alienated? With whom will we sing, eat, gossip, and laugh then? Who will accompany us in these harrowing moments of penetrating alienation and loneliness (Nystrom, 2006), when we can no longer communicate as we did before? Who will we be if we have changed so much?

MAKING THE SUBJECTIVE ABSTRACT AND OBJECTIVE

In the same way that Marx focussed on how captains of industry value the product of labor, rather than the qualities of the *person* producing that product (Marx, 1978), so in the field of medicine and health, clinicians can often focus on the illness and labels of illness, rather than on the experiences of the people producing such illnesses or ill health. Therefore, a dynamic, complex, and conscious system (a person) is reduced to static, linear, and simplistic labels; and the human experience of illness and suffering is somehow often overlooked. Because of this disregard for phenomenology, useful information could be lost, thus leading the practitioner to miss something vitally important to the client and to the client's health. But this process of labeling the client and undervaluing their experiences of illness, could also lead clients to inhabit positions that single them out as contaminated or deserving of isolation (see Chapter 9 on stigma in the profession).

According to Ollman (1976), alienation is a problem of the individual becoming an abstraction. What Ollman meant by this is that individuals who have become alienated have apparently lost the qualities that signal their recognition as being part of the rest of the world. "Thus denuded, the alienated person has become an 'abstraction' " (Ollman, 1976, p. 134). In other words, their unique and personal characteristics become invisible; instead replaced with abstract labels. It is this process of becoming an abstraction that is at the core of alienation according to Ollman. In the process of becoming depersonalized and objectified, individuals are estranged from their life activity (Ollman, 1976).

This process of depersonalization and alienation is demonstrated in the following conversational extract with Veronica,[1] a patient who had suffered from cancer of the tongue, and who consequently needed speech therapy. She explained to me the process of receiving a diagnosis of cancer of the tongue from a private surgeon.

Veronica: Exactly, well. You sit and you wait and you're called in. The consultant that I went into first hardly looked at me; he just looked over my head. He said, "Open your mouth." He never called me by my name and he said, "You can pay on your way out." . . . He didn't want me to ask him how he was. He said, "I'm well how are you?" Now obviously the man had a lot of people waiting for him. But I don't find that an excuse. He didn't want to know anything more about me. I was just a number. That is awful.

In this account, Veronica was acutely aware of a sensation of not being real to the surgeon. In her experience, she was merely an abstraction to him, a number – one of many numbers that needed processing for his job to be done. It is in this moment that Veronica becomes alienated. She experiences what it is like to lose one's intrinsic value in the eyes of another. In some perverted way, Veronica has become a life support system for cancer – a topic of interest for the surgeon. Wallach Bologh (1981) criticizes some practitioners of medicine who "disregard the patient as anything but a possessor of the body or illness" (Wallach Bologh, 1981, p. 190). Veronica seems invisible to the clinician; but she sees the surgeon. He does not relate to her as a real person who laughs, sings songs, and who gossips with her friends. Therefore, Veronica is simply something abstract – a number to him. In Veronica's words, "That is awful."

Of course, many would argue they would rather have an excellent surgeon with poor bedside manners than a clumsy surgeon who was very "nice." However, there may be a link between bedside manner and recovery in patients. Evidence in the field of neuroimmunology is emerging that indicates that there are multiple relationships between the central nervous system, the immune system, and the general health of the individual, which support this argument (Evans, 2003; Kop & Gottdiener, 2005). In short, the relationships between client and professional may have a real effect on the immune system and the healing process.

These ideas from neuroimmunology ring true to me. I recall myself going for an eye operation recently. The anesthetist, a senior houseman, came to take a history. I took an intense and immediate dislike to him, as I didn't like his scraggly beard, his poor pragmatics, and his unintelligible accent. Moreover, he did not seem to understand the reasons for my surgery. I was ready to book myself out of the planned surgery because I believed that an incompetent person would be in charge of keeping me alive during surgery. Luckily, shortly after this, an older and wiser professor of anesthetics, who was supervising the procedure, put my mind at ease by touching my arm, using a calm and reassuring voice, and by giving me clear information. This difference in tone certainly mattered to me; and it is clear from Veronica's comments above, that the surgeon's tone had an alienating impact on her.

LOSS OF IDENTITY, SOCIAL RECEDING, AND EMBARRASSMENT

Seeman (1959) hinted at the universality of the concept of alienation when he noted that themes of alienation permeated common sociological topics such as "powerlessness," "meaninglessness," "normlessness," "isolation," and "self-estrangement." These associations with alienation are similar to those described by Van Riper and Erickson's (1996) explanations of the multifactorial impact of the loss of speech and communication. These authors highlighted how communication disorders are associated with penalties, guilt, frustration, hostility, and anxiety; and it is not difficult to see how these labels are related to Seeman's themes of alienation.

If we no longer seem to be who we were, then perhaps we are no longer ourselves. Instead, we are strangers who our friends may not recognize: once our identities are no longer sure, then neither we nor others know how to relate to this new me. Maureen, a woman who had aphasia following a stroke, described to me the embarrassment of friends who when meeting her on the street would not stay and chat for a while: "They wouldn't want to talk to you. But I know – I can understand. Well I'd say, 'Look, it's OK, if you don't stop,' because I understand that I am a different *person*." Maureen told me that they would say "they were flying" or "going someplace else." She reported understanding that these individuals did not want to talk to her; and while she did not blame her friends for this avoidant behavior, she noted that "they couldn't do it for themselves"; and that she understood this behavior because she was "a different person." While these comments are stoic, they nevertheless hint at a loss of identity and a sense of disconnectedness from others and from herself after the onset of aphasia. Maureen said to me about this experience of losing her previous communication abilities: "When our speech is gone really and truly a lot is gone of your person, of your whole being, is gone."

This is not an insignificant statement – it is one that I have encountered with other research participants who have told me the stories of their loss of communication. It suggests that the work of speech and hearing clinicians is more than simply promoting a return to communication; and that it may involve "dis-estranging" the client and those relating to the client. This implies that clinicians need to think of ways of helping the client find continuity between their present and their past identities.

Many therapists do this. For example, some participants in my study said that their speech clinicians recognized this loss of self-identity and responded to it in a meaningful way. Veronica told me that her clinician was able to respond to this perceived loss of identity and inspired her to remember her intrinsic value.

Veronica: She pointed out to me that I haven't changed. The only thing that has changed about me is the way I'm speaking, and that's part of me *now* and I have to face up to it and that's the kind of the attitude she adopted which I felt was only *wonderful* you know. [My therapist] soon pointed out to me that I had no disability. I spoke differently and face up to that and that's it. She helped me that way.

According to Charmaz (1983), ill individuals may cause discomfort in those who relate to them, because illness strips away the social/public face of the individual. Similarly, Emerson and Enderby, in their study examining attitudes to communication disorders, reported that most of the participants in their study who had aphasia associated interactions with the general public as negative (Emerson & Enderby, 2000). This discomfort in others may then result in re-evaluations of the self and a corresponding withdrawal from those with whom the individual previously associated (Younger, 1995). It also has negative implications for employability following the onset of communication disorders.

It is this withdrawal that is caused by unfavorable evaluations by others in relation to their own comfort that may result in alienation. Younger (1995, p. 54) explains that "people who were previously friendly become embarrassed and strained in their [the sick person's] presence." Loss of communication particularly involves the loss of a socially salient activity that forms a major point of articulation between the individual and others in the individual's environment. Breakdown in this ability therefore represents an obvious discontinuity of contact between individuals.

This loss of social contact may also manifest as a perception of being invisible to others. For example, Alfred, a professor who had dysarthria, explained his sense of invisibility to others and his perception of not being taken seriously anymore. He explained how he had become aware of his dwindling social impact following the onset of Parkinson's disease, and that people paid him less attention and took him less seriously. Moreover, he found that his wife was doing all of the talking for him.

Alfred: People with diseases like mine are not inclined to be taken seriously and speech is part of this . . . If you're in a group of say five people and you're chatting, they center the attention on anybody but me. That's what I feel sometimes. It doesn't bother me because I can just stand and listen . . . My wife notices it too. She says she finds she has to do a lot of the talking if we're talking in a group, she'll do nine-tenths of the talking. I know that people don't take me as seriously as they did 10 years ago.

According to Bunning (2004), changing role allocations are an important influential factor to be considered by speech-language therapists. In the case of Alfred, it seemed that he was painfully aware of this loss of identity and his changing role. This sense of being invisible was evident in others I interviewed. For example, Jack, a client with aphasia who had suffered from stammering prior to his stroke, said the following to me: "I cannot say things fast enough. If there is a group speaking, I feel that I cannot speak very well in that group to attract their attention. I'm too slow. I was always sidelined, but I'm more so now." In this situation, Jack was unable to find a meaningful self in an unequal interaction and then lost his "identity as [a] meaningful contributor to the interaction process" (Twining, 1980, p. 426).

Taken to an extreme, alienation may involve not only estrangement and withdrawal from others, but may also involve an estrangement from the self. One dimension of self-estrangement may involve an estrangement from one's physical body. Clarkson (2003, p. 213) referred to this type of alienation as being "alienated from your own physiology." This sense of estrangement from your own physiology was evident in Priscilla, a singing teacher I interviewed, who herself had suffered from vocal cord nodules. Her difficulties producing a singing voice had led to embarrassment and disappointment in her abilities as a singing teacher. She told me: "And it's embarrassing. There are days that I'm their singing teacher and I can't sing what my students are doing, you know, and that's really a horrible situation to be in you know. I know how they should do it. I know how they should approach it, yet I can't do it myself."

Seeman (1959) related self-estrangement to the idea that the individual might only understand their value in relation to their usefulness to others, and not in terms of their own intrinsic value. In this situation, Priscilla understood her own significance contingent upon the presence of a good voice – and her embarrassment and disappointment revealed an attenuated self-valuing associated with the problem of vocal cord nodules. To me, Priscilla seemed really demoralized by her persistent vocal cord nodules.

DEMORALIZATION

Most of the participants in my research on the therapeutic relationship (Fourie, 2009), were demoralized. This demoralization can also be seen as a type of alienation similar to Seeman's (1959) themes of "powerlessness," "meaninglessness," "normlessness," "isolation," and "self-estrangement." While most individuals must face such existential issues in their lives (Spillers, 2007), the onset of a communication disorder is likely to accentuate such processes. For example, Ian, who had suffered from dysphagia following cancer, explained his sense of demoralization: "I first came here *very* sick not feeling good at all. I feel a lot better than I did when I first came. I was very pretty, I won't say depressed, but I mean down in the dumps." Ian was not alone in this regard. Veronica, the participant who had suffered from tongue cancer, and had subsequently received a partial glossectomy, told me that when she first came to therapy, she believed: "[she] would never ever be able to pick up the pieces that [she had] left over and [teary voice] were gone."

Writing from the perspective of psychotherapists, Frank and Frank (1991) explained their theory that most individuals seeking help in therapy seemed to do so, not because of their symptoms *per se*, but for the resultant sense of demoralization they experienced because of their symptoms. These authors referred to this as their "demoralization hypothesis." More specifically, they defined demoralization as an individual's inability to "live up to their own or others' expectations for mastering a situation or controlling their own responses to the world around them" (Frank & Frank, 1991, p. 53). This is similar to Seeman's (1959) description of meaninglessness in alienation, as the valuing of productive efficiency over autonomy and insight.

Conceivably, this may also be the case with clients who have communication disorders; or the parents or children of clients. In my own research on the therapeutic relationship (Fourie, 2009), alienation was cited as the starting point for narratives regarding participants' experiences of therapy; and the enactment by speech-language therapists of various therapeutic qualities and actions resulted in the alleviation of alienation (Fourie, 2009).

Perhaps this highlights that the ultimate goal of speech-language therapy is linked to helping clients live through and maybe resolve existential issues such as alienation and loneliness, which are often the inevitable resultants of the loss of communication (Nystrom, 2006). Therefore as clinicians concerned with communication, we need to be looking between the lines. Ostensible reasons for receiving therapy or (re)habilitation may be obvious: stuttering; loss of voice; aphasia. But the real reason for seeking or accepting help may not be so much the disorder itself, but because of the demoralization associated with the loss of social interconnectedness, cohesion, and the security inherent in group life. Our connection with others provides every individual with a sense of shelter, well-being and protection from the harshness of life. Perhaps our job then is also to "re-moralize" and help restore connections and the well-being that is associated with gossiping, listening, laughing, and singing.

DISCONNECTION AND THE LOSS OF DIALOGUE

Younger notes that alienation may not be so much about the suffering created by adversity *per se*; but about the secondary loss of connectedness and community the adversity elicits in the individual. It is therefore a *second* level of suffering that compounds the first (Younger, 1995). This is in harmony with the ideas of Twining (1980), who suggested that alienation should be viewed as a relational concept that involves a consideration of how the individual relates to family and social situations (see also Chapter 16 on stress and burnout to understand how this may also apply to the therapist). Ollman (1976) conceives of alienation, stripped down to its essential components as a disintegration or decomposition of elements that belong naturally together – a sort of dis-synergy. Therefore, those who are alienated do not feel that they belong, or are in harmony with a collective unit. The "other" is therefore a "face in the rain." Similarly, Twining states that alienation can be defined as: ". . . an interactional, or relational, consequence of a negative encounter of some duration which involves the degree of felt separateness from fundamental social situations in which self is being defined" (Twining, 1980, p. 422). Twining suggests that alienation is essentially relational in character and that unless the individual can interpret interactions with others positively or with an alternate focus, alienation follows. This is particularly the case when the individual interprets an interaction as resulting in a loss of control/power and/or a negative evaluation of the self (Twining, 1980).

According to Younger (1995, p. 56), suffering undermines an individual's ability to communicate what they are experiencing to others: "The tendency of pain and suffering is not simply to resist expression but to destroy the capacity for speech by breaking off the autonomous voice, making it cry out when agony wants it to cry and be silent when agony wants its silence, turning it on and off without the autonomous will of the person." This is the double-edged sword of the communication disorder: both autonomy and dialogue are damaged. First, in terms of the physical loss of speech ("loss of the outer voice"); and second, by the loss associated with the internal or psychological ("loss of inner voice") which may accompany any eating or communication disorder.

Younger cites Erik Erikson's belief that it is the professional's work to care for the client in this position by " 'cherishing' and 'caressing' that which in its helplessness emits signals of despair" (Erikson, 1982, pp. 59–60, cited in Younger, 1995); and thereby give expression to the inner voice, which is made silent in its experience of loss. Loss of speech, language, and hearing, therefore impairs mutual dialogue and common purpose. Perhaps then, at least some of the work of the clinician should be aimed at dealing with this "inner aphonia."

DIALOGUE AND COMMON PURPOSE

According to Rowan and Jacobs, in psychotherapy, particularly in the Jungian traditions "being together," mutuality, and the equality that fosters meaningful dialogue are highlighted as an essential part of therapy. Dialogue arises when the therapist experiences the client as they truly are (Rowan & Jacobs, 2002). In other words, this meaningful dialogue is only possible when both partners do not view each other as abstractions. This is no different for clinicians working with speech, language, and hearing disorders. Many clients of speech-language therapists describe the experience of being accepted by the speech-language pathologist as they truly are, without explanation or reason as significant for regaining a sense of mutuality and common purpose (Fourie, 2009). Loss of dialogue brings up the existential position of loneliness – and the anticipation of endless aloneness. Part of the meaningfulness of therapy can be generated when the clinician consciously enables a natural connection with their client (Nystrom, 2006; Spillers, 2007, and Chapter 17) (For a contrasting example, see Robillard's, 1999, experience of a speech-language therapist, reported in Chapter 8, this volume). Therefore, it is not difficult to see how the role of the speech and hearing clinician in therapy may involve helping the client deal with such existential positions within the context of meaningful dialogue. By understanding the context of a speech or hearing disorder, and by communicating ordinary social interest, the therapist and client engage in a process of entering a real, two-way person-to-person relationship, which may facilitate a willingness to engage and be transformed in the process of relating to one who understands (Fourie, 2009).

Perhaps also, the clinician is transformed in this dialogic interaction (see Chapter 13 on transference, counter-transference and projective identification). Rowan and Jacobs (2002, p. 50) state the following: "Dialogue is what emerges when you and I come together in an authentically contactful manner. Dialogue is not 'you plus I', but rather what emerges from the interaction, which may happen when both parties make themselves present."

This conception of dialogue as genuine interaction, is reminiscent of Rogers' (1961) person-centered approach. Rogers cited research by Whitehorn and Betz (1954) in which the researchers found that clients preferred it when personal *meaning* was explored in psychotherapy, and when goals related to personality were set, rather than simplistically examining sets of symptoms (Whitehorn & Betz, 1954). While many of the goals of speech and hearing clinicians are often linguistic or medical in nature, perhaps we need to also focus on working with clients to help reinstate the meaningful dialogue that may have been lost or degraded at the onset of a communication disorder. Moreover, this work should also examine the impairment on a phenomeno-logical level. In other words, we need to help reinstate both the autonomous inner and the outer voices of our clients. If this is true, then how we as a profession assess clients may need to change focus. Speech and hearing clinicians often start rehabilitation with tests and assessments; only paying minimal lip-service to "establishing rapport" (see Chapter 5 in this volume). Many of us are very focussed on providing explicit correction and feedback, which is not a part of natural conversation (see Chapter 4 in this book). There is therefore the risk that a focus on this type of analysis and assessment could indeed further demoralize or alienate an already alienated client. In other words, the client's unique and personal characteristics become invisible, instead replaced with abstract labels. It is this process of becoming an abstraction, which is at the core of alienation, and one that I believe we as speech and hearing clinicians need to avoid with great diligence.

However, in the process of assessment and diagnosis, it becomes very easy to make the client "abstract" by reaching for formal tests and by attaching diagnostic labels. The client's "usefulness in speaking" is measured and made explicit; and this could obscure the client's inner voice and intrinsic value, thus preventing the client and therapist from entering into a meaningful dia-logue with each other. Therefore, while psycholinguistic assessments may be invaluable to clinicians for determining their own agendas in therapy, these assessments will not explain to us how to enter into the demoralized client's world, nor will they assess the client's ability to express their demoralization or alienation. They may stipulate the linguistic impact of a communication disorder; but often they fail to reveal the personal impact of a communica-tion disorder. In other words, quantification of a communication disorder, instead of being helpful to a client, could, when used improperly by a clin-ician, lead to further alienation.

The International Classification of Function (ICF), as described by the World Health Organization (WHO) can be used to think about this issue (WHO, 2001). Speech-language therapists may, at the outset of therapy, begin with a phenomenological assessment of the client's world and partici-pation restrictions; and then work backwards to activity limitations, and finally impairment as assessed by formal testing. Then, the clinician could negotiate the necessary remedial actions required to reinstate a sense of dialogue in the client while simultaneously reducing the client's sense of alienation. This does *not* mean that the therapist refrains from formal assessment, but that assessments are driven by existential and phenomenological considerations in the first instance, instead of as an afterthought. Many clinicians will attest to the power of this approach and the level of information it yields in the process of diagnosis.

THERAPEUTIC RELATIONSHIPS

Participants in my research on the therapeutic relationship in speech-language therapy were able to indicate some characteristics and actions their therapists possessed and enacted, which they believed helped them settle into therapy; and which may have facilitated their treatments (Fourie, 2009). For example, descriptions of their therapists contained shared features that surfaced as a coherent depiction of the qualities and progression of the relationships they had with their therapists. In this study, participants described therapeutic qualities (TQs) and therapeutic actions (TAs) that interacted dynamically and resulted in a therapist with "restorative poise." It was therefore possible to describe, from the client's viewpoint, the therapeutic relationship in speech-language therapy as an emergent and ongoing property of a complex interaction between a number of therapeutic attributes and actions.

More specifically, participants described therapeutic qualities in their speech-language therapists that referred to *attitudes* of being understanding, being gracious (polite, "nice," and time generous), being erudite (knowledgeable and easily able to explain things), and being inspiring. In addition, they described therapeutic actions that referred to the things therapists *did* that were therapeutic such as being confident, being soothing, being practical (concrete), and being empowering (pointing out choices for the client). In general, the participants valued the patient understanding, social skills, and the calming, practical, and empowering support provided by their clinicians throughout their treatment for acquired speech-language disorders (Fourie, 2009).

To illustrate, Veronica, cited above in relation to her negative experiences of being diagnosed with cancer of the tongue, explained how her speech-language therapist was able to use the above therapeutic attributes and actions in a way that she valued as a client.

Veronica: Oh yes, she told me . . . You have a lisp and if you can improve on it, improve on it, if you can't, she said, you're still the same person and don't apologize, say in your own mind, "This is me, this is how I am talking now and take it or leave it," that kind of an effort, which I smiled at and thought "good on you" . . . I was inclined to apologize, I'd say I've had surgery in my mouth you'll have to bear with me, and all this. I've given up all that now and I talk as I am talking and it's all due to Niamh, it's just the self-confidence she instilled in me. I couldn't explain exactly the way exactly that she got to me. But it was a beautiful way.

It is clear from this piece of narrative that Veronica's clinician was able to reinstate the dialogue that she had lost. It was through being authentically present for her client that the clinician was able to recognize despair, and to allow the voice of suffering to speak. In making a space for this voice, the client was empowered to see beyond the suffering of cancer and the loss of speech – reminded of her true essence ("I talk as I'm talking"). It is in this reconnection that the client is brought home – out of the rain – and in which alienation is no more.

CONCLUSION

Clinicians can and must deal with the psycholinguistic and audiological aspects of communication disorders. However, we also need to consider that the core reasons for clients coming to us are not about impaired, or lost, or disordered speech and hearing. People need us because they are demoralized and alienated (Frank & Frank, 1991). They are asking themselves, "who am I now?" But if our response to this is to make our clients abstract by giving them a label; or if we cannot accompany the client through this journey of suffering (Spillers, 2007), then our efforts to reinstate communication are surely in vain.

When clinicians work to understand their clients' worlds and the restricting, often alienated nature of these worlds, then they may provide more appropriate help. Indeed, the therapeutic relationship may provide the catalytic context for arriving together in dialogue at appropriate goals, assessments and treatments, which may in turn reconnect the client into wholeness from the position of alienation.

NOTE

1 Veronica and all other names are pseudonyms referring to participants in my research on the therapeutic relationship, for which ethical approval was sought and granted; and whose terms and conditions permit inclusion of this data in this book.

3 Shaping practice

The benefits of really attending to the person's story

Rozanne Barrow
Beaumont Hospital, Dublin

INTRODUCTION

> "I was just looking at the pictures and that I said it wasn't . . . that word . . . and the pictures that they're not . . . they didn't mean anything to me."

(Pat Gath)

In a column entitled "A Doctor's Best Attributes" in the *Irish Times* Health Supplement in January 2008, Muiris Houston wrote about the responses he received to an earlier request asking people to share their thoughts about the sort of doctor's attributes that best served their needs. The overwhelming response was "time": time for the person to tell their story and have its meaning acknowledged. Houston concluded that time helps to "unmask medical mystery." This struck a particular cord with me as I remember some time ago Pat, a woman with aphasia, giving a rich description of how she felt confined by the 15 minutes allocated for each of her appointments with her doctor. She related how this made her feel very anxious – and anxiety only increased her difficulties in saying what she wanted to say. Her difficulties were further compounded by what she described as the "attitude" of her doctor. Throughout consultations the doctor would look at the computer screen and for Pat, this conveyed the message that he was not listening to her – "maybe he was listening but it tells me he doesn't want to know – it's his attitude." These factors together with others resulted in unsatisfactory consultations for Pat: "I can only get out one thing – I just want to get out as soon as possible."

Pat's story resonated with others that I had heard. They led me to ask myself the following questions about how we practice.

- As practitioners what can we do to support the telling of the person's story?
- What techniques can we use that would help to ensure that we *really* hear the story?
- What is the role of all this in shaping intervention?

- What are the implications and risks for the person when a health or social care professional fails to hear their story?

I agree with Charon (2006) who said that giving a person time to tell their story provides one with "a rich, resonant grasp of another person's situation as it unfolds in time" (Charon, 2006, p. 9). A core skill in achieving this "resonant grasp" of the individual's situation is the ability to really listen for and witness the person's story as being listened to helps us to unfold and expand. It lies at the heart of working practice. Atkinson (1998, p. 35) states: "Listening well produces a safe place built on the twin pillars of trust and acceptance. There can be no room for making judgments of any kind at all. Listening well means caring for, respecting, and honouring the other person's life and story. Listening well is both an art to be learned and a gift to be given."

In attempting to answer the questions posed, I start this chapter with setting the scene by situating practice within its cultural context as it relates to illness and disability and acquired communication disability in particular. This is followed by a brief discussion around paying attention to the "particular" that draws on *narrative* both in terms of practice and in terms of "the stories we live by." *Stories we live by* are grounded in our beliefs, values, and views of the world built up over time that are shaped by our personal, societal, and cultural contexts (Barrow, 2008). I go on to explore the application of narrative as a way of working encompassing such clinical processes as assessment, intervention and therapy, tracking change and documentation. Throughout I will draw on qualitative data from both research and working practice.

SETTING THE SCENE

"Illness comes unbidden into the person's life and may then proceed to steal away his/her roles and dreams" (Swain, Clark, Parry, French, & Reynolds, 2004a p. 125). The same could be said of any acquired disability. It constitutes a significant life change that creates a "fork in one's lifeline" resulting in the need to revise one's life story. For someone who acquires a communication impairment, this poses a particular challenge as communication is the medium through which we negotiate and construct our identity for others to acknowledge and validate (Shadden, Hagstrom, & Koski, 2008).

The social meaning of a particular illness, impairment or disability strongly influences how the person and others make sense of it (Swain et al., 2004a). These meanings shape how they accommodate it into daily life. In general our understandings of illness and disability are gained through the media, folk knowledge, stories from friends, and our own prior knowledge (Gwyn, 2002). In addition, each culture draws on master narratives that serve as summaries of socially shared understandings that help us to attach meaning to experience (Nelson, 2001). People bring these understandings to health and social care encounters.

In Western culture the dominant master narrative of health care is that of modern medicine with its focus on "body-as-machine" that can be fixed (Banja, 1996; Nettleton, 1995). A qualitative study exploring the narratives (i.e. the stories one lives by) of people living with or touched by stroke and aphasia highlighted the complexity and multiple views people hold about stroke and aphasia as well as physical and communication disability (Barrow, 2004).

The narratives of the participants in this study were overwhelmingly informed by the public narratives of illness and disability. Ways of thinking about and understanding disability from this perspective can lead to a reductionist view of disability; a view that privileges a way of being that fits with our cultural predetermined norms. This is usually referred to as the medical or individual model of disability (e.g. Brisenden, 1986; Oliver, 1996). Drawing on such models of disability has been found to diminish a person's sense of personal agency (e.g. Swain, French, Barnes, & Thomas, 2004b), to be isolating with its view of singular self rather than self linked with others, and to discourage diversity as such views are shaped by global norms about life (White, 2007). Therefore, for some there is a risk that such a view may get in the way of moving forward in living life with disability that incorporates positive feelings of self-esteem and self-worth.

NARRATIVE-BASED PRACTICE AND PAYING ATTENTION TO THE PARTICULAR

One of the key aspects about being an individual is that each of us *is individual*. Each of us views life and all that it deals us differently: each of us can be an exception to the rule. This highlights the importance of taking a person's unique experiences into account (Grypdonck, 2006). Narrative provides us with a frame of working that allows us to do this as it opens up practice and helps us to pay attention to the particular, to singularize intervention and to recognize our ethical and personal duties (Charon, 2006; Shadden, Hagstrom, & Koski, 2008). Qualitative methodologies are ideally suited to narrative-based practice as they recognize that our knowledge and experience of the world are "profoundly shaped by our subjective and cultural perspective and by our conversations and activities" (Yardley, 2000, p. 217). They allow us to explore the consequences and impact of illness, impairment, and disability while attending to the meanings, experiences, and views of the individual concerned. In this way, they facilitate exploration of the particular and address the "how" and "why" questions that emerge in everyday practice. In so doing they allow us to look behind the mask of communication disability to the individual's lived experience of it within the overall context of their life story (Barrow, 2000).

Drawing on the work of Schön (1983, 1987), van der Gaag and Anderson (2005) discuss practice in terms of the "solid high ground" and the "swampy lowlands." The solid high ground focusses on the application of technical skills toward specific impairment-related difficulties while the swampy lowlands deal with the issues related to the complex and messy challenges of living with disability. They suggest that to address the many issues that people face living in the wider world, practitioners need to work from the swampy lowlands. Working in these lowlands helps us to focus our assessment and intervention in ways that anchor to the person's everyday life. This has been found to lead to better outcomes (Faircloth, Rittman, Boylstein, Young, & Van Puymbroeck, 2004).

The Polish American philosopher and scientist Alfred Korzybski (1879–1950) believed that we should approach the world with an attitude of "I don't know; let's see" in order to better discover and reflect on reality and not be blinded by one's own criteria. Such an attitude fits well with considering practice from the swampy lowlands.

APPLYING NARRATIVE AS A WAY OF WORKING

I find the metaphor of journey accompanied by analogies of maps and territories (see also Sontag, 1991; van der Gaag & Anderson, 2005; White, 2007) useful as a means to reflect on and shape my practice. Like White (2007) I find the notion of a map helps to remind me that working with a person with communication disability is like embarking on a journey to a destination that cannot be precisely specified via routes that cannot be precisely predetermined. This, together with Korzybski's famous premise "the map is not the territory" (Korzybski, 1990, p. 299) reminds me that I can only gain access to a representation (i.e. the map) of the person's experience (i.e. the territory). To draw the most valid and meaningful map, I need to gain as clear an understanding of the territory as possible. On first meeting with a person with communication disability I have either a blank or a very sketchy map; together we have to draw a more detailed map if we are to chart a way forward towards the individual's desired goal(s). For some, a simple map may suffice while for others a more detailed comprehensive map is required for us to work together effectively. In our quest to add detail to this map, Charon (2006) suggests that we need to recognize the person in the face of impairment, to respect their strengths, to accompany them through the territory of illness and/or disability and to honor the meaning they attach to their experience.

Considering practice in this way can be helpful as it brings to the foreground the fact that clinical practice is neither a simple nor a linear process. I have found it is rare that we move from "assessment" to "therapy" and back to "assessment" again in a strictly linear fashion. In the next section I discuss some of the processes we engage in as part of our practice. They include:

- Assessment – which I entitle "hearing the story."
- "Therapy" – by which I mean the way in which we work with the person to bring about changes that will enable them to move forward in living a more satisfying life in the context of communication disability.
- Tracking change and documentation.
- The implications of this way of working in terms of benefits and risks.

Although I present these in a linear fashion, they rarely follow a strictly sequential order of activities in practice. Early on there may be more of an emphasis on hearing the story and less on therapy, later there may be more of an emphasis on therapy and less on hearing the story. However, the reality is that we oscillate between the various different processes as each informs and shapes the other. They then merge to form what can be referred to as practice (Figure 3.1).

Hearing the story

According to Charon (2006) when we first meet a person we should invite them to tell us all that they feel we need to know. She suggests that we just "absorb all that he emits" (p. 177), keeping writing to a minimum as this can distract from giving the person your full attention. Adopting this attitude entails being inwardly and outwardly quiet. This technique is often referred to as mindfulness and involves the ability to "actively mute inner distractions" (p. 132) and suspend the self in order to concentrate on the person. It is about being in the present. Such a stance opens one up to absorb all that the person emits and so is central to narrative-based practice and really hearing the story.

Charon's (2006) notion of stereophonic listening; which she describes as "the ability to hear the body and the person who inhabits it" (p. 97), is useful

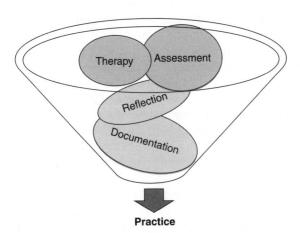

Figure 3.1 Some of the oscillating processes that merge to form practice.

as it reminds us to listen for and pay attention to the different aspects of living with impairment and disability. This listening with more than one ear helps us to focus simultaneously on such aspects as the impairment itself, impairment effects (i.e. restrictions in activity due to the impairment), barriers-to-doing (i.e. environmental, informational, and social barriers), and barriers-to-being (i.e. hurtful and hostile behavior of others that affects self-esteem and how one feels about oneself now and in the future) as described by Thomas (1999, 2007).

Charon (2006, p. 99) states "If the professional listens stereophonically for what the person says and also what the body says, he or she has the rare opportunity not only to hear the body out but also to translate the body's news to the person who lives in it." Frequently the person comes to us with a particular view of our role (i.e. critic, expert, fixer, helper, supporter, etc.) that will shape the way in which they tell their story. Similarly, as listeners to their story we come with our own set of expectations and so we need to be careful that we do not confine ourselves to our limited view of the world. Hearing the story is not just a matter of one person listening to and receiving another's story; rather the listener is a co-creator of the story and the stance taken at the time of listening shapes the understanding of that story. We actively co-create the story by probing, asking questions, forming hypotheses, looking for clues, etc. in our quest to hear the authentic voice of the person (Charon, 2006). To do this effectively we have to open ourselves up to numerous interpretative approaches in order to select the "best fit" for that individual.

There are a number of techniques that can prove useful to consider when trying to gain a sense of what life is like for the individual living with communication disability. They can help to add detail to the map of the territory. They include the following.

1   *Listening for stories.* The notion of listening *for* stories rather than listening *to* stories makes us more aware of the metaphors and images the person uses as well as their allusions to other stories. This helps us to gain a sense of the meaning they attach to their situation (Charon, 2006; Frank, 1995). Moreover, listening *for* stories makes us consider why the person is telling this story, in this way, to us, at this particular point in time. In addition, it helps us to acknowledge and understand why we are responding in a particular way. Listening *to* stories on the other hand, tends to focus on the facts and the content; whereas listening *for* stories recognizes what the teller is revealing "between the lines." Listening in this way helps us to gain a deeper understanding of the territory the individual inhabits.

2   *Externalizing the problem.* The concept of externalizing the problem forms the basis of narrative therapy (White, 2007; White & Epston, 1990). It involves separating yourself from the problem thereby helping to relieve the pressure of blame and perceived failure. Making the problem

distinct from the person in this way allows them to map the influence of it on their life as well as allowing facts that contradict the dominant story (referred to as "unique outcomes" in narrative therapy) to emerge. It opens the door for the individual to form a different relationship with communication disability; one that may help them to develop an alternative story or narrative that incorporates the creation of a positive identity in the context of disability.

3   *Negotiating an "experience-near" definition.* The notion of negotiating what White (2007) refers to as an experience-near definition of the challenges associated with living with communication disability engages the person more actively in the process of externalizing the problem. In so doing, it helps them to increase their awareness and confidence in their own resources. This differs from an experience-distant definition; which is one more commonly found in the realm of professional and expert jargon.

I have found listening *for* stories helpful to guide and shape intervention. For example, a number of years ago I reported on two individuals with aphasia (Barrow, 2000). "David" acquired aphasia 8 years prior to our work together. At that time he exemplified the contradictory nature of living with disability: while he wanted his aphasia cured, he wanted to get on with life; while he desired to be ordinary he wanted to deal with difference (Pound, 2004). When we first met I was struck by how problem-saturated his story was. To support him in his goal to get on with life our work together focussed on externalizing the problem (aphasia) and its influence on his life. In a remarkably short period of time he began to view his aphasia in a different light and became more aware of the many resources he had that could help him to control the influences of it in his life. On the other hand, "Richard" and I met just a few days following his stroke. While not linear, I witnessed a gradual progression from the confusion of the early days, to a period of wanting his aphasia cured through to the gradual emergence of a future life plan incorporating aphasia. There were times I had to resist the path that I felt we should follow as it seemed more important and meaningful for Richard that I accompany him along his chosen path rather than coercing him along a path of my choosing. For example, during the first year intervention focussed on remediation of the impairment, yet at this time he frequently spoke about the emotional and social consequences of aphasia in his day-to-day life but was reluctant to explore these in any depth at that particular time.

   There are times when we see people who are not able to tell their story in the conventional way. For example, in the very early days following the onset of acquired communication impairment the individual is often too ill or shocked to be able to actively engage in the meaning-making necessary to tell their story. However, this should not preclude us from trying to gain some sense of their experience of communication disability in these very early days. Listening to and for the stories of others close to the individual or those working with them can help us to begin to gain insight into their situation. Also, drawing on some of the techniques used in qualitative research can provide invaluable insights in shaping intervention. For example, ethnographic notes from even brief periods of observation can guide the development of an environment that supports inclusion and autonomy.

Therapy

Shadden et al. (2008) believe that one of the key ways that practitioners can help people with acquired communication disability and those close to them is to focus on their life stories and how communication impairment has affected how they live life. In this way therapy is inextricably linked with assessment and hearing the story.

It is well documented that telling one's story is therapeutic in its own right as the stories we weave allow us to make sense of our own lives. The telling helps to situate communication disability in the context of everyday life, it gives permission to express emotion, it reduces one's sense of isolation, and it increases awareness of goals, barriers, conflicts, and resources. Moreover, it assists in the process of attaching meaning to what has happened and in re-authoring one's life in a positive way (Atkinson, 1998; Charon, 2006; Swain et al., 2004a; White & Epston, 1990). Creating the conditions for a person to tell their story allows them to give voice to their experience and to frame it into something meaningful.

Many people come to therapy with the goal and expectation of having their communication impairment cured or fixed. For many this is an important focus for therapy as it was for Richard described earlier. However, for others the sole goal of cure may not be realistic as they struggle to live with communication disability in the present while contemplating the future. This chapter focusses on this aspect of the therapy process and not remediation of the impairment which is documented extensively elsewhere.

I have found the methods used in narrative-based practice and solution-focussed brief therapy (see Burns, 2005) to be extremely useful to inform my work with people with communication disability. As described earlier, a key feature of narrative practice is externalizing the problem (White & Epston, 1990). This process of making the problem distinct from the person allows the person to identify and map the things that affect communication in day-to-day life. It helps to make the problem more manageable as it breaks it down into bits each of which can provide a focus for specific intervention. During this process and with careful questioning, things that go against the dominant problem-saturated story are identified (i.e. unique outcomes) and ways that problems have been effectively managed in the past emerge. Previously hidden resources that the person brings can then form the basis of a "toolkit" that they can use to manage communication in daily life. This practice of externalizing the problem formed the basis of therapy with two people ("Eleanor" and "Maeve") with whom I worked some time ago.

Eleanor identified her difficulty in finding words as the main problem that contributed to her experience of communication disability. This made her "tighten" which resulted in making it even more difficult for her. Our conversations centered on what other factors influenced her ability to find words. She quickly identified fatigue, not being able to depend on others being right (i.e. when they talked for her), others being impatient, a fear of what others might think and not being able to trust her memory for certain things. Together we drew up a representation of this (Figure 3.2) to provide us with a point of reference for our work together. Conversations then turned to which of these influences she felt she could affect change together with the development of a plan about how she might approach this. These discussions revealed the many resources Eleanor had upon which she could draw to bring about her desired change. In so doing, not only did she report that she felt increased control over her communication but her self-esteem improved through the rekindling of the resources she had forgotten she had.

Maeve identified the stroke as the main source of all her difficulties as it was this that made her speech difficult which in turn made her feel "upset," "down," "confidence bad," and that "no one was interested." Our work together was two-pronged: it focussed on direct work on the impairment while simultaneously exploring other influences on her experience of communication disability. In this way her goal of "getting on with life" in the context of aphasia could be charted. Like Eleanor, Maeve identified numerous things external to her that impacted on her experience and which she felt made her aphasia worse. These included when she felt she had to give an answer, when there were lots of things going on around her, if the other person was in a bad

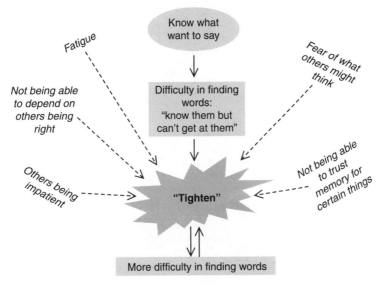

Figure 3.2 Information from externalizing conversations with Eleanor.

humor, "looks through you," in a rush or treats you as if "not there." The representation in Figure 3.3 formed the basis for conversations about how she could influence these external factors to make them work for her rather than against her. The many resources that Maeve had on which she could draw were revealed during this process.

As practitioners, we have the opportunity to play a role in opening doors to new ways of thinking about acquired communication disability that may lead to the development of a self-affirming alternative narrative of disability; one that incorporates living "healthily" with communication impairment. Such alternative narratives constitute a revised understanding by resisting the dominant narratives of disability that view the person as damaged or less than whole (Oliver, 1996; Swain et al., 2004b) and replacing it with one that commands respect (Nelson, 2001). Ideas to support the development of such alternative narratives include the identification and thickening of "unique outcomes," the provision of opportunities to hear how others live satisfying lives in the context of acquired communication disability, and the development of opportunities for discussion and debate about meanings of communication disability (Barrow, 2004, 2008).

Documentation and tracking change

Anchoring intervention to things that are meaningful for the person in everyday life has been found to produce better outcomes (Faircloth et al., 2004). However, the approach to practice that I have outlined does not lend itself to the more traditional standardized methods of tracking change over time. Shadden et al. (2008) differentiate between documentable and measurable

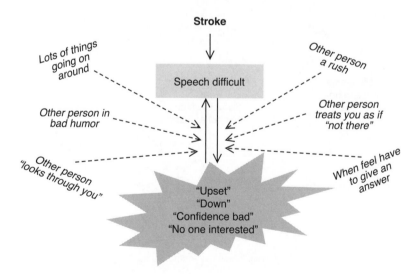

Figure 3.3 Information from externalizing conversations with Maeve.

evidence. *Measurable* evidence assumes an endpoint while *documentable* evidence allows for dynamic and open-ended change. I believe *documentable* evidence is better suited to this type of work than measurable evidence. In this way evidence of change over time can be documented using a variety of methods that include ethnographic notes taken from even brief periods of observation, snapshots of comments made by the person and about the person, self-story "handouts," use of simple visual analogue scales, lifestyle grids (Jeffers, 1987), or such resources as the "tree of life." Therapists in the discipline of narrative therapy regularly use a wide variety of documents as a means to represent and celebrate the gains a person has made (White & Epston, 1990).

If we are to work effectively in this way we need to be aware of our own values, beliefs, and attitudes that come to bear in practice. Becker and Kaufman (1995) found that the ways in which doctors managed and treated people who had a stroke were strongly influenced by the way in which they viewed stroke. Many expressed hopelessness and equated severe stroke with a "living death" or a "disaster." These meanings influenced how they approached treatment. Our core beliefs about illness and disability can get in the way of really hearing the person's perspective so the ability to reflect and to become self-aware is crucial (see also Chapters 14 and 15).

IMPLICATIONS AND BENEFITS ASSOCIATED WITH THIS WAY OF WORKING

Swain et al. (2004a) believe that notions of health and treatment that focus on pathology together with disabling models of care jeopardize enabling and therapeutic relationships. *Therapeutic* relationships are founded on a genuine desire to find out the individual's perspective. However, all too often a person's narrative is cut short or derailed by very focussed closed questions and/or constraints of time. Over-directed interviewing risks obscuring the very issues we need to be aware of (Gwyn, 2002). Therefore, if we impose a framework of case-history taking that asks questions in a checklist fashion we may sacrifice gaining valuable and highly relevant information that would guide intervention. Charon (2006, p. 99) contends that we "mine far, far more knowledge" if we spend more time listening for stories in our everyday practice.

Figure 3.4 provides a representation of how really attending to the person's story reaps benefits for all on a number of levels. It helps us to gain access to important information relevant to diagnosis and intervention and so improves clinical decision-making. This results in improved outcomes that lead to greater job satisfaction and less stress for the practitioner. This in turn opens one up to really attending to the person's perspective.

If we fail to listen to the person's perspective we risk affecting clinical decision-making resulting in possible diminished intervention outcomes;

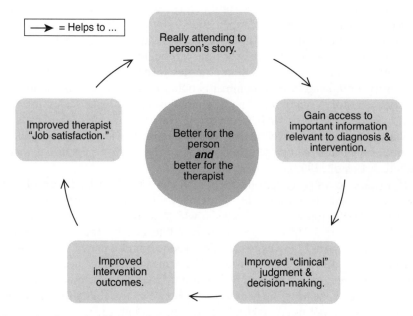

Figure 3.4 "Hearing the story" – the benefits of really attending.

which can lead to increased stress and reduced job satisfaction for the practitioner. Unfortunately "attentive listening does not feel enough like a clinical action" (Charon, 2006, p. 199). Yet therapeutic conversations as described in this chapter provide us with opportunities to support the person towards a revised understanding of communication disability. In so doing, they contribute to the recreation of an identity that incorporates communication disability in an affirmative way. To achieve this we need to allow our "therapist expertise to interact with but not overpower the expertise of the person" (Pound, 2004, p. 41) through providing a context where our views can be genuinely challenged and a space for the individual's voice can be genuinely heard.

CONCLUSION

At the beginning of this chapter I posed four questions, my responses to these questions formed the body of the text and are summarized below.

As practitioners what can we do to support the telling of the person's story?

It can be challenging to open ourselves up to really hear the story when we work in a health and social care system that is aligned with a logico-scientific mode of thought that privileges "general knowledge." Paying attention to the particular experiences of the individual on the other hand aligns with a narrative mode of thought (White & Epston, 1990). Practice that purports to keep the person at its center needs to ensure that the "general" fits with the "particular" rather than the particular conforming to the general.

What techniques can we use that would help to ensure that we really hear the story?

Many of the techniques used in narrative therapy can help to create the conditions for collaborative work with people with acquired communication disability. Such techniques include mindfulness, trusting in the resources of the individual and a genuine attitude of "I don't know – let's see." In addition, for some people, techniques to support conversation (see Kagan, 1995, 1998) are required to help them to tell their story. These, together with an ability to suspend one's own beliefs about illness and disability as well as an ability to reflect on their role in our work, are critical in ensuring that the person's voice is heard.

What is the role of all this in shaping intervention?

Hearing the perspective of the individual makes intervention more meaningful and relevant for the person who comes to us with their unique set of meanings, priorities, concerns, and resources. All of which can be capitalized upon to chart a way forward in your work together.

What are the implications and risks for the person when a health or social care professional fails to hear the person's story?

If we fail to create the conditions for the person to feel free to tell their story then we risk not having access to important information that could be crucial for both diagnosis and planning intervention. Also, if intervention is not meaningful for a person then there is an increased likelihood that they will not engage in the process resulting in poorer "outcomes."

Attending to the person's unique story of living life with communication disability lies at the heart of practice as it helps to ensure that the person is kept at the center. People value practitioners who listen and tailor therapy to their particular concerns, issues, and lifestyle; and who have warmth, empathy, and unconditional positive regard (Cott, 2004; Fourie, 2009; Pound, 2004; Swain et al., 2004a).

Final comment

You will recall that at the beginning of this chapter I told you about Pat, a woman with aphasia, and how the attitude of her doctor made her feel not listened to. This affected Pat's ability to tell the doctor all which she felt he needed to know. Pat would come away from these consultations feeling frustrated and marginalized. She has since changed doctors and now attends a general practitioner who she says "knows her as a person – listening and has all the time in the world." Yet these consultations take no longer than her consultations with her previous doctor. Clearly, her new doctor attends to her story in such a way that allows her to expand and unfold and so to feel valued. She is of the opinion that *both* she *and* her doctor gain more from the encounter as a result.

ACKNOWLEDGMENTS

I would like to thank Pat Gath for her insights, drawn from her experience of living with aphasia, on ways to support a person in telling their story.

4   Exploring clinical interaction in speech-language therapy

Narrative, discourse and relationships

Nina Simmons-Mackie
Southeastern Louisiana University

Jack S. Damico
University of Louisiana, Lafayette

INTRODUCTION

I remember that the day was lovely with blue skies and a fresh breeze, but my mother and I were too anxious to enjoy the weather. I had accompanied her to a neurologist because she had tingling and mild weakness in both hands and arms. The computed tomography and magnetic resonance imaging scans ordered by her internist had been unremarkable, so we hoped that the trip to the neurologist would be informative. The neurologist asked her questions regarding her symptoms and conducted a neurological examination. He reported to us that "she probably had a mild stroke" that did not show up on the scans. My mother asked him to explain what sort of stroke would produce that set of "bilateral symptoms." Ignoring her use of relatively "informed" terminology, the neurologist proceeded to define stroke and risk factors in very simplistic terms. He recommended physical therapy and an aspirin each day. Although my mother was polite and seemed attentive within the doctor's office, on the way home she angrily announced "He didn't get it right! I'm not doing anything he says – he thinks I'm an idiot, but he's the idiot." My mother rejected the diagnosis and the physician's recommendations, even though both exercise and aspirin therapy are scientifically supported forms of intervention. By failing to acknowledge my mother's interests, background and knowledge, this physician failed to construct a shared narrative of what happened, why and what to do about it, resulting in wholesale rejection of his recommendations. My mother's contribution to the unsuccessful interaction was her failure to demand further explanation, and her implicit acquiescence to the "doctor as dominant" style of medical encounter.

In essence, the *clinical interaction* was the pivotal flaw in the above encounter. Clinical interactions are equally important in speech-language therapy. In fact, the social interaction and relationship between client and clinician is the essence of the therapeutic event. Thus, Clarke (2003, p. 83) describes his life after aphasia: "It was . . . the quality of the relationship between myself and the speech therapist that I was to learn from." Therapy tasks and activities are a medium for achieving goals and socially constructing the therapeutic interaction that fosters change. Although it has long been assumed that the clinician's behavior in speech-language therapy affects the client's behavior in such a way as to effect change (Brookshire, Nicholas, Krueger, & Redmond, 1978), the influence of the client's behavior on the clinician has less often been appreciated. In fact, therapy is not a unidirectional process of clinician "doing to" client, but a collaborative activity in which both parties work to effect change. The client and therapist work together to achieve a co-constructed event that requires both parties to implicitly agree to a social contract. In this respect, speech-language therapy *is* the clinical interaction. As soon as the therapist and client meet, they begin to negotiate their unique social relationship and construct their respective roles and identities. Through the interaction, each distinctive story of therapy begins to unfold. In her discussion of "therapeutic emplotment" in occupational therapy, Mattingly (1994) describes clinical encounters as the creation of a plot structure within clinical time. The "plot" gives meaning to actions within therapy and helps to situate sessions within a larger narrative. The unfolding story is influenced by the local context, emerging discourse, and broad elements (e.g. cultural background, expectations, institutional constraints).

Like the interaction between this author's mother and her neurologist, some speech-language therapy interactions focus on symptoms, facts, or tasks without integrating participants' lived experiences. Consequently, therapy "becomes" the picture cards or the naming task, and the multiple layers of experience that participants bring to the task are ignored. When therapy interactions are overly focussed on procedures aimed at improving speech or language, then participants fail to arrive at a shared narrative that can accommodate both the therapist's and client's life worlds and they cannot make changes relevant to future life worlds. Narrative-based approaches focus on integrating lived experience and future aspirations into the therapy interaction as a means of achieving relevant, socially oriented goals (Hinckley, 2008).

WHAT MAKES A THERAPY?

Byng and Black (1995) have asked "what makes a therapy?" This seemingly simple question is, in fact, quite complex, yet crucial to understanding how therapy works. Although the literature tends to define therapy idealistically in terms of controlled tasks and procedures, "real life" therapy enactment is a messy business. Aspects of the interaction are improvised as therapy unfolds and the way that participants deal with the interaction is an important ingredient of the therapy. For example, how does the therapist deal with a humorous remark made by the client? Does the clinician exert control and redirect to the task, explicitly acknowledge the client's humor as evidence of communicative competence or simply laugh? Where do we learn to make these online clinical decisions? How do these choices affect the outcomes of therapy? Such questions are important to delivering effective and efficient therapy.

Although subtle aspects of the clinical interaction can positively or negatively affect the therapeutic relationship, the interactive element of therapy is not often described in effectiveness research or evidence-based practice reviews (Horton & Byng, 2000). Clinicians are typically attuned to their therapy interactions as exemplified in comments such as "it went well today" or "we were out of sync today," but when questioned critically, clinicians tend to have trouble articulating exactly what made the session go well or poorly. Rather, many give generalized comments (e.g. "he was in a bad mood," "the pictures were too hard"). Similarly, clients are rarely able to articulate what happens in therapy (Parr et al., 1997). It would seem that information beyond the objective descriptions of tasks and procedures is needed to fully answer important questions such as: What are the characteristics of "good" versus "poor" therapy? How do we teach the therapeutic process? How do we recognize what therapy is and what it is not? There must be recognizable elements within the clinical interaction that "make a therapy." The remainder of this chapter will review an emerging literature on clinical interaction in speech-language therapy and offer suggestions for a narrative-based clinical practice.

ANALYZING CLINICAL INTERACTION

By studying clinical interactions we gain valuable insight into the ways clinician and client narratives are played out in therapy. Every communication exchange represents multiple layers of information such as linguistic, personal (e.g. what is in the "head" of each participant), local (e.g. what is happening at the moment), social and cultural aspects of the story. We can study the macrostructure of the interaction, the physical context, the content (e.g. what the participants talk about), analyze discourse on a micro level (e.g. structural and semantic elements), or pursue story telling within the interaction. On a broad level, qualitative paradigms such as ethnography can explain how culture is realized in an interaction (e.g. Agar, 1986; Hymes, 1966; Kovarsky & Maxwell, 1992; Simmons-Mackie & Damico, 1999a). Narrative analysis and phenomenological approaches (e.g. Giorgi, 1985; Mishler, 1986; Riessman, 1993) focus on what is meaningful to particular stakeholders such as clients and family members. At a more micro-level of analysis using methods such as sociolinguistic discourse analysis (Hengst & Duff, 2007; Leahy, 2004), functional systemic linguistics (Armstrong, 2005; Ferguson & Elliot, 2001; Togher, 2003) or conversation analysis (e.g. Damico, Oelschlaeger, & Simmons-Mackie, 1999; Wilkinson, 1999) we might analyze how the participants use social actions and language in ways that both display and create relationships. Finally coding systems have been proposed in an attempt to organize or "map" elements of clinical interaction (e.g. Horton & Byng, 2000). For our purposes, findings from these various streams of research have been organized into three categories: (1) interactional style, (2) contextual and discourse variables, and (3) identity negotiation.

Clinical interaction styles

Much of the research on clinical interaction suggests that traditional speech-language therapy is a different type of interaction from everyday conversation outside of therapy (Ferguson & Armstrong, 2004; Panagos, 1996; Simmons-Mackie & Damico, 1999b; Togher, 2003). In fact, different interactive styles of therapy are recognizable based on particular characteristics (Kovarsky & Duchan, 1997). These "types" of therapy interactions are variously described as clinician/adult/teacher versus client/child-centered therapy.

Clinician-centered therapy

Clinician-centered therapy involves interactions in which the clinician exerts control over the therapy interaction to ensure that goals of therapy are addressed (Cole & Dale, 1986; Damico, Simmons-Mackie, Oelschlaeger, & Tetnowski, 2000; Duchan, 1993; Fey, 1986; Kovarsky & Duchan, 1997; Norris & Hoffman, 1990; Panagos, 1996). There are many reports of therapy sessions that are dominated by the therapist (Becker & Silverstein, 1984; Bobkoff & Panagos, 1986; Damico & Damico, 1997; Horton, 2003; Kovarsky, 1990; Kovarsky, Kimbarrow, & Kastner, 1999; Kovarsky, Shaw, & Adingono-Smith, 2007; Leahy, 2004; Prutting, Bagshaw, Goldstein, Juskowitch, & Umen, 1978; Ripich, Hambrecht, Panagos, & Prelock, 1984; Silvast, 1991; Simmons-Mackie & Damico, 1999b; Simmons-Mackie, Damico, & Damico, 1999; Simmons-Mackie & Schultz, 2003). Reported indices of therapist dominance and interactional asymmetry include: controlling turns, evaluating performance, requesting known information, talking more than the client, controlling topic introduction, and controlling interpretation of meaning.

Clinician-centered therapy as described in the speech-language pathologist literature has been associated with traditional overtly "impairment-focussed" therapy in which activities target specific aspects of the individual's disorder. For example, a therapy session might consist of naming pictures to improve word finding, imitating "s" words to improve sibilant articulation, or remembering lists of items to improve memory. A discourse sequence that is frequently described in clinician-centered interactions is the *request–response–evaluation* sequence (RRE) involving a therapist request for performance, client compliance with the request, and evaluation of client performance by the therapist as follows.

1   Clinician Request: "What is the name of this? [shows picture of tree].
2   Client Response: "Tree."
3   Clinician Evaluation: "Good."

The RRE is a form of tutorial discourse that has been identified in adult and child speech-language therapy, individual and group therapy, and teacher-centered classrooms (Cazden, 1988; Duchan, 1993; Horton, 2003; Kovarsky et al., 1999; Markova, 1991; Panagos, 1996; Prutting et al., 1978; Ripich & Panagos, 1985; Simmons-Mackie & Damico, 1999b; Sinclair & Coulthard, 1975). Similarly, researchers have described "test questions" that require the client to provide known information in response to a query (Kovarsky & Duchan, 1997). While these routines typically are associated with "teaching," the asymmetrical interactive structure casts the client in the relatively passive position of responding to requests from the therapist.

Related to the RRE structure is the prevalence of extended repair sequences in clinician-centered interactions. When the "response phase" of the RRE is not correct, then the therapist typically offers a correction or a cue to encourage the client to fix the error as follows.

1   Clinician request: What is this? [shows picture of chair].
2   Client response: Uhhh sss sart.
3   Clinician correction/cue: Wait! It's a CH. . . . . . [points to own mouth].

Such attempts at repair in therapy interactions differ from repair in ordinary conversation. For example, repair (or correction) in therapy can and often does proceed over several turns with the therapist working to get the client to produce the correct response (Kovarsky & Duchan, 1997). In contrast, few turns are typically required for repair in ordinary conversation and the goal is typically mutual understanding (Schegloff, Jefferson, & Sacks, 1977). Relatedly, research has identified a high frequency of exposed corrections in clinician-centered aphasia therapy; exposed corrections occur when a speaker's error is highlighted and the listener offers an explicit correction (Simmons-Mackie & Damico, 2008). In peer conversation blatant exposed corrections are handled delicately and often avoided since they risk impugning the competence of the error maker. It appears that interactional work aimed at practicing a correct response is often protracted and unnatural in clinician-centered therapy.

These asymmetrical interactional characteristics evident in the discourse of clinician-centered therapy are often interpreted in light of overarching socio-cultural themes and broader cultural narratives. For example, uneven distribution of humor attempts and feedback in therapy has been interpreted as a sign of the power differential in favor of the clinician (Simmons-Mackie et al., 1999; Simmons-Mackie & Schultz, 2003). Clinician-centered interactions also exhibit an asymmetrical distribution of shared personal information – the therapist asks what the client had for breakfast, but the client rarely asks this of the clinician (Togher, 2003). These interactional asymmetries reflect the power asymmetry of therapy as well as overarching sociocultural orientations of the profession (Damico, Simmons-Mackie, & Hawley, 2005).

Client-centered therapy

Client-centered therapy is characterized by less clinician control and a more egalitarian interactional relationship (Bobkoff & Panagos, 1986; Cole & Dale, 1986; Duchan, 1993; Fey, 1986; Kovarsky & Duchan, 1997; Leahy, 2004; Norris & Hoffman, 1990; Panagos, 1996; Simmons-Mackie, Elman, Holland, & Damico, 2007). Several characteristics have been identified in client-centered therapy including prevalence of "natural" discourse routines, following the conversational lead of the client, avoiding rigid discourse structure (e.g. RRE), fostering the "feel" of discourse equality, symmetrical usage of multimodal communication (e.g. gestures, writing), and strategies to promote turn taking by clients (Kovarsky & Duchan, 1997; Simmons-Mackie et al., 2007). Client-centered therapy tends to evidence fewer exposed corrections and less evidence of repairs aimed at "accuracy." Rather client-centered therapy involves more hidden corrections or repairs such as modeling during conversation or asking for clarification. Client-focussed interaction typically involves discourse that more closely resembles peer interactions in which clients establish and follow-up on topics of choice and initiate discourse sequences (e.g. ask questions). Emphasis shifts from a focus on defined tasks to a focus on the communicative interaction (Simmons-Mackie et al., 2007). Therapy is crafted to be informative and empowering, and the client–clinician relationship is one of partnership.

The clinical interaction as context

The clinical encounter as a sociocultural context has been studied using a variety of approaches such as those familiar in the ethnographic tradition (e.g. Cicourel, 1992; Strong, 1979) and in sociological research (e.g. Garfinkel, 1967; Goffman, 1974; Lofland & Lofland, 1995). Context exerts a powerful influence on the clinical interaction. Context refers to the common knowledge that is shared by the participants in an interaction (Edwards & Mercer, 1987) including physical aspects of the environment, shared experiences and expectations of the participants, and acknowledged goals of the encounter. Importantly, context is not a concrete entity for the participants; rather, it is an intersubjective mental phenomenon. Context is constructed within the therapeutic encounter through our social interactions and discourse. In this sense, contextual markers are evident in the shared narratives that individuals use to make sense of situations. These markers of context reflect professional culture, personal histories, and shared experiences, and as these markers are incorporated into discourse, the clinical context is created and reinforced (Geekie, Cambourne, & Fitzsimmons, 1999; Worrall, 2000). Thus, context provides us with expectations of how to act and what to say in any given situation (Bakhtin, 1986). For example, speech-language pathologists often speak and dress in a way that distinguishes them from clients and these patterns of behavior may become incorporated into the shared narrative. In addition to superficial markers such as manner of speech or dress, therapy participants also convey hidden cultural messages regarding values, beliefs, and the prevailing narratives in which they are immersed. Consider the following creation of context:

> AH, a 50 year old housekeeper who had recently suffered a stroke, was seated at a large oval conference table along with multiple rehabilitation professionals for her initial case conference. The physician began the conference with a brief report on her medical status and called for reports from the other professionals seated at the table. The physical therapist reported that AH had "spasticity in her lower right extremity but was ambulating X3 with an AFO." AH sat quietly while each team member gave a similar report.

The allocation of turns, content of reports, and use of professional jargon immersed AH in a story (likely an incomprehensible story) created by health care providers; a story in which AH is a passive "patient" whose role is to listen to the experts describe what has or would be done to her. The created context involves a disempowering social position; one in which she was not expected to question or collaborate with the authorities or assume responsibility for her rehabilitation. A large literature addresses contextual constraints evident in the institutional discourses of education and medicine, close relatives of speech-language pathology. For example, analyses of medical encounters have revealed that doctors are awarded dominant social and authoritative roles during doctor–patient interactions (e.g. Cappella, 1983; Cicourel, 1992). Other health care providers also use markers that create "medicalized" stories such as the use of professional jargon (as above) and evaluative words (e.g. appropriate, unmotivated) to describe patient behavior. From a contextual perspective, MacDonald and Murray (2007) argue that the use of words such as appropriate "facilitates the smuggling of values into clinical encounters, which can marginalize patients and compromise therapeutic relationships" (p. 59). Research suggests that interactive elements similar to those found in medical encounters are also present in traditional speech-language therapy (Bobkoff & Panagos, 1986; Cole & Dale, 1986; Damico & Damico, 1997; Duchan, 1993; Fey, 1986; Kovarsky & Duchan, 1997; Norris & Hoffman, 1990; Simmons-Mackie & Damico, 1999b; Simmons-Mackie et al., 1999).

Within this discussion of the construction of the therapeutic context, however, we should not forget that this contextual construction is actually a *co*-construction. What are the mechanisms for the client's contribution? How does a dominant professional culture pervade speech-language therapy if this is, in fact, a co-constructed event? It is likely that clients arrive at therapy with knowledge of similar types of events. When an event carries cultural markers that are similar to known events, then we tend to act based on known experience. That is, since the contextual elements of traditional speech-language therapy are similar to other familiar contexts such as visiting the doctor or taking a lesson, these familiar institutional discourses help clients frame their interactions and respond in ways that they deem acceptable. Speech-language pathologists arrive at sessions with a particular cultural orientation that is displayed for clients; clients recognize these sociocultural markers and accommodate interactions accordingly; the shared context is created. Thus, therapy sessions might mimic aspects of familiar classroom and medical encounters.

Institutions and organizations also create, reproduce, and instantiate the contextual orientations displayed within clinical interactions. Speech-language pathology culture is learned via replication through educational institutions and clinical experiences. Institutional enculturation is also perpetuated in written texts (Duchan, 1999; Ferguson, 2008, 2009). For example, an analysis of American Speech-Language-Hearing Association evidence-based practice documents revealed pervasive institutional orientations (Kovarsky & Curran, 2007). These investigators reported that the "voice" of the client is missing in these professionally oriented documents, likely because the stories of clients are not valued as "objective" or quantifiable. The authors argued that "evidence-based practice should be reconstructed to include the voices of clients as a form of evidence" (Kovarsky & Curran, 2007, p. 50; Kovarsky, 2008) – a notion in keeping with narrative-based practice. Thus, both obvious and hidden cultural and contextual orientations influence the unfolding therapy relationship and the narratives that are co-constructed.

By adopting familiar event structures borrowed from socially similar situations, therapy participants can more easily and automatically attend to the interaction and tasks without having to create a macrostructure within which to function. However, when clinical interaction adheres rigidly to certain cultural expectancies and fixed narratives, then the communicative roles of the participants might be limited and misunderstandings can occur based on unfounded expectations (Simmons-Mackie & Damico, 1999b). For example, medical stories often proceed from diagnosis and treatment to discharge associated with recovery or cure. For many individuals with communication disability the "cure" narrative is not applicable and expectancies cannot be fulfilled. Hersh (2001) studied discharge from aphasia therapy and found that clients with residual disability often did not understand why they were being discharged. Possibly the narrative ascribed to by these individuals ends in cure, rather than living with disability. This mismatch in the narratives of client versus clinician can result in disappointing outcomes.

In addition to the obvious professional culture of speech-language pathology, both clinicians and clients bring unique social and cultural experiences to the therapy interaction. These far reaching influences can have significant effects on clinical interactions and the outcomes of therapy. A narrative view of therapy requires that we attempt to understand and acknowledge cultural influences and work to co-construct the therapy story in such a way as to integrate past and present, and work toward the best possible "futures" for the participants including both clients and clinicians.

Discourse and clinical interaction

The way we interact in therapy not only assists in establishing the context, it also conveys social meanings and helps us understand the stories that drive the clinical relationship. In other words, what we say along with subtle variations in voice, gesture, gaze, and movement provide information on the participants' perspectives and stances towards the interaction. As the therapy event is co-constructed, the story that is woven defines who the participants are and how they will function in therapy. By analyzing these interactions we gain insight into the roles and relationships established by participants. The following excerpts display recognizable roles in therapy interactions via the discourse. In the following example, the therapist is preparing to introduce a task and is working to establish client compliance.

Example 1
Clinician: Um, I know you're having trouble with your [talking]
Client: [nodding in agreement]
Clinician: So we're going to do some work to help with your talking, okay?
Client: [nods head yes.]

The use of wording such as "you're having trouble" and "some work to help" situate this as a "helping" relationship. The therapist has assumed the role of "helper" and the client has assumed the role of "person who needs help." This relatively pervasive role relationship in speech-language therapy reflects a larger "seeking help" story reminiscent of the "quest narrative" described by Frank (1995) as one of several narratives that result after illness. As discussed previously, the importance of these larger meanings within therapy discourse is that they can affect how therapy proceeds. For example, when clients expect the therapist to "effect a cure" then they might become passive communicators, might not realize their own power and responsibility in effecting carry-over, or might lose confidence in their residual competencies.

In the next example, the client is naming pictures during the "doing tasks" segment of therapy (Simmons-Mackie, 1999; transcription conventions are taken from Silverman, 2006 – see Appendix).

Example 2: Client is shown a picture of a bowling ball
Clinician: Tell me the name of this.
Client: This a::::: bowly ball
Clinician: Listen, ((points to own lips)) It's a bowl<u>i</u>ng ball.

Here the clinician plays the role of judge, pointing out errors and correcting the client's productions. The use of the commands "tell me" and "listen" establish the clinician as the authority, while the offer of the corrected production carries an implied request for the client to say it correctly. Again the client is cast in the relatively passive role of doing what the clinician asks. The client is the "error maker" while the clinician is the "error fixer." One wonders what effect the role of "error maker" has on the life story and self-image of a client? What aspects of the therapy interaction serve to dispel the notion that the client is incompetent? Do these interactive roles become internalized?

In the following excerpt the clinician and adult client are engaging in conversation prior to beginning tasks (Simmons-Mackie, 1999).

Example 3
Clinician: Hey, by the way, did you see the tennis match?
Client: Yes, yes. It was fru . . . fantastic.
               And Marvel had it too with me.
Clinician: I videotaped it . . . it was great.

Although the client is distinguishable by his errors, the clinician and client *roles* are indistinguishable as they engage in relatively natural conversation about a shared interest. The dyad focuses on the propositional content rather than on the impairment. This sharing of an interest in tennis affirms the relationship and reinforces client identity as more than "the disorder." The participants are engaging in "small talk"; Walsh (2007) suggests that small talk paves the way for task achievement and is an important element of the therapy relationship.

Certainly, these excerpts do not represent therapy as a whole. However, they provide clues to the stories and roles that are being played out in therapy. If the clinician orients to the client as incompetent, then the client might begin to accept his/her incompetence and avoid communicative risks outside of therapy. His or her life role becomes the disorder. Such psychosocial consequences of clinical interaction cannot be ignored. In fact, many believe that psychosocial consequences are as important as objective change in language or speech performance (Holland, 2007; Sarno, 1993, 2004; Simmons-Mackie, 2000, 2001). Only by incorporating attention to lived experience can we address both communicative and psychosocial consequences of communication disorders.

The clinical interaction and negotiation of identity

Through clinical interaction clients and clinicians negotiate who they are and the roles that they play in the therapy story. While each of us represents a cast of characters that collectively constitute a composite identity, clinical interactions sometimes limit the realization of multiple selves within therapy.

Studies of therapy discourse have demonstrated how social position and identity are established and maintained within therapy. For example, Horton (2006) analyzed aphasia therapy interactions and demonstrated clinicians' use of topic control to maintain specific participant roles and identities. The topics selected by therapists hindered the development of a client identity associated with "competence."

Simmons-Mackie and Damico (1999b) analyzed a therapy session in which the therapist failed to recognize a client's identity as a competent consumer who wanted input into task selection. This narrow appreciation of the self beyond the disorder resulted in the client's termination of the session. Kovarsky and colleagues (2007) described the negotiation of identity in group therapy for adults with traumatic brain injury. In the following excerpt (Example 4) the clinician (Monica) has asked a client (Peg) to explain the rules of a therapy game to the group (p. 61) (Transcription conventions are taken from Silverman, 2006 – see Appendix).

Example 4

7	*Monica:*	=Okay. Well Peg would you explain it to Jim then since he hasn't played it.
8	*Peg:*	No. School teacher's days they tell me are over now. I'm not allowed to explain it anything anymore.
9	*Monica:*	You're allowed to explain somethin' in here.
10	*Peg:*	No I'm super serious. I would really prefer not to=
11	*Monica:*	=Alright=
12	*Peg:*	=I'm still kind of upset that I can't go back to teaching.
13	*Monica:*	Okay then Bobby would you explain to Jim how this is played.

Notice in lines 8 and 12 that Peg laments her lost career and her future as a school teacher, yet the clinician does not follow-up on the introduced topic. In the discourse we see a missed opportunity to address an important issue that would probably ring familiar to other group members – the story of lost identity and fear of the future. Interactive "tells" such as Peg's comment about her teaching career provide clues to important messages within therapy interactions and serve as windows into relevant life narratives. It should be noted that the construction of negative identities is not unique to clinical speech-language therapy. Extensive recent work addressing issues of chronic back pain (Smith & Osborn, 2007), Parkinson's disease (Bramley & Eatough, 2005), fibromyalgia (Paulson, Danielson, & Soderberg, 2002), and multiple sclerosis (Reynolds & Prior, 2003) have demonstrated that the patients' "lived experiences" of pain are often directly mediated by the narratives constructed for them by the medical communities and that without attention to the patient's self-narrations, seemingly organic phenomena like pain can be greatly impacted. Speech-language therapy undoubtedly includes practices that detract from client goals and positive outcomes as well as practices that benefit our clients. We suggest an action-oriented and informed approach to the exploration and implementation of a narrative-based approach to clinical interaction that focusses on maximizing clinical interactions.

FRAMING CLINICAL INTERACTIONS IN A NARRATIVE-BASED APPROACH

When therapy interactions differ from typical daily communication, then the therapy story becomes a limited narrative, separated from "real life." The interactions focus on facts or activities without integrating the lived experiences, events, and places of participants into the interaction. For the clients we serve, this may be a serious problem. Who they are in therapy differs from who they are outside of therapy. How they communicate differs in and out of therapy. While it is not possible for the two situations to be identical, it is likely that a marked discrimination of therapy interaction hinders generalization of changes to other contexts.

To address these issues, clinical interactions should be reframed to more closely approximate speaking situations typical of the person's life (Kovarsky & Duchan, 1997; Simmons-Mackie, 2000, 2001; Togher, 2003). That is, a more authentic narrative-based and relationship-centered approach should be undertaken. Narrative-based approaches focus on integrating lived experience and future aspirations into the therapy interaction as a means of achieving relevant, socially oriented goals. Listening for the "tells" in clinical interactions as well as conducting interviews and eliciting stories are methods of accessing the experiences of clients (Hinckley, 2008).

Clinical interaction and evidence

Relevant to this stated need, Horton and Byng (2000, p. 372) posed an important question relative to therapy interaction: "Is there any indication that interactions which take place above and beyond the prescribed therapy content ... have an impact on the outcome of the therapy? The simple answer is that we do not know." In fact, data are lacking to determine the objective influence of the clinical relationship on speech-language therapy outcomes. While research is needed to answer this question more definitively, there are indications that the answer to the question is "yes." For example, there are reports that interactive style and communication affect compliance with recommendations and patient satisfaction (e.g. Christensen, 2004; Kummerer, Lopez-Reyna, & Hughes, 2007; Safran, Taira, Rogers, Kosinski, Ware, & Tarlov, 1998; Stewart et al., 2000). Additionally, clinical interaction can have a pervasive influence on what clients think about the world and about themselves (Damico & Damico, 1997). Clinical interaction also affects psychosocial factors that are important to communication. As discussed previously, clients and therapists establish and negotiate identity within interaction (e.g. Horton, 2007; Shadden, 2005; Shadden & Agan, 2004; Simmons-Mackie & Elman, in press).

When a robust identity and communicative confidence are established in therapy interactions, then the client is more likely to take communicative risks and participate in communication outside of therapy (Mackay, 2003). Moreover, the interactive elements of therapy directly affect engagement of clients and clinicians in the therapeutic process itself. When elements of the interaction are not "successful," then clients are not likely to participate even though objective procedures are followed (e.g. Simmons-Mackie et al., 1999). In other words, clinicians employ a host of subtle interactive strategies to enlist the participation of clients in therapy. For example, feedback after completion of a task is often altered as needed to insure the client's continued engagement in the task (e.g. "good" versus "GOOOOD! You got it!") (Simmons-Mackie et al., 1999).

When such engagement strategies are ignored, then clients might discontinue therapy. Simmons-Mackie and Damico (2009) analyzed aphasia group therapy interactions in which therapists either succeeded or failed to engage a group member in group interactions. In the unsuccessful group, the "unengaged" group member withdrew from therapy soon after the session under study. While no cause and effect relationship was established, the analysis raised an interesting question for further research and demonstrated that interactive behaviors can be studied in a systematic manner. In a similar incident, Simmons-Mackie et al. (1999) described a client who discontinued therapy due to a misunderstanding within a session. Conclusions about the impact of the clinical relationship on outcomes must also include the personal perspectives reported by therapy participants themselves, rather than simply objective test scores or the judgments of clinicians (Carradice, Shankland, & Beail, 2002; Gilbert, 2000; Parr et al., 1997). For example, Worrall, Davidson, Ferguson, Hersh, Howe, and Sherratt (2007) reported that "what people with aphasia want" from rehabilitation is not always congruent with therapist goals.

Analyzing narrative mismatches

DM, a young client who had sustained a brain injury during an inner city fight, spent several weeks as an exemplary rehabilitation inpatient and learned to communicate quite successfully with staff and visiting family members via an electronic device, written support, and other methods of augmenting speech. He and his family were "cooperative" and agreeable throughout the rehabilitation process. However, upon discharge DM refused to take the communication device home or use compensations because he feared rejection if friends saw him using "school talk."

This young man's life was organized within particular cultural rules, values, and attitudes that differed from those of his rehabilitation team and this markedly affected outcome. While this client played the patient role convincingly as an inpatient, his life experiences were not integrated into therapy. He accommodated to the culture of rehabilitation, while he temporarily set aside his life world. He could not incorporate the two diverse lives or identities and – to some extent – the therapy failed. When the narrative that dominates therapy and the narrative that represents a client's world are not integrated, then disappointing outcomes can result. Part of our responsibility as clinicians involves learning about the lives and personal narratives of clients.

Narrative mismatches need not be completely negative. They can provide windows into hidden plots in therapy or implicit rules and constraints that dictate what is appropriate or inappropriate in therapist–client encounters. For example, therapists have reported moments of feeling "out of one's element" when a client raises a delicate personal issue such as a spousal relationship or personal finances. Penman and deMare (2003, p. 93) describe a typical therapy response to delicate personal issues as follows. "I would briefly acknowledge the personal comments but then quickly move back to the communication task at hand or else 'subvert' the comments into communication activities." By shifting away from the delicate topic, the therapist communicates to the client the hidden rule that such delicate subjects are not admissible in therapy. Even if the clinician is unable to assist the client, acknowledgment of issues might be validating and provide an opportunity to seek others to help negotiate the life issue. Clinicians have also demonstrated discomfort in moving away from the "control" typical of much speech-language therapy. For example, Leahy (2004) analyzed a stuttering therapy session in which the clinician attempted to change the session into a more client-centered therapeutic conversational exchange. The client hesitated demonstrating a recognition that the session was deviating from the usual interaction structure. The clinician quickly abandoned the effort and returned to the traditional discourse structure involving structured evaluations and corrections. The discomfort of the participants signaled the existence of established interactive rules that fit into an agreed upon story of therapy (i.e. the clinician controls the discourse in order to help the client). This awareness can signal the need and the impetus for change. Within a narrative-based approach such realization can help parties appreciate the impact of the power differential and work to become more egalitarian when possible. While therapy interactions must have some implicit rules and limits on comfortable, appropriate, or admissible topics, maintenance of overly strict professional boundaries can limit the therapeutic relationship and prevent the participants from addressing authentic communicative needs. As Holland (2007) has described, the therapy relationship should include a greater awareness of the narrative-foundations of the interactions and this may result in a counseling orientation in order to ensure that the psychosocial components of communication are tackled and that individual experiences are validated.

Awareness of interactional power

While power asymmetries, acting out of professional culture and use of professional language are elements of professional identity, these do not allow the healthy, personal narratives of our clients to be revealed and negotiated in therapy. By studying our own clinical interactions we learn how to sort out "habitual" and overgeneralized cultural practices from ways of responding that foster relevant change. When power is not strategically used during therapy, the session can become a controlled and stifling situation. Therapy is an occasion to empower the client and move the client towards autonomy or independence as a communicator, not an occasion for the therapist to exhibit and perpetuate power. By analyzing our own interactions in therapy we identify disempowering and habituated practices. For example, speech acts designating power might include evaluating, instructing, or requesting known information, while equalizing acts might include soliciting advice or acknowledging competence. Holland (2007) suggests that the therapy relationship might be reconfigured to adopt "positive psychology" principles by focussing on the positives and on how to make things as right as they can be through a collaboration between the client and clinician.

Acknowledging and accommodating identities

As addressed earlier in this chapter, a crucial aspect of the therapeutic process is identity construction of clients as they review and incorporate their lived experiences into their future selves. While evidence of identity destruction has been associated with clinical interactions that cast the client as the "incompetent patient," positive identity negotiation within clinical interaction has been described as well. For example, Ferguson (2008) describes intervention approaches in literacy development in which different types of discourse are taught as a means of empowerment. Others describe group therapy for aphasia in which the clinician adopts an interaction style that encourages positive self-assessments and reinforces group identity (Simmons-Mackie & Elman, in press). Hagstrom (2004) suggests using narratives to incorporate issues of identity within therapy. By increasing our awareness of our own identities, we can better understand how to "fit" with client expectations and build positive identities. Furthermore, recognition that clients are people with multiple selves, roles, beliefs, and experiences, helps us look beyond the unidimensional "client with a disorder" identity (Hengst, Duff, & Prior, 2008). In a narrative approach, therapy is designed to access many aspects of personhood in order to make communication changes that are relevant to lived experience (e.g. Pound, Parr, Lindsay, & Woolf, 2000; Simmons-Mackie, 2000, 2001). By encouraging discourse that projects positive identity and multiple selves, a robust identity can prevail. By assigning value to experiences and life narratives, we implicitly assign value to the individual and bolster confidence. This does not mean that we share secrets, describe intimate moments or reach beyond the realm of professionalism. It does mean that we attempt to understand more about what participants want out of therapy and out of life as a first step in actually getting there (Hinckley, 2008; Holland, 2007). It means that our clinical interactions strive to be authentic relationships based on shared goals and mutual respect.

Relationship-centered therapy

Although the literature tends to describe client-centered and clinician-centered therapies as opposing interactive styles, it is likely that hybrid forms exist such that therapies form a continuum from therapist-centered to client-centered, and that variation might occur from client to client or even within a session (Fey, 1986; Kovarsky & Duchan, 1997; Simmons-Mackie et al., 2007). For example, although group therapy sessions analyzed by Simmons-Mackie and colleagues (2007) were considered "client-centered," the authors describe how clinicians subtly managed and controlled sessions to achieve successful communicative interactions and effect change in communicative behaviors. Thus, neither the clients nor the clinicians dominated the session. Also, particular client characteristics might impact the degree of client-focus during interactions. Research on doctor–patient encounters suggests that doctors were more patient-centered with patients they perceived as more engaged, more positive, better communicators, more satisfied, and more likely to follow their recommendations (Street, Gordon, & Haidet, 2007). The authors concluded that "reciprocity and mutual influence have a strong effect on these interactions in that more positive (or negative) communication from one participant leads to similar responses from the other" (p. 586). It is likely that similar reciprocal influences occur in speech-language therapy. Completely client-centered therapy is probably not therapeutic. Rather, the therapist must exert some form of control in order to achieve objectives and to "be" therapy (Damico & Damico, 1997). However, such control must be managed so as to prevent disempowerment and encourage creative and flexible communication. Thus, it is the task of the clinician to achieve a "relatively" egalitarian relationship in which interactional power shifts between client and clinician in a way that effects change and bolsters self-esteem. When the clinical interaction shifts to a more egalitarian one, then this is reflected not only in the structure of the discourse, but also in the willingness to share information, roles, and experiences; and more natural communication tends to emerge. Conversely, when clients are placed in an interactive social situation in which they are passive participants, do not make active choices, do not contribute to decisions, and are constrained in terms of contributions, then it is unlikely that the therapy will contribute to a robust sense of self, promote engagement in communicative activities or increase social participation.

Toward these objectives, clinicians and clients might strive for "relationship-centered therapy" within a narrative-based approach by fostering more natural communicative interactions, acknowledging shared power and expertise and uncovering individual narratives that will help drive a successful therapy partnership. By incorporating the three previous suggestions within a narrative-based interactional format that recognizes and accommodates to the lived experiences of the clients, this "relationship-centered" interactional style can be accomplished.

STRATEGIES FOR ACHIEVING NARRATIVE-BASED PRACTICES

The preceding discussions suggest a number of strategies that can move clinicians toward more narrative-based therapeutic interactions.

1   Seek to understand one's own and one's clients' life narratives, and how these intersect within the therapeutic interaction. This can be accomplished by listening carefully to clients' stories, considering obvious narrative mismatches, looking for interactive "tells," and analyzing discourse misunderstandings. As we gain an understanding of narratives that drive therapy, clients, and ourselves then it is more likely that therapy will facilitate changes in the client's communication life.
2   Recognize and minimize the interactional power differential that acts to the detriment of the client during therapy. In part, this can be accomplished by monitoring one's own discourse as well as sharing responsibility for therapy activities and goals.
3   Build positive identity development into the therapy encounter by creating empowering communicative activities and sharing responsibility for change.
4   Adopt an interactive style that fosters partnership rather than clinician-centered interaction. Methods such as collaborating on goal setting, following the conversational lead of the client, acknowledging conversational offerings as valid and interesting, and providing a genuine communicative experience will create a more relationship-oriented session and serve to foster not only improved communication but also increased communicative confidence.
5   Avoid institutional practices within the discipline that do not account for experiential and phenomenological facets of human life. For example, therapy should reflect not only interventions supported by research evidence, but also interventions that are suited to a particular client's goals, culture, lifestyle, personal history, and values.

CONCLUSION

Ultimately, the goal of speech-language therapy is to foster improved communicative participation of clients with communication disorders. Traditionally our role has focussed on reducing the "disorder" with the assumption that improved speech or language will foster increased participation in communicative life. However, over the years the authors have experienced many clients whose test scores improved considerably, yet their participation in communicative life and life satisfaction did not follow suit. After much reflection and study we have come to appreciate the need to go beyond working on the disorder and explicitly incorporate methods of working with clients to improve their communicative lives. This involves attention to domains beyond those measured by most formal speech or language tests. Rather, it involves attending to how a disorder impacts the life world of the client and how therapy can address these unique consequences. The implication, of course, is that we must attend to therapy interactions as much as we attend to tasks, materials, and concrete goals if we are to achieve the desired outcomes of our therapies. We offer a narrative-based approach as a means of addressing the life world of clients and building relationship-centered therapy interactions.

This chapter has argued that embedded within each clinical interaction is a story. In this story the participants assume a variety of roles and enact an unfolding plot. By attending to the meanings that our actions portray in the therapy narrative and working "with" clients instead of "on" impairments, then the many sides of the self of client and therapist are allowed to emerge in therapy. Thus, a narrative-based approach to speech-language therapy incorporates the myriad lived experiences and individual characteristics of participants. This includes listening to the stories that our clients relate as well as co-constructing clinical interactions in such a way as to create authentic relationships aimed at effecting relevant change.

5 Product and process depictions of rapport between clients and their speech-language pathologists during clinical interactions

Irene P. Walsh
Trinity College, Dublin

Judith Felson Duchan
State University of New York at Buffalo

INTRODUCTION

While most clinicians and researchers in the field of speech-language pathology would agree that the positive relationships between clinicians and their clients can be central to client progress, there has been little direct attention paid to the topic. Neither textbooks nor the clinical research literature have written much on how relationships get established or negotiated in clinical interactions. Instead, their primary focus has been on communication impairments and how clinicians should go about identifying, diagnosing, and remediating those impairments. If the clinical relationship is attended to at all, it is discussed briefly under the rubric of "rapport."

In this chapter we try to redress this general neglect of the study of rapport in speech-language pathology contexts by focussing on it directly. We will be examining how writers have conceptualized rapport in the past in the hope of coming up with a framework for best conceptualizing and studying it in the future.

TYPICAL DEPICTIONS OF RAPPORT

Dictionary definitions have treated rapport as a fixed entity, a connection or a sympathetic relationship between two people. For example, the *Collins English Dictionary* (2007, p. 1342), defines rapport as "a sympathetic relationship or understanding." The *Concise Oxford Dictionary* (1985, p. 857) defines it as "(useful) communication, (harmonious) relationship or connection, (in rapport with)."

Two attributes, sympathy and empathy, are commonplace in definitions of rapport. Sympathy is usually taken to mean *feeling* another's emotions.

Empathy, on the other hand, is the *understanding* of another's emotions. In this vein, sympathy is seen as being emotionally based, and empathy as conceptually based or as a person with aphasia has put it: "Perhaps sympathy is 'feeling for' someone else, while empathy, is 'feeling with' the other person" (C.D. in Joanette, Lafond, & Lecours, 1993, p. 34).

These definitions portray rapport as if it were an object, made up of raw materials such as feelings for and understandings of the other person in the relationship. Once rapport is created, the feelings and understandings become features of the relationship. This portrayal, which we will be calling a "product" view of rapport, treats rapport as if it were a desk or other crafted product, created and assembled from materials such as wood and nails. The product view of rapport is dominant in the speech-pathology literature. In textbooks dealing with clinical skills (e.g. Goldberg, 1997; Schum, 1986; Warner, Byers-Brown, & McCartney, 1984), rapport is discussed as something that must be constructed by clinicians early in their clinical sessions. Schum (1986, p. 28) comments: "As clinicians enter a clinical situation, they might recall that the goal of the first phase of the clinical process, be it diagnostic or therapeutic, is to establish rapport. In establishing rapport, clinicians want to get to know the client and to gather information from the client." Lesson plans often have as their first element, "establish rapport" (Hegde & Davis, 1999). The implication is that it is the clinician's responsibility to create this rapport and then, once rapport is "established," treatment can begin.

Textbooks also tend to treat rapport as being created out of and under the influence of clinicians. Indeed, Goldberg (1997) replaces the term sympathy with emotional empathy. He describes emotional empathy as involving: ". . . feelings clinicians experience by personally identifying with clients and their distress. On a very simplistic level, it is the equivalent of the current phrase 'been there done that'" (p. 167). Goldberg (1997) observes that the "been there done that" mentality has been applied to training in stuttering in which students were encouraged to stutter voluntarily in public places (Reitzes, 2007; Van Riper, 1973). The aim of the exercise was to give students experience of how it felt to stutter and how others reacted. Goldberg distinguishes emotional from cognitive empathy. He defines cognitive empathy as "an understanding at an objective level of what the client is experiencing" (Goldberg, 1997, p. 167). He elaborates (p. 167):

> To understand how clients may feel about the effects of a specific condition does not necessarily mean that clinicians have had to experience that communicative disorder. Emotions and feelings are not uniquely tied to specific communicative disorders. The feelings of humiliation that clients who stutter or have aphasia experience, when unable to effectively communicate, are probably no different than the feeling of humiliation an individual experiences when publicly berated by a supervisor for poor performance.

Another building block of rapport found in the literature on clinical relationships is "empathetic genuineness" (Haynes & Oratio, 1978). Haynes and Oratio (1978, p. 28) found four indicators of empathic genuineness that adult clients rated as important for therapeutic effectiveness: "The clinician listens attentively to me. The clinician possesses a good sense of humor. The clinician accepts me as a person and not just another case. The clinician is himself and does not play a false role."

Genuineness has been discussed in relation to various aspects of the speech-language pathology clinical relationship. A *genuine understanding* (Davis, 1983, p. 292), a *genuine concern* (Goldberg, 1997, p. 164) and showing a *genuine professional interest* (Warner, Byers-Brown, & McCartney, 1984, p. 22) are all seen as important attributes of clinical rapport.

The clinician's *serenity* is another element that has been forwarded as a helpful material in the construction of rapport. Cyr-Stafford has suggested that "the serene attitude of the knowledgeable professional who is familiar with these situations is reassuring to the person with aphasia" (Cyr-Stafford 1993, p. 108). By "serene attitude" Cyr-Stafford seems to mean one in which the clinician is calm and composed. A clinician who can hear a patient's troubles and concerns in a calm and focussed way may help to appease the distress a person is experiencing.

Along with empathy and patience, Davis (1983, 2000) discusses the notion of "unconditional positive regard" that has been seen as "a positive climate for therapeutic change" (Davis, 2000, p. 258). To ground this aspect of rapport, Davis (2000) draws from Carl Rogers (1961, p. 62) who feels clinicians need to have "an outgoing positive feeling without reservations, without evaluations." This feeling of acceptance provides an atmosphere in which the client feels free to express feelings of frustration or depression without fear of reprisal.

More recently, Fourie (2009) explored clients' perceptions of speech-language therapy and therapists. Through his analysis of interviews with adults with acquired communication or swallowing disorders, Fourie (2009, p. 979) identified a number of "attitudinal and behavioural characteristics of an ideal speech and language therapist from the perspective of the client." Attitudinal characteristics included constructs such as being "understanding," "gracious," "erudite," and "inspiring." Behavioral characteristics included being "confident," "soothing," "practical," and "empowering." Fourie concluded that although qualities such as these could be a reflection of the personalities of the therapists concerned, such constructs could certainly be useful in training "to provide learners with a model of ideal therapist contributions to a therapeutic relationship, so that therapists in training might reflect on how therapy is conducted rather than possibly only focusing on what therapy is conducted" (p. 996).

Thus far then, we have shown how rapport has been depicted in a dictionary definition as well as in clinical usage. It is seen by many as a product created by clinicians out of certain traits such as empathy, genuineness, serenity, graciousness, and an inspiring attitude. The clinician is the creator of the product, just as a carpenter assumes the role of creator of their product.

RAPPORT AS PROCESS

There is an emerging second view to the product rendering of rapport in the speech-language pathology literature. In this second view, rapport is portrayed as a dynamic process that is co-created and experienced in an ongoing way by both participants whenever they interact. This process view focusses on how rapport is created and how it evolves rather than what its fixed features are. This process view of rapport is not new. Indeed, it can be traced all the way back to 400 BC when Hippocrates and his followers talked about the importance of patients and doctors gradually feeling at ease with one another over time (Chapter 12). In the process view, rapport is ever changing, and not confined to particular segments of a therapy session. Emerick and Haynes (1973, p. 17) support this position when they state: "Rapport is developed over a period of time and is not easily established in a single session or during a few minutes at the initiation of one therapeutic encounter. Rapport must not only be developed it must be maintained, and this calls for continued effort."

Evidence for this more pervasive existence of rapport comes from recent research on clinical interactions. Ferguson and Elliot (2001), for example, explored elements within speech-language pathology sessions with people with aphasia. They compared sessions undertaken by two novice clinicians (an inexperienced and an experienced student in training), with that undertaken by an experienced clinician. They found that a greater proportion of conversational "moves" (p. 233), were taken up with rapport building by the experienced clinician (i.e. 17.9% of moves), than for student-led sessions (e.g. 7.4% for the inexperienced student and 0% for the experienced student). An interesting pattern emerged when rapport-building was tracked through such moves:

> The inexperienced student's session is a straightforward linear progression from establishing rapport, outlining tasks to follow, conducting two tasks, outlining the plans for the next session, reviewing the session as a whole, and then leave taking. The experienced student's session contains no separable segment where rapport building is the main focus. However, there is a cheerful and lively rapport between the student and her client, and it may be that in the movement from ward to the clinic room considerable rapport-building ensued
>
> (pp. 235–236).

> The experienced clinician spent considerable time specifically devoted to the building of rapport, while the student clinicians relied on the interchange during the conduct of tasks to facilitate rapport.
>
> (p. 237)

Coupland (2000), Walsh (2007), and Leahy and Walsh (2008) found that "small talk," a kind of social talk that can occur throughout clinical interactions, can serve a key role in the co-construction of rapport. A specific example of small talk illustrates this point.

The following interaction occurred within a session between a 13-year-old client (C) with a fluency disorder and his therapist (T) (from Leahy, 2004 and discussed in Leahy & Walsh, 2008). The session was already well underway when the following nontask-related topic emerged (Leahy, 2004, p. 78). Transcription conventions in this chapter are taken from Silverman (2006) – see Appendix.

Extract 1: "Are you getting your son that dog he wants?"
1 *C:*   are you getting your son that dog he wants?
2 *T:*   ((laughs)) he's still talking about it ooh ((laughs))
3 *C:*   don't you want one then?
4 *T:*   yeah I think so. It's just we would need to
5 *C:*   quite hard work . . . what breed do you think he will be?
6 *T:*   slightly slower
7 *C:*   wha:t breed do you think he'll be?
8 *T:*   I don't know what do you reckon?

Extract 1 is an example of small talk emergent in clinical discourse in that it involves nontask-related talk (initiated by the client) about topics such as the weather, hobbies, or enquiring after family members. In the opening lines, the small talk segment represents "an avoidance of rigidly structured discourse" (Simmons-Mackie et al., 2007, p. 10), such rigidity being more typical of a clinician-controlled practice session. Interestingly, however the therapist exerts clinician control in line 6 as she asks the client to go "slightly slower" when speaking, probably to aid or increase his fluency. The fact that the client makes this attempt in line 7 indicates trust in their relationship: the child cooperates with what he is asked to do, and the conversation continues following the minor disruption. What starts out as nontask-related talk, becomes task-related as the therapist weaves a probable session goal into the ongoing talk.

This idea that rapport infuses all interactional time in the clinician session is not new. Some authors have identified positive or successful experiences in the therapy process as crucial for creating "a positive atmosphere for therapeutic change" (Davis, 1983, p. 290; Goldberg, 1997, p. 162). If experiences are positive for both clinician and client, enjoyment and increased motivation are more likely. Rapport is therefore nurtured as therapy tasks unfold. Similarly in Brookshire's (1997) outline of a typical session plan for working with people with aphasia, he promotes the use of "error-free tasks" and a "positive conclusion" as essential parts of a therapy session. In Chapter 12 of this book, in her review of the history of clinical relationships, Duchan describes the recommendation by Avicenna, a medieval physician, that practitioners use "gladdening influences" to promote healing (Duchan, 2009, p. 12). Avicenna's gladdening influences may well have included those feelings of success that both clinicians and clients feel when therapy objectives are jointly met or therapy activities have been mutually enjoyed.

A second area of research that differs from traditional product views is one that portrays rapport as being co-created by the client and the clinician. The process view depicts rapport as ongoing and persistent, as permeating therapy sessions. It is typically co-constructed through talk. The client, in this view, assumes responsibility for rapport building and maintenance along with the clinician.

There are certain therapeutic contexts that tend to foster more client control and thereby offer a rich view of how rapport is co-constructed. For example, there are often occasions when clients engage in talking about their problems or in what has been called "troubles-telling" (Coupland, Coupland, & Robinson, 1992; Jefferson, 1985; Walsh, 2007). Troubles-telling often emerges within small talk or social talk sequences. Some authors have cast such talk as an undesirable departure from the work at hand. For example, Davis (2000, p. 244) makes an appeal for steering the patient away from this kind of talk:

> On some days a patient may just want to talk, and a clinician may want to be sympathetic to the patient's desire. However, the clinician has to make a judgment as to whether listening for a while is necessary for achieving successful stimulation on that day. The patient may need to vent, which should clear the air to resume treatment. In general, the clinician needs to manage valuable treatment time by gently steering the patient into planned activities.

Although Davis advocates that the clinician may listen for a while to troubles-telling, he advises the clinician to consider whether it is "necessary for achieving successful stimulation on that day" (p. 244). Coupland et al. (1992), Coupland (2000), and Walsh (2007) however, have argued for the important sociorelational function of troubles-telling in health care interactions. Listening to and engaging with troubles-telling, which can emerge at any time during a clinical session or episode, can pave the way for more successful and positive therapeutic relationships and in fostering rapport.

In the following extract (from Walsh, 2008, p. 87), a client (C) explains his diagnosis (i.e. schizophrenia) to his therapist (T) and to the speech-language pathology students present. The explanation was triggered by the client's own concern about some delusional thoughts he had had earlier in the day. The sequence therefore could be considered a troubles-telling one, where sharing of worries is aired in the session.

Extract 2: "That must be very upsetting"

1 C: it's a stupid disease
2 T: It's a stupid disease what makes it stupid?
3 C: it's a disease you think you've done something bad but you haven't
4 T: yeah
5 C: it's a disease I'm a paranoid schizophrenic that's my name my
       illness is
6 T: that's your?
7 C: the name of my illness is paranoid schizophrenia
8 T: that's right yeah yeah and it makes you think you've done things
9   and you haven't done them
10 C: yeah
11 T: that must be very
12 C   [it's a funny disease]
13 T: [upsetting yeah]

In this extract, the client's talk about his illness temporarily casts him in the expert role in the interaction. The client describes his condition as "*a stupid disease*" (line 1), before giving it its medical term in lines 5 and 7 (*paranoid schizophrenia*). In line 8 the therapist reiterates the client's description of the "disease" possibly for the sake of the students present. She then goes on to say, empathically, in lines 11 and 13 "*that must be very upsetting*", while the client simultaneously concludes that schizophrenia is "*a funny disease.*"

The uncertainty in the therapist's use of "that must be very upsetting" is respectful in this context, as she has no idea what it must be like to have schizophrenia. She acknowledges empathically that is must be very upsetting when the condition makes you "*think you have done something bad but you haven't.*" Rather than considering this troubles-telling as a departure from the work at hand, the talk is allowed to unfold over a number of turns. Additionally, there is some attempt to share perspectives or beliefs in this example too, where a "funny" disease in terms of its peculiarities (i.e. client's perspective) and it being described as "upsetting" (i.e. the clinician's perspective) are mutually aired, if not fully shared.

Another key ingredient of "rapport-as-process" is *trust*. Schum (1986, p. 16) states:

> The trust relationship is a critical factor in determining whether or not a client will accept counseling or any other assistance from the clinician. Clinical treatment, be it counseling or speech therapy or aural rehabilitation, involves getting a client to make changes. If clients felt capable of making changes on their own, the changes would have been made without a clinician's help. In many clinical cases clients cannot generate new alternatives or are frightened to try something new or radically different.

Clinicians encourage them, as an act of faith, to take a leap into the unknown, to try something different and maybe even scary. Clients must trust the clinician if they are to make that jump. They must believe that the clinician would not ask them to jump if it were dangerous and that the clinician will stay with them until they safely land.

In a more general reference to "rehabilitation counseling," Walker (1995, p. 619) comments: "by providing information and respecting the views of clients and family members, the rehabilitation counselor builds a relationship of mutual trust and conjointly constructs a rehabilitation plan."

The notion of *mutuality* is also important here, that is, in a trusting relationship, the clinician believes the client is committed to cooperating with them and, in turn, the client similarly believes that the clinician has his/her best interests at heart. Trust, therefore, is a two-way street. As Schum (1986, p. 16) concludes:

> Any conscious or unconscious resistance on the part of the client will hamper the effectiveness of clinical service. When clients resist, they are not trusting the clinician . . . Trying to talk clients into trust is not effective. Rather trust is enhanced when clinicians show interest in the clients, when clinicians listen to clients, and when clinicians learn each client's unique story.

A final aspect of rapport-as-process that has been reported on is the role of shared perspectives. For example, Goldberg (1997, p. 162) comments "[Rapport] is the establishment of a commonality of interest between two people or a mutual understanding of each other's values, beliefs, and experiences." An observation by Wulf (1979 p. 50), a speech pathologist with aphasia, emphasizes the importance of commonality of *interest:* "Speech therapy's rare talent is this: being able to hop on anybody's wave length and stay there . . .". Here we see how sharing a common *interest* can ultimately facilitate the joint establishment of goals between client and clinician. Having a commonality of *values* is another key aspect of being "on the same wavelength" (Goldberg, 1997, p. 162). Bunning (2004, p. 55) elaborates:

> Conflicts with the individual's personal value system may happen. A therapeutic goal may clash with the personal ideals held by the individual. e.g. a goal to work on drawing as a means of communication is felt to be of little value compared with speech. The personal style of the SLT and the resultant quality of rapport established between client and therapist may affect the individual's ability to contribute to assessment and therapy activities. A positive rapport between client and therapist is evidence of mutual appraisal and regard, and acknowledgement of the other person's right to contribute.

A significant point raised by Bunning (2004, p. 55), in her consideration of positive rapport, is the client's "right to contribute." This right to contribute may be interpreted to mean both contributing to the content of *what* is being discussed and *how* it is discussed. It is apparent in the analysis of clinical discourse that speaker–listener roles may be asymmetric and very different to those that operate in more casual conversation (Fisher & Todd, 1986). Sarangi and Roberts (1999) have discussed how institutional authority manifests in the discourse of medical encounters, while Cortazzi and Jin (2004), Walsh-Brennan (2002), Walsh (2004), and Leahy and Walsh (2008) discuss this phenomenon in speech-language pathology contexts. In such contexts, the clinician wields more "power" than the client in the unfolding talk. This power is most usually characterized by the clinician initiating topics to be discussed and terminating others and in establishing the turn-taking routine (e.g. "initiation–response–follow-up", akin to the structure of classroom discourse (Sinclair & Coulthard, 1975). In the following extract, it is clear who is holding the power in the interaction.

This extract is of a classroom language lesson in which a classroom teacher (T) is conducting a lesson to teach her student with autism (S) the names and functions of everyday objects (Duchan, 1983, p. 56).

Extract 3: "What do we do with a napkin?"

1	*T:*	What is this? ((holding up a napkin))
2	*S:*	((no answer))
3	*T:*	A napkin. What is this Robbie?
4	*S:*	A napkin.
5	*T:*	What do we do with a napkin?
6	*S:*	We play . . . ((sung))
7	*T:*	We wipe our mouth with a napkin. Wipe our mouth?
8	*S:*	Wipe our mouth?
9	*T:*	And hand?
10	*S:*	And hand?
11	*T:*	Wipe our mouth and our hand when we eat.
12		What do we do with a napkin?
13	*S:*	When we eat.

In this rigidly structured question–answer excerpt the teacher and student exhibit very little enthusiasm for the task. Nor do they seem to be responding positively to one another's challenges, feelings, or accomplishments. The only indication that an answer by the student is acceptable is that the teacher moves on to the next exchange in the sequence (turns 4, 9, 11). While the lesson is being co-constructed (the teacher asks the questions, the student responds), all the power is in the teacher's hands. We include this extract to illustrate a task in which there is very little positive rapport. The partners contribute in a perfunctory way. The student has neither power nor interest in the task at hand.

An informative power contrast to Extract 3 is the following in which the power between the clinician and client is fluid, with the clinician in control during the first part of the session and the client wielding more power later in the session.

In Extract 4 (previously discussed in Leahy & Walsh, 2008), the therapist (T) and client (C) are reviewing what was discussed in a previous session, that is, the client's reported tendency to say inappropriate things at times "out of the blue." The client's reported "disinhibition" in communication causes her a lot of stress. It had been decided in earlier sessions with her therapist that this pragmatic difficulty would become a focus for therapy.

The extract opens with a recap of what was discussed in the previous session, with the therapist attempting to reassure the client that the client herself understands the cause of her difficulty and has already generated her own possible solutions to the problem (Leahy & Walsh, 2008, p. 236):

Extract 4: "I could write a science book"
T: but you were saying to me the last day that those things are related you were explaining to me and you know best you're the expert on this not me – you're the expert that when your rate speeds up you're more inclined to blurt out those things
C: yeah
T: isn't that what you explained to me
C: that is true that is true
T: so it makes sense then if you try and slow your rate down
C: because I'll tell you what it's so fast it comes out so fast I haven't it in my mind to think about it first you know . . .
T: mm
C: you know when you are going to say something you say it in your mind
T: yes you do
C: well this you don't say it in your mind it just comes out
T: it just comes out without any warning
C: no no warning nothing
T: so there's kind of no rehearsal
C: nothing ((laughs)) I could write a science book
T: you could what?
C: I could write a science book ((loud laughter))
T: you could write science books ((laughs))
C: the Guinness Book of Records
T: the Guinness Book of Records
C: ((laughs))

The dynamic nature of power relations in talk can be identified in this extract. The opening lines see the therapist very much in control of the talk, only to relinquish that control to the client ("because I'll tell you what..."). Having given the therapist further detailed information as to the nature of her difficulty, the client concludes in a joking manner, that in the context of her knowing so much about her difficulty and its possible cause, she "could write a science book." She goes on to suggest that because she is able to describe her difficulties in such detail, she may qualify for an entry into the *Guinness Book of Records*. In this extract, we can see that the client feels she is indeed the "expert" on her own difficulties, as her therapist had suggested to her in the opening lines.

There are several indicators of comfort, egalitarianism, and enjoyment that exist between these participants. The positive affirmation from the therapist, along with the joking tone of the client and resulting joint laughter, are indicators that the interaction is a positive, rapport-building experience for both client and therapist. This segment can be seen as unusual, since most initiations, jokes, and teasing in clinical interactions have been found to be initiated by the clinician (Simmons-Mackie, 2004).

It follows therefore that, at times, sharing or relinquishing the power in talk that is usually "held" by the clinician in such interactions, may be conducive to nurturing and maintaining rapport (Walsh, 2004). When power is shared, clients have equal rights to talk; they are afforded a chance to initiate or air their concerns, to ask questions and to truly discuss and share opinions in an open and receptive environment. This is akin to a positive therapeutic process described by Simmons-Mackie et al. (2007, p. 9) in the context of group work, as "establishing the feel of discourse 'equality'." How open a clinician is to relinquishing the control of talk can often influence the resulting quality of rapport with the client.

We conclude, then that rapport-as-process is primarily characterized by joint involvement and mutual trust. Rapport can best be built through speaker–listener roles that are more equal in nature, that is, where control of talk and talking time is shared, where troubles are aired and where therapy objectives are jointly negotiated and planned. Rapport is built and nurtured throughout the period of therapeutic involvement. Moreover, rapport is enhanced when the activities between clinician and client are enjoyable and positive for the client and when the clinician and client share interests and values, especially those that pertain to the well-being of the client and his or her family.

CONCLUSION

In our examination of the literature we have found two separable views of rapport, one that construes rapport as a product and the other a process. Literature presupposing the product view depicts rapport as a fixed construct that is created by clinicians at either before or after the "work time" in a clinical session. It is the time when clinicians devote their attention to trying to "get to know" their clients. Clinicians who are seen as most successful in establishing rapport, under this view, are those who empathize with their clients, who manifest a genuine attitude toward them and who exhibit serene and inspiring personality traits. Rapport, in this view, is created by the all-powerful clinician, and is achieved through relationship talk that largely takes place outside the core work time of clinical sessions.

An alternative view found in the literature regards rapport as a co-constructed dynamic process that is achieved by both participants in an interaction. That is to say, it is experienced and created by both partners throughout the therapeutic interaction as a more egalitarian feel – or tone – to the interaction emerges. We provide evidence for the validity of this view by showing manifestations of rapport in the talk throughout the clinical interaction.

Table 5.1 outlines some of the differences between product and process views of rapport that we have outlined. We believe that doing a more extensive discourse analysis, along the lines of the excerpts above, would yield more insights into the nature and quality of rapport building and negotiating process between clinicians and clients. Attention to such talk-in-interaction can result in an increased awareness of discourse styles that may prove to inhibit or facilitate the negotiation of rapport. We found that manifestations of rapport were closely tied to power sharing, wherein the more egalitarian exchanges were those that gave space for clinicians to respond empathically

Table 5.1 Differences between product and process views of rapport

	Rapport as a product	*Rapport as a process*
Nature of rapport	Like an object – stable, with identifiable attributes	Like a negotiation – dynamic and fluid
How it comes to be	Constructed by clinicians	Constructed together by clinician and client
When it takes place	Beginning or ending of sessions set aside for "rapport building" and/or at discrete moments of time between therapy activities	Throughout the therapy session and episode; infuses all interactional time between client and clinician
What helps it become established	Clinician's personality traits such as empathy, serenity, friendliness. This can be trained by having clinician assume the role of the client, i.e. "be in their shoes"	Clinician and client both influence rapport negotiations. Some contexts that are rich for constructing rapport are small talk and telling one's troubles, and error-free activities that are enjoyable to both participants. Shared perspectives (interests, values) also help
Power and control	Clinicians have control of establishing rapport	Clients need to be empowered to negotiate rapport on their own terms.

and get to know their clients throughout their interactions. Clients too were afforded space and time to talk with their clinicians in a relaxed and open way. These rapport-experiencing characteristics could be the focus of training student clinicians to become more egalitarian and responsive to their clients as they work together to achieve mutually created clinical goals.

6 Clinical linguistic proficiency

Managing multiparty interactions

Alison Ferguson
University of Newcastle, New South Wales

INTRODUCTION

Therapeutic relationships are created and maintained through interaction, and so the way that talk, posture, and gesture are managed within clinical interactions provides one way to understand the nature of these kinds of relationship. The communicative interaction skills of clinicians can be seen as part of their essential tool kit, as these skills provide the medium through which therapy is conducted. This chapter will focus on interactions where the clinician needs to establish a therapeutic relationship with more than one person, as this situation presents specific challenges to the management of the clinical interaction. The chapter will explore two commonly encountered multiparty interactions: assessment through case-history interview when the client is accompanied by a family member, and group therapy. The nature of the clinical linguistic proficiency needed within these interactions will be explored through the analysis of case examples, making use of methodologies developed for the purpose of investigating interaction, namely conversation and discourse analysis. The implications of understanding the interactive achievement of therapeutic relationships for skill development will also be discussed.

CLINICAL LINGUISTIC PROFICIENCY

Good communicative skills are well recognized as a central requirement for practice across the range of health professionals. Clinicians who work with individuals with communication disability typically are highly skilled communicators, whose metalinguistic skills have been trained and practiced in order to enable them simultaneously to interact with clients and observe, analyze, and manipulate their own and their partners' communication. While many professionals are highly skilled in active listening and in communicating information and feelings clearly, I suggest that the simultaneous operation of receptive and expressive metalinguistic skills is most closely associated with the demands of the work involved in speech-language pathology and auditory rehabilitation. While all these aspects of communication are involved in clinical linguistic proficiency, it is the online application of metalinguistic observation, analysis, and manipulation that is the focus on this chapter.

The types of clinical linguistic skills required are currently underspecified. However, some preliminary information can be drawn from a study by Moore (2008) who investigated the clinical linguistic skills perceived to be required by clinicians and student clinicians. She posed three hypothetical clinical scenarios to 16 participants in focus groups involving 3 experienced speech-language pathologists and 13 speech-language pathology students (4 students prior to their first clinical experience, 4 students with preliminary experience in both adult and child settings, and 5 students in the final stages of their professional program). Using qualitative analysis, she found that the most commonly identified skills across the scenarios and across the range of clinical experience involved communication accommodation and the ability to ask questions. The most commonly mentioned communication accommodations involved adjustments for the nature of the communication disorder or the age of the client, simplifying language, using alternative and augmentative communication modes, slowing rate of own speech, and allowing extra time for responses (Moore & Ferguson, 2009). Moore (2008), who conducted a focus group with beginning students of speech-language pathology, noted that they were aware that clinicians needed practice asking questions in a way that is skilled and appropriate.

This chapter aims to illustrate some of the main features of clinical linguistic proficiency, and to do so looks particularly at one situation which places high demands on clinicians' linguistic proficiency – the situation in which he or she is working simultaneously with more than one person.

MULTIPARTY INTERACTION

The situation in which the clinician is working simultaneously with more than one person is described in this chapter as constituting a multiparty interaction. Linguists have suggested this term instead of the more commonly encountered description of a group interaction, in order to avoid pre-empting the nature of the interaction (Osvaldsson, 2004).

For example, a group interaction implies some degree of cohesion or common purpose, but some situations may involve multiple interactants without them necessarily being connected in any way. Analyzing multiparty interactions can be approached in many ways (Leahy, 2004), but this chapter makes use of two very different perspectives that have a substantial history of application to speech-language pathology: conversation analysis (Schegloff, 2003), and an approach that can be seen as falling within the general domain of discourse analysis – systemic functional linguistics (Armstrong, 2005). Conversation analysis is primarily concerned with the structural dynamics of how speakers manage the conversational floor, for example, who speaks when and for how long. Systemic functional linguistics is a semantic perspective primarily concerned with how language is used to exchange meanings concerned with experience and the interpersonal relationship. Each of these perspectives provides insights into the nature of clinical linguistic proficiency and point the way to how such proficiency might be observed, trained, and improvements measured.

Multiparty case-history interview

Possibly one of the first encountered challenges in managing multiparty interactions for most clinicians arose during their early student experiences when beginning to work with children, when they needed to take a case history from the parent with the child present. The clinician aims to find out sufficient information to understand the nature of the problem, with a view to identifying the options for further assessment and potential directions for intervention. The clinician needs to establish enough rapport with the parent to be able to ask probing and often personal questions, and to listen carefully in order to interpret the possible significance of the information being provided, and thus to be able to explore further with ongoing discussion. At the same time, there are purely practical reasons for keeping the child occupied in order to allow for both the clinician and the parent to concentrate. However, there is also the need to begin the process of observation of the child's communication (including the child's communication with the parent).

In previous research using case studies of assessment and treatment sessions for child stuttering (Ferguson, 1998), student clinicians were observed to do one thing at a time, spending only a short time in general chat for rapport building before going on to take a case history, and commencing observational assessment. The experienced clinician ("Caitlin") was observed to multitask, making use of the case history and observational assessment to build rapport with both the parent ("Mary") and the child ("Brad"), and returning to clarify points of the case history following particular observations (pseudonyms are used). Example 1 illustrates how Caitlin managed Brad's "interruptions" by taking the opportunity to develop rapport with Brad and Mary in shared play. Her later comments made it clear that she had also been using these moments to observe Brad's communication ("Listening to him he sounds terrific") and to compare these observations with Mary's reports regarding Brad's recent stuttering. The moments that involved all three occurred as often as the moments in which only Caitlin and Mary were involved in discussing the case history.

Example 1: Child case history interview
1 *Caitlin:*   Yes, um, perhaps I could ask you on, on this scale,[1] how, what would his speech be at the moment? What sort of range would it be?

 2 *Mary:* Like this morning?

 3 *Caitlin:* Mm, the last week.

 4 *Mary:* [Overlap] The last few days . . . this last week.

 5 *Caitlin:* Yeah.

 6 *Mary:* Probably about, maybe about three.

 7 *Caitlin:* Mm.

 8 *Brad:* Mum. [Brad playing with train set]

 9 *Mary:* Yes?

10 *Brad:* This train will have a big load.

11 *Mary:* It has got a big load hasn't it?

12 *Brad:* It's really got a big load.

13 *Mary:* Mm

14 *Brad:* Where's this one go?

15 *Caitlin:* That could fit on the back there. [Caitlin adds carriage] That's it.

16 *Brad:* Where's this go mum?

17 *Mary:* Where could that one go?

18 *Brad:* Mm.

19 *Mary:* Well, you could turn this one upside down. [Mary plays toy figures, putting into carriage]

20 *Brad:* Mm.

21 *Mary:* And put, put it on there for a change. How's that?

22 *Brad:* Good. Where's this one go?

23 *Mary:* Oh that one could go maybe on top of there. It might be a spare one.

24 *Brad:* Yeah.

25 *Mary:* How's that?

26 *Brad:* Good, how come the train can't go?

27 *Mary:* You'll have to pull it along sweetheart.

28 *Brad:* It's stuck.

29 *Caitlin:* [Overlap] We're gonna wear these things off now.

30 *Brad:* It's stuck. It's stuck mummy

31 *Mary:* [Sitting back in chair] Mm, is it? Oh dear maybe it's just stopped at the station.

32 *Brad:* Mm.

33 *Caitlin:* How about this morning, what have you heard?

The clinical linguistic skills evident in Example 1 are Caitlin's active listening and attention to the interaction between Brad and Mary (lines 8–14), resulting in her joining in the play (line 15). Both Mary and Caitlin participated in nonverbal play concurrently through lines 15 to 29, putting carriages and toys onto the train. The timing of Caitlin's return to direct case-history questioning followed Mary's cue (line 31) where she withdrew from physical contact with the toys and sat back.

In analyzing this sample of interaction from the perspective of conversation analysis, the main point of interest is how the interruption was managed (Schegloff, 2000). At no point did either adult attempt explicitly to take back the floor. Instead, the adults contributed to the child's focus of attention through turns involving repetition and reformulation of the child's utterances (Mary, lines 11, 17), and suggestions in the form of statements (Caitlin, lines 15, 29; Mary, lines 19, 21, 23, 27, 31). These data point to the recognition that this moment in the case-history interview was not perceived as an interruption by the interactants, but rather as part of the main business of the interview, i.e. since the purpose of this adult conversation was to discuss the child's speech, this opportunity for communication with the child was seen as part of the process.

Additionally, through the semantic perspective of systemic functional linguistics, this exchange can be recognized as talk that accompanies action, rather than constituting the action itself (Martin & Rose, 2003). It is the nonverbal play with the child that was the shared focus of meaning for the interactants, and so the verbal contributions of both adults were eliciting primarily nonverbal play rather than longer verbal responses. Thus, while this moment in the interview provided the clinician with some opportunity to observe the child's speech, she needed longer verbal utterances from the child in order to measure disfluency, and indeed she moved on to this stage of observation later in the assessment session ("I might talk to Brad for a little while and then I've got some more things I want to ask you").

The issues for multiparty interaction involving child clients also involve questions as to the extent to which information or wording needs to be modified for the overhearing child, particularly for older children who need to be included where possible. For adult clients, it is when the communication disability is severe that the complexity of multiparty interaction in case-history interviews arises. Severe communication disability such as severe aphasia is in itself sufficiently challenging for professionals-in-training to require specific assistance with skill development (Holland, 1998; Legg, Young, & Bryer, 2005). However, with severe disability a further challenge arises since it is common for a family member or carer to accompany the person for outpatient medical or other health-related appointments. The clinician has to balance the need to obtain relevant case-history information with the need to observe the client's communication as well as seeking to help the person with aphasia maintain face even when assisted. The interaction can be described as a complex sequence of alternating "speaking for" (Croteau, Le Dorze, & Morin, 2008), "speaking help," and "speaking about" (Ferguson & Harper, 2009; Harper, 2008). Example 2 illustrates the commonly encountered moment in case-history taking where the client ("Alfred") is asked to provide basic biographical details in the presence of his wife ("Wilma"). Note that pseudonyms and substitute details have been used for the husband and wife, and that I was the interviewer (Ferguson, 1993, p. 410).

Example 2:   Adult case history interview

  1 *Alison:*   Um, just, names and ages and things like that.
  2 *Wilma:*   Uh huh yeah. Go on. You go first. [gestures to Alfred]
  3 *Wilma:*   Alfred. You want his full name?
  4 *Alison:*   Yep.
  5 *Wilma:*   Alfred Benjamin Cook.
  6 *Alison:*   And how old are you? [to Alfred]
  7 *Wilma:*   Seventy five.
  8 *Alison:*   And your date of birth? [to Alfred]
  9 *Alfred:*   This address?
 10 *Alison:*   Date of birth.
 11 *Wilma:*   No, no 1st of January.
 12 *Alfred:*   Oh.
 13 *Wilma:*   1925.
 14 *Alison:*   How long were you at school, Alfred?
 15 *Alfred:*   Ah, f-, fifteen, wasn't it? Am I right darl? [to Wilma]
 16 *Wilma:*   I don't know. I didn't know you then.
 17 *Alfred:*   I, I think so, yeah.

In example 2, I made a number of attempts (lines 6, 8) to obtain the information directly from the person with aphasia (Alfred), but his wife (Wilma) often spoke for him (lines 3, 5, 7, 11, 13). However, Wilma held back from taking the floor on two occasions, initially (line 2), and again when she did not know the information (line 16). While such joint productions would be unusual in other circumstances, in the presence of aphasia, this kind of teamwork can be seen as a valuable resource, and one that is explicitly sought by the person with aphasia in the above example (line 15). When fast information exchange is needed, such teamwork can be useful for all interactants, and additionally can allow the clinician to observe the strategies and effectiveness of the communicative partnership. For example, in the case of Alfred and Wilma, further analysis of their nonverbal communication revealed that it was only when Alfred looked directly toward Wilma that she would speak on his behalf, and even during lengthy word-searches in which he would look down or away, she did not speak for him (Ferguson, 1993).

   Conversation analysis of this sample highlights the way the turn-taking structure was used by the interactants to mediate repair of trouble in the communication (Schegloff, Jefferson, & Sacks, 1977). Wilma made use of a trajectory for repair described as "same turn other repair," which is relatively uncommon in everyday communication between nonbrain-damaged inter-actants, i.e. she corrected the speaker who had the floor, within that speaker's turn. It might be suggested in therapy that Wilma made less use of this trajectory, while continuing her very effective use of "next turn other repair." Also, Alfred's ability to make use of the repair trajectory "self-initiated other repair" helped him to contribute to the conversation while indicating his communicative competence through explicit recognition of trouble, and this could be encouraged.

From a systemic functional linguistics perspective, this sample highlights an important role for shared knowledge in the exchange. The most salient aspect of the context of situation for this exchange is the role relationship of the interactants, namely husband and wife (high shared knowledge) with myself (no shared knowledge). My use of dynamic conversational moves to support the exchange of meaning is thereby limited to repetition of immediately preceding utterances ("co-text," see lines 8, 10). This is in sharp contrast to Wilma's ability to contribute substantive (or "synoptic") conversational moves on behalf of Alfred. When knowledge is not shared (lines 14–16), then the exchange of meaning becomes uncertain. This insight has implications for working with Alfred, since it highlights how dependent he is on the presence of his wife (or other familiar people) to be able to communicate effectively. Directions for intervention would need to provide ways to build the shared knowledge of communicative partners (for example, through Alfred carrying relevant written information with him to give to others).

In both the examples of multiparty case-history interviews, it can be seen that the presence of the third party was an essential component of the total assessment process. It is also apparent that the clinician in such situations is required to expand the scope of metalinguistic attention to include the concurrent observation of all parties. While the clinician will also need time devoted specifically to the individual with the communication disability, multiparty interactions provide highly informative opportunities to assess communication in interaction. Such observations provide rich insights into directions for further assessment as well as for intervention.

GROUP THERAPY

In everyday life, communication frequently involves multiple partners and so group therapy provides an authentic situation for both children and adults to practice and explore ways to increase their communicative effectiveness. Additionally, the group therapy context provides opportunities for individuals with communication disability to receive the support of others who are best able to empathize with their difficulties, and to observe and support others with similar difficulties (Elman, 2007). For these reasons, clinicians may seek to provide therapy within a range of group contexts. However, group leadership or facilitation is not necessarily an experience that is familiar to novice clinicians. In relation to group therapy, the previously mentioned study by Moore (2008, p. 16) posed the following hypothetical scenario to the participants in focus groups of clinicians and students: "You are attending a group for people who have had a stroke and as a result have difficulty communicating. The aim of the group is to maximise communication and build confidence. What communication skills does a speech pathologist group leader need to have?" Two skills were identified for this scenario that did not arise in the other scenarios discussed: facilitation of conversation among the group members, and the use of humor.

The recognition of the role of facilitation accords with literature that indicates the importance of this role for the clinician in aphasia therapy groups (Simmons-Mackie et al., 2007). Moore (2008) noticed that participants recognized that facilitation was a deliberate activity that required planning and practice on the part of the clinician to become skilled in its application.

In the literature on aphasia therapy, humor has been described as an important facilitator of interpersonal dynamics and suggested as a primary pathway toward adjustment and re-establishment of identity in both individual and group therapy (Madden, Oelschlaeger, & Damico, 2002; Norris & Drummond, 1998; Sherratt, 2007; Simmons-Mackie, 2004). For the focus group participants in Moore's study, humor was seen as a way of doing the conversational work of saving face for participants when the clinician needed to take a directive role in opening up the floor for group members with more severe communication disability.

While the facilitation of conversation among group members was recognized by students across the range of experience, the role of humor was discussed only by the experienced clinicians (Moore & Ferguson, 2009). Perhaps the experience of the clinicians had contributed to their recognition of this skill, and potentially to their deliberate use of humor in managing group interactions. So how are these clinical linguistic skills of experienced clinicians demonstrated within an actual group therapy session?

The interaction presented in Example 3 occurred in an aphasia therapy group which met weekly, usually with around eight members with aphasia, two speech-language pathologists and two speech-language pathology students. The intervention model for this aphasia therapy group was life participation (Elman, 2005), where the goals for members were jointly negotiated within the broader aims of maximizing communicative competence and confidence within increased opportunities for social participation (Alston, Sherratt, Ferguson, & Vajak, 2006; Sherratt, Alston, & Ferguson, 2007). In the following example, pseudonyms are used, with clinicians' names starting with "C" (Catherine, Christine), the names of group members with aphasia starting with "A" (Ann, Adele, Alan, Adrian), and the wife of a group member with aphasia (Wendy). As well as these seven participants, three other people with aphasia and two students were present and engaged through shared attention and laughter.

Example 3: Aphasia therapy group

1 *Catherine:*   OK, good-oh. All organized. It'll be a good night.
2 *Adrian:*   [Laughs].
3 *Catherine:*   Anyone going to do some ballroom dancing while you're there?
4 *Ann:*   No [laughs].

5 *Christine:*	[To Ann] Apparently they do ballroom dancing there.
6 *Alan:*	[To Christine] Yeah I used to do ballroom dancing there.
7 *Christine:*	[To Alan] Really.
8 *Catherine:*	[To Ann] Did you?
9 *Catherine:*	Adrian and Wendy, you might get up and have a dance?
10 *Adrian:*	Oh yes.
11 *Adele:*	[To Alan] You?
12 *Alan:*	Eh?
13 *Adele:*	You, Alan, get up and dance?
14 *Alan:*	Can't understand [jokingly] [General laughter from group].
15 *Catherine:*	Any excuse, any excuse.

In Example 3, the group was discussing a planned outing to a local club. Catherine's skill in facilitating contributions from a number of members can be seen through the combination of the general and directed questions she used (lines 3, 9). The success of the facilitation of interaction among group members can be seen from lines 11 through to 15, where Adele (who had moderate–severe expressive aphasia) drew out a further contribution from Alan. This moment in the sample provides an illustration of the role of humor (as discussed above) in group therapy, since Alan feigned a disinclination to dance by pretending first not to hear and then playing on his aphasia and pretending not to understand – a joke greatly appreciated by the group in general. This was a complex interplay invoking past and present social identities in a very supportive social environment. One of the clinicians (Catherine) described her communicative work in this setting as closely reflecting Elman's metaphor of jazz music to describe group therapy interactions (Elman, 2004).

Klippi (2003) has applied conversation analysis to describe the nature of interaction in aphasia therapy groups, and emphasizes the collaborative nature of such group conversations. This high degree of collaboration can be seen in the above example between the two clinicians, from the way Christine (line 5) provided Ann (who had significant auditory comprehension problems) with a repetition of the information about the topic of the question posed by Catherine, allowing for a second attempt by Catherine (line 8) to clarify Ann's previous response (line 4).

From a systemic functional linguistics perspective, it is of interest to note the way the interactants made use of the lexicogrammatical resources of mood and modality to negotiate the proposal of future dancing. The mood of a clause consists of the subject (S) and the finite (F), and the choices speakers make as to their ordering for making declarative statements (S + F) or interrogative (F + S), shift the negotiability of what is being discussed. In this example, Catherine omitted the finite (line 3) and in line 9 she used a statement structure (S + F) with added rising intonation rather than a direct question. Additionally, Catherine added to the negotiability of the proposal by using the linguistic resources for modality in line 9, when she used "might" rather than the more straightforward future "will". While the speakers with aphasia had relatively reduced access to these lexicogrammatical resources due to their aphasia, both Adele and Alan negotiated the future possibilities by making use of a command structure (line 13) from Adele, countered by Alan's negative and modalized "can't" response in line 14.

Anecdotally, students undertaking such roles as part of their clinical experience often describe their surprise at the difference between watching experienced clinicians facilitating a therapy group (perceived as relatively simple) and actually running such a group themselves (perceived as very difficult). Clinicians can find themselves in a kind of conversational "ping-pong" where they are taking the bulk of the initiating turns and group members are thereby limited to responsive turns, and this kind of group interaction has been described in the literature (Kovarsky, Kimbarow, & Kastner, 1999; Wilcox & Davis, 1977). The analysis of such moments within group sessions (through either transcription or watching video recordings) provides clinicians with the opportunity to "unpack" the linguistic skills that are needed in this kind of situation. This kind of structured and active reflection assists in identifying skills needed by the clinician, as well as sharpening the observation of the group members' roles and contributions so assists with therapy planning.

IMPLICATIONS

This chapter has drawn attention to two situations involving multiparty interactions that are commonly encountered by clinicians and that require highly developed communication skills. The analysis of such multiparty interactions has been suggested to provide clinicians with directions for assessment and intervention, while also providing important insights into the development of such aspects of clinical linguistic proficiency (for both novice and experienced clinicians). But how then does clinical linguistic proficiency develop – to what extent might such proficiency reflect pre-existing communication skills and to what extent can it be improved through specific professional education and ongoing professional development activities?

The previously mentioned research by Moore (2008, p. 26) identified that both students and clinicians saw clinical linguistic skills as pre-existing (in the sense that students enter professional programs with skills developed through their life experience to date) as well as learned through their academic and clinical experiences. For example, "I just find some students do have the package that far more readily can be fine-tuned but some have to be taught it quite specifically so I'm not actually sure that it is developmental. I think you can get better at it but some students certainly come in with a developed package" (Experienced clinician focus group).

From such comments as these it could be suggested that both pre-existing skills and additional learning experiences underpin the exercise of the clinical linguistic proficiency needed to work with clients within multiparty interactions. An important step toward developing greater skills is the ability to describe what is to be learned, but within methods used to assess the development of student clinical competencies; the description of communicative competence needs to be sufficiently broad to apply across a wide range of clinical situations (McAllister, Lincoln, Ferguson, & McAllister, 2006). Fortunately, in order to be able to specify aspects of clinical linguistic proficiency more finely, the clinical professions have a number of analytic tools available to assist. The necessary shift is to turn the application of such analyses back on our own therapeutic interaction.

Past research has tended to approach the training of communication skills from a behavioral perspective (Boone & Prescott, 1972; Klevans, Volz, & Friedman, 1981). However, more recently Horton and colleagues (Horton, Byng, Bunning, & Pring, 2004) have reported teaching speech-language pathology students a linguistic framework to analyze therapeutic interactions. Their preliminary research suggests that it is possible to promote this kind of learning within a classroom setting, but further research is needed to establish whether such learning assists in the students' clinical interactions.

CONCLUSIONS

From the issues presented in this chapter, it can be seen that clinicians who work with individuals with communication disorders require a high level of communicative ability to enable them to develop and maintain therapeutic relationships, since the medium through which such relationships are managed is itself both the problem and the means for resolution. These challenges to the therapeutic relationship exist for all clinical interactions, and particularly for multiparty interactions, given the complexities of managing diverse levels of communicative proficiency as well as different needs for therapeutic support that exist across the interactants. Two analytic approaches offered insights into clinical interaction, namely, conversation analysis and the discourse analytic approach of systemic functional linguistics. It is clear that the understanding of how skilled clinicians communicate effectively with their clients is still developing, and further research is needed to deepen our knowledge and its potential application to promoting the high levels of clinical linguistic proficiency needed for mediating therapeutic relationships.

NOTE

1 Using a severity scale for parent report within the Lidcombe Program for early stuttering (Onslow, Packman, & Harrison, 2003)

7 Challenges to therapeutic processes

The cross-cultural context

Linda Hand
University of Auckland

INTRODUCTION

There has been an increasing awareness of issues of cultural diversity in the work of speech-language therapy over recent times (Battle, 2002; Isaac, 2002; Martin, 2009). Indeed, there are few parts of the world in which speech, language and hearing clinicians operate without "challenges" of cultural and linguistic diversity. However, most models of speech-language therapy/ pathology are based on the monolingual speaker in a monocultural context, in which "normal language" is the language employed by a monolingual (English) speaker. Therefore "normal language development" is that of a monolingual learner; and therapeutic talk and interaction is based on dominant culture[1] norms. Sometimes clinicians are aware of some of these issues, and bi/multi-lingualism and bi/multi-culturalism are superimposed onto those models. In this way, Spanish norms might be adopted for English tests; or additional courses may be added in to educational programs that deal with cultural issues and the adaptations that clinicians may need to make to span language and cultural barriers.

CROSS-CULTURAL CONTEXTS IN CLINICAL PRACTICE

There is much that could be said about practice in multilingual or cross-lingual contexts. However, the focus of this chapter will be on communication where both client(s) and clinician(s) are speaking the same language, in this case, English; but are speaking it from different cultural perspectives. In practice, as Gee (2005) illustrates so effectively, we are all members of multiple cultural and communication groups. We are professionals, clients, parents, siblings, children, sports players, concertgoers, and there are many ways in which diversity can manifest itself, both across and within people. There is no lack of advice in the literature with regard to spanning cultural and language barriers. However, this advice tends to be about backgrounds, about information, about "us" knowing more about "them"; and in general, the cultural discourse of "otherness" as Shi-xu (2005) phrases it.

Inherent in this advice, is the lack of a critical theory perspective that takes into account the inseparability of *difference* from *power* issues, or *difference* from *discrimination* as Roberts, Davies, and Jupp (1992) termed it. Neither does this approach sufficiently focus on discourse or the interactional issues involved. Recent work has used critical approaches and socially informed linguistic theory to give insights into power and control, among other things, into workplace interactions, but these have not included speech, language, or hearing therapy contexts (Drew & Heritage, 1982; Fairclough, 2001; Gee, 2005; Halliday & Matthiessen, 2004; Holmes & Stubbe, 2003; Martin & Rose, 2003).

Instead, these recommendations in the speech-language therapy literature have dealt with issues of content (i.e. information to the clinician with regard to other cultures or topics that need to be covered in assessment); the norms of interaction in different cultures; or variations in service delivery that take into account cultural norms. Moreover these recommendations have covered culturally sensitive details such as forms of address, issues of religion (e.g. avoiding particular dates, references, or foods), or particular cultural details (such as not showing the soles of your feet to a person from Thai culture) (Hodge, 1986; Hyun & Fowler, 1995; Wilson, 1996). Such advice also makes suggestions as to how clinicians might change test items in assessments and intervention in order to be culturally appropriate (Hamayan & Damico, 1991; Isaac, 2002; Wyatt, 2002). Indeed, most advice (e.g. almost all the contributing authors in Battle, 2002) relates to how the clinician needs some kind of background knowledge about the culture and the nature of the languages of their client; as well as the relationship between such languages and the dominant language – in this case English. This background know-ledge is presented as essential for any assessment or intervention. Some authors include a need for the professional to work to become a cross-cultural communicator, with cultural awareness training and a willingness to examine their own attitudes and practices (e.g. Terrell & Terrell, 1993).

However, it is not only background issues that are monocultural in their starting points. The therapy interactions in speech-language therapy/path-ology and possibly audiology may also be implicitly monocultural. What constitutes "good communication" or "good therapy practice" in the work-place is based on values about things such as explicitness and positive affect, which are essentially cultural notions borne out in cultural features of communication. These issues may be related to issues of "rapport," seen by many as an essential part of the therapeutic task (see Chapter 5 for more on this point). Therefore, although most of the advice given is relevant to discourse, it rarely becomes as precise as actual client–professional discourse; nor does it discuss how this discourse (i.e. the local interaction in language) might be changed. Some of these recommendations are more precise than others, and the significance of background knowledge can become very clear, as it is in the following example from Bryce's work (2002, p. 619). This author is an Australian non-Aboriginal doctor working in northern Australia:

It is important to recognise that Yolngu [this Aboriginal group's name for themselves] (particularly older people) do not consider themselves in any way to be educationally inferior to non-Aboriginal people. If a doctor explains a health issue in a way that is confusing or does not make sense, then it is usually assumed that the health professional does not really know what is going on. That is to say, the confusing story is assumed to be an attempt by the health professional to hide his or her ignorance. Even worse, it may be assumed that the doctor has more sinister intentions. Conversely, if a Yolngu patient hears their health story in a way that makes sense to them then this is considered proof that the health professional is competent and on the right track. Good communication is an important way to establish credibility.

Acknowledging, understanding, and being skilled in cross-cultural communication is therefore not just a feel-good issue. It is central to effectiveness and satisfaction, for both clients and clinicians.

DISCOURSES AND OUR ROLES IN THEM

There are a great many parts to communication, and many of them are involved in cross-cultural discourses. For example, there is a major relationship between politeness systems in discourse, and culture (Brown & Levinson, 1987; Scollon & Scollon, 2001). Politeness factors in discourse are myriad: they include the extent to which directness is appropriate, the amount of deference to authority, the extent to which differences of opinion are tolerated and how they might be expressed and by whom; and a whole range of minutiae of communication (such as lengths of pauses, lengths of turns, eye contact, proxemics, gestures, frequency of feedback/discourse markers, the judgment placed on overlapping talk or interruption, meanings of prosody, use of modality, choices of lexis, and forms of greetings) (Brown & Levinson, 1987; Hodge, 1986; Pauwels, 1995; Roberts et al., 1992). Differences in the use and meaning given to these signals between communicators in an interaction commonly result in a perception that politeness has been violated – the person has been rude, or not very friendly or respectful, the interaction is not comfortable or satisfying, or has been downright offensive (Roberts et al., 1992; Scollon & Scollon, 2001; Wierzbicka, 1991).

It is very difficult to be consciously aware of these features. They are internalized, and associated with values the speaker may be only partly aware of having. Some that tend to feature in Western speech-language therapy contexts are being "a nice person," being "friendly," being "approachable," being "appropriately professional." We convey many of these values in our communicative behaviors. However, when we interact with those who may have different values attached to different communication features, cross-cultural miscommunication could occur. For example, we may smile, make compliments, offer our first name and call a client by their first name. If a person is expecting formal signals, these may seem "over-friendly" or "over familiar" or just be sending confusing signals – what is going on here? What is this person conveying to me? What is their role?

Speech-language therapists are experts in communication. However, this does not mean they are necessarily any better than other groups in cross-cultural communication. When professionals get serious about working with diversity, it is easier to deal with "facts" than it is to deal with discourses, or interactions. However, there may be great value for us in looking at discourse, and the analysis of our professional discourses, for the insights and the recommendations they may provide (see Ferguson, 2009, for an excellent discussion of critical discourse analysis applications in speech-language therapy).

For the remainder of this chapter, I shall illustrate my points with some data gathered from speech-language therapy clinics in Sydney, Australia. These data came from 12 initial interviews between speech-language therapists, all members of the dominant culture, and parents of children with suspected communication difficulties who came from culturally and linguistically diverse backgrounds (Lebanese, Chinese, Iraqi, Iranian, Syrian, Chilean, Cook Island, and Spanish). All the parents judged themselves to be fluent in English and not to require an interpreter, and none of the sessions was characterized by more than minor misunderstandings based on language itself. The clinicians were all female, seven had less than 5 years of experience, while five clinicians had been working for 5 to 15 years. The sample represented a typical range of clinician and client characteristics for this region.

THE CROSS-CULTURAL DISCOURSE

There are many ways that cross-cultural discourse manifests in texts, as was briefly indicated above. Some are pervasive and subtle, while others appear to be more obvious. There were many other points where this was relevant, but the most obvious points of cross-cultural discourse in these texts was when culture and language issues appeared as topics in themselves, and these direct topics were remarkably interesting. It was not only the aspects of the topic of culture and language that appeared, but also those that did not, how they appeared, what was done with them in the processes of the discourse that illustrated the challenges of cross-cultural discourse in the speech-language therapy context.

The topic of language and culture might be expected to figure in all these sessions, given the nature of the clients. There might also be expected to be a baseline set of points raised and discussed, which would be reasonably consistent across sessions. However, this did not prove to be the case. In two sessions, there was no talk about culture and language (i.e. non English language) at all (see Table 7.1). When such talk did occur, the actual topics did not cover anything like the range of language and culture-related topics

Table 7.1 Content of talk on language and culture

Content of talk on language and culture	No. of sessions (N = 12)
Central	
Language; child and cross-language issues re disorder	4
Language; child's development in their languages	4
Peripheral	
Language, pronunciation and spelling of names	3
Language; parent's languages, country of origin	5
Language; parent on child's suitability for ESL class	1
Culture; clinician re parent's religion	1

ESL, English as a second language.

suggested in the literature (e.g. Battle, 2002; Hammer & Marting, 1998) and varied greatly from interview to interview. The majority of the topics raised, I classified as "peripheral" topics to the core business of speech-language therapy, for example a concern about the spelling and pronunciation of names. There were no questions from the clinician that probed any cultural values or issues of specific family practices that appeared to be motivated by an awareness of intercultural communication issues. Similarly, there was no discussion about the cultural differences between the dominant Australian culture and the home culture of the family.

The initial point revealed by this picture is that although the material in the literature has been there for some time, and Australians are very aware of their identity as a multicultural nation, the recommendations do not appear to have yet penetrated very far into the practices of the profession.

Why might such advice apparently be ignored? There are some clues as to why this might be the case even at this surface level. For example there was more (non-English) language- and culture-related talk in the sessions when it was raised by the parents, and 4 of the 12 clinicians did not raise any language or culture-related topics. It may be that the clinicians found it difficult to bring up these topics because they were following the politeness rules of their own culture. Or the clinicians were encountering the discourse boundaries that inhibit talk on such issues in ordinary conversations. This seemed to be particularly true in relation to culture, as there was no evidence of discussion relating to the topic of culture and language in areas such as child-rearing practices, beliefs about child language development or disorders, or the patterns of communication at home, all of which are important and relevant, and clearly discussed in the literature. Where such talk did arise, it was mostly about languages spoken and countries of origin and birthplaces of the people concerned, and most of that was not in the professional domain, as we shall see later. Only one topic on culture, as opposed to language, occurred, and it was in "social" mode, beginning with whether the family celebrated Christmas or not.

More revealing than topics or their absences was the actual discourse. The topics concerning names and pronunciation indicated a number of aspects of ease and unease in cross-cultural discourse on the part of clinicians.

Extract 1: C = clinician (speech-language therapist), P = parent (mother of child)

364 *C:*   (to mother) [what's] your first name
365 *P:*   L_____. [spells first two letters]
366 *C:*   yup
367 *P:*   [spells next 2 letters]
368 *C:*   yup
369 *P:*   h-e-z
370 *C:*   h-e-z?
371 *P:*   yeah
372 *C:*   how's that pronounced?
373 *P:*   L_____
374 *C:*   L L_____
375 *P:*   yeah that's it. don't say it again and get a mistake [points at C, both laugh]
376 *C:*   we'll keep it at that once
377 *P:*   or you can call me L_____ [an English name, phonetically close] [laughs]
378 *C:*   L_____, oh isn't that interesting
379 *P:*   yeah just write "L_____" next to it
380 *C:*   okay. well, we don't mean to insult you by using the English term it's just that it's a lot easier to get the mouth around
381 *P:*   [laughs] yeah that wasn't too bad, you know, when you said it

This is a relatively short episode in the session, but interesting in terms of the work that it did. It labeled the clinician as relatively incompetent; she cannot pronounce or spell names. It also labeled the parent's cultural group as clearly "other" in relation to the service, as the professional would be unlikely to not know names that were "ordinary" (see turn 380 – a nonexplanation but a kind of apology for incompetence). It is also however an indicator of cultural awareness: the clinician presents herself as knowing that names are important and she is anxious not to offend, rather than ignoring the issue. It is taken seriously as a topic. The relatively "incompetent" role is emphasized in the "teasing" exchange initiated by the parent in turn 375; and in her praise of the clinician in turn 381. This is in essence a role reversal, in expert–consultee relationships, and both sides show it in their discourse.

The discourse in this case is therefore an interesting juxtaposition of cultural competence and incompetence; and these are conflicting discourses for the clinician. But they also convey that it is apparently acceptable for a clinician to be incompetent in cross-cultural communication on the principle that if it involved too much loss of face for them, it would not be raised. The other occasions in the texts where incompetence becomes normalized appeared when topics were clearly "social," where the professional had no obligation to be expert. These issues are at best ambiguities and raise the question: is cultural competence a professional competence or not? The discourse of these clinicians tended to label it as not.

There were five broad topics that concerned a language other than English and the families concerned. There seemed to be almost an inverse relationship between the centrality of these topics to the issues of cross-cultural communication and their appearance in this discourse: the most common topics were the least central to the issues. Seven of the 12 interviews contained talk about languages spoken by a parent, about countries of origin, and/or about spelling or pronunciation of names. They concerned only broad or relatively minor matters of nondominant language (see Extract 2).

Extract 2: C = clinician (speech-language therapist), P = parent (mother of child)
(3 minutes settling into chairs etc.; talk not intelligible due to competing voices, furniture noises, and distance from microphone.)

1	*C:*	[looking at notes] I noticed that . . . Spanish is spoken in the home
2	*P:*	yes
3	*C:*	is that right?
4	*P:*	m-hm . . . we do
5	*C:*	does everyone speak Spanish?
6	*P:*	we're still getting . . . not much
7	*C:*	[to child] do you like speaking Spanish?
8	*C:*	is it a good language?
9	*C:*	you don't? ohh [gasps slightly]
10	*P:*	he doesn't speak
11	*C:*	at all?
12	*P:*	no
13	*P:*	a little words but [shakes head]
14	*C:*	nothing much
15	*P:*	[unintelligible]
16	*P:*	now we try him to speak more Spanish but
17	*C:*	yeah. . just the English
18	*P:*	yep
19	*C:*	ah . . . okay . . . alright . . . so when did you come, did you come, where, from Spain or from
20	*P:*	no she's ah, she born here
21	*C:*	yep
22	*P:*	and we went back when she were 3
23	*C:*	oh right, okay
24	*P:*	and then we come back again and we stay
25	*C:*	when did you come back?
26	*P:*	about 2 years ago

27 C: was it to Spain that you went?

28 P: yeah [5 sec pause – C writing notes]

29 C: it had "Spanish" on another family and I was saying they'd been to Spain and they were saying "Argentina" [C shakes head] [P laughs, shakes head]

30 P: no, from Barcelona [P shakes head and laughs, C nods quickly while writing]

31 C: [5 sec pause – writing notes] okay so you were there for 2 years, or thereabouts

32 P: 2 years

33 C: in Spain

34 P: yeah [_____] (nods)

35 C: [5 sec pause – writing notes] okay

36 C: [to child] can you remember much from that time? [child shakes head slowly]

37 C: just a bit? not much? [child nods slightly]

38 C: mm, okay

With the exception of two short sections totaling 15 turns, this is all the talk about cultural and linguistic diversity in this interview. It is a short episode, but interesting in terms of what it reveals. Although the clinician raised the topic of the languages spoken at home and did so at the beginning of the session, which would imply she is treating it as an important issue, she did not systematically investigate it. After two questions on "facts" (turns 1 and 5), she moved to "involving the child" (turns 7 and 8), indicating this as a priority in the session. This becomes a "tease" sequence, indicated by the gasp in turn 9. Even in these first two requests for information, little that is systematic is gathered.

The clinician used first an indirect question in the form of a statement relating to what she had read in the intake notes on the client, to which she requested a simple confirmation (turns 1–4). She followed this with another yes/no question, "does everyone speak Spanish?" – wherein it is unclear as to what was meant by "everyone." This way of introducing the topic had limited the parent's contribution to yes/no answers and whatever she could add in this space if she took the initiative to do so. The clinician also referred to "the home" (turn 1) rather than "your home" or even "at home," and made it a passive construction – there is no agent of this language use – which has the effect of distancing the topic and depersonalizing or objectifying it. The topic of language use was presented in the discourse as an issue related to "facts"; and not one related to values and personal or subjective actions and emotions. This is a pointer towards what Scollon and Scollon (2001) called the "utilitarian discourse," originating in the age of enlightenment at which point objectivity became valued over subjectivity. This utilitarian discourse could be said to be underlying the discourse of the clinician, and it is itself a cultural discourse.

The clinician then diverted the discourse into some relationship-talk with the child (turns 7–9). She asked her for an explicit judgment about Spanish, again in a yes/no question format, using the terms "like" and "a good language" (subjective terms), and then reacted to the child's answer. This was after only 6 short turns on the language issue. It was then that the parent re-focused the talk onto "the facts" of how much the child speaks Spanish, and who rescued her child from this potentially face-threatening exchange (turns 10–18). The clinician contributed only by confirming or checking acts during this section, and marked a change of topic (with discourse markers "ah . . . okay . . . Alright . . . so" (in turn 19) to ask about the parent's country of origin. Thus the most salient information to this point, about what languages and how much the child spoke, and some indications of the family's and the child's attitudes to their languages, was not raised by the clinician, and not elaborated upon when raised by the parent. The clinician's formulation in turn 17 explicitly labels her conclusion and implies that further investigation is considered unnecessary; "just the English."

The topic of country of origin received more attention from the clinician. Over this topic (turns 19–35) she asked some details of how long the family had been in each country, during which she took notes consistently, signaling she was taking this information seriously. This could have been leading up to discussing cultural communication issues about Spain and Australia, which could have motivated this section. However, the reason for the clinician paying attention to this topic area seemed to be revealed when she tells a story of how she made an incorrect assumption in the past about a client's country of origin in relation to language spoken (turn 29). This seems to offer an explanation of why she had raised the topic right at the beginning, to avoid a face-threatening mistake; and it places the value of the information in the realm of professional credibility. However, to say so directly is self-face-threatening, and seems to act as another positive politeness strategy to place the interactants on an equal footing and thereby decrease social distance – an "anyone could make these mistakes" move. This is primarily relationship-work, rather than giving the language and culture issue the inherent importance it should have had in relation to children with communication disorders. If this supposition is correct, the clinician has shifted the value of the information from the importance for the child and family to the importance for her own face needs.

The value apparently conveyed by this clinician's immediate raising of the topic is therefore undermined in the discourse itself. The topic of languages spoken at home is not covered in any systematic questioning, any ethnographic method of enquiry, nor any space for talk of cultural values or roles of talk. The clinician's agendas of relationship work, "fact" gathering and protection of face are all that are in evidence in the discourse on this topic. This pattern is consistent with the points about what is revealed in the discourse about pronunciation and spelling of names.

There were other consistent indications in these transcripts that the discourse on the topics of language and culture were either "facts" or they were "lay" discourses, with mainly social purposes. For example several parents raised the topic of their own inadequacies in English, and the clinician tended to meet this with reassurance; for example in Extract 3 below, seen in turn 197.

Extract 3: C = clinician, P = parent, [xx] = overlapping talk
188 *P:*   and I talk too fast too
189 *C:*   right
190 *P:*   some people they understand but I go really fast because I more or less [rushing] everything
191 *C:*   [is] is English your second language?
192 *P:*   yes
193 *C:*   right right
194 *P:*   yes yes, because. yeah that's right and. yeah because sometimes I find I got to pronounce some words because I go fast and then I don't pronounce. [well]?
195 *C:*   [yeah]
196 *P:*   but [now I]
197 *C:*   [I find] you quite clear to hear
198 *P:*   yeah? no, I. certain words not all the [time] but
199 *C:*   [yeah]
200 *P:*   when I'm a bit likely get upset or
201 *C:*   that's even a result in people who don't have English as a second language as soon as you get upset or something [you talk much] faster
202 *P:*   [that's right] yeah
203 *C:*   and its very clouded
204 *P:*   no, so my family my family alright yeah my ____ he's alright cos my husband is – from Asian background
205 *C:*   yeah yeah. were there any people had sort of had – speech problems or just in general
206 *P:*   yeah just like stuttering and ____ just um-
207 *C:*   oh, stuttering, right

This is a social rather than a professional discourse. The reassurance was followed up in slightly more "professional" sounding language in turn 201; however the clinician's point about talking faster when upset is also lay knowledge (it is not clear whether it is always the case in fact), and the first reaction from the clinician was to compliment the parent (turn 197). The purpose of this seems to be to reassure, a social purpose rather than a consequence of professional role or knowledge. A further opportunity to follow relevant topics in this interview was lost when the parent raised further diversity issues in the family in turn 204 "my husband is from Asian background." This potentially opens a large topic of investigation about the relationships between languages and cultures and the child's proficiencies, but it was not taken up. Instead, the clinician pursued the topic of communication problems in the parent's own family, and this point about the father's language and culture received no further attention.

These discourse patterns reinforce the lack of expertise on cross-cultural issues on the part of the clinician. Even though these topics would seem to relate to professional expertise, the speech-language therapist uses lay discourse rather than expert discourse to respond to them. The agenda of "establishing a 'positive' relationship" seemed again to dominate the discourse.

The analyses in this section have revealed that at least some clinicians position themselves in these interviews ambiguously; specifically, with regard to the value they place on cultural and linguistic diversity issues, and as nonexperts in the area. This can be seen in the way clinicians raised few topics in this area and investigated those which were raised very little. There was a consistent failure to follow up with relevant follow-ons when relevant topics were raised by the parents. On those few occasions where cultural and linguistic diversity relevant topics were discussed by the clinicians, the focus was on the clinician's pronunciation of the parent's or children's names, or the parent's proficiency in English. Both of these are peripheral to the main purposes of the interview in terms of content, and this peripheral status was underlined by their construction as primarily social discourses, with the clinician giving compliments and reassurances and/or in the role of interested and supportive listener. No clinician incorporated the cultural and linguistic diversity issues raised here into the professional expert discourse, in spite of all the clients coming from cultural and linguistic diversity backgrounds.

IMPLICATIONS

There were many other ways that cross-cultural issues surfaced in the discourses of these interviews that we do not have space to deal with here. Examples were the positioning of the role of children versus adults, the use of tone or intonation that appeared to be potentially misunderstood by both sides, the use of compliments, the use of humor, and expectations of work versus fun for the child. However, even when examining this limited data set, it is evident that by analyzing discourse in a number of ways very useful insights can be achieved. These insights in turn have important implications for clinical practice. These data suggest that the advice offered in the literature about culturally competent practice has not yet been naturalized in the clinical practice of speech-language therapists. This is so even in an apparently favorable context where the applicability to the client group was obvious and in a country where multiculturalism is conscious and favored. It indicates that the profession has still some way to go in making its practices in culturally diverse contexts equal to those of the monocultural model.

I suggest a number of possible steps that could be taken to improve this situation. First of all, the advice to increase own-culture awareness is not as strong in the literature as other-culture awareness, and the data discussed in this chapter shows that such awareness shows in the clinicians' discourse. Knowing your own discourse practices is an important step to seeing how they operate in the field.

This extends beyond the individual clinician to the profession as a whole. It is my contention that a more socially and critically aware profession, that sees a reflexivity of vision as one of its basic competencies, would thereby see its own positioning and be able to take responsibility for it more easily. Anecdotally, discussions on the speech-language therapy role in potentially supporting "power" and "racism" make most clinicians react anywhere from bewilderment to offence, and yet as Clarke and Smith (1992) and Rampton (2001) point out, a lack of mention of culture in communication issues is not only a lack of professional expertise, it is a representation of dominant culture, and a form of color blindness. The lack of discussion, which may on the one hand be a desire not to offend, or a recognition of potential face-threat, is also treating the area as ignorable, as invisible, and hence operating to maintain the social (de)valuing that is implied by dominance. Therefore speech-language therapy discourses follow the institutional discourse line and do not challenge social power structures in this respect.

Coupland (2000, p. 8) points to the possibilities here: "perspectives on interethnic or intercultural communication will differ greatly depending on whether we theorise intergroup relations in politically neutral terms or in the context of post-colonialism." Rampton (2001) sees the obligation of the institution from a "difference" perspective is "to be hospitable to diversity" whereas from a "domination" perspective it is "to combat the institutional processes and ideologies that reproduce the oppression of subordinate groups" (p. 261). Antaki (1994) makes the point that a "culturally informed reading of content" (p. 121) may be necessary to understand the pervasiveness of the inequality in discourses. He writes:

> Suppose you were interested in seeing whether the educated elites who write and control news reports acknowledged or denied racism in society. A plain content analysis would be happy to make a category list of predefined things which would count as "acknowledgements" and "denials", specifying perhaps certain combinations and phrases and then scour the material to count how often each type appears. But a Discourse analyst would say that this is to rely too much on mechanical recognition of just when something is an acceptance or a denial, and wouldn't capture the subtleties which are arguably still more significant than what is obvious. Take, for example, the following extract from a British newspaper editorial, which appears at first sight to be unexceptionable:
>
> > No one would deny the fragile nature of race relations in Britain today or that there is misunderstanding and distrust between parts

of the community. (*Daily Telegraph*, 1 August 1985, quoted in van Dijk, 1992, p. 106)

> It may look plain enough, but van Dijk calls our attention to the discursive work that the concessionary form of the piece is doing: it sets the tone as being one of judicious objectivity (there is a problem) but, he argues, smuggles in a prejudicial definition of the problem under its cloak of evenhandedness. To define racism *as the fragile nature of race relations* is to strip it of any implication of inequality of power in society, and to call the parties involved *parts of the community* is to imply that they are equal, and equally to blame. Van Dijk's reading uses his analysis of society (that "races" have unequal power) to spot the discursive work done by linguistic devices (here, implication and presupposition) which play tricks with the surface content. The net effect is to unearth the kind of semi-hidden message that a word-level count would miss or misinterpret.
>
> (Antaki, 1994, pp. 121–122)

I have used the word "culture" in this chapter thus far. It is a neutral term, from a discourse of "difference" rather than of "discrimination" (Roberts et al., 1992; van Dijk, 1992) or "domination" (Rampton, 2001). Critical analysis would use "racism" or "dominance," as an acknowledgment of the social positioning that accompanies cultural difference. In that sense I am guilty of exactly what van Dijk's analysis highlights – a neutralizing that serves to maintain the current power structures unchallenged. It is the utilitarian discourse operating, with its adherence to "objectivity" in both research and professional practice. This point is also made very clearly about scope of practice documents in Ferguson (2009).

Clarke and Smith (1992) talk about color blindness as a form of racism, so that the failure to talk about issues of race at all takes it off the agenda and conceptualizes racism as having a strictly individual pathology rather than a cultural or institutional one. It denies the existence of racism and associated race privilege. I have never heard the word "racism" in discussing speech-language therapy by speech-language therapists in Australia. It would probably be perceived as aggressive and insulting to do so, and would offend many who are doing their best to manage and accommodate diverse needs and who do not perceive themselves or their profession as racist. Similar reactions can and have occurred in education contexts when agendas such as those of Clarke and Smith (1992) have been raised there.

Dealing honestly with cultural and linguistic diversity requires professions being more prepared to discuss these issues. Discourse analysis, with its critical theory and ethnography associations, gives some tools to help this dialogue, as can be seen in such works as those by Ferguson (2009) and Kovarsky, Duchan, and Maxwell (1999). In spite of the 10 years between these two publications however, there has not a noticeable increase in the discussion or the use of the tools in the profession.

Educational programs in speech-language therapy need to play their part. A list of specific and basic elements to be discussed in all sessions involving cultural and linguistic diversity needs to be developed and taught to students and professionals. Cultural self-awareness should be a basic part of all curricula, followed by awareness and skills in cross-cultural communication, added to the existing stock on "facts" about other cultures and languages. These should be assessed as competencies for all clinicians. Reflexive thinking on what constitutes therapeutic talk and interpersonal relationships as part of the therapy task should also be a part of clinical education programs and clinical services.

All of these areas need more research. More specifically, critical, discourse, and ethnographic research, and other qualitative methods that are sensitive to power dynamics and which value the subjective experiences of participants, need to have an increasing profile within the profession. As evidence-based practice is an accepted part of professional practice, clinicians should research, or enter collaborative relationships with researchers, to study a wider range of issues pertinent to outcomes, including the knowledge, attitudes, and skills of clinicians; satisfactions and other service delivery outcome measures for clients, and assessment and therapy outcomes for clients.

The power of discourse to illuminate cross-cultural issues can be found in many works, such as the example above from Bryce (2002), and Bishop and Berryman (2006). There is much we can do to use such resources to help improve our practices. However, the challenge of the cross-cultural context is an ongoing one, and as Shi-xu reminds us, we still lack a way of theorizing discourse "from in between cultures" (2005, p. 43). More work lies ahead. However, willingness to use the tools and the theories we already have, will put us on track and enable us to continue to meet the challenge.

NOTE

1 The term "dominant culture" refers to those practices most visible and most taken for granted in a given place. If the mainstream education, newspapers, street signs, and government documents are all conducted in one language, then that is the dominant language. If introductions take place in a certain way, shoes are removed on entering dwellings, eye contact is not made between strangers or nonfamily members and these kinds of practices are taken for granted by the majority, then they represent dominant culture.

8 Exploring gender and power in clinical encounters

Mary-Pat O'Malley
University of Ireland, Galway

> I am the nurse from hell and do not try any of that communication shit with me.
> (Robillard, 1999, p. 56)

INTRODUCTION

The purpose of this chapter is to explore issues of power and gender in clinical discourse: specifically between individuals with communication disorders and the speech and hearing clinicians they may encounter. These topics have been somewhat neglected in health care research, which is surprising, given the relatively high numbers of female professionals in areas such as speech-language therapy and audiology. While power in clinical interactions has been explored relatively extensively, it tends to be generally considered in the context of doctor–patient interactions and from the perspective of the doctor. I will therefore incorporate the client's perspective in this chapter, by exploring some first person accounts of power in health care settings. Similarly, I will examine the interactions of professionals in training. In addition, I will examine speech-language therapy clients' experiences of power in institutional settings; and how these clients attempt to resist the established roles institutions encourage them to adopt. Finally, I aim to provide the reader with an opportunity to reflect on their interaction styles in practice and what they may unwittingly be communicating to their clients.

POWER AND INSTITUTIONAL CONTROL OF THE CLIENT

Many investigations of power in medical or health care interactions have been carried out to date (Danziger-Klein, 1978; Fisher, 1986; Heritage & Maynard, 2006; Mishler, 1986; Tannen & Wallat, 1993). However, these investigations have tended to focus on the perceived "powerful" member of such dyads, such as the doctors in doctor–patient interactions; or nurses in a nurse–patient interaction. Consequently, the client or patient's activity or perspective within these studies is sometimes obscured.

According to Wang (2006, p. 529), power is "inherent in all dialogues, whether in casual conversation or in an institutional dialogue." In a general sense, power tends to be associated with rank and status, with power being determined by the institutional role of the "professional." The central concern of this chapter is power in a discursive sense; specifically in the context of clinical interactions involving speech, language, or hearing clinicians. Fairclough (2001, p. 46) states that "power in discourse has to do with powerful participants controlling and constraining the contributions of non-powerful participants." In institutional settings, the distribution of power may be clear to participants before the beginning of a verbal interaction, with clear role expectations existing in advance of the clinical encounter. Moreover, institutional discourse tends to be highly conventionalized, such as when question–answer–evaluation/next question exchange structures are used in clinical encounters (Mishler, 1984).

Institutional interactions tend to be goal-oriented, for example, when doctors conduct a physical examination, or when speech-language therapists assess language comprehension, or when audiologists test hearing and give feedback on test results, and so on (Danziger-Klein, 1980). This goal orientation of clinicians may in turn, lead to certain biases or inferences with regard to how interlocutors interpret client utterances. More specifically, Wang believes that "due to various asymmetries of knowledge and interests, participants are often thought unequal in institutional settings, where professionals tend to ask questions, and laymen have to respond" (Wang, 2006, p. 535).

Another example of clinician-controlled power relations can be seen in the overt use of questions to control the conversations within clinical encounters. This is illustrated by Wang (2006), who examined the use of Yes/No and Wh-questions in such interactions, resulting in the differential exercise of power. To illustrate, the relative higher frequency of Yes/No questions in institutional domains such as courtroom cross-examination and medical interactions can be interpreted as an attempt to restrict and control topics and to thereby exercise power. Similarly, Yes/No questions constrain the addressee's possible responses to a greater degree than Wh-questions. Wang concludes that powerful participants' Yes/No questions and Wh-questions "serve the function of maintaining control over the content of conversation and exercising dominance over the less powerful" (Wang, 2006, p. 545). Accordingly, such a pattern could result in the assured dominance of "the biomedical perspective within which patients' statements are interpreted and allows doctors to accomplish the medical tasks of diagnosis and prescription" (Mishler, 1984, pp. 62–63).

O'Malley (2005) examined the silencing of service users' perspectives in conversation, as a means of sustaining the *status quo* in relation to antenatal care. The women in this study were all attending a midwives' clinic for their antenatal care. The researcher showed them how to introduce their own life world perspectives on pregnancy and birth in interaction with midwives. Specifically, they learned how to append their stories to their responses to midwives' questions. By introducing such spontaneous accounts at transition-relevant places during their visits, service users were able to be more powerful in such interactions (Fisher & Groce, 1990; Sacks, Schegloff, & Jefferson, 1974). The midwives, however, were found to have ultimate control in terms of responding to these narratives or not, and to interpret these stories of participants' subjective experiences of pregnancy according to a medical model of pregnancy and birth. Therefore, the medical model of pregnancy and birth was found to prevail in this context and alternatives that did occasionally surface, essentially remained irrelevant to the midwives, with the ultimate preservation of the *status quo* in relation to pregnancy and birth as a result.

Menz and Al-Roubaie (2008) explored whether doctors and patients exhibited different patterns of nonsupportive interruptions in their communication with each other, and found this was indeed the case. For example, doctors in general used more nonsupportive interruptions than their patients did. However, this difference was more prominent when the doctor was a senior one, and less prominent when the doctor was female. Supportive interruptions were defined as those "characterised by the physicians' maintenance and co-construction of patient-initiated topics" (Menz & Al Roubaie, 2008, p. 649). Nonsupportive interruptions were described as those which constituted a "violation of a speaker's rights and/or being dominance-related due to their non-supportive interruption style" (Menz & Al-Roubaie, 2008, p. 651). Contrary to what might be expected, the more physicians interrupted, the lengthier were the interviews, as the patients repeatedly endeavored to have their main complaint heard. They found that status may be the decisive variable in medical encounters, rather than gender, with those of higher status interrupting more often than those of lower status. They report that "aside from minor significance, however, our data do not reflect any statistically significant difference regarding gender" (Menz & Al-Roubaie, 2008, p. 660). However, they did find that both female patients and female doctors produced more supportive interruptions and maintained the speakers' interests, despite interruption, thus supporting Tannen's findings that women's linguistic style tends to be more relationship oriented (Tannen, 1990).

Gender in relation to communication gives rise to contradictory results arising from differences in methodologies and contexts of data collection. For instance, while Holmes (1992) and West (1998) report that female doctors were interrupted more often by patients, regardless of patient gender, Menz and Al-Roubaie (2008) found status to be the more influential variable in relation to nonsupportive interruptions.

REDRESSING THE BALANCE IN THE CLIENT'S FAVOR

There are some attempts to redress the balance in terms of paying attention to the voice of the client in institutional encounters (Lorentzen, 2008;

O'Malley, 2005). Faber and Mazlish (1995), in relation to the field of education, consider teachers and pupils not necessarily equal in knowledge or experience but equal in dignity and it is the element of dignity in relation to service users that stands out in the accounts below.

The lived experience of communication in clinical encounters

The opening quote of this chapter is taken from Robillard's autoethnographic account of his experience of motor neuron disease and refers to a first encounter with a nurse in an intensive care unit in Hawaii, where he spent 3½ months following an acute episode of pneumonia.

In the intensive care unit, his main means of communication with the doctors and nurses was through the use of an alphabet board; which gave rise to several problems. The most common problem encountered was that the nurses did not appear to be able to remember the letters of the words as he selected them from the board and they "would not write the letters and words down" (Robillard, 1999, p. 55). Furthermore, he observed that they would reverse letters, forget the last letter of the sequence, and forget the first word, by the time he had spelled out a third word. He also noticed that the nurses had difficulty translating the combination of letters into a word that they recognized. Other problems included people anticipating words as he was spelling and completing his sentences thereby "making me say something that I had not intended" (Robillard, 1999, p. 61). Short-term contract nurses, anticipating such communication troubles with the alphabet board, often refused to use it, leading Robillard to conclude that they thought that working with someone in his condition could be accomplished without communication. He reports that "my insistence on talking and being heard, expecting what I said to influence behavior, led to a spiral of mutual antagonism between myself and the flying nurses" (Robillard, 1999, p. 56). No male nurse attempted to use the alphabet board to communicate with him and he also reports that "males, in general, appear not to have the patience or the multiple communication rhythms to be able to use alternative means of communication" (Robillard, 1999, pp. 57–58).

Other problems in communication that he encountered in this setting were described as "not now" and "out of context." He noticed that he would be told "not now," either when he indicated that he wanted to say something; or while he was formulating a sentence, "as a way of breaking the interactional focus, rearranging the interaction to permit something else to happen." He was likely to be "cut off" when he was speaking about a particular procedure that he was undergoing, although he may have been trying to communicate to the nursing staff important information about how to best handle his body during the procedure in question. Nursing staff appeared to have three avenues for "not now." The first avenue was simply saying the words when Robillard was attempting to communicate. The second was when he was mid-communication and nurses could cut him off by attending to another task and by walking away while he was in mid-sentence. The third avenue was when another person interrupted his conversation, "taking over the inter-actional focus."

"Out of context" occurred when he was able to resume the initial topic but nurses had forgotten the original topic and therefore were unable to appreci-ate the relevance of his contribution. He writes in detail of his experience in intensive care, reporting that he could not control what was happening to his body, nor could he control "the interactions that largely made up my person." Doctors, under time pressure suggested that he formulate what he had to say before they visited him, omitting the possibility that he may have wanted to participate in the conversation as it was taking place in the room. Robillard's account highlights the relatively powerless position of the patient in this context. However, he together with his wife, devised a communication system that involved him communicating by spelling out words by moving his lips, with his wife or graduate students acting as translators or interpreters of his messages. Later he recounts his meeting with the speech-language therapist in the same hospital:

> Speech therapy was first, I will always remember the frown of disap-proval on the speech therapist's face as I failed one speech assessment after another. She told me I had a collapsed upper palate and would never recover. The therapist seemed particularly officious when she told Divina and me that the lip-signing and lip-reading system we had fash-ioned on our own was inefficient. She assumed no-one could learn it and I would be restricted in communication if I did not acquire an artificial voice. "You know, no-one will understand you. You will be dependent on your wife and mother-in-law. Don't you want to be independent?" I was dismissed from the presence of the speech therapist with this question. I had no opportunity to respond.
>
> (Robillard, 1999, p. 124)

Robillard's detailed autoethnographic account provides rich insights into the client's experience of clinical encounters, both with staff trained specifically to work with people with communication disorders and with other health care staff. In terms of clinical education, his account can be considered a valuable resource both for introducing clinicians in training in the participa-tion elements of the International Classification of Function (WHO, 2001), the social and medical models of impairment, and to autoethnography as a methodology for exploring experiences of disability.

Smith (2008) in his account of his experience of hospital and rehabilitation following the discovery of a demyelinating lesion of the medulla oblongata, recounts his own experience of speech-language therapy. The focus of the extract below is a group speech-language therapy session:

> I can't recall what the group was talking about and it doesn't matter

anyway but I remember it was this man's turn. He could not find the words. He struggled like a man in chains as we willed him on. Tears of frustration were waiting but he was holding them back, holding it all back. Finally, he burst out:

"This . . ."

"Yes?"

"This fucking illness."

With passion. It was a magnificent, triumphant moment. I applauded. Well I would have done but my hands missed like some spastic seal, but the thought was there. I turned to the young speech and language therapist taking the group and saw she was horrified. Not at his predicament but at his *behaviour*. She began to tell him off. For swearing. This gentle man who had so articulated with his small profanity the huge profanity perpetrated upon him and his family was being scolded by some jumped-up, buttoned-up little bitch of a girl who did not have one ounce of his wit or grace.

(Smith 2008, pp. 223–224)

Lorentzen (2008), explored resistance in women's experiences of medical interactions that she found took the form of direct challenges to medical truth claims, avoiding confrontation altogether by ending the relationship, and locating what she describes as "compliant physicians" (Lorentzen, 2008, p. 74). Robillard (1999) engages in resistance by directly challenging the nurses in the intensive care unit regarding their use of time and their treatment of patients, while Smith (2008) attempts to unsettle the balance of power in an interaction with the speech-language therapist in the extract below. The setting for this extract is a group therapy session focussing on swallowing with which Smith was experiencing difficulty:

I'm on a mission to swallow and it becomes clear as she talks in a very slow voice to us dribbling maniacs that she apparently knows as much about it as the primary school teacher she should have been in the first place. She draws a bad diagram of the mouth, oesophagus and larynx. I tell her she's missed out the soft palate and the pyriform sinuses and she knows she's in for a bad afternoon. She decides attack is the best form of defence. "Why don't *you* tell us how swallowing works, Nigel?" she challenges. So I do. In ludicrous detail, with some bits I chuck in just to sound good . . . there was some proper stuff in there just to let her know I quite possibly knew more than she did. I gave a Nobel performance. I stopped. "But I could be wrong," I sneered. "How do *you* think it works?" We stared at each other and suddenly there was a wonderful power shift. First I knew somehow we were equal. Then astoundingly, something gave and I was in charge. I was back in my office, she was a stupid researcher who'd pressed the wrong button on the TV Avid recording machine and wiped the tape. And I was going to discuss that with her. In my fucking office. Over a hot P45. She met my eyes and that was astounding because very few people had. And I don't know what she saw in there because I wasn't entirely sure what was behind them, but she ran in tears from the room.

(Smith, 2008, pp. 279–280)

Smith also claimed that from the patient's perspective, "the real battle in hospital, the one you have to win, is for dignity" (Smith, 2008, p. 280). These may be seen as two extreme examples in terms of power and gender from the patients' perspective, which by no means undermines their relevance to the clinician in training. Beck (1999) described her experience of the language and cognitive testing of her son who had Down syndrome. During testing, it became apparent to her that her son Adam, had realized that testing stopped after a certain number of items were failed, and was deliberately responding incorrectly to get the reward for finishing: a can of Sprite. However, when she broached this possibility with the tester, she reported him as replying that "I know it's hard to accept, but we need to be realistic about your son's abilities" (Beck, 1999, p. 113). She reports:

eventually I did get the examiner to write my interpretation of that test down on his records. I caught a glance of it later on. It said, "Subject unable to answer Level One vocabulary. Mother claims subject is 'faking it'." . . . I can still picture the school board sitting with that document, sadly shaking their heads over my inability to come to terms with my child's limitations.

(Beck, 1999, p. 113)

The above examples suggest that "being a client" involves being in a relatively powerless position in terms of topic initiation, maintenance, termination, and meaning; mirroring what Fairclough describes as "powerful participants controlling and constraining the contributions of the non-powerful participants" (Fairclough, 2001, p. 46). It appears difficult for the client to resist the structures of power imposed in institutional discourse, possibly resulting in what may appear to be extreme responses. The examples further reflect the preponderance of the medical model of disability where the "problem" is construed as located within the individual as opposed to the social model of disability where the disabling nature of society is equal, if not more pertinent (Threats, 2006). Within the social model, "disability is perhaps not a tragedy but part of life" (Holland, 2007, p. 6). Holland construes the client as one expert in a constellation; the expert living in the disorder, in addition to those living with the disorder (family members and significant others) (Holland, 2007). These accounts raise complex issues in relation to gender and power, that in turn raise the question of how clinicians in training handle power in clinical interactions. The next section explores this topic.

LEARNING TO DO "BEING PROFESSIONAL"

For the clinician in training, there appear to be several delicate factors at play when dealing with clients. For instance, they may be dealing with somebody who has many more years of life experience than they do; or someone of a similar age, someone of a different gender, someone experiencing the receipt of a difficult diagnosis of which the clinician in training has no direct experi- ence. All of these factors may make it difficult to interact in a way that facilitates a sense of equality in terms of the dignity of both participants. Alternative approaches can be found such as narrative-based therapy that facilitates clients telling their personal stories to "increase insight into their problems, promote motivation to change, and .. create the circumstances wherein psychological change can occur" (Leahy & Warren, 2006, p. 320). Furthermore, direct instruction in relation to clinical discourse is an import- ant element of undergraduate training for speech-language therapists, at least in some degree programs (Leahy & Walsh, 2008), involving them in record- ing, transcribing, and analyzing discourse in various contexts. In some pro- grams, clinicians in training also use methods of discourse analysis applied to clinical discourse for example in the discipline of speech-language therapy at the National University of Ireland, Galway. This section focusses on speech-language therapy interactions, and draws on a session in which two clinicians in training are involved in information gathering with a male client of a similar age to the clinicians. The first extract is from the start of their second session. (In this chapter transcription conventions are taken from Silverman, 2006 – see Appendix.)

Extract 1: SLT = speech-language therapist, C = client
   1 *SLT1:*   so how have you been keeping since the last day we were speak-
                ing to you? (.)
   2 *C:*   ahm alright now (.)
   3 *SLT1:*   yeah
   4 *C:*   ((block)) ah I'm doing a lot of long hours at school like
   5 *SLT1:*   really studying away
   6 *C:*   (2.0) mm I'm home at like (.) half ahm nine or ten at night so
   7 *SLT1:*   god that's tough going
   8 *C:*   [rough stuff rough stuff]
   9 *SLT1:*   [yeah yeah sixth year all over]
  10 *C:*   yeah ((laughs))
  11 *SLT1:*   well what I want to say to you today is that I'm going to do the
                start of the session
  12 *C:*   yeah
  13 *SLT1:*   and just kind of ask more questions kinda more questions about
                what we were speaking about last
  14   week
  15 *C:*   kay

16 *SLT1:* 'cos we felt you were so good last week and you were really open
about how you felt and

17   every (.) stuff about your stutter and just we kinda just wanna
kinda get more into kinda the details

18   of it and be a bit more specific a bit things like that (.) so I'm
gonna do the first bit and ask you

19   more questions and stuff like that and then I'm gonna hand you
over to X

21 *C:* right ((smiles and looks at SLT2))

22 *SLT1:* and she's gonna do (.) she's a couple of things to do with you
as well

23 *C:* okay

24 *SLT1:* if that's okay (.) and em (.) the first thing I just need to get some
of your details like surname date

25   of birth and stuff like that cause we didn't get them the last day

The interpretation of this extract draws on Brown and Levinson's (1987) framework for politeness, Tannen's (1993) work on framing, and Fairclough's (2001) work on the manifestation of power in discourse. I have found these resources can be used in exploring discourse analysis with clinicians in training. The participants in this interaction have met at a previous session and the early part of the extract (lines 1–10) appear to focus on rapport building. At the start of the extract, the participants appeared to be aligned to what Walsh (2007) describes as a sociorelational frame of talk. The participants of this conversation are engaging in small talk at the start of the session before the therapy tasks are commenced. However, this early phase of the encounter can be seen as suffused with what Fairclough terms power in discourse as the speech-language therapist in training opens the interaction with a question (Fairclough, 2001).

However, in line 3, which could have represented a turn transition in which one clinician could have legitimately taken the floor again, instead responds with a back channel response (*yeah*); following which, the client introduces the topic of school work and long days (lines 4–6). Then, the clinician, having recently been in a similar position in terms of phase education is able to draw on shared experience. She can then be seen as attempting to convey empathy using similar informal lexical choice e.g. "that's tough going, yeah yeah sixth year all over."

Although the client laughs, the clinician in training does not take up the invitation to laugh (Glenn, 2003), possibly because she is readying herself for a transition to therapy tasks and therefore has difficulty being attentive to the sociorelational efforts of the client. This is a delicate transition for the clinician in training as she attempts to balance rapport building with the goals that have been established for the session. She takes the floor in line 11 and directly introduces *her* agenda for the session using a discourse marker ("well") which Kovarsky (1990) has described as being used as session-regulating devices. This discourse marker indicates a transition from rapport building or small talk to therapy tasks: "well what I want to say to you today is that I'm going to do the start of the session . . . and then I'm going to hand you over to X and she's gonna do (.) she's a couple of things to do with you as well . . if that's okay (.) and em (.) the first thing." Here it appears as if the clinician is *announcing* the format of the session in terms of therapy tasks that need to be completed by her and the second clinician in training who also participates in the session ("I'm going to do the start of the session . . . she's a couple of things to do with you as well"). Her use of *I* in "what I'm going to do" and "I'm going to hand you over to X" can be seen as representing the clinicians in training as the more powerful participants controlling the agenda.

There is a sense of the client being informed about what is to take place without being offered an opportunity to actively engage at this point. What may be influencing the clinician in training is her awareness of background information that needs to be collected and which was forgotten in the previous session (line 25), "cause we didn't get them the last day." The clinicians in training at this point can be seen as juggling tasks in term of establishing rapport and gathering contact information. Their position as clinicians in training may make it difficult for them to relinquish control of the proceedings. They would have completed a session plan in preparation for the session and there may be an inclination for clinicians in training to rely on the plan to manage the session, thereby unwittingly heightening the asymmetry in the interaction and effectively excluding the client from choices about the direction of the session.

Furthermore, her explanation for the rationale for the proposed agenda, can be seen as communicating to the client what constitutes a "good client" in this context. In line 16, having introduced her intention to ask questions, the clinician in training talks about her rationale for asking questions using what Wodak (1996) refers to as *pluralis hospitalis*, that is the use of *we*; which can be seen as a marker of power in the interaction:

16 *SLT1:*   'cos <u>we</u> felt you were so good last week and you were really open
             about how you felt and
17   every (.) stuff about your stutter and just <u>we</u> kinda just wanna
             kinda get more into kinda the
18   details of it and be a bit more specific a bit things like that

These utterances are interesting from an analytic point of view in that they can be seen as revealing discourses concerning what constitutes a "good client." From the clinician in training's comment here ("we felt you were so good last week") co-located with "and you were really open about how you felt and . . stuff about your stutter," it may be inferred that a good client is one who is open about how they feel, which may place pressure on the client to perform in a particular way in the session.

Politeness theory can be used to explore expressions such as "just kind of ask more questions kinda more questions" (line 13), "just we kinda just wanna kinda get more into kinda the details of it" (lines 17–18), and line 18 *"so I'm gonna do the first bit and ask you more questions and stuff like that."* The clinician in training may be seen as attempting to lessen any sense of imposition on the client in the requests for information by her unspecific and informal use of vocabulary i.e. she can be seen as paying attention to the client's negative face needs (Brown & Levinson, 1987) here while maintaining the focus on therapy tasks. However, the frequent use of unspecific vocabulary such as *"kinda, the first bit, stuff like that"* and so on may be heard as vague and confusing to the client. The difficulty of juggling relationship building and therapy tasks may be a significant burden on the clinicians in training, who in this instance are being video recorded and observed by their clinical supervisor.

Other potentially influential factors that need to be considered here are age and gender. The two therapists in training are female and the client is male and of a similar age; and while this may be facilitative in terms of rapport building, it may also create discomfort, as the clinicians in training attempt to move into more formal therapy tasks, where they are attempting to apply theoretical knowledge in a real-life context. Davies (2003) examined gendered discourse styles in small classroom discussions and found that all-girl groups tended to produce friendly talk that fulfilled both social and educational work goals. This was similar to Coates' observations of how talk forms the basis of women's friendships (Coates, 1996). On the other hand, the talk in the all-boy groups was characterized by using talk to "police each others' behaviour and to establish a pecking order of masculinity" (Davies, 2003, p. 125). Similarly, Mills (2003) considered gender as an act or a verb; something which is enacted within specific environments. In relation to this encounter here, gender is considered as a potential variable to be borne in mind with the clinicians possibly attempting to use friendly talk to accomplish both social and therapy goals. On the other hand, status may be the more significant variable at work here as evidenced by the setting of the agenda by speech-language therapist 1 in lines 11–19.

CONCLUSION

Leahy and Walsh (2008) point out the importance of discourse analysis for attending to the role of the client *and* the role of the clinician in clinical encounters. Gender and power in institutional encounters are useful entry points for clinicians in training to examine their interactions with clients. By exploring their own contributions in interactions, as part of their clinical training, learners can draw on the rich body of extant work in discourse analysis. Moreover, discourse analysis as part of health care curricula could allow clinicians in training to analyze and reflect on their own styles of interaction with clients and to understand the influences of their talk on what develops in the clinical encounter; and on the representation of the client that emerges. Also, it can be useful for identifying ideology in relation to what constitutes a "good client." Exploring clinical discourse can also be useful for educators and clinicians in training alike in terms of understanding sessions that do not appear to have gone as planned; and to understand the variables that could be at play in negatively impacting upon clinical interactions.

9   How audiologists and speech-language pathologists can foster and combat stigma in people with communication disorders

David Downs
Wichita State University

INTRODUCTION

"Professionals don't stigmatize deaf persons. Society does." That was the response to a question I posed to one of the speakers following their presentation at a national symposium on deafness about a decade ago. The speakers, an audiologist and a physician had just discussed how future developments in genetics could eventually allow teams of professionals to identify "deaf genes" and then engineer them to prevent genetically based deafness – ultimately reducing the incidence of persons who were deaf. During the question and answer session, I asked the speaker, "Are you concerned your work stigmatizes persons who are deaf by suggesting deafness is so bad their genes might be altered to prevent it?"

When the speaker answered that society, not professionals, stigmatized deaf persons, I replied, "But aren't professionals a part of society?"

"Yes, I suppose we are. But we're not going to get into it here," he said.

I dropped my questioning. But I did not drop my interest in how professionals, including myself – a clinician, teacher, and researcher in audiology – can stigmatize individuals with communication disorders. Indeed, this incident and similar ones over my career have led me to ask the following questions that I will address in this chapter.

- What is stigma?
- What is professional stigmatization?
- How can professionals, like audiologists and speech-language pathologists, foster and combat stigma in people with communication disorders?

WHAT IS STIGMA?

In his seminal 1963 book, *Stigma: Notes on the Management of Spoiled Identity*, Irving Goffman ascribed the origin of the word "stigma" to marks, burns, or cuts that early Greeks branded unto a person's body to stain them as having a lower status (e.g. a criminal or slave). Early Christians expanded stigma's meaning to wounds (i.e. stigmata) on the crucified Christ, as well as to signs of physical disorders on a person's body. Goffman also popularized a modern meaning of stigma in the preface to his book, "The situation of the individual who is disqualified from full social acceptance" (Goffman, 1963, preface). Individuals who are stigmatized are viewed as different, abnormal, or less than human by others who consider themselves normal. People, in turn, may consciously or unconsciously treat stigmatized individuals harshly by depreciating, discrediting, ostracizing, or discriminating against them at home, work, school, church, recreation, and in media (Baumann, 2007; English, 1977a, 1997b; Gilmore & Somerville, 1994).

Spurred by civil rights movements and legislation of the 1950s, 60s, and 70s, research on stigma has grown rapidly during the past 50 years – especially by scholars in sociology, anthropology, social psychology, and rehabilitation. Initially, researchers investigated how people from majority groups (e.g. who were young, white, or Christian) stigmatized people from minority groups (e.g. who were old, black, or Jewish); or how people from powerful "in" groups (e.g. who were richer or more educated) stigmatized people from less powerful "out" groups (e.g. who were poorer or less educated). Scholars soon turned their attention to how, throughout history, (a person or) people without disabilities have stigmatized (a person or) people with disabilities (Smart, 2001). For many people with disabilities, psychosocial effects of stigmatization have been more handicapping than biophysical limitations imposed by the disability itself. Alonzo and Reynolds (1995) have suggested that the trajectory of psychosocial effects of stigma on lifestyles of people with HIV/AIDS may vary from limited and controllable to expansive and pervasive at various biophysical stages of the disease. Stigma, moreover, may not only affect people with disabilities, but may be generalized to their families (especially parents) and friends (Smart, 2001).

I once consulted at an excellent clinic on an American Indian reservation that provided early identification and intervention for children with developmental disabilities. During its start-up years, however, this clinic was mislabeled by some persons on the reservation as only serving children with fetal alcohol syndrome. Many mothers of children with any type of disability became reluctant to bring their child to the clinic for fear of being unfairly stigmatized as a mother who drank during pregnancy.

Disability research has also included a growing literature on stigmatization of people with communication disorders by (a person) or people without communication disorders. Although anyone with a communication disorder may be stigmatized, most research has focussed on persons with fluency and voice disorders, individuals who are culturally Deaf,[1] or those who are hard-of-hearing and use hearing aids. As shown in Box 9.1, the degree of stigmatization may differ among people with disabilities,

---

Box 9.1 Degree of stigmatization as a function of type, onset, and visibility of disability (adapted from Smart, 2001)

TYPE OF DISABILITY
Least Stigmatized

- Person with physical disability (e.g. vision, hearing, speech, & mobility disorders)
- Person with cognitive disability (e.g. learning disabilities; some types of traumatic brain injury)
- Person with intellectual disability (e.g. mental retardation; autism)
- Person with mental disability (e.g. many psychiatric disorders)

Most Stigmatized

ONSET OF DISABLITY
Least Stigmatized

- Person with disability from honorable endeavors like war or work (e.g. traumatic brain injury; noise-induced hearing loss)
- Person with congenital disability (autism; inherited hearing loss)
- Person with acquired disability who did not contribute to it (e.g. presbycusis; aphasia)
- Person with acquired disability who contributed to it (e.g. parents of children with fetal alcohol syndrome; traumatic brain injury from driving car while intoxicated or motorcycle without helmet)

Most Stigmatized

VISIBILITY OF DISABILITY
Least Stigmatized

- Person with invisible disability (e.g. hearing loss without hearing aids; central auditory processing disorders; certain articulation and language disorders; many mental illnesses; learning disabilities)
- Person with mildly visible disability (e.g. hearing loss with completely-in-the-ear hearing aids; low vision with contact lenses)
- Person with moderately visible disability (e.g. hearing loss with behind-the-ear hearing aids; low vision with eyeglasses; aphasia; cleft palate; some dysarthrias)
- Person with highly visible disability (e.g. hearing loss with sign language; low vision with cane; speech disorder with assistive technology; mobility disorder with wheelchair)

Most Stigmatized

---

including those with communication disorders, in complex, and sometimes unpredictable, ways.

Individuals with physical disabilities, like many with communication disorders, tend to be less stigmatized than those with mental disabilities. People with communication disorders incurred in an honorable endeavor may be less stigmatized than those who incurred them in a less responsible way. Those individuals whose disorders are more visible may be stigmatized more than those whose are less visible. They also may be stigmatized differently depending on demographic characteristics like age and gender. Younger people and women with hearing losses, for example, may be stigmatized more than older ones or men with hearing losses (Garstecki & Erler, 1998). Researchers have even shown that people with communication disorders and their families may stigmatize one another. Deaf children of Deaf parents may feel they are more culturally Deaf and, therefore, superior to Deaf children of hearing parents. Likewise, parents who raise a deaf child primarily through oral communication and education may discredit parents who raise their deaf child primarily though manual communication and education, and vice versa (Baynton, 1996; Moore & Levitan, 2003).

WHAT IS PROFESSIONAL STIGMATIZATION?

Goffman (1968) coined two terms, "the own" and "the wise," to describe segments of society that are potentially more sympathetic to effects of stigmatization. In the case of people with disabilities, "the own" are persons who share the same disability and, therefore, may be subject to stigmatization themselves. "The wise" are people without disability who may have greater empathy for stigmatized people with disability because they know them personally (e.g. as family, friends, or employers) or serve them professionally (e.g. as teachers, doctors, audiologists, speech-language pathologists, etc.). Researchers, nevertheless, have reported that professionals often do consciously or subconsciously stigmatize people with disabilities – sometimes more severely than segments of society not deemed as "the wise" (Faugier & Sargeant, 1997). This professional stigmatization of those with disabilities can be blatant or subtle and can occur through direct clinician–client interactions or indirect professional activities. It, ultimately, can harm quality of care by discouraging individuals with disabilities from seeking professional services, spoiling the client–clinician relationship, and reducing the likelihood that those with disabilities and their families will comply with follow-up recommendations (Baumann, 2007). Conversely, professionals can also play an important role in combating the stigma of people with disabilities (English, 1977a; Schulze, 2007).

The growing literature on professional stigmatization of people with disabilities has been conducted most with two groups of clients who have experienced some of the greatest stigmatization by society: individuals with HIV/AIDS (Alonzo & Reynolds, 1995; Barrick, 1988; Gilmore & Somerville, 1994) or with mental illness (Deacon & Boulle, 2006; Schulze, 2007).

Literature on stigmatization of individuals with communication disorders by audiologists and speech-language pathologists, conversely, is almost nonexistent; may actually be in decline; and, as detailed later in this chapter, has been primarily anecdotal, historical, or descriptive reports of professional stigmatization of individuals who are culturally Deaf, or of parents of children with communication disorders. As shown in Box 9.2, a limited literature on professional stigmatization of people with communication disorders is only one of many reasons audiologists and speech-language pathologists may know so little about how they can foster or combat stigma.

Box 9.2 Possible reasons audiologists & speech-language pathologists know so little about professional stigmatization of people with communication disorders (PWCD)

- We are unfamiliar with existing literature on professional stigmatization of people with disabilities.
- We have a meager literature on professional stigmatization of PWCD.
- We do not consider our profession to be a significant part of society that stigmatizes PWCD.
- We like to feel our interactions with PWCD always are benevolent.
- We assume we already are taking sufficient steps to combat stigma with PWCD.
- We may not recognize when we stigmatize PWCD as it may be subtle or unconscious.
- We may have a difficulty admitting that we stigmatize PWCD.
- We may worry about negative consequences if we are "whistle blowers" to stigmatization of PWCD by ourselves or colleagues.
- We may have limited contact or follow-up with PWCD making it difficult to know whether our professional stigmatization carries over outside of the clinic.
- We identify PWCD as our clients and are unaware how we can stigmatize their families.
- We may stigmatize PWCD indirectly through professional actions and associations.
- We don't recognize how our actions to combat stigma in PWCD may unwittingly foster it.
- We view fostering and combating stigma as outside our scope of practice.
- We rarely discuss stigma in our professional training programs.
- We increasingly emphasize our professional training and research include "harder" sciences (e.g. physics, physiology) versus "softer" sciences (e.g. psychology, sociology, anthropology) and humanities (e.g. existential philosophy).
- We increasingly employ medical models rather than ecological, functional, and rehabilitative models in our professional training and practice.

HOW CAN PROFESSIONALS FOSTER AND COMBAT STIGMA IN PEOPLE WITH COMMUNICATION DISORDERS?

In a classic essay, *Stigma: An Enigma Demystified*, Lerita Coleman suggested stigma was multidimensional and, therefore, was studied best holistically across disciplines (Coleman, 1997). Specifically, Coleman suggested stigma has three interrelated components: a *behavioral* component, which addresses what people do when they stigmatize other people; a *cognitive* component, which addresses how people view those they stigmatize; and an *affective* component, which addresses how people feel about individuals they stigmatize. These three components of stigma, in turn, involve several interrelated mechanisms for stigmatizing people with disabilities. I will now describe these three main components of stigma; define their stigmatizing mechanisms; suggest stigmatizing messages some professionals may send to people with communication disorders via these mechanisms; offer real-world illustrations of how these mechanisms are manifested when audiologists and speech-language pathologists foster stigma in those with communication disorders; and propose some ways to combat stigma.

Behavioral component of stigma

Coleman (1997) suggested that the behavioral component of stigma is primarily manifested through social control of others. Specific mechanisms through which professionals exert social control of people with communication disorders include paternalism, marginalization, dependency, and scapegoating.

Mechanism of social control: Paternalism

Definition

Managing a person in the manner of a father with his child.

Message sent

"I know what's best for you."

Illustration

"In another 50 years we will no longer have any Deaf people," proclaimed the featured speaker, an otolaryngologist, at another national conference of audiologists and ear, nose, and throat specialists I attended 15 years ago. Most of the audience applauded the speaker's point: future developments in early otological and audiological interventions with deaf children, especially cochlear implantation and genetic engineering, would dramatically reduce the world's prevalence of deaf people. A smaller number of persons in the audience, including me, did not applaud. All I could think of was, "I hope there are no deaf persons here."

I was well aware that many members of the Deaf community have long been wary of, ostensibly, benevolent efforts of professionals to "serve" them. Indeed, a term, "audists," has been employed in Deaf studies (Lane, 1999) to describe the historical paternalism from a "hearing establishment" of audiologists, speech-language pathologists, otologists, and educators of deaf children: from the eugenics movement in the mid-nineteenth century in which prominent figures like Alexander Graham Bell advocated outlawing intermarriage and procreation by deaf adults; to hearing teachers of deaf students during the next hundred years favoring oral education while forbidding students to use sign language in their classrooms; to cochlear implant teams in the late twentieth century promoting auditory–verbal therapy while proscribing total communication approaches; to genetic testing and engineering of deaf people by audiologists and physicians in the twenty-first century (Baynton, 1996; Lane, 1999; Moore & Levitan, 2003; Scheetz, 2001).

Paternalism, arguably, is becoming more common among audiologists and speech-language pathologists as they base more of their professional training and practices on a medical or "doctoring" model of disability, in lieu of ecological, rehabilitative, or functional models (Anderson, 1977; Smart, 2001). Following a medical model can lead them to be active and their clients passive during evaluation, treatment, goal setting, and decision-making; rather than having clinicians and clients both active. In a medical model, moreover, client trust of clinicians is formed mainly through a professional's credentials (e.g. Doctor of Audiology), rather than by an ongoing relationship developed between client and clinician. And, more often than not, in a medical model clients are more likely to return repeatedly to the clinician for advice when problems arise, rather than problem solving by themselves (Anderson, 1977). Accordingly, a medical model may be preferred during some clinical practices with people with communication disorders (e.g. during site-of-lesion testing by audiologists). When applied willy-nilly to other clinical practices, however, a medical model can lead to paternalism of individuals with communication disorders.

Combating paternalism

1　Encourage active participation of clients in all clinical areas: interview, evaluation, goal setting, treatment, termination, and follow-up.
2　Respect decision-making of client even if you do not always agree with them.

Mechanism of social control: Dependency

Definition

Turning a person's freedom, control, and autonomy over to others.

Message sent

"You can't live without me."

Illustration

In his superb book, *Counseling Persons with Communication Disorders and Their Families*, David Luterman (2001, p. 53) described a lifelong relationship of interdependency between Helen Keller and her teacher Annie Sullivan, and then concluded: "The goal of teaching, like the goal of parenting, is to encourage the child to be independent. Annie could not do this because she had such a strong need to be needed that had not been fulfilled in her life. In many ways, she needed Helen more than Helen needed her." Sullivan epitomizes a speech-language pathologist as "rescuer" (Luterman, 2001; Smart, 2001).

Rescuing makes the person with communication disorders more dependent on them, often to fulfill the clinician's own professional and personal needs. When I have assigned Luterman's book in my classes, many audiology and speech-language pathology students have said he was unfair in his criticism of Sullivan. I was not surprised by their reactions. Over the years, I've read hundreds of essays by students explaining why they applied to our communication disorders programs. Most applicants wrote they wanted to "help" individuals with communication disorders either because they, or someone close to them, had a speech and hearing problem; or they "loved" to work with children; or they were a "people person"; or sometimes all of these. Some students even wrote they first thought of becoming an audiologist or speech-language pathologist after being moved by the movie, *The Miracle Worker*.

When some of these students were clinicians in clinics I've supervised, their "helping" sometimes has verged on "rescuing." Too often they fostered dependency when they set goals, made decisions, and prescribed recommendations *for* their clients, rather than *with* their clients. Likewise, over the past two decades, I've worked with dozens of children who have received cochlear implants. Nearly all of them showed significant improvements in their listening and spoken language. Yet, I have one major misgiving about cochlear implantation of early deafened children. In previous generations, many of these children would have employed American Sign Language for their communication and education and entered Deaf culture to fulfill many of their socialization needs. In other words, they would have been relatively independent of "audists." Conversely, the advent of cochlear implants for deaf children has made most of them and their families more dependent than ever on otologists, audiologists, and speech-language pathologists for their surgeries, therapies, mapping, hearing evaluations, etc. (Lane, 1999),

Combating dependency

1 Examine motives for becoming an audiologist or speech-language pathologist: are you a rescuer?
2 Avoid over-involvement in the life of clients by not making their problems your problems.
3 Remember that people with disabilities may view dependency differently than professionals who work with them (e.g. for some Deaf persons a hearing aid may signal dependency, while a sign language interpreter may not) (Smart, 2001).

Mechanism of social control: Marginalization

Definition

Relegating a person with a disability or their family to the sidelines.

Message sent

"You just stay out of my way."

Illustration

Another gripe Luterman (2001) had with Annie Sullivan was that she effectively limited Helen's mother's participation in her daughter's therapy and education. Professional marginalization of parents of children with communication disorders, unfortunately, continues: from having parents sit in a waiting room while an audiologist tests their child's hearing; to having parents sit behind two-way mirrors as they watch a speech-language pathologist with their child doing "parent–infant training"; to professionals, rather than parents, doing most of the talking and less of the listening during interdisciplinary meetings; to professionals leaving fathers completely out of their child's evaluations and treatments. Indeed, I once attended a 2-day workshop on autism presented by a well-known speech-language pathologist. One of her major emphases was the vital role of parent involvement so that interventions demonstrated by the therapist during weekly therapy sessions could be carried over by parents during the rest of the week. The presenter played numerous videos of her therapy sessions, including several with a child with autism that she had worked with for over 7 years.

Yet none of the videos showed any parents in the therapy room. When I mentioned this to the presenter, she candidly confessed, "I know parent training is important. But, to be honest, it's just easier to work with the kids myself."

Combating marginalization

1 Involve families of clients (that includes dads!) in evaluation, treatment, and follow-up even if it's easier to do it yourself.
2 Talk to and, especially, listen to clients and their families during interdisciplinary meetings.

Mechanism of social control: Scapegoating

Definition

Blaming others for our own inadequacies.

Message sent

"It's your fault."

Illustration

When professionals stigmatize individuals with communication disorders through social control mechanisms like paternalism, dependency, and marginalization they may run into a problem if things go wrong. After all, if the professional and not the client is in control of clinical management, isn't it the professional's fault when management doesn't go as planned? Not necessarily when the professional scapegoats the client or their parents. Rather than saying, "I don't know what caused Jennifer's stuttering," speech-language pathologists, pediatricians, and psychologists, etc., once blamed it on parents calling excessive attention to Jennifer's normal nonfluency. Rather than saying, "I don't know what caused Michael's autism," speech-language pathologists, pediatricians, and psychiatrists, etc., once blamed Michael's mother for her impersonal childrearing. Rather than saying, "There are a number of reasons why Courtney's communication may be improving slower than we would prefer," a mother is told, "You are the key to Courtney improving her speech." And rather than writing in a clinical report, "I was unable to test Johnny's hearing," audiologists employ the passive voice, "Johnny could not be tested," or, as discussed later, they label Johnny as "difficult-to-test."

Combating scapegoating

1   Admit you do not know when you do not know.
2   Take responsibility when you make mistakes.
3   Write clinical reports more in active voice.
4   Don't imply parents of children with communication disorders are the sole determinants of their child's progress.

Cognitive component of stigma

Coleman (1997) suggested that the cognitive component of stigma is primarily manifested by categorization of people. Mechanisms through which professionals categorize people with communication disorders include stereotyping, labeling, shading, infantilization, and scrutinization. At the heart of any of these categorization mechanisms is a concept called "master status": the tendency for professionals to focus on the one attribute, a communication disorder, that makes a person with such a disorder most different, while ignoring many positive attributes that make them similar to those without such a disorder (Higgins, 1980; Scheetz, 2001). Accordingly, it is not stigmatizing to recognize that a person has a communication disorder; it is stigmatizing to assume the communication disorder defines the person (Smart, 2001).

Mechanism of categorization: Stereotyping

Definition

Exaggerated negative beliefs that pigeonhole people into a particular category.

Message sent

"You're all alike."

Illustration

Stereotyping people with communication disorders is the stigma mechanism that audiologists and speech-language pathologists seem to be most familiar with as well as try hardest to combat. Most of us, for example, use politically correct person-first language ("Philip is a man with aphasia") and avoid value-laden or sensationalizing language ("Pamela suffers from cerebral palsy"). Some of us have been involved in exercises to simulate having a communication disorder (e.g. wearing highly visible hearing aids in public for a few days). A few of us have even received some extensive cross-cultural training (I got over 3 months when I was a Peace Corps volunteer). What I've learned from all of these experiences, as well as from writing this chapter, is that there are no absolutes about stereotyping. While most scholars proscribe professionals using stereotyping language, people with disabilities may rate a professional's skill level and effectiveness as more important than politically correct language (Arokiasamy et al., 1994) or self-change (Cunningham, Sobell, & Chow, 1993). Short-term simulations of stigma by people without such disorders, moreover, can be counterproductive by underestimating the amount of stigma a person with a disability experiences over a lifetime and by not accounting for their compensatory and coping skills (Smart, 2001).

Combating stereotyping

1   Do not assume simple solutions are sufficient to reduce stereotyping.
2   Use stigma simulations sparingly, if at all.
3   Have dealings with people with disability on an equal basis outside of the professional–client relationship.

Mechanism of categorization: Labeling

Definition

Assigning a person a description to classify them.

Message sent

"You're one of them."

Illustration

Several years ago I read a satirical editorial about health care associations inflating incidence, prevalence, and severity statistics of persons diagnosed with various illnesses or disabilities. The more people they could label with an illness or disability, the more private and public funding the association might receive. Yet, as the editorial joked, if these statistics were accurate, all of us would be too ill and too disabled to even get out of bed. On a more serious note, Faugier and Sargeant (1997) distinguished between two types of labeling of people with disability: Unofficial labeling by family and friends of someone and official labeling by educators, government officials, and health care professionals. Whether unofficial or official the labeling can, at best, help a person with disability get services, and can, at worst, stigmatize them by becoming a self-fulfilling prophecy (Faugier and Sargeant, 1997; Harris, Milich, Corbitt, Hoover, & Brady, 1992). That is, a person with a disability may assume a stereotypical "sick role" and become even more dependent on professionals. Professionals, meanwhile, may treat the individual differently once they are labeled. Many children with autism have been labeled, inappropriately, as "difficult-to-test" with behavioral audiometric techniques. This has led many audiologists to delay testing them behaviorally or testing them with more expensive and less informative electrophysiological measures like auditory brainstem response audiometry (Downs, Schmidt, & Stephens, 2005).

Combating labeling

1   Professional associations for people with communication disorders should avoid inflating their statistics.
2   Clinicians should avoid pejorative labels like difficult-to-test.

Mechanism of categorization: Shading

Definition

Overgeneralizing effects of a disability to other attributes of a person with a disability.

Message sent

"You're not very attractive, either."

Illustration

A prominent example of shading among individuals with communication disorders is called the "hearing aid effect" (Blood, Blood, & Danhauer, 1977). Researchers traditionally measured it in laboratories by having subjects rate the appearance, intelligence, personality, etc. of persons photographed wearing or not wearing hearing aids. Some studies have shown subjects rating persons wearing hearing aids less favorably (Blood et al., 1977; Danhauer, Blood, Blood, & Gomez, 1980; McCarthy, Hall, & Peach, 1985). Unlike real-life conditions, however, the inanimate photographs used in these studies may have biased subjects by drawing attention to their hearing aids. Other researchers have suggested children (Riensche, Peterson, & Linden, 1990), adolescents (Stein, Gill, & Gans, 2000), and older people (Iler, Danhauer, & Mulac, 1982) may be more accepting of persons wearing hearing aids. Nevertheless, many individuals with hearing loss do feel stigmatized and may prefer to wear less visible hearing aids (Hetu, 1996). Many audiologists and hearing aid dealers have accommodated their preferences by selling them less visible hearing aids.

This can lead to "passing," a well-documented practice in which people with less visible disabilities choose to not disclose their disability to others (Smart, 2001). The hope of people with communication disorders is that benefits of passing (aka, non-disclosure of their disability) will outweigh the costs of passing or, conversely, benefits of not passing (aka, disclosure of disability or "coming out"). Their hope is often fleeting, as passing may backfire for them; making their lives more problematic than if they had "come out" (Smart, 2001). Indeed, many persons with hearing losses experience costs to trying to pass as a person with normal hearing when they are discovered "bluffing" their understanding of a conversation; or when they wear less visible hearing aids and, thereby, hear worse than they might with more visible hearing aids; or when, as adolescents, they take off hearing aids or FM amplification at school only to experience increased difficulty understanding in the classroom.

Combating shading

1   Conduct shading research (e.g. on hearing aid effect) in field settings.
2   Let clients try a variety of hearing aid styles if concerned about shading.
3   Discuss advantages and disadvantages of passing with the client.

Mechanism of categorization: Infantilization

Definition

Viewing adults as if they have never grown up

Message sent

"You're still a kid."

Illustration

"Please tell your students my name is Mr. Stafford, not Jimmy." I have heard comments like this one from many clients – especially from deaf adults, older adults, or adults of any age who have other disabilities in addition to a communication disorder. Their underlying message is not only that they want to be treated with respect, but that they are not a child. Having lived and worked with persons from many cultures in the USA and abroad, I suspect this infantilization of adults with communication disorders may be worse when customs and media promote youthfulness and instant familiarity more rather than deference to persons who are older. Personally, I do not particularly enjoy restaurants where waiters bring crayons to write on the table and sit down next to me to take my order. I cannot hardly imagine how stigmatized I might be if I had aphasia and a clinician called me Davy, used toys during therapy, patted me on the back, and constantly yelled, "Goooood!"

Combating infantilization

1   Avoid diminutive names and patronizing gestures with adults.
2   Employ age-appropriate evaluation and treatment materials.
3   Don't say "Gooooood!"

Mechanism of categorization: Scrutinization

Definition

Sizing up a person in greater detail than done with others.

Message sent

"You don't measure up."

Illustration

The Americans with Disabilities Act (ADA) was enacted, in part, to prevent discrimination in hiring of people with disabilities. Much of this discrimination included employers having higher standards for hiring those with disabilities than those without. I have worked at several places in which a person with a communication disorder was being considered for a job. In most cases, the employer did not know the applicant until he or she was brought in for a face-to-face interview after being deemed, "the best choice on paper." In none of the cases did the person with the disorder get hired. Cognizant of ADA prohibitions, no one involved in hiring ever mentioned an applicant's communication disorders as a reason for not being hired. Reasons were given, instead, in vague statements like, "I get the feeling he may not be able to do the job as well as others," or, "I just think others might present a better image for our place than her." What was most disturbing was that these statements were made by audiologists and speech-language pathologists.

Combating scrutinization

1   We should not set higher standards for individuals with communication disorders than for those without.
2   We should welcome more people with communication disorder becoming audiologists and speech-language disorders.
3   We should oppose discrimination of people with disorders even when it is by our colleagues.

Affective component of stigma

Coleman (1997) suggested the affective component of stigma is primarily manifested by people without disability out of fear of people with disability. Health care workers, for example, may stigmatize clients with HIV/AIDS out of fear of contagion, while mental health workers may stigmatize clients with psychiatric disorders out of fear for safety. Although fear of contagion and safety may be less common among professionals serving those with communication disorders, limited anecdotal evidence does suggest many audiologists and speech-language pathologists may have a fear of stigma-by-association (aka, courtesy stigma) (Goffman, 1963).

Mechanism of fear: Stigma-by-association

Definition

Real or perceived stigma attached to persons close to those with a disability.

Message sent

"Stay away from me."

Illustration

Empirical evidence is accumulating, especially in mental health literature, that many persons who work closely with people with disability are also stigmatized (Sadow, Ryder, & Webster, 2002; Smart, 2001). Whether this fear is legitimate or unfounded, it usually results in those without disability maintaining their distance from, or acting different towards, the clients they serve. Stigma-by-association may be so severe that some professionals leave their jobs to avoid it. Ironically, people with the greatest education, experience, and expertise in health care may avoid stigma-by-association by distancing themselves the furthest from those with disabilities (Sadow et al., 2002). Stigma-by-association may explain, in part, why the American Speech-Language-Hearing Association annually gives its highest award, the Honors of the Association, to a skewed demographic of audiologists and speech-language pathologists (ASHA, 2009b). Specifically, biographies of the 68 persons who received Honors of the Association from 2000 to 2009 indicated all had exceptional careers and they, undoubtedly, assisted numerous persons with communication disorders. Closer inspection of their biographs, however, indicates that virtually all of them were honored primarily for their achievements as academics in university or research settings. This differs strikingly with overall demographics of ASHA (2009a) membership in which 79% of its members work primarily as clinicians, whereas only 3% of its members work primarily as academics. In other words, the vast majority of

ASHA members who spend most of their time working as clinicians with people with communication disorders are never recipients of ASHA's highest honor. Could it be that these full-time clinical audiologists and speech-language pathologists are recipients of stigma-by-association from ASHA?

Combating stigma-by-association

1   Our professional associations should reward persons who provide the most direct services to clients.
2   Audiologists and speech-language pathologists should engage in more research on stigma-by-association.

CONCLUSION

In a fascinating essay entitled *Deaf and Dumb in Ancient Greece*, Martha Edwards (1997) proposed that much of what we know historically about people with communication disorders is based upon writings of elite philosophers and playwrights including Aristotle, Plato, Herodotus, and Aristophanes. Because these men admired rhetorical skills so highly in themselves and others, they were likely less empathetic and more stigmatizing of individuals with communication disorders than the general populace. Things have not changed much in this regard over the past two millennia.

Many university training programs in communication disorders in the USA grew out of programs in speech communication and performing arts. It is not surprising that many audiologists and speech-language pathologists of my generation (I started college in 1971) matriculated as speech communication, theatre, or music majors. As mentioned earlier, many students now major in communication disorders, in part, because they, or a person close to them, had a communication disorder. In other words, persons in our field likely value communication skills more than most other segments of society, both personally and professionally. This bias can make us especially prone to being critical of persons who don't speak or listen as well. Society can stigmatize people with communication disorders. But so can we.

NOTE

1 The word "Deaf" is capitalized to indicate the sociolinguistic and cultural dimensions of the biological correlates of deafness.

10 Establishing relationships in speech-language therapy when working alongside people with mental health disorders

Irene P. Walsh
Trinity College, Dublin

Dana Kovarsky
University of Rhode Island

INTRODUCTION

The following example is taken from the beginning of a session between a psychotherapist and a client (Ferrara, 1999, p. 347). (Transcription conventions throughout this chapter are taken from Eggins & Slade, 1997, p. 5 – see Appendix.)

Client:	I thought most of today that I had so much to tell you. . . . Now that I'm here! I don't have much else to . . . tell you.
Therapist:	Do you think it's the tape?
Client:	No: I had forgotten about the tape.
Therapist:	Hm.
Client:	No. I had forgotten about it.
Therapist:	But you see, we don't believe you forget. Remember . . . We've worked together long enough. You ought to know what I believe about the unconscious. The unconscious doesn't forget. It's all in there.
Client:	My conscious didn't know it.
Therapist:	Well, I think it probably does have something to do with why you feel funny about what's to say. That's my guess.
Client:	Well [6 secs].

When the client confides that she has simply forgotten what is worthy of discussion, the therapist rejects this claim by invoking a professional perspective on the nature of the unconscious that goes back to the work of Freud and says "we don't believe you forget . . . you ought to know what I believe about the unconscious." Even though the client attempts to oppose this explanation, it is the interpretive voice of the therapist that, by speaking for an entire profession ("we"), dominates and helps establish a relationship of evaluative expert versus incompetent novice (Ferrara, 1999, p. 347).

Although positive interpersonal relationships are important to any number of clinical encounters, they take on a special significance when working alongside people with "ongoing mental problems" that demand "a greater level of skill and sensitivity" on the part of the therapist (Perkins & Repper, 1996, p. 39). By the very nature of their psychiatric presentation, people with mental health disorders may have significant difficulties relating to others. Exercising professional expertise in a way that does not create a situation in which the client loses "face" (or public self-image) and that builds rapport, can be particularly important. Comments like those made in the previous example may only serve to undermine the kind of positive relationships that professionals seek to build.

For those with mental health disorders like schizophrenia, bipolar affective disorder, or anxiety disorder any additional speech, language, or hearing disabilities may only serve to further compound difficulties in interpersonal communication (Emerson & Enderby, 1996; Walsh et al., 2007); and in the establishment and maintenance of social relationships. Therefore, for those with mental health and communication disorders, language and communication are both the media and the objects of intervention, with the therapeutic relationships being the conduit for this work.

In this chapter, we will explore how speech-language therapists and audiologists might use some core concepts related to building clinical relationships with people with mental health disorders. Extracts from speech-language therapy discourses that are drawn from individual and group sessions will be used to illustrate these concepts. The sessions involve professional speech-language therapists and their students working with people with schizophrenia, one of the most serious and common mental health disorders in adults (Lavretsky, 2008; Levine & Levine, 2009; Tandon, Keshavan, & Nasrallah, 2008).

However, before addressing these core concepts, it is important to understand the special nature of communicative relationships when interacting with adults with mental health disorders.

DEVELOPING THE THERAPEUTIC RELATIONSHIP WITH PEOPLE WITH MENTAL HEALTH DISORDERS

The process of building rapport is considered an important part of clinical work in speech-language pathology (see Chapter 5). However, this process takes on an even greater significance in mental health populations due to the often slower, more protracted pace of relationship development between clients and mental health professionals: "Psychiatric patients are often outsiders; they do not feel and see things in the same way . . . and many of the taken-for-granted rules and meanings of other people do not hold for them" (Benner, 1984, p. 67).

Many mental health service users will come to the clinic with a cocktail of troubling feelings including fear, anxiety, and distrust; feelings that arise from confused emotions or thinking associated with their presenting condition. Because people with mental health disorders meet psychiatrists and other mental health professionals "when they are experiencing considerable distress and psychological disturbance" (Watkins, 2001, p. 46), relationship building in clinical contexts can prove especially difficult. These clinical encounters are so sensitive that some individuals may present themselves in uncommunicative ways that reflect a long history of "interpersonal scarring," while others will immediately and more urgently divulge their psychiatric difficulties (Watkins, 2001, p. 46). This variability in client presentation poses a challenge to the clinician who seeks to develop a stable working relationship with that person. How a person engages in face-to-face interactions is not necessarily determined by their psychiatric diagnosis. To illustrate, regardless of diagnosis, the demeanor of an individual with schizophrenia or a bipolar disorder, may be highly variable from day to day, or even from moment to moment, within a particular interaction. From displays of reticence and hostility, to discussions of highly personal symptoms and experiences, client variations in the presentation of self can pose particular challenges to clinicians. However, these challenges are not insurmountable; and positive, effective, and lasting therapeutic relationships can be nurtured and sustained. However, this cannot happen unless practitioners respond to what individuals with mental health disorders want or need in their relationships with their therapists.

RELATIONSHIP BUILDING WITH PEOPLE WITH MENTAL HEALTH DISORDERS

The turmoil of a mental health disorder can leave a person feeling helpless and frustrated, and aware of their inability to interact in the clinical context. Therefore, these individuals recognize the need for, and desire, a positive therapeutic relationship with mental health professionals. Janet Frame, a well-known novelist from New Zealand who had repeated experiences of mental ill health, describes this sense of helplessness as follows:

> I cannot talk about myself. I cannot. Every month I go to the hospital and [see] one of doctors from Seacliff, . . . I have been able scarcely to say a word to them . . . I just go into a kind of dream probably to escape their questioning. And my voice won't work. And if it did I would utter what they would think to be utter nonsense . . . I keep silent because physically, I cannot speak.
>
> (Frame, 1949 as cited in King, 2000, p. 103)

All too often, clinicians characterize people like Frame, who struggle to even begin to establish a therapeutic relationship with those who are there to help them, as "uncommunicative." The difference between how a person with a mental health disorder may be perceived by a clinician and how they really are feeling at any given moment is key to understanding how relationships can succeed (or fail) in mental health contexts. Frequently, for many people with these disorders, the default option is to remain quiet; silencing rather than sharing their thoughts, concerns, or ideas. O'Hagan believes that problems in interpersonal communication between health care practitioners and patients expose "the fundamental reason why mental health services so often fail to help people" (O'Hagan, 1996, p. 44). However, others describe their therapeutic relationships in more positive, if somewhat simple terms. For example, Emmons and colleagues report how a person with schizophrenia described his relationship with his psychiatrist as follows:

> There was one psychiatrist who
> would always shout
> when he talked to you.
> But he was different from all
> the other psychiatrists I met.
> First, he took your communication seriously.
> And second, he always
> had time to talk to you
> So what if he did shout?

(Emmons, Geiser, Kaplan, & Harrow, 1997, p. 57)

Taking a person's "communication seriously" and having "time to talk" seem to be key ingredients at least in this successful therapeutic relationship.

RELATIONSHIP BUILDING: SOME THERAPEUTIC PROCESSES

There are four core processes that are particularly relevant for speech, language, and hearing clinicians when developing working relationships with people with mental health disorders. These processes, though not mutually exclusive or exhaustive, include engagement, self-disclosure, presencing via silence, and humor/playfulness. We will show how each of these principles is manifested in speech-language therapy discourse involving individuals with schizophrenia; but the principles and processes may apply equally to people with mental health disorders in general.

Engagement

According to Tannen, cited in Kovarsky, Curran, and Zobel Nichols (2009, p. 28), engagement refers to:

the intensity and manner of interpersonal involvement displayed by participants, and it reflects the extent to which they are mutually engrossed in, and alive to, the unfolding interaction. This kind of involvement represents "an emotional connection individuals feel which binds them to other people as well as to places, things, activities, ideas, memories, and words."

(Tannen, 1989, p. 12)

Because it is considered an important part of the language learning process and the development of clinical relationships, engagement has been studied in a variety of speech-language therapy contexts, including interactions involving adults with traumatic brain injury (Kovarsky et al., 2009), aphasia (Simmons-Mackie & Damico, 2009) and dysphagia (Walsh & Leahy, 2009). These studies reveal that engagement is an interactional achievement. In fact, Tannen (1989) describes a number of "involvement strategies" that function communicatively to build engagement in interaction. One such strategy is *repetition*. The following examples reveal how engagement can be realized through repetitions found in small talk about the weather, that occur during a speech-language therapy session involving people with schizophrenia.

Extract 1: T1 = therapist; T2 = student; C = client
1 *T1:* it's DRIZZLING is it?
2 *C:* drizzling.
3 *T1:* but it's not too COLD.
4 *C:* cold enough
5 *T2:* is it?
6 *T1:* wasn't it VERY cold the weekend?
7 *C:* it was.
8 *T2:* terrible-absolutely terrible [3 secs] so were you just down at the SHOP?
9 *C:* just at the shop. [4 secs] went towards Joe's then . . .

Extract 2: T1 = therapist; T2 = student; C = client
1 *C:* it's great they had THAT CONCERT for Princess Di near her–near the palace in England over the weekend.
2
3 *T1:* oh did they HAVE IT? ==
4 *C:* ==they had a concert==
5 *T1:* ==they HAD the concert . . . oh right I thought they were just selling the tickets were they not?
6
7 *C:* I – I thought it was on over the weekend
8 *T1:* ==oh?
9 *C:* == I saw it I think
10 *T1:* a concert for princess Diana's ==
11 *T2:* ==oh yeah ==

12 *T1:*   ==em I . . . CHARITY wasn't it
13 *C:*   ==charity
14 *T1:*   ==charity concert
15 *C:*   ==charity . . . charity

In both examples, there is an echoing of particular words ("drizzling" and "cold" in Extract 1; "charity" and "concert" in Extract 2) and grammatical patterns (lines 4 and 5 in Extract 2: "they had a concert"). Repetition according to Tannen, "functions on the 'interactional level of talk: accomplishing social goals, or simply managing the business of conversation' by 'providing back-channel response', 'showing listenership' and 'ratifying another's contributions' " (Tannen, 1989, p. 52). Furthermore, ". . . repetition not only ties parts of discourse to other parts, but it bonds participants to the discourse and to each other, linking individual speakers in a conversation and in relationships" (Tannen, 1989, pp. 51–52).

It is interesting to note in the above extracts, that repetition is not just a conscious involvement strategy used by therapists, it is a process shared by all participants, signaling an involvement or engagement that is interactionally achieved in talk.

Self-disclosure

The use of self-disclosure on the part of a skilled mental health clinician is a topic that has received considerable attention in the literature (e.g. Perkins & Repper, 1996; Seligman, 2009). Seligman (2009, p. 210) comments: "A survey of the research on clinician self-disclosure suggests that a small amount of self-disclosure can enhance the treatment alliance and build trust between client and clinician. However, self-disclosure must be used judiciously and with a purpose. . . ." As Perkins and Repper (1996, p. 42) note, such self-disclosure does not occur in a vacuum and involves some type of cautious reciprocal sharing:

> If the person is telling of their life, then it is important for the staff worker to tell something of their own, otherwise a two-way interaction cannot occur. Clearly, staff should not engage in painful and sensitive self-disclosures, and the way in which any disclosures may be understood (or misunderstood) by the client must be given careful consideration. Most of us have areas of our life that are safe to share in the process of relationship formation – our views, holidays, cats, interests, leisure and sports pursuits. Telling about ourselves for our own benefit must be avoided, the key question is how will any self-disclosure affect our relationship with the person we are trying to help?

In keeping with this, Seligman (2009) discusses "usually unacceptable" and "usually acceptable" types of self-disclosure. For example, in the usually unacceptable category, he includes: "very personal information about the clinician" and "information on clinicians' own problems and difficulties that is unlikely to help the client." In the usually acceptable category, Seligman includes "minimal sharing of neutral factual information" and "gently offering new perspectives based on your own feelings" (Seligman, 2009, p. 210).

Different degrees of self-disclosure can be seen in the following extracts. The content of many of these self-disclosures could be described as "safe topics" (Brown & Levinson, 1987, p. 112). For example, in Extract 3 below, we see how the therapist is apparently taken aback as the client reciprocates by asking about her weekend (line 2).

Extract 3: T = therapist; C = client
1 *T:* how are you?
2 *C:* not too bad. How are you? D' you have a ==good weekend?
3 *T:* ==I'm not too bad. Did I have a good weekend? I did actually yeah?==
4 *C:* ==did you do anything exciting?
5 *T:* did I do anything exciting? Actually I did I went to a concert last night.

Although the therapist responds to the questions asked of her, there is some hesitation as she repeats the same questions almost verbatim in lines 3 and 5 (did I have a good weekend? did I do anything exciting?) However, the therapist does disclose something about her weekend activities (line 5) and the conversation proceeds. Reciprocally sharing some weekend news makes for a more equitable conversation instead of the more usual trend of the therapist questioning the client. Therefore, Extract 3 above and Extract 4 below are interesting in that, at first glance it seems that the role relations are reversed and the client (C) is "interviewing" the therapist (T), instead of the other way around.

Extract 4: C = client; T = therapist
1 *C:* how are you?
2 *T:* I'm grand thanks
3 *C:* were you in family's p-parents house Christmas?
4 *T:* for a short time = = I was
5 *C:* = = short time. You weren't Christmas day were you==?
6 *T:* ==yeah for a little little while
7 *C:* just visiting
8 *T:* yeah but I cooked I cooked Christmas dinner = = myself
9 *C:* = = for them?
10 *T:* no
11 *C:* for my- yourself==
12 *T:* ==my husband's family
13 *C:* your husband's family?
14 *T:* mhmm yeah so we'd a grand day I didn't burn the turkey this year

Here we see the client asking the therapist many questions about Christmas. It is interesting to note that instead of taking the opportunity to "shut down" this small talk after line 7 – where the topic could have been easily brought to a close – it is the therapist who maintains the "safe" topic by adding more information about cooking the Christmas dinner herself in line 8. Extract 4 is also similar to Extract 3 above in that just enough – but not too much – information (in this instance about family and Christmas) is shared, to keep the conversation going in a relaxed and equitable way.

The final example of self-disclosure to be discussed here is one where age is being talked about in relation to people taking up a new career (Extract 5). The topic arose within a conversational group therapy session with people with schizophrenia.

Extract 5: C1 = client 1; C2 = client 2; T = therapist
 1 *C1:*   a chef . . . a good chef em I think to meself I'm too old now to be a chef
 2 *T:*   what age are ya?
 3 *C1:*   twenty-nine
 4 *T:*   twenty-nine?
 5 *C1:*   yeah
 6 *T:*   do you think that's old?
 7 *C2:*   ==no
 8 *C1:*   ==yeah
 9 *C2:*   I don't think so
10 *C1:*   it is
11 *T:*   I'm twenty-nine I don't think that's old

In the last line of this extract, we see the therapist voluntarily sharing her age with members of the group. Although Seligman (2009) may class this as an "unacceptable type of self-disclosure" in terms of "very personal information," it can be interpreted simply as a mutual sharing of topically related information. It is a truly reciprocal and equitable process in this example, given that the therapist asked the client his age in the opening lines of the extract (line 2), not for any case history purposes, but for purely conversational ones.

In the conversations discussed above, self-disclosures emerge on the part of the clinicians. These help to cast the therapist in the role of a "person" as well as a "therapist" in much the same way as therapists attempt to see the "person" behind the "patient" in therapeutic interactions (Perkins & Repper, 1996, p. 42). The give and take of conversation is important in these contexts.

Presencing via silence

A third core feature involved in establishing a relationship among people with mental health disorders is called "presencing" – a term coined by Benner (1984), and one we suggest can include silence. Speech-language therapists are all too aware of the need "to talk" in order to fill the silences in an inter-action, considering those silences to be vacant, empty, or awkward. In mental health contexts particularly, silence is highly valued because it provides a space for reflection and time out from what can sometimes be considered "cognitive overload" (Frith, 1979). Watkins comments:

> Conversations that are too probing or intense can overload vulnerable people and lead to withdrawal, avoidance, or the exacerbation of acute symptoms. Others may be so sunk in depression they seem difficult to engage with. Others may be troubled and distracted by unusual thoughts or voice hearing. In all these scenarios sensitivity and awareness . . . is required.
>
> (Watkins, 2001, pp. 47–48)

Dirschel (1998, p. 77) indicates that presencing goes "beyond doing for a patient, as is seen in parts of the rehabilitation process, to the state of being with a patient". Benner (1984, p. 57) uses the following reflection from an expert nurse to illustrate presencing:

> It is a person-to-person kind of thing, just being with somebody, really communicating with people . . . You talk about empathy or whatever, but somebody is frightened and just sitting down and listening to people, it's not that you even have to say anything. And I think that is an important thing, because I tend to always want to have an answer. But when I have just kept my mouth shut and just listened, it's been much more effective; just the fact that somebody is there to listen to somebody express their concerns, and that you don't necessarily have to have an answer or a suggestion or solve the problem, but just because they've been able to have someplace to talk about it. It makes it easier.

Truly "being with" a client who has had disturbing experiences or thoughts in a clinical session can be challenging for the speech-language therapist. The reported delusional or hallucinatory experiences of a person with schizophrenia – when discussed within a speech-language session – require sensitive handling. Whether these experiences are "hushed" or "heard" often depends on the agenda of the clinician (Walsh, 2008). Psychiatrists may avoid talk of delusions during sessions with a person with schizophrenia (McCabe, Heath, Burns, & Priebe, 2002). However, being with a client in the presencing sense, is not about avoidance. Rather, it requires listening to such talk, without feeling the need to respond, interpret, or provide a solution to the problem. In the following extract, the therapist (T) is talking with a client with schizophrenia (C):

Extract 6: T1 = therapist; T2 = student therapist; C: client
  1 *T2:*   ( ) how was the weekend anyway

2   [5 secs]
3 *C:*   em [4 secs] I was a bit depressed but it passed away
4 *T2:*   ( )
5 *C:*   after a few hours
6 *T1:*   [5 secs]
7 *T1:*   is that how it hits you John? hits you for a few hours an' then
         passes

8
9 *C:*   sometimes
10 *T:*   mm yeah and do you still hear voices John or is that kind of stopped
         your voices stopped or are they still at you?

11
12   [11 secs]
13 *C:*   I'm still hearing' they're mild mild voices==
14 *T:*   ==oh right right ... so you say mild are they quiet? they quiet?
         are they?

15
16 *C:*   I HAVE heard quiet voices
17 *T:*   right yeah what kind of things do they say [6 sec] or are the [quiet] ( )
18   [9 secs]
19 *C:*   might tell me to take up wrestling or do plenty of exercise
20 *T:*   take up wrestling?
21 *C:*   mm
22 *T:*   would you like to take up wrestling?
23 *C:*   I wouldn't be much good==
24 *T:*   ==no I don't think I would either I don't like the way bodies get
25   thrown around the rings
26 *C:*   mm
27 *T:*   so they tell you – positive things ==do they?
28 *C:*   ==mm
29 *T:*   yeah uh/ (not so bad then) uh and do they annoy you do they
30   bother you?
31   [6 secs]
32 *C:*   they do a bit yeah
33 *T:*   mm ... yeah ... so the weekend did you go up to your Mum?

Although the therapist in the above extract asks a lot of questions of the
client (lines 1,7/8,10/11,14/15, 20, 22, 27 and 29), she does so in a nonchal-
lenging or nonthreatening way, as she gently extends the client-initiated topic
of his depression (line 3: I was a bit depressed but it passed away) by nudging
the conversation forward to talk of the client's auditory hallucinations (line
10). Although the therapist is concerned with talk about the client's depression and his experience of hearing voices, she also offers a "break" in such
emotive and troubling talk as she moves the hallucinatory topic of "wrestling" onto safer ground, in terms of whether or not one would be good at the

sport (lines 22–26). In doing this, she validates the client's hallucinations as "real" for him. The therapist then revisits talk of the nature of auditory hallucinations *per se* in line 27 (so they tell you positive things do they?) and line 29 (do they annoy you do they bother you?). The client is given time to air his concerns in a relaxed and supportive environment, through the conversational behavior of the therapist. Through presencing, the therapist does not attempt to avoid, interpret, or judge the client's telling of his feelings or experiences. Rather, she scaffolds, through questioning, the patient's expression of his concerns and the patient's own problem solving in relation to his feelings of ill health.

The relatively long inter-turn pauses in this extract are also of particular interest (see lines 2, 6, 12, 18 and 31). In more typical interactions, overly long inter-turn pauses may result in conversational breakdown, especially in the context of adjacency pairs (e.g. question–answer sequences). More usually, inter-turn pauses last no longer than a "conversational beat" or less than a second (Nofsinger, 1991, p. 81). It is interesting that in this interaction the therapist does not attempt to fill these overly long pauses with follow-up questions, instead allowing them to occur. Long inter-turn pauses happen to be a feature of this client's communication style, evident also in sequences of small talk at other times in sessions, as the following extracts demonstrate.

Extract 7: T = therapist; C = client
1 *T:*   is your Mum well?
2 *C:*   she's not too bad T
3 *T:*   good that's great! is there anything in the news over the weekend that
4   you – caught your interest?
5   [22 secs]
6 *C:*   it's great they had THAT CONCERT for Princess Di near her – near
7   the palace in England over the weekend.
8 *T:*   oh did they HAVE IT? ==
9 *C:*   ==they had a concert

Extract 8: T1 = therapist SLT; T2 = student; C = client
1 *T1:*   yeah. so any other news now? 'cos it's nearly a month since we've
           seen y
2 *T2:*   mmm
3 *T1:*   imagine!
4   [30 secs]
5 *C:*   crash in the land rover up north was terrible
6 *T1:*   oh?
7 *C:*   two soldiers ( )
8 *T1:*   oh when was that C?
9 *C:*   a few days ago

The long pauses between the questions asked of the client and the subsequent responses given by him (22 seconds in Extract 7 and 30 seconds in Extract 8) would, in other circumstances, most certainly result in a conversational breakdown, yet are tolerated by the therapist in this context.

In these examples, the therapist's behavior may be described as a form of presencing behavior, where silences are tolerated and talk is facilitated by proceeding on the client's terms, without any need to problem solve. Although the therapist does not remain silent, she does not attempt to add content or interpretation to the talk, just facilitates it to move forward in a conversational and nonthreatening way at the client's pace. In other words, the therapist is finding a "way of being" or "way of behaving in talk" with the client (Walsh, 2002, p. 141).

Such presencing may be attributed to what Coupland, Coupland, Giles, and Henwood (1988) call "discourse attuning" factors. Discourse attuning is a feature of communication accommodation (Coupland et al., 1988), where interlocutors adapt their communication to one another in order to facilitate the interaction. The therapist's silence functions communicatively as a way of attending to the client's "productive performance," attuning to his discourse style by waiting for him to answer. At the same time, the therapist is accounting for the client's "interpretive competence," allowing him considerable time to process the question asked. In other words, there is an asymmetric convergence where the speech-language therapist attunes to the client's communication style by permitting longer than usual pauses between turns.

Humor and playfulness

A final concept to be discussed in our exploration of the establishment of relationships with people with mental health disorders is humor or playfulness. In the first author's (Walsh's) experience of working alongside people with mental health disorders for over a decade, humor and playfulness have figured largely – if somewhat unexpectedly – in interactions. Wilson (2007, p. 151) talks about playfulness in the context of family therapy as follows: "Play and playfulness can enhance the repertoire of the therapist and family to find some new communicational avenues to the usual self-defeating scripts they hold on to."

In the following extract, a more positive and "new communicational avenue" is opened up to the client, who, while initially engaged in troubles telling, begins to joke or be playful about how he is feeling.

Extract 9: T1 = therapist SLT; T2 = student; C = client
1 *C:*   when I get me teeth done I'll be better [sniffles]
2 *T2:*   yeah
3 *T1:*   you will ==
4 *C:*   ==I'll feel better anyway I feel better I feel lousy
5 *T1:*   do you feel lousy?==
6 *C:*   ==I don't feel so good that's why I'm not concentrating

7 *T1:* yeah==
8 *C:* ==I'm all shook up () Elvis Presley [laughs]
9 *T1:* [laughs] all shook up all shook up like Elvis Presley are you?
10 *T2:* [laughs]
11 *T1:* all shook up [laughs]
12 *T2:* [laughs]

Line 8 sees the client comparing himself to the singer Elvis by being all shook up. This comment occasions laughter, thus leaving behind the troubles telling. Joking and laughter, in this case, lessen the negativity of the troubles telling or the impact of the complaint gone before. Put another way, joking functions as a social accelerator that promotes camaraderie (or positive face) among the participants (Brown & Levinson, 1987).

According to Jefferson (1985), laughter during troubles telling indicates "troubles resistivity" where the teller communicates that he/she is able to cope with the troubles in question. The joking and subsequent laughter thereafter result in what Coupland et al. (1992, p. 225) describe as a "momentary suspension from the impact of troublesome life circumstances." What is important here is how both student and therapist align to this joking sequence instead of quashing it as inappropriate or irrelevant in therapeutic talk.

The following extract is taken from an interaction with a client who had earlier expressed that he had wanted to sign himself back into hospital, as he had been feeling unwell the weekend before. He was concerned that he was out of hospital "for 3 years" and usually did not "stay out that long." The therapist (T1) seeks to reassure the client that he is generally doing well.

Extract 10: T1 = therapist; T2: student; C: client
1 *C:* ==I've been out THREE YEARS you know I usually don't stay out that long
2
3 *T1:* right? I think that's 'cos you've been doing SO WELL?
4 *C:* ... ah I don't think I've been doing [well].
5 *T1:* do you not?==
6 *C:* ==well I SUPPOSE I AM. I have to be
7 *T1:* I think you've been doing VERY WELL I think Mary thinks you've
8   been doing very well ==
9 *C:* ==DOES SHE ?
    .... [talk continues]
10   she thinks you are doing VERY WELL yeah? so you didn't feel so well so ... you were thinking of signing yourself back in.
11
12 *C:* I've an awful lot of ENERGY ENERGY and maybe I take up
13   A SMALL BIT OF JOGGING in the spr – in the summer==

14 *T1:*   ==OH RIGHT? that might be an idea would you LIKE – would you
15   ENJOY that
16 *C:*   . . . I wouldn't say I'd ENJOY it mind you
17 *T1:*   [laughs]
18 *C:*   [laughs]
19 *T2:*   [laughs]
20 *T2:*   it'd be GOOD for you.
21 *T1:*   [laughing] but IT would get you out and about
22 *C:*   yeah

In line 16, the client contradicts, in a humorous way, the suggestion that he might enjoy the "small bit of jogging" (14–15). The client's use of the "mind you," coupled with the additional stress placed on "enjoy," transform this into a humorous response as is evidenced by the ensuing laughter. Here, laughter and humor help suspend the troubles telling for all concerned and allow the interaction to move forward without minimizing the seriousness of the client's earlier assertion about the need to sign himself back into hospital.

Wilson (1993, 1998) has written of the need to create a seriously playful context for practice in family therapy, and these examples illustrate that need. Note that in Extracts 9 and 10, it is the client, not the therapist, who initiates the joking sequences. How joking sequences are attended to by the therapist and the students is of importance: they join in the jocularity, if only moment-arily and they do not laugh at but laugh with the client – an important distinction to be made in this context (e.g. see Glenn, 2003). The camaraderie they achieve through their joint efforts is conducive to the building and maintenance of positive relationships.

CONCLUSIONS

Working alongside people with mental health disorders in speech-language therapy can be both challenging and multifaceted, especially when it comes to relationship building. People with mental health disorders are complex in their clinical presentation and demeanor, potentially the result of long or protracted histories of "interpersonal scarring" (Watkins, 2001). While clinicians may find such complexity overwhelming, we examined how engagement, self-disclosure, presencing via silence, and humor and playfulness as manifest in talk, can all function to foster positive relationships in clinical contexts. We have described these processes as they were interactionally achieved in talk. We do not see these processes as prescriptive. Rather we see these processes as descriptive, serving to illuminate what building relationships with people with mental health disorders might look like in conversations and in a clinical context. These are general strategies that must then be applied judiciously in situated contexts according to the individual needs or wants of clients. To do this, it is important to recognize the person and not just the psychiatric diagnosis. By nurturing positive relationships, people with mental health disorders can be enabled in their efforts to re-access their social worlds through language and communication.

11 Constructivism and adaptive leadership

Framing an approach for clinicians to overcome barriers to counseling

Anthony DiLollo
Wichita State University

INTRODUCTION

For speech-language pathologists and audiologists, integrating counseling into existing practices faces four primary barriers:

1   lack of knowledge of *counseling techniques*;
2   not knowing *what* aspects of the client's problem require counseling;
3   not knowing *when* to do counseling; and
4   not having the *time* to do counseling.

These are real barriers that need to be taken seriously if clinicians are to change the way they engage clients in the therapeutic process. By the end of this chapter, my goal is to have provided at least tentative ways to address each of these four barriers, with the hope that clinicians might use this as a starting point for reconstructing their clinical practices. Let's start out with a bold statement: The role of professionals who work with individuals with communication disorders, that is, speech-language pathologists and audiologists, is *not* simply to remediate disorder. Yes, individuals who come to us for treatment for a communication disorder do so with the hope of improving or remediating the disorder, and, on the surface, this would appear to be a relatively simple "transaction." In this simplified view, the individual comes to therapy and the therapist uses his or her expertise to facilitate changes in the person's communicative behaviors. In reality, however, such therapeutic interaction is far from simple. The purpose of speech and language is communication; and communication is inextricably woven into the very fabric of human existence, becoming bonded to the individual's understanding of self, the world, and the role that the self plays in the world. When faced with significant change to communicative ability (i.e. remediating an old problem or dealing with a new one), individuals must "reconstruct" their understanding of self and their role in the world by *meaningfully* integrating new behaviors into their established self and world image.

In this chapter we will investigate a framework around which speech-language pathologists and audiologists might construct therapeutic processes to help facilitate reconstruction of clients' lives in relation to their communication problems. That is, help clients *meaningfully* integrate new behaviors into their self-image in order for them to effectively enact alternative, more functional, communicative roles. The use of this framework can be incorporated within traditional approaches to treatment, in many cases allowing clinicians to continue doing essentially what they have always done, but with a different focus and understanding. As we will also see, this framework may be useful for clinicians working with clients with any type of communication disorder, based on the concept that all individuals need to *meaningfully* integrate new behaviors gained during therapy and the knowledge that many will require specific help from the clinician for this to occur. Finally, I will close the chapter by taking a look at how clinicians might put this framework into action. To do this we will explore the idea that "doing" counseling or, in fact, simply being an effective clinician, might be viewed as an act of *leadership* in which clinicians work to help clients deal with both "technical" and "adaptive" aspects of their problem.

A CONSTRUCTIVIST FRAMEWORK FOR COUNSELING INDIVIDUALS WITH COMMUNICATION DISORDERS AND THEIR FAMILIES

This framework draws heavily from personal construct theory (PCT) and narrative therapy; two constructivist approaches to therapy that I believe are well suited for use with persons with communication disorders (see also Brumfitt, 1985). Detailed descriptions of PCT and narrative therapy have been presented elsewhere and will not be repeated here. The reader is referred to George Kelly's (1955) original work on PCT and descriptions by Fransella (1972), Stewart and Birdsall (2001), and DiLollo, Neimeyer, and Manning (2002) regarding how PCT might be used by speech-language pathologists. Similarly, the work of Michael White (1989, 1995) has been central to the development of narrative therapy, and the reader is referred to White and Epston's (1990) *Narrative Means to Therapeutic Ends*, as well as introductory texts by Morgan (2000) and Payne (2006) for more detail. Finally, Dilollo, et al. (2002), and Wolter, DiLollo, and Apel (2006) have described the use of narrative therapy by speech-language pathologists, and DiLollo, DiLollo, Mendel, English, and McCarthy (2008) described the potential use of narrative therapy and PCT by audiologists. My goal in the following section of the chapter is to synthesize the material from PCT and narrative therapy to provide a constructivist framework that might be useful for clinicians in guiding their clinical practice.

Therapeutic stance: The client as expert

Neimeyer (2004) described constructivism as a theory of knowledge (an epistemology), rather than as a system of psychotherapy per se. Constructivists believe that knowledge is constructed through interpretation and a search for meaning; that we essentially live in an "interpreted space" between the self and the real world. One implication of this constructivist view of knowledge is that knowledge is relative and provisional, meaning that the knowledge that clients possess about their problems may be seen as equally valid and important as the "scientific" knowledge possessed by clinicians. Consequently, when working within a constructivist framework, clinicians need to "give up" their expert status and role of "problem fixer" and recognize that clients have unique knowledge of the problem and their own personal resources. As such, clients should be *active* participants in the therapeutic process, not *passive* recipients of the clinician's "expertise."

Diagnosing the situation: Beyond case history

Allowing the client to take the role of expert and lead therapy is often a problem for clinicians, in part because of the tension between using techniques and being person-centered. What aspects of the client's problem require direct "technical" intervention with specific speech, language, or hearing techniques and what aspects require a more person-centered, counseling approach? This is the clinician's dilemma; our role is not entirely one of being a *counselor*, nor is it sufficient for us to merely provide *technical intervention*. Working within a constructivist framework, clinicians pay particular attention to gathering rich, thick descriptions of the client's situation that should help the clinician distinguish these different aspects of the client's problem.

Typically, as speech-language pathologists and audiologists we are very good at finding out all the relevant details of the speech, language, swallowing, or hearing problem that our clients present. We ask specific questions, often from a list of "standard" case-history questions (e.g. Shipley & McAfee, 2009), we use standardized tests, we take speech samples, and we do instrumental testing. All of these activities are important, but all focus solely on the *problem* and not the *person*. One of the basic tenets of this constructivist framework is that the clinician must engage the client in a conversation, the aim of which is to go beyond what White (1989) called the "problem-saturated" story and investigate the impact of the problem on the life of the person.

The primary "technique" (if you want to call it such) used by the clinician at this stage is to ask clarifying and extending questions. DiLollo et al. (2002) used the term "curious questioning" to describe this interaction, with the clinician taking the role of an *interested conversational partner*. White and Epston (1990) suggested that this is a process for clients to "map the influence of the problem in their lives and relationships" (p. 42). By this process of curious questioning clinicians can help clients provide more detail about ways in which they are experiencing difficulty and, most importantly, the effect of these on their life.

Alternative ways of construing: Subplots that lead to alternate self-narratives

Another implication of the constructivist view of knowledge is that, as knowledge is based on interpretation, there may be an endless number of ways in which a specific event or problem may be interpreted. From a constructivist perspective, then, all interpretations of a situation may be considered valid, even if those interpretations do not match those "expected" by the dominant cultural or social group in which the individual exists. Of course, some interpretations (or ways of construing) may provide more functional and satisfying ways of living than others, and this forms the fundamental aspect of the constructivist framework as it relates to communication problems. *If a communication problem is producing emotional and/or social consequences, it is likely that alternative ways of construing that problem may prove helpful for individuals and their families.*

Personal narratives

One way of helping clients to start the process of construing a communication problem in a different way is to focus on their self-narrative or story. Winslade and Monk (1999) suggested that people understand their lives through their "storying" of lived experience, a concept echoed by Morgan (2000, p. 4) when she stated that:

> As humans, we are interpreting beings. We all have daily experiences of events that we seek to make meaningful. The stories we have about our lives are created through linking certain events together in a particular sequence across a time period, and finding a way of explaining or making sense of them. This meaning forms the plot of the story. We give meanings to our experiences constantly as we live our lives. A narrative is like a thread that weaves the events together, forming a story.

In discussing this concept of self-narratives, however, White and Epston (1990) have suggested that only a fraction of our lived experience can be storied and expressed at any one time, resulting in a significant amount of lived experience falling outside the dominant stories that form the basis of people's understanding of their lives. The implication for counseling, then, is that "those aspects of lived experience that fall outside of the dominant story provide a rich and fertile source for the generation, or re-generation, of alternative stories" (White & Epston, 1990, p. 15).

Unique outcomes

White and Epston (1990) referred to these aspects of lived experience that fall outside of the dominant story as "unique outcomes." From a clinical perspective, these potential alternative storylines may be found in the conversations between the client and clinician. They show themselves as occasions when the client describes fleetingly overcoming the influence of the problem, dealing with the problem in some creative way, tapping into mostly forgotten personal resources, or even simply forgetting, for a brief moment, that the problem existed.

The challenge for the clinician is to locate these unique outcomes in the elaborated descriptions of the problem and its effects on the person – the conversations with the client. Payne (2006) suggests listening for "clues" that the client provides, usually in a passing allusion to some taken-for-granted reference of resistance to the dominant story. An example of a "clue" might be when a client briefly mentions how she is able to "cheat" and "bluff" her way through each day so that no one at her office realizes that she has a literacy problem. This might lead to a storyline that focusses on creativity, adaptability, and resourcefulness rather than her current dominant story of helplessness and inadequacy. White and Epston (1990) and Payne (2006) also suggest that if a client struggles with revealing clues to unique outcomes, specific questioning might be used to help the client locate some of those ignored events (see also DiLollo et al., 2002, and Epston & White, 1999, for examples of such questions).

Once identified, the client is invited to expand on the circumstances and nature of the unique outcome, providing as much detail as possible. The clinician again uses curious questioning to focus attention on how these events do not fit with the problem-saturated story as previously told. Questioning may include aspects of the person's feelings, thoughts, and actions, and may also invite speculation on how other people who may have witnessed these unique outcomes may have understood them. In this way, a richer story of the person's life may begin to emerge.

Externalizing

Another way that can be useful in helping clients to construe their problem in a different way is the use of "externalizing" language. White and Epston (1990) describe externalizing as an approach that "encourages persons to objectify and, at times, to personify the problems that they experience as oppressive. In this process, the problem becomes a separate entity and thus external to the person or relationship that was ascribed as the problem" (p. 38). The effect, according to White and Epston, is to shift the focus of conversation to *the relationship between the person and the problem* rather than on a "problem-person," encouraging greater focus, feelings of control, and options for "dialogue, rather than monologue, about the problem"

(p. 40). This enables the clinician and the client to work together to resist the effects of the problem as opposed to the expectation that the clinician will "fix" some broken aspect of the client.

Typically, a single word or short phrase might be used to "name" the problem as a way of creating opportunities for the client and clinician to engage in "externalizing conversations." The clinician should always ensure that the name has specific, consistent meaning for the client. For example, I recently worked with a person who decided to use the term "stuttering" to name his problem. We proceeded to try to incorporate externalizing language in all of our subsequent conversations, talking about how "stuttering" had "outsmarted" him when he had carefully prepared a presentation for school, practiced it, and was confident of success, only to have a severe block on his name, which he could usually say quite smoothly.

Experimenting

As alternative interpretations of situations or problems emerge (i.e. as an alternative personal story begins to be told), they are initially rather tentative and, not surprisingly, feel strange and unfamiliar to the client. One process that may be useful for clinicians in these circumstances is to engage the client in *experimenting* with the alternative interpretations. Such experiments may begin in the therapy room, in the form of role playing, and later be extended to real-life roles in outside situations. Interestingly, the concept of experimenting with new behaviors is not unfamiliar to most speech-language pathologists and audiologists, as many clinicians assign "homework" to their clients to "practice" new behaviors outside the therapy room. The primary difference, however, is in the focus of the experimenting. Usually, when a clinician asks a client to experiment with a new behavior, the focus is on successful execution of a learned therapeutic technique or behavior. For example, an audiologist who is working with a client on being more assertive in asking for clarification when he has not heard someone clearly, might ask the client to experiment with that behavior at his next church meeting. Typically, preparation for the "experiment" might involve practicing the behavior and making sure the client knows what he might say. Then, following the experiment, the clinician might ask the client how successful he was at implementing the behavior and might review how the client could have performed better.

Within a personal construct framework, however, experimenting takes on a slightly different look with a different focus. Instead of the focus being on successful execution of the technique or behavior, the focus is on how the experience compares with the individual's existing constructs or interpretations of the situation. Continuing with the above example, then, an audiologist working within a constructivist framework might assign the same experiment but with a few modifications. In this case, preparation for the experiment would involve asking the client to make specific predictions (both negative and positive) regarding how he expects the experiment to unfold, both from his perspective and from the perspective of others (these would be his existing *constructs* that will be "tested"). He is then invited to find evidence for his interpretation during the course of the experiment. Following the experiment, the audiologist would specifically discuss with the client how well the evidence that he gathered matched his earlier predictions. In this way, the clinician can help the client process his experiences in a way that helps him meaningfully integrate those experiences, thus helping to solidify the emerging alternative story.

Recognize the loss

Any time significant personal change occurs, as in the case of remediating a long-standing speech, language, or hearing problem or trying to adjust to a recent decline in speech, language, or hearing ability, individuals will experience emotional reactions. Working within a constructivist framework, clinicians can be better prepared to understand and deal with clients' emotional reactions. Kelly (1955) described a constructivist view of emotions such as fear, threat, anxiety, guilt, and hostility, providing a slightly different understanding of these terms compared with traditional definitions.

The constructivist view of *fear* and *threat* is that they represent an awareness by an individual that, based on current experiences, his/her belief system (what constructivists would call the "construct system") must change (Landfield & Leitner, 1980). Put another way, if a new construct (or belief) is introduced to an existing construct system but is incompatible with that system, then fear or threat will occur. These new constructs or changes do not have to be negative, and, in fact, they often are desired changes such as remediation from a long-standing disorder. Landfield and Leitner provided such an example, stating, "if a person has defined his life-role in terms of sickness, the prospect of successful therapy could be traumatizing" (1980, p.12). This concept can help us to understand the paradoxical "resistance" that is often noted at later stages of therapy for communication disorders. This was noted by Fransella (1972) when she reported that people who stutter, having defined their lives in terms of "stuttering," often appeared to find the prospect of taking on the role of a fluent speaker to be traumatizing, leading to resistance and potential relapse from successful treatment.

From a constructivist perspective, *anxiety* reflects an awareness that events with which one is confronted lie mostly outside the individual's previous experience and their ability to predict how those events might unfold (Butler, 2009). For example, a person who stutters may feel high levels of anxiety when speaking fluently because he has little experience in that role and does not really know how others will react to him or how he should react to the situation.

Another emotion often encountered as therapy progresses is guilt. *Guilt*, in constructivist terms, occurs when a person acts in a way that is contradictory to his/her core understanding of self (Butler, 2009). The frequent reports of persons who stutter feeling as though they are "deceiving" people by acting as "fluent speakers" (Manning, 2001) may be examples of this constructivist view of guilt.

Finally, the constructivist definition of *hostility* suggests that a person is acting in a hostile manner when he or she is persistent in trying to validate a social prediction in the face of repeated invalidation of that prediction. DiLollo, Manning, and Neimeyer (2003) reported examples of this with individuals who stutter who persistently predicted a return to "stuttering" even during extended periods of "fluency."

Co-construction

Although we have discussed the narrative therapy concept that people weave together their experiences in order to form meaningful self-narratives, this process does not occur in isolation. In essence, "we are not the sole authors of our stories" (Winslade & Monk, 1999, p. 3), as there are social, cultural, political, and historical influences that play significant roles in shaping our personal narratives. It is often from these additional influences on an indi- vidual's self-narrative that problems begin to emerge. Indeed, Neimeyer (1995) pointed out that, "clients often seek or are referred to therapy when they are identified with their problems and subjected to a 'dominant narra- tive' that disqualifies, delimits, or denies their personhood" (p. 22). These dominant narratives are derived from stereotypical, taken-for-granted descrip- tions or labels on individuals (e.g. gender expectations, ethnic stereotypes, political stereotypes) that limit not only their own view of the world but the range of "acceptable" behaviors that they can choose from in their role (Gergen, 1994a, 1994b; Raskin & Lewandowski, 2000; Winslade & Smith, 1997).

This concept that our stories are essentially "co-authored" by outside influences has certain implications for conducting therapy within a construct- ivist framework. First, clinicians need to be aware of the stereotypical social, cultural, and political influences that might be contributing to the client's story and actively work to "push back" against such "default" interpretations. Second, clinicians must understand their own role in co-authoring the client's story. Working within a constructivist framework, clinicians accept that they *will* play a role in co-authoring the client's story through their interpret- ation of the client's situation, the questions that they ask, and the retellings of the emerging alternative story that they provide. This underscores the importance of clinicians being *client-centered* and their need to guard against imposing their own values and beliefs on the direction that the client's story takes. Finally, the social construction of self-narratives means that, as the client's alternative story begins to emerge, it is important that it be told to and by others outside the therapy room. This may initially involve inviting significant others from the client's life to come to therapy and witness the client's retelling of the alternative story, with them providing feedback and comments that act to further elaborate the story. In addition, "outsider witnesses" (White, 2007), individuals who do not know the client, can be invited to, again, hear retellings of the alternative story and provide feedback, ask questions, and engage in their own retelling of the story, sometimes facilitating elaboration of the alternative story in unexpected directions.

Summary

By getting familiar with the principles of the constructivist framework described above and engaging in their own *experiments* with some of the techniques and processes, clinicians can begin conceptualizing clients differently and incorporating counseling into their regular therapeutic processes. The basic processes described in this framework may be incorporated into regular therapy sessions but will require a change in focus from techniques to the whole person and his/her lived experience. One of the primary challenges facing clinicians, however, is how to make this move from a technique focus to a more person-centered focus. Neimeyer (2004), in a video discussing and demonstrating constructivist counseling, suggested that constructivist counseling involves "leading from one step behind." With this in mind, the next section of this chapter will focus on one way that might be helpful for the clinician to take up a more person-centered focus: conceptualizing therapy as an act of *leadership* rather than *service*.

THERAPY AS AN ACT OF LEADERSHIP

Consider the following quote: "you have to help people navigate through a period of disturbance as they sift through what is essential and what is expendable, and as they experiment with solutions." This would appear to be a neatly summarized description of the role of the clinician using the constructivist framework for counseling that was just described – the idea that the clinician takes the role of guiding the client as he/she works through what constructs can and cannot be changed and then experiments with potential solutions. Interestingly, this quote does not come from a textbook or article on counseling, nor does it come from any source related to speech-language pathology or audiology. In fact, it comes from a book on leadership, written by authors from Harvard University's John F. Kennedy School of Government, for people working in the business world. Here is the *complete* quote with my emphasis on the parts originally omitted: "*To practice adaptive leadership*, you have to help people navigate through a period of disturbance as they sift through what is essential and what is expendable, and as they experiment with solutions *to the adaptive challenges at hand*" (Heifetz, Grashow, & Linsky, 2009, p. 28).

Adaptive leadership

Typically, when we mention the word "leadership" people think of someone in a position of authority or power – a chief executive officer, a principal, a senator. The stance taken by Heifetz and his colleagues (e.g., Heifetz et al., 2009; Heifetz & Laurie, 1997; Heifetz & Linsky, 2002), however, is that "leadership is an activity, not a position" (Cohen & Tedesco, 2009, p. 5). They see authority, power, and influence as useful *tools* but state that these tools "do not define leadership" (Heifetz et al., 2009, p. 24). They describe all authority relationships as "power entrusted for service" (p. 24), suggesting that individuals attain positions of authority with the expectation that they will provide some kind of service to those under them. In contrast, Heifetz, et al. (2009, p. 14) describe what they term "adaptive leadership" as "the practice of mobilizing people to tackle tough challenges and thrive."

At the core of the concept of adaptive leadership lies the distinction between technical and adaptive challenges. *Technical problems* can be solved by an authority or expert. They have a known solution. *Adaptive challenges*, on the other hand, have no known solution, and the skills and answers lie outside the regularly applied behaviors and ways of thinking (Heifetz & Laurie, 1997; Heifetz & Linsky, 2002). O'Malley (2009) succinctly described the differences this way: "Technical problems live in people's heads and logic systems. They are susceptible to facts and authoritative expertise. Adaptive challenges live in people's hearts and stomachs. They are about values, loyalties, and beliefs. Progress on them requires the people with the problem to do the work, and the work involves refashioning those deeply held beliefs" (p. 9).

Adaptive leadership and therapeutic processes

The above definition of adaptive leadership, taken in the context of therapy, accurately describes the role of the clinician working in a constructivist framework – *mobilizing clients to tackle tough challenges and thrive*. The key here is the term mobilizing as it reflects the role of the clinician as a motivator and guide and focusses us on the active role of the client in tackling the challenges. In addition, the distinction between authority and leadership made by Heifetz and colleagues also speaks directly to our earlier discussion of constructivist counseling practice and the suggestion that clinicians give up their (authoritative) expert status in order for clients to take greater responsibility and active control of the therapeutic process (i.e. being more person-centered or client-driven).

In a similar way, the distinction between technical and adaptive challenges mirrors the decision-making process in therapy whereby clinicians must decide what aspects of their clients' problem require treatment with specific techniques and what aspects require counseling. O'Malley's (2009) description of technical and adaptive challenges, again, could be lifted from a text on constructivist counseling for communication disorders therapy. For speech-language pathologists, for example, technical problems would involve the specific behavioral (speech, language, or swallowing) aspects presented by their client, whereas the adaptive challenge would involve the impact that the problem behaviors have on the individual's life and self-concept or story. Addressing the technical problems may be effectively and appropriately accomplished through application of the clinician's *expert* knowledge. Addressing the adaptive challenges, however, will require the clinician to step back and realize that these challenges relate to emotional aspects of values, loyalties, and beliefs, and that progress will require the person with the problem to do the work. Table 11.1 includes these and other connections between

Table 11.1 Similarities between aspects of constructivist counseling and adaptive leadership

	Constructivist counseling		*Adaptive leadership*
1	Diagnose the situation: Distinguish between specific behaviors that need changing and effects of the problem on the person that require counseling	⇔	Distinguish between technical and adaptive challenges
2	Therapeutic stance: Give up expert status and give power and responsibility back to the client	⇔	Relinquish authority status – give the work back to those who have an investment in the solution
3	Focus on the whole person rather than just the specific problem	⇔	Get on the balcony – step back to get the whole story
4	Alternative ways of construing: There are alternative constructs or stories available to the client in any given situation	⇔	There are multiple stories/ interpretations for any given situation
5	Push against "default interpretations" (stereotypes) that co-author "dominant narratives"	⇔	Push against "default interpretations" of the situation
6	Elaborate on unique outcomes – focus on experiences that conflict with the dominant story to facilitate development of an alternative story	⇔	Manipulate the "heat" to orchestrate conflict within the system; this leads to discourse that reveals alternative interpretations
7	Experiment with alternative behaviors/roles	⇔	Experiment with interventions that relate to alternative interpretations
8	Address fear, threat, and guilt at loss of dominant story	⇔	Speak to loss – adaptive challenges involve changes to "the way things have always been done"
9	Use of outsider witnesses – provides opportunity for varied feedback and elaboration of alternative story in unexpected directions	⇔	Engage unusual voices – provides varying perspectives and may lead to unexpected interpretations

constructivist counseling and adaptive leadership, suggesting that the two share a similar understanding of human nature and the process of change and may be applied in a complementary way to the process of therapy.

Adaptive leadership as a model for enacting counseling

Heifetz et al. (2009) proposed an iterative model of adaptive leadership that might be effectively adapted for use by speech-language pathologists and audiologists as a way of incorporating counseling into their therapeutic processes. The definition of an iterative model is that it is a systematic repetition of a cycle that progressively moves toward the desired result as the number of iterations increases. The model proposed by Heifetz et al. involved three key activities: (1) observing events and patterns; (2) interpreting observations (i.e. developing hypotheses); and (3) designing interventions based on the observations and interpretations to address the adaptive challenge. For speech-language pathologists and audiologists, this model might be adapted as in Figure 11.1.

Data collection, as the first step in the cycle, involves collecting all the available information about the client. This includes listening to the "thick" description (Payne, 2006) of their story, as opposed to simply the "problem-saturated" story (White, 1995), and listening for "clues" to potential alternative storylines that might be hidden within the client's account of the problem. Heifetz and colleagues (e.g. Heifetz et al., 2009; Heifetz & Laurie, 1997; Heifetz & Linsky, 2002) have proposed a technique that they term "getting on the balcony" as a helpful way of being able to see the overall patterns in a situation. This technique may also be useful for speech-language pathologists and audiologists to help them be more client-focussed and to look at the big picture regarding their client. Many times, clinicians can become so distracted by the "technical" things we are supposed to be doing

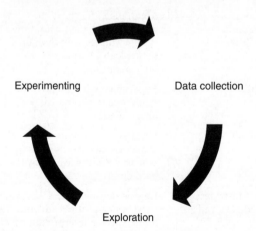

Experimenting   Data collection

Exploration

Figure 11.1 Iterative model for adaptive leadership for therapy.

in therapy (i.e. living up to our "expert" status), that it is difficult to focus on simply listening and contemplating the client's story. The metaphor of "getting on the balcony" may be helpful in avoiding such difficulties.

Exploration of meaning involves moving beyond simple observation and listening. It is at this point that many clinicians will opt for trying to throw a technical solution at the problem rather than go through the process of connecting with the client, exploring their potential unique outcomes, and challenging their default interpretations. A technical solution is "safe ground" that allows clinicians to stay within their comfort zone and maintain their "expert" role within the relationship. Taking on the adaptive challenges involved in helping clients alter their interpretations requires greater investment on the part of the clinician. Indeed, Heifetz et al. (2009, p. 38) stated that, "Acts of leadership not only require access to all parts of yourself so that you can draw upon all of your own resources for will, skill, and wisdom; but to be successful, you also need to fully engage people with all these parts of yourself as well."

As discussed earlier, *experimenting* is an integral part of a constructivist approach to counseling. In the context of adaptive leadership, experimenting carries essentially the same meaning and importance. Adaptive leadership requires that the clinician develop hypotheses about the problem based on the data collected and the exploration of those data. Of course, these hypotheses should be discussed with the client to ensure that they are in line with the client's understanding of the problem. The clinician and client can then design a series of experiments to test these hypotheses, in the same way as described in the "experimenting" section of the constructivist framework. Such experimenting can help address the values, loyalties, and beliefs that are at the heart of adaptive challenges. In addition, Hiefetz et al. (2009) point out that experimenting can open up unanticipated possibilities, which lead to the further data collection, exploration, and experimenting that characterize the iterative process.

CONCLUSION

At the beginning of this chapter, I listed four primary barriers that clinicians face in integrating counseling into their existing therapeutic practices and stated that my goal was to provide at least tentative ways to address them. Let's finish up, then, by reviewing each of those barriers.

1   *Lack of knowledge of counseling techniques:* As part of my description of the constructivist framework, I did present a few counseling techniques that might be useful to clinicians – the concept of experimenting (and how the constructivist version differs from what clinicians already do) and the idea of listening for "clues" to alternative storylines – but the message that I hope came through loud and clear is that *techniques* are

not the most important aspect of counseling. By conceptualizing clients using the constructivist framework, clinicians can liberate themselves from concerns about techniques. Every clinician knows how to be an *interested listener* and to ask *curious questions* (we do it every day with our family and friends) and these are the primary skills of an effective counselor.

2   *Not knowing what aspects of the client's problem require counseling:* Thinking of clients' problems in terms of *technical problems* and *adaptive challenges* should help to clarify this aspect of therapy. I love the way O'Malley (2009) contrasted these two aspects, highlighting the "head" versus "heart" aspects of technical and adaptive challenges. Of course, the concept of integrating counseling as a part of therapy means that you don't really "do therapy" and then "do counseling." By conceptualizing therapy as adaptive leadership and using the constructivist framework as a system for organizing and interpreting their understanding of clients, clinicians should be able to easily integrate the technical and adaptive aspects of therapy.

3 and 4   *Not knowing when to do counseling; and not having the time to do counseling:* I want to deal with these two barriers together, as they really address the same problem. These barriers only become a problem for clinicians if they conceptualize counseling as something they have to do *in addition* to their regular therapy. My point throughout this chapter has been that counseling should be an *integrated part* of everything that clinicians do with their clients. The constructivist framework for counseling fits well with this idea, with the focus being client-centered, and the primary activities being experimenting (which we already do) and conversation (which we already do, at least to some degree). Furthermore, the proposal that clinicians conceptualize therapy as *adaptive leadership* also promotes therapy being more holistic and client-focussed.

My hope is that speech-language pathologists and audiologists can take the information from this chapter and grow as clinicians, taking up the challenge of adaptive leadership and focussing on *mobilizing clients to tackle tough challenges and thrive* rather than on their own performance of technical procedures.

12 The social construction of relationships in healing interactions from ancient times to the present

Judith Felson Duchan
State University of New York at Buffalo

INTRODUCTION

It is evident from the literature in speech-language pathology that the way clinicians interact with their clients is, in large part, predetermined (Kovarsky, Kimbarow, & Kastner, 1999; Simmons-Mackie & Damico, 1999a). It is also apparent from the literature and from direct observation, that the clinician controls interactions. This means that the *clinician's* construal of responsibilities, goals, and competences is more likely to influence the interaction than that of the client. So, when extracting factors that determine the nature and course of clinical interactions, it is perhaps fruitful to look first at the clinician perspective.

The lively debate now taking place among speech-language specialists is a clear example of the ways clinicians influence interactions with clients (Duchan, 2001). This debate is between proponents of the social and medical models of practice. Clinicians working within the social model, regard exclusion, disempowerment, and negative sanctions as being central to the experience of disability. Therefore, social-model proponents have focussed their clinical efforts on working together with their clients to identify and reduce social barriers and to support their clients to gain access to communication.

On the other hand, medical-model advocates work to reduce the causes of communication impairments and to improve their clients' communication skills. They reason that because impairments are the cause of many communication problems the primary focus of diagnosis and therapies should be on eliminating or minimizing those impairments.

These social and medical frameworks not only result in different therapy goals, they also alter the ways clinicians talk with their clients. Introductory meetings between social-model proponents and their clients are likely to involve narratives or an open-ended problem-solving conversation about what the client sees as the barriers to communication access; and about what might be done to minimize or eliminate those barriers. On the other hand, first-time interactions between clients and practitioners endorsing a more medical model are likely to be centered on obtaining a case history about the course of the person's impairment through question–answer exchanges, with the clinician asking the questions.

In this chapter I will analyze various historical examples of what I will be calling *healing interactions*. I name them healing because some of the interactions are not clinical in nature, nor are they necessarily with professionals; yet they all are dedicated to improving the health of someone. In addition, I will examine what a few of our historical predecessors have said and thought about such healing interactions. I will present several examples from ancient and medieval practitioners and will then jump to the mid-nineteenth century for a final example of how healing interactions may have taken place during that period. To conclude, I will summarize the ways historical figures have explained the nature of healing interactions. My focus (and bias) is to favor egalitarian interactions, so I will end by considering what clinicians can learn from our past and how clinicians can best promote egalitarian interactions with their clients.

ANCIENT TIMES

Herodotus (484–425 BCE), who was believed to be the world's first historian, wrote about Babylonian health practices (Lendering, 2009). In his book on *The History of the Persian Wars* (Herodotus, trans. 1862, p. 197) he described the following Babylonian treatment of those who are sick:

> They have no physicians, but when a man is ill, they lay him in the public square, and the passers-by come up to him, and if they have ever had his disease themselves or have known anyone who has suffered from it, they give him advice, recommending him to do whatever they found good in their own case, or in the case known to them; and no one is allowed to pass the sick man in silence without asking him what his ailment is.

This practice of advising one another prefigures today's self-help support groups. It suggests that Babylonians felt obliged to take care of one another. That moral stance also led to the notion that the disabled or ill were experts on their own condition by virtue of having had experience with it. In addition to the support provided by lay experts, the sick and disabled of ancient Babylonia also relied heavily on prayer. They prayed to rid themselves of demons and evil spirits, each of whom specialized in a specific disease or impairment. Below is a Babylonian prayer to placate and expel the Demon of Consumption:

> Wicked Consumption, villainous Consumption, Consumption which never leaves a man, Consumption which cannot be driven away,

Consumption which cannot be induced to leave, Bad Consumption, in the name of Heaven be placated, in the name of earth I conjure thee!

(Buck, 1917, p. 13)

Like their Babylonian predecessors, the ancient Greeks also appealed to the gods to rid them of their illnesses or disabilities. A favorite among the gods of healing in Ancient Greece was one called Asclepius. By 200 BC every large town in Greece had a temple where the sick and disabled could pay tribute to the god Asclepios in the hope of finding a cure for their ailment. These temples contained spas, overnight sleeping arrangements, and even amphitheatres used for viewing entertainment during their stay at the temple. Pilgrims seeking advice would go to the temple where they appealed to the god through prayer and tributes. If things went well, Asclepius would provide the pilgrim with a healing vision in a dream. When pilgrims awoke from their "temple sleep" they would either be cured or have their dream interpreted by a priest at the temple for information about a cure (Farnell, 1921).

One would imagine, then, that the ancient doctor–priests would need to spend a considerable amount of time listening carefully to the pilgrim–patient's dream. Also, the doctor must have been interacting with the person in the course of their dream interpretation. Interactions in these situations would need to have been individualized, and the doctor–priests must have treated the patients' words as worthy of considered and respectful attention. Therefore, the doctor–priest interacted as an intermediary on behalf of both the god Asclepius and the ailing patient (Holowchak, 2001).

However, then, as now, abuses of the intended system took place. An example is in the following description reminiscent of current hospital waiting room practices where one Asclepian priest by-passed the dream analysis, and instead prescribed remedies based on the complaints of the patients: "Every morning a certain Asculapid has fifty or sixty patients in his waiting room; he listens to the complaints of each, arranges them into four lines, prescribes a bleeding for the first, a purge for the second a clyster for the third, and a change of air for the fourth" (Foucault, 1975, p. 15).

Another early source describing a crass circumvention of respectful interactions required for Asclepian dream analysis tells how a speechless child, maybe the first reported case of elective mutism, was cured:

He came as a suppliant to the temple for his voice. When he had performed the preliminary sacrifices and fulfilled the usual rites, thereupon the temple servant who brings in the fire for the god, looking at the boy's father, demanded he should promise to bring within a year the thank-offering for the cure if he obtained that for which he had come. But the boy suddenly said, "I promise." His father was startled at this and asked him to repeat it. The boy repeated the words and after that became well.

(Inscriptiones Graecae, 2009, 4.1.121–22.5 Text 1.3)

The most famous of the priest–doctors within the Asculpian tradition was Hippocrates of Cos (c. 460–370 BC), who nonetheless departed significantly from that tradition. Rather than being a priest and intermediary for the god Asclepius, Hippocrates and his followers dealt directly with their patients. They based their diagnoses and treatments on observable symptoms as well as the complaints their patients described. He says that physicians need to talk to patients to learn about their ". . . habits, regimen, and pursuits." He taught that physicians should also attend to their patients' "conversation, manners, taciturnity, thoughts, sleep, or absence of sleep, and . . . [about] what and when [dreams] . . . occur" (Hippocrates, 1946, p. 368, Book 1, Section 3, para 10).

These quotes from Hippocrates and those in his school indicate that they considered the lives of their patients, as well as discourse with them as relevant and key elements of healing. Furthermore, this suggests that those in the Hippocratic school would be willing to listen at length to their patients in order to gain the information needed for diagnosis, therapy, and prognosis.

The relationship between the Hippocratic doctor and his patient is also revealed in the original version of the now-famous Hippocratic oath. The oath contains a principled pledge about how the doctor must maintain boundaries with his patients and protect their privacy:

> Into whatever homes I go, I will enter them for the benefit of the sick, avoiding any voluntary act of impropriety or corruption, including the seduction of women or men, whether they are free men or slaves.

> Whatever I see or hear in the lives of my patients, whether in connection with my professional practice or not, which ought not to be spoken of outside, I will keep secret, as considering all such things to be private.
>
> (North, 2002, p. 1)

Hippocrates advised doctors to visit the patient frequently so they could be at ease with the person, and so they could check out whether the patient was reporting information truthfully by detecting changes in the patient's answers: "Make frequent visits; be especially careful in your examinations, counteracting the things wherein you have been deceived at the changes. Thus you will know the case more easily, and at the same time you will also be more at your ease" (Porter, 1997, p. 58).

Hippocrates also cautioned doctors that they could be unfairly blamed for problems arising from patient negligence: ". . . Keep a watch also on the faults of the patients, which often make them lie about the taking of things prescribed. For through not taking disagreeable drinks, purgative or other, they sometimes die. What they have done never results in a confession, but the blame is thrown upon the physician" (Porter, 1997, p. 58).

Lastly, Hippocrates wrote about the need to convince patients and others to follow his sage advice: "Life is short, and the Art long; the occasion fleeting; experience fallacious, and judgment difficult. The physician must not only be prepared to do what is right himself, but also to make the patient, the attendants, and externals co-operate" (Hippocrates, trans. 2009). In sum, Hippocrates regarded the information provided by his patients to be of considerable importance. He was interested not only in the symptoms of their conditions, but also in their personalities, their dreams, and their daily habits. He advocated frequent home visits so that the information provided by the patient could be verified; so that the physician could distinguish between valid and false information. Talking to one's patient frequently could, according to Hippocrates, result in greater cooperation from the patient; and less likelihood that the patient or the family would blame the doctor for things gone awry. Also, interaction between the doctor and patient should be one in which they both feel at ease, one in which private information is kept private, and one that has clear boundaries with regard to social intimacy. Yet, it is apparent from the quotes above that the doctor was very much in charge. It was the doctor who decided what information needed gathering and it was the doctor who created the conditions of cooperation.

Plato (428–348 BC), like Hippocrates, saw the interaction between doctors and their patients as being crucial to healing (King, 1954; Moes, 2000, 2001). However, Plato gave the patient's contribution more credibility than did Hippocrates. Plato considered humans to have inherent powers for self-construction, self-maintenance, self-repair, and self-transformation. He drew parallels between doctor–patient discourse and the discourse between philosophers and their students. When writing about Socratic dialogues, Plato described Socrates as asking the slave Meno guiding questions so he could remember what he already knew but had forgotten in the shock of birth (Schildknecht, 1996).

So too, according to Plato, the medical practitioner should facilitate the revelation of known therapeutic solutions from his patients. This process using dialogue to remember what was already known was called *anamnesis* by the Greek philosophers. While the term is still used in medicine today, it is now associated with obtaining case-history information through a question–answer discourse in which the doctor aims to discover clues to a diagnosis. However, in the time of Plato, the discourse of anamnesis was more open ended, perhaps more similar to a modern psychotherapeutic interaction in which the doctor's goal would be to provide the patient with a discourse scaffold for discovering a pathway to health. Plato believed that the job of good doctors, like that of good teachers, was to recognize when to step in and to assist a natural urge to healthy development.

Neither Plato, nor Hippocrates, nor the followers of Hippocrates spelled out details for how to question the patient. It was Rufus of Ephesus who was the first to do this, some 300 years later. Rufus, who lived between late first century BC and mid first century AD, was a Greek physician who was schooled in Alexandria, and who had lived in Rome. In 100 AD he wrote a treatise, called *Medical Questions* or *The Interrogation of the Patient* (Brock,

1929). The book emphasized the importance of gathering information from his patients and gave advice for how to go about it "One must put questions to the patient, for thereby certain aspects of the disease can be better understood, and the treatment rendered more effective" (cited in Brock, 1929, p. 113). Rufus, like Hippocrates, (but not Plato) believed that "Patients should be questioned in order to learn about the nature of their disease, to facilitate the negotiation that follows" (Cited in Van Tellingen, 2007, p. 361). When his patients were unable to answer his questions, Rufus interviewed bystanders who knew the patient "Bystanders could be of use if the patient is not able to convey the information asked. One should reckon with possible obstacles like madness, apoplexy, unconsciousness, exaltation, speechlessness, stupor, complete exhaustion or imposed silence, for instance in pulmonary bleeding" (cited in Van Tellingen, 2007, p. 361).

Among the questions posed to his patients, were ones having to do with the time of onset and the nature of the illness. In the words of Rufus:

> Time of onset of the affliction involved is of major importance for specific treatment and in recognition of critical days or moments. In order to get a hold on the clinical course hitherto one should form an idea of regularity, irregularity and evolvement of symptoms, whether the onset is acute or intense, or if the outbreak of disease is sudden and rapid or slow and gradual.
>
> (Cited in Van Tellingen, 2007, p. 361)

Besides asking about the circumstances surrounding disease onset, Rufus gave considerable attention to learning about the patient's pain. To this end, he advocated finding out about the specific nature of a pain as well as working to distinguish between true and exaggerated or made-up reports of pain:

> One should ask about the nature of pain, although it is possible to reach a fair judgment looking at the moaning and groaning, the restlessness, timidity, attitude, color, weakness and the movements of the hands. Nevertheless, it is necessary to discriminate true pain from lamentation and therefore interrogation is mandatory for a proper diagnosis. For it is known that many of the patients, driven from weakness or timidity, pretend to suffer from pains that are no less simulated than the pains displayed in drama. Because most pains tend to be episodic one should make inquiries about this aspect too.
>
> (Cited in Van Tellingen, 2007, p. 361)

As can be seen from the questions posed by Rufus, and the way they are framed, the doctor–clinician is the one in charge of the interaction. Accordingly, it is the doctor who selects the questions and evaluates the answers. Rufus's focus is on obtaining information about the onset of the disease and the nature of the pain, rather than on what the patient thinks about the problem.

Summary of ancient practices and their conceptual underpinnings

In ancient times, healers or physicians interacted with their patients in different ways depending upon their construal of the situation, their roles in the situation, and upon their understanding of the patients' abilities and disabilities. Five different types of interactions can be identified from the writings of the time. In one, described of the ancient Babylonians, the patient interacted with peers with whom they shared symptoms and who had recovered. In this peer-based interaction, the lay person was regarded as an expert by virtue of having had experience with the disease. In the second type of interaction that took place in both Babylonia and ancient Greece, the ill person interacted directly with a specialized god, using prayer as the medium. In a third interaction, doctor–priests in Greece acted as interpreters; facilitating communication between the ill or disabled and the god Asclepius. In a fourth type of interaction, one promoted by Hippocrates and his followers, the physician took control of the situation, asking questions and evaluating answers. Lastly, following the philosophy of Plato, physicians promoted open dialogue with their patients, so that patients could access their own innate ideas and arrive at solutions for how to deal with their illness or disability.

MEDIEVAL TIMES

Among the most famous of medieval historical figures was a man called Ibn Sina, or Avicenna (980–1037 AD) (Haque, 2004). A Muslim and native of Persia, he worked as a physician, scientist, philosopher, statesman, and poet. He wrote over 100 books on science, religion and philosophy, with the most famous being his textbook, *Canon of Medicine. The Canon* contained a comprehensive review of medicine and medical practices of the time (Cameron, 1930).

Avicenna believed that the heart was the locale for both intelligence and feeling. The heart in his view, was affected by emotions such as pleasure, sorrow, joy, grief, revenge, anxiety, and exhilaration. The emotions also influenced mental and physical health. Avicenna therefore recommended therapies that promoted good emotions. For example in order to promote joy, Avicenna recommended the following "gladdening influences":

1   obtaining that which is wished for;
2   satisfying an intention without meeting opposition;
3   preferring to do something peaceful;
4   confidence;

5   the memory of past and future joys and hopes;
6   think about ambitious things;
7   mutual argumentation with kindred minds;
8   contact with curious (interesting, unusual, remarkable, new) things;
9   uplifting of the mind;
10   meeting friends and friendly surroundings;
11   overcoming deception in small matters (Shah, 1966).

His search for ways to promote positive emotions would have led him naturally to discussions with patients about their personal experiences and aspirations. He and they were likely to have talked about ways of bringing more joy (and thereby health) into the patients' lives. His philosophy associating joy with health would have offered the needed groundwork for him to relate to his patients on a more personal level.

A widely reported example of Avicenna's therapy with one of his patients offers insights into how he attended to and, indeed, embraced his patients' expressed point of view. When working with a patient who had delusions due to what Avicenna would say was melancholia, he entered into the patient's delusionary world. For example, a prince of Persia imagined that he was a cow. He stopped eating because he worried that he was about to be killed and made into stew. Avicenna was called in to convince the man to eat and to help rid him of his delusion. The doctor posed as a butcher who was coming to the prince's house to slaughter him. When Avicenna arrived, he asked "Where is the cow so I may kill it?" The patient mooed to signal his whereabouts. As Avicenna approached the prince, he said "The cow is too lean and not ready to be killed. He must be fed properly and I will kill it then." The prince was then offered food. He ate it and gradually "gained strength, got rid of his delusion, and was completely cured" (Haque, 2004, p. 376).

Avicenna also prescribed impairment-based medical remedies, ones that did not require that he take the perspective of the patients (Rahman, 1952). For example, he recommended the use of ice packs to treat various neurological illnesses; and for epilepsy, he advocated having the patient swim in tanks with electric eels. It was perhaps no accident that Avicenna resorted to patient-centered practices for problems that he regarded as having emotional rather than biological origins.

NINETEENTH CENTURY

During the mid-nineteenth century an argument took place between those who subscribed to a positivist view of illness and those who promoted what today would be called an interpretive view (Mishler, 1984). The proponents of the two sides referred to themselves as *organists* and *spiritualists*. A representative of the organist position was Jean Baptiste Bouillaud (1796–1881), a French physician and medical researcher who worked in

Paris. His philosophy was countered by Jacques Lordat (1773–1870) who was a physician and professor of anatomy and physiology, at Montpellier's University of Medicine in France.

The differences between the two schools of thought can be readily discerned from how representatives of each described their patients with aphasia. One of Bouillaud's case-history reports was of a 44-year-old woman of a "nervous-sanguine" constitution who Bouillaud described as follows:

> On 10 December 1822 she suddenly lost her voice, and some time later made her way to the hospital Cochin. She heard and understood perfectly everything that was said to her, but was unable to utter the least word. She expressed her ideas clearly by means of writing, and advised us in this manner that she had a pain in the forehead, etc. Annoyed by her muteness, she grew impatient, gesticulated vigorously, and wept. Following a copious bleeding, this woman recovered the full use of her speech after a few days.
>
> (Bouillaud 1825, p. 28, translated in Jacyna, 2000, p. 45)

In this description, Bouillaud keeps to the facts. While drawing from the reports of his patient about her ability to understand, her inability to talk, her pain, and her annoyance, he conveys all this information as depersonalized and objective facts – as observable behavior rather than experienced truths. Bouillaud describes even her emotional frustration in behavioral terms. Nor does Bouillaud talk about his own subjective impressions or actions; even referring to his bloodletting procedure in passive terms.

Lordat's case depiction differs considerably from that of Bouillaud. He described how his patient, when realizing that he was unable to talk, had a strong emotional reaction. Moreover, Lordat also conveyed in vivid detail the situational setting of the stroke, approaching it as would a narrator. His patient was an artist who had experienced his stroke in the countryside where he went to paint a landscape at the home of a friend. Lordat's account begins with his detailed description of the patient's experience before the doctor's arrival:

> He took a light lunch of bread and an orange, and made his way to the designated place. He promptly set to work. He was in the open air, under the sun, furnished with a large hat. While sketching he had need to give an order to a servant who was nearby; he realized that he had forgotten the name of this individual, he cried out, and when he wished to express the order, he saw that he had not a word at his command. This discovery astonished and terrified him.
>
> (Lordat, 1843, p. 422, translated in Jacyna, 2000, p. 29)

In another of his case histories, one about a priest who had experienced a stroke resulting in aphasia, Lordat arrived at the priest's home and was received graciously by his host:

> When I arrived the supposed apoplectic was seated on his bed wide awake; he received me with a courteous and open manner. He seemed more concerned about me than about himself. I had come on horseback; the weather was bad. He made signs to indicate that I should first get warm and have a meal. This language, silent as it was, was sufficiently significant that everyone moved and obeyed.
>
> (Lordat, 1843, pp. 425–426, translated in Jacyna, 2000, p. 30)

Lordat presented himself here in first person terms. He also described his patient as a competent man of the house, treating his physician as his guest. In the words of Jacyna:

> Lordat figures in these narratives as one of a number of characters. There is a genuine dialogue between him and those whose ills he is called upon to treat. What is notable is not merely the egalitarian relations that obtain between doctor and patient, but also the complete visibility of the former within the narrative. Lordat's status is straightforward; his entrance upon the scene is clearly marked and brings with it a shift in perspective. He is one of a number of empirical narrators whose combined testimony affects the story.
>
> (Jacyna, 2000, p. 38)

CONCLUSION

Box 12.1 offers a summary of the various examples of healing interactions described in this chapter. The examples differ in illustrative ways, including the time periods they were drawn from.

One influential difference has to do with who is doing the interacting. Most of the examples were between physicians and their patients. Two exceptions were the healing interactions between lay experts and novices, and between ill people and a specialist god. These examples were selected to reflect how healers of different kinds and from different periods in time might have interacted with their clients.

It is apparent that the different healers in the examples viewed their responsibility differently. Some saw their primary roles as *diagnosticians* and *curers* of diseases, rather than as healers of people. As a result, they structured their clinical interaction to obtain information. Physicians of the Hippocratic School, for example, saw interactions as a way to maintain their control over their patient's illness. Accordingly, they interacted with the patient to make sure the person was accurately describing their symptoms and was following prescribed regimens. Their role then was as a curative agent. These interactions were likely to be depersonalized and authoritative, with the physician as active curer and the patient as the mere embodiment of disease and the (hopefully) cooperative object of cure.

Box 12.1 A few examples of different types of healing interactions from different periods in history

Ancient times
- Peer advice was given in the marketplace. Advice given by those who have experienced an illness or disability to the newly afflicted. This was done in a city marketplace, according to Herodotus's reports.
- Direct appeal to gods through prayer. Those with health problems prayed to deities specializing in their disease. They appealed to the gods to rid them of the demons causing the illness (Babylonians and Ancient Greeks).
- Those with health problems consulted with doctor–priests working in religious temples. The doctor–priests served as intermediaries between the ill or disabled and the god Asclepius. Asclepius sent his advice to the patient in the form of dreams and the doctor–priests interpreted them and administered the cure, when needed. Physicians, trained by Hippocrates, administered to the ill in their homes. The patients were questioned by the doctor about their lives and their symptoms. Rufus of Ephesus, 400 years later provided explicit advice for how these interviews were to be conducted.
- Doctors engaged with patients in patient-centered discourses. These extended and open-ended interviews were designed to help patients discover remedies for their own maladies. They are reminiscent of today's psychotherapy techniques. The method, promoted by followers of Plato, was parallel to the Socratic dialogues described by Plato in the Meno in which they were helped to remember information that they knew, but had forgotten.

Medieval times
- Doctors worked with patients to create conditions for improving their emotional lives. Avicenna recommended ways to achieve joy as a means for promoting health. He also designed a therapy for his delusional (melancholy) patients in which he entered the imagination of the patient.

Nineteenth century case histories
- The choice between subjective and objective portrayals of a case is associated with how the social interactions are portrayed in the case description. Lordat, who took a subjective perspective, described his patients in complex roles and in their real-life contexts. He allowed the voices and points of views of both patient and doctor into his descriptions.
- Bouillaud, on the other hand, portrayed cases in more objective terms, by reporting on case histories, symptoms, remedies and the outcomes of treatment.

There were several notable exceptions to healing interactions based on the view of the healer as a curer of diseases. One was the view of the doctor–priest of the Asclapian temple who saw their role as *interpreter*. In this case a successful healing interaction required that the physician attend to and showed respect for the words and thoughts of the ill or disabled person.

Indeed, in was through the words of the pilgrim in the temple that the god Asclepius revealed himself. The God spoke through the pilgrim's dream and the doctor–priest interpreted the dream for both Asclepius and the patient.

Another exception to the healer as curer was the Platonic view of healer as facilitator or *elicitor*. In this case, the healer engaged in dialogue with the ill person so as to reveal the patient's ideas about how best to achieve a healthy state.

The interactions also differed in their perceived purpose. Some interactions were designed to obtain or reveal information to be used in the healing process. Hippocratic physicians and positivist physicians of the nineteenth century such as Bouillaud worked to obtain information. Platonic physicians or those who dialogued about emotions, worked with patients to reveal information. These information gathering or revealing processes were more likely to be conducted during the first meetings with patients, when the physician was diagnosing the problem, than later ones, where he was remediating it.

Some interactions, such as ones taking place in the Babylonian marketplace were designed to *convey advice* from those experienced with the disease or disability to those who were new to it. And still others, like those involving prayers, made an appeal to the gods to expunge the demons and evil spirits from their bodies.

The interactions designed to keep the patient honest and to encourage cooperation were likely to be more egalitarian than the ones that were information based. The interactions involving dream interpretation or ones that were open enough to allow patients to express their personal narratives, such as those reflected in Lordat's case histories, were probably more egalitarian. The most egalitarian interactions may have been the ones like those held by Avicenna and his followers who worked together with patients to attain positive feeling states such as joy.

Another key element affecting healing interactions is the healer's regard for his patients. This involves making judgments about their competence. The peer expert in the Babylonian marketplace was likely to presume his advisee to be his equal except for his advisee's relative naïveté about the disease or disability. Lordat also saw his patients with aphasia as fully formed, and competent, except for their inability to speak. He portrayed them in his case reports as worthy of considerable biographic detail; as key characters in their personal dramas. Bouillaud, on the other hand, regarded his patients as mechanical objects, whose parts were broken. Hippocrates and followers as well as Rufus and his school judged their patients in terms of their honesty and cooperativeness. Plato, because he believed people held valuable knowledge that required discovery, judged patients as *wise*, holding the secrets to their own recovery.

So in the past as well as the present, the attitudes, frameworks, and feelings of the clinicians have strongly affected the quality and nature of interactions between healers and their clients. The historical review shows the potential effects of the healers' sense of the responsibility, goals, and judgments about the competence of those they interact with. If the goal of the healer is to achieve interactions that are egalitarian and relevant to those in need, then one can find the following lessons from the historical examples presented. From the Babylonians, one can see that clients can become authorities on their own disabilities or illness, by virtue of having had experience with it. From the Greeks, one can find ways to create Socratic dialogues with clients that reveal their ideas about their own health. From medieval physicians, such as Avicenna, one can see that interactions that focus on persons' feelings about disease or disability are likely to be more involving and egalitarian than those that focus on skill training or remediating physical impairments. And from the biographical and subjective case histories provided by Lordat one sees how a narrative-based focus promotes ways to acknowledge and foster interactions based on the client's point of view and life experience.

Part II
Focussing on the clinician

13   The transference relationship in speech-language therapy

Kirsty McDonald
Northern General Hospital, Sheffield

> *The mind, that ocean where each kind*
> *Does straight its own resemblance find;*
> *Yet it creates, transcending these*
> *Far other worlds, and other seas*
> (Andrew Marvell 1621–1678; The Garden, 2003, p. 157)

INTRODUCTION

Whether it is in the school or hospital environment, in clients' homes or within social education centers, in professional meetings or on a one-to-one informal basis, speech-language therapists and audiologists spend most of their working day in relationship with someone. Their primary purpose as clinicians is to enhance communication and to adopt the skill of directing communication at a level appropriate for the listener. However, developing sufficient rapport with clients is a core skill gained through understanding and the fine-tuning of their skills in the processes of active listening, empathy, and nonverbal communication.

Possessing such skills and utilizing them on a daily basis with other people makes "relationship" within the work place inevitable. When in relationship with another human being we are communicating both at a conscious and unconscious level. As clinicians, we are likely to be more aware than a lay member of the public of "how" someone is communicating; whether it be at a motor speech level, language level or pragmatic level; i.e. we will immediately be able to spot if someone has a dysarthria or word finding problems or is verbose. Less tangible, are the everyday unconscious processes that may be in progress and can lead to fluctuations in one's feeling state.

THE TRANSFERENCE RELATIONSHIP

Feeling states emerge in relationships which are both positive and negative. Think if you will of someone you have met who exudes warmth, affection, and acceptance, invoking in you feelings of comfort and safety. Similarly, think of someone you have met who is apprehensive, distrustful, and evasive. They will tend to invoke in you feelings of hostility, fear, and potentially contempt. Sometimes the depth of feeling can be intense, quick to engage and difficult to fathom. In either case, the unconscious process of "transference" is likely to be in operation.

In this chapter, I hope to shed some light on this enigmatic phenomenon and on other associated terms coined by Freud at the turn of the last century. My aim is to assess the relevance of the transference relationship for the field of speech-language therapy and audiology; with some case illustrations, demonstrations as to how transference may manifest itself, explanations as to why it may be in operation, and how best to deal with it as a clinician when it does occur.

Transference is a psychoanalytic concept, which Jones defined as "an unconscious relocation of experiences from one interpersonal situation to another" (Jones, 2005, p. 1177). Accordingly, thoughts, feelings, and expect-ations of significant others from the past are relived in the present, thus affecting current relationships (Jones, 2004). It is primarily an unconscious process, which the recipient of the transferred feeling experiences as surpris-ing, unwarranted or at the least, out of proportion (Freud, 1912 cited in Parker Hall, 2009, p. 53). The terms transference, counter-transference and projective identification are inherently complex and have developed alongside the field of psychotherapy.

Freud's original definition of transference focused on the idea that the sub-ject has stereotyped ways of conducting their erotic life (Freud, 1912, cited in Evans, 2007). Erotic in this instance refers to how one relates to love objects (parents, children, pets). Freud posited that within the transference relationship the subject relates to the other in the light of their "infantile prototype" (Laplanche & Potalis, 1973, p. 455) or "childhood pattern," which may be abnormally positive (idealized) or abnormally negative (hostile), depending on their childhood experiences. Transference is thought to occur as a compromise between the urge to express and the urge to defend. The subject is afraid of remembering aspects of the past and yet difficult memories press for discharge (Smith, 1996). When this occurs, there is a disruption to any close relationship that a person might be developing (Tantum, 2002).

Subsequent definitions of transference have placed less emphasis on child-hood experiences, since evidence has suggested that more recent events can have more impact than more remote ones (Rutter, 1980 cited in Tantum, 2002, p. 245). Thus, it may be more pertinent to emphasize that displaced feelings and attitudes may be derived from memories of previous significant figures that may or may not have been experienced in childhood. "Our self image is formulated to a large degree upon the reflected appraisals we per-ceive in the eyes of important figures in our life" (Yalom, 2002, p. 47). In transactional analysis terms,[1] the analogy of a *rubber band* is used in which interactions within the present situation can catapult us back to an earlier situation. Stewart and Joines (1993) suggest that because our parents are such important figures in our early life, they are often to be found at the far end of these metaphorical rubber bands. They go on to describe transference as "putting a face on someone." In the current situation we are literally super-imposing an historic significant figure on the face of the person with whom we are interacting. Therefore, the present day interlocutor is unconsciously being used as a surrogate for images of significant figures from the client's past (Smith, 1996). Figure 13.1 is a visual depiction of this process.

It is important to note that few theorists have empirically validated psychoanalytic concepts by conducting scientific research (Bateman, 2004). Despite this, there is a rich psychoanalytic literature describing these hypo-thetical phenomena and it is important to consider that absence of proof is not the same as proof of absence. From an evolutionary perspective, Charles Darwin as early as 1872 proposed that it is a basic mammalian capacity to pick up on the nonverbal cues about the emotional state of fellow beings in order to decipher if they are friend or foe (Bateman, Brown, & Pedder, 2000).

Related psychological terms include counter-transference and projective identification, and it would be useful at this point to provide a definition of these processes.

Counter-transference

Counter-transference is a response to transference and is influenced by the particular qualities of whatever material is being transferred (Jones, 2005). To illustrate, a person might feel induced to respond to another in a particular way, e.g. as caretaker in response to dependency feelings and behaviors being transferred from the other. Furthermore, counter-transference is invoked by specific qualities of the transference and is characterized by an emergence of

Figure 13.1 Transference.

feelings or behaviors that seem inappropriate in intensity for the current relationship. A case example might include the client or the colleague for whom we find ourselves working unusually hard to make sure they are okay by problem solving for them; perhaps rearranging our diary to meet their needs at the expense of everyone else. Alternatively, one might feel ignored or bored in response to the client, colleague, or carer who has a tendency to ramble, has limited curiosity in a shared topic or who never enquires about the clinician's well-being. In more subtle cases, we can be induced into feeling beholden and grateful to clients when they make attempts to ingratiate themselves to us through self-sacrifice. In certain cases, clinicians may begin to feel sexually aroused. In such instances, sexuality may be the only reliable way a client has learned to keep people in relationship (Cashdan, 1988). Such thoughts and feelings are understandably disconcerting.

It is important to note that the clinician's own unresolved emotional difficulties and unconscious conflicts also form part of the counter-transference (Smith, 1996). One example is a clinician who fears her own aggression and placates a client whenever she senses hostile feelings coming from the client; or a clinician who needs to feel important and therefore keeps clients dependent on him, precluding the client's independence and self-responsibility (Aveline, 1996). Features of transference and counter-transference can often be subtle and difficult to identify. Manifestations of the phenomena are often inferred by strong feelings and behaviors towards another, which seem out of place (Jones 2005). Self-scrutiny of the clinician's interventions is highly beneficial to ensure appropriate, safe, and optimal patient care.

Projective identification

Projective identification was first described by Melanie Klein (1946), and is even more elusive than transference and counter-transference. It can be described as an unconscious communication in which the experience being communicated is beyond words, relating to verbally inexpressible experiences; or to preverbal experiences (Casement, 1985). Casement further explains that: ". . . the projector disowns some aspect of the self and attributes this to another. If this communication by projective identification is successful, it reaches the other person as an affective resonance within the recipient, whose feelings take on a 'sameness' based on identification" (Casement, 1985, p. 81).

Whereas transference and counter-transference do not necessarily evoke overt responses in the other, projective identification involves behavioral and emotional manipulation, leading the interlocutor to act out the identified material (Cashdan, 1988). Masterson (1993) refers to the subject behaving in such a manner so as to coerce the other into actually accepting and feeling the projection.

Such behavior can be quite covert, consisting of such things as facial expressions, tones of voice, and body postures. To illustrate, certain clients who are themselves unable to accept their sadness, fear, or confusion, may powerfully affect the therapist who, as they walk away from the client might in fact experience a strong urge to *act out* or experience the client's tears, their feelings of anger, their inner terror, or their confusion. Many writers within the field of psychotherapy describe this as a powerful subjective onslaught of emotion (Casement, 1985; Orbach, 1999). "Consciously I felt well equipped and prepared for what lay ahead. Unconsciously, I responded like those animals that sense an imminent earthquake" (Casement, 1985, p. 97).

MANAGING TRANSFERENCE IN CLINICAL RELATIONSHIPS

So how is transference relevant to the fields of speech-language therapy and audiology? Without question, the phenomenon of transference has a central place in the psychological therapies, since it permits reflection and interpretation of damaged self-constructs, with the ultimate goal of clients improving their relationships with themselves and others. However, transference is part of any human interaction to a considerable degree, and is certainly part of any therapy where the participants have a close relationship (Aveline, 1996). This includes not only speech-language therapists but also a wider range of health and social welfare disciplines e.g. physiotherapy, social work, and teaching. As stated earlier, one of our main roles as clinicians is to optimize communication for clients and their families. When communication breaks down there is always an emotional consequence; either for the client or for the interlocutor, or both (Brumfitt & Barton, 2006; Daniels, 2007; Glozman, 1995; Gordon, 1991; Klompas & Ross 2004). Therefore, as clinicians we have the potential to elicit strong transferences and counter-transferences that if understood, could be managed to ensure a safe and positive outcome; but if ignored could lead to a myriad of relational hazards.

In my career as a speech-language therapist, I have experienced my share of both positive and negative transferences. Whether it was the affection bestowed on me by an elderly stroke patient who found that I resembled her granddaughter; or the parent of a child with severe learning difficulties who leveled contempt and scorn against me for seemingly being too young (at the time) to provide any helpful management of care. Thus as clinicians, we may be viewed positively with feelings of care and comfort being invoked; and negatively with counter-transferential responses of bitterness and antagonism being elicited. Prior to my psychotherapeutic training, I was unable to discern these complicated processes emerging, and I tended to become either over- or underinvolved with my clients as a result.

While being on the receiving end of a positive transference can be a pleasurable experience, it is important for clinicians to ensure they are not giving preferential treatment to particular clients who are transferring these positive attributes. Similarly, on realizing that we are the recipient of a negative transference, it is important to be cautious and sensitive to how we will respond in our caring role, while being cognizant of our potential to withdraw, to avoid, and to punish.

Therefore, it is essential to recognize when powerful transferences are in operation, and that we are likely to be on the receiving end of an exerted pressure or expectation that may be unrealistic or misplaced. Thus, the client who is acutely apprehensive, may expect us to reject, criticize or humiliate him, just as he was treated by perhaps either or both of his parents, or his grandmother, or his uncle. Similarly, the client who is admiring, complimentary and affectionate, may expect and compel us to provide certainty and security, just as her primary carers overly protected her. The pressure to meet these expectations can be considerable, which is why it is so important to reflect on the responses we make as clinicians.

In the following illustrative cases, I hope to highlight some examples of transference, counter-transference, and projective identification, thus bringing to light how the transference materializes and how these feelings and behaviors are experienced. In addition, I will offer some suggestions for how the transference relationship could be managed.

Case 1

"David" is a speech-language therapist with 5 years of experience working with adults. He works on the acute inpatient wards and has been treating a patient called "Jeremy" on the Intensive Care Unit (ICU) for the last 3 months. Jeremy has suffered a traumatic brain injury following a road traffic accident. He has a tracheostomy in place and is communicating by eye pointing. David has been teaching Jeremy's partner "Clare" to use an eye recognition alternative communication system. David's visits to the ICU have recently increased in frequency. The following interaction takes place after the eighth session as Clare and David are exiting the ward.

C: Thank you so much for your support over the last few months. I don't know what we would have done without you. [Clare is holding David's arm and her eye gaze is intense]
D: That's not a problem, all part of my role. [David is caught between feeling flattered and affectionate and slightly uncomfortable since this is the third time Clare has emphasized his importance in the last 2 weeks]
C: I hope you don't mind but I got you a little something as a measure of our appreciation. [Clare hands David a gift wrapped parcel]
D: Oh that is really not necessary. [David feels a combination of delight and acute embarrassment and blushes readily, unsure of whether to accept the gift or not]
C: Please accept, you really have done so much for us and I feel so lucky and safe in the knowledge that we have had you to look after Jeremy.

In this illustrative case, David is on the receiving end of a positive idealization transference. Clare goes above and beyond what is necessary in terms of communicating praise, interest, and respect for David. If he is not careful, David might be drawn into providing the extra care and security that Clare longs for. Clare is re-experiencing David in the present as a parental figure from the past. Clare's ill mother was unable to hold Clare's anxiety as a child, and as a result, she constantly looks to others in positions of power to "hold" (allay) such feelings of anxiety and uncertainty for her. Clare's unconscious provocation is to engender caretaking feelings within the object (David) onto whom she transfers feelings of awe, dependency, and certainty. How should David respond?

There are a number of options available to David.

1   He could react in a way that Clare expects him to behave, as an all-powerful, heroic therapist who can reassure her that everything is going to be ok and that her partner will regain independent breath support and normal speech and language. As you may imagine this course of action is a risky strategy, with the high potential for Jeremy not to make a full recovery. In the event of Jeremy not returning to his premorbid level of functioning, David will be required to back track at a later stage in the patient's recovery and explain the reality of the situation.
2   An alternative approach could be taken. David could receive the gift, rush back to the department and ask his colleagues to take over his client thus avoiding any future discomfort. However, the ethics of this maneuver are in question, considering the harmful effects to the client and his carer in losing this relationship.
3   David could respond to Clare by stating that although it is very kind of her to offer him a gift, he will need to refer to his manager and the trust policy to make sure it is okay for him to receive the gift. He could also ask Clare about her concerns about the future and Jeremy's recovery, keeping Clare as close to the reality of the situation as she can manage. If Clare finds it difficult to accept the reality of her partner's condition, David could direct her to further counseling or family support services; thereby ensuring Clare receives the appropriate level of support from a qualified practitioner.

David's awareness of unconscious processes in this scenario will help him to direct Clare in the most beneficial direction, which will ultimately help Jeremy.

Case 2

"Mary" is a speech-language therapist with 2 years post-qualification experience. She has a busy pediatric caseload covering mainstream nurseries and schools, special needs schools, and community clinics. One of her clients in mainstream nursery, "Toby," has recently been diagnosed with autism.

She has met with the parents on two occasions to discuss the diagnosis and to offer advice on how best they can support Toby's communication. Mary is aware that both Mr and Mrs Pemberton are having considerable difficulty accepting Toby's diagnosis and communication skills. Mary feels nervous prior to their treatment sessions and is overly conscientious in organizing treatment materials. On their third meeting the following interaction occurs.

Mr P: I'm not sure what the plan is here, but Toby doesn't seem to be getting any better. [Mr P is restless in his chair, his head is reclined and there is limited eye contact with Mary or his wife]

Mary: Have you read any more of the literature I gave you in our previous sessions on the features of autism? [Mary is beginning to feel discomfort; her voice wobbles as she feels a pressure to explain herself]

Mr P: To be honest, I've been very busy with the business. You've looked at it haven't you Stacey? [Mr P has a dismissive, arrogant tone]

Mrs P: Yes but it's been upset . . .

Mr P: We're finding this all very difficult to make sense of and wonder when Toby will start to see you on a one-to-one basis and when we will start to see some progress?

Mary: As I . . . explained at . . . at our last session, Toby will benefit from an. . . . advisory speech-language therapy role so that helpful communication skills and tech-techniques can be adopted by those who are in daily communication with Toby. [Mary's communication is halted and dysfluent. She feels hot, and her pulse has begun to race. Mary becomes aware of growing feelings of hostility within herself towards Mr P]

In this illustrative case, it is possible that Mr P is projecting his negative feelings of hostility onto the therapist. In addition, he may be disowning his (unacceptable) feelings of grief and despair at the situation and is therefore projecting them onto (or *into*) the therapist; thus inducing her to feel incompetent. On the other hand, Mary's "counter" responses are intensified by her own memories of an overdemanding mother. The reason for Mr P's hostility is the result of both his distress and confusion in relation to his son's diagnosis, and his inner representation of a previous relationship with a highly critical father. This former significant relationship is being re-enacted in the present as Mr P mirrors his inner critical parent while Mary identifies with his rejected child state, which is manifesting itself at a physical level. Mary is perhaps being invited unconsciously to act towards Mr P in a particular way, i.e. with hostility and avoidance, in the same way as Mr P's father did to him.

The inner critic may not only be the result of a highly critical primary carer, but may also be the result of feelings of deprivation at being abandoned via parental departure or death, "misattunement" (Erskine, 1998), in which a parent or significant other was physically present but emotionally unavailable; this may have been due to parental illness (Smith, 1996).

You would not be blamed at this point for thinking that this description involves a somewhat complicated and convoluted chain of events. However, if nothing else, psychological theories go some way to explain how the brain, with its highly complex primitive drives, motives, and emotions (for survival and protection), interacts with an evolving newer brain that can reason, reflect, and be self-aware. So the internal mind with memories and synaptic anomalies interacts with the external social environment; and thus, emotional triggers are in operation (both internally and externally) that are not always so easy to regulate (Gilbert, 2009).

What are Mary's options for handling the situation? As Mary has limited clinical experience, being only 2 years post-qualification, she would do well to access her clinical supervisor to talk through and plan her future management of this case. Mary would benefit from talking through her feelings of fear and incompetence with her clinical supervisor, ensuring that, at a conscious level, she is not taking responsibility for either Toby's diagnosis or Mr P's personal feelings of anger and despair. It may well be worth organizing a meeting with the medical pediatrician to go through the implications of Toby's diagnosis once more with the parents. Once Mary has worked through her feelings of distress and has gained sufficient support in managing them, she may feel prepared to address Mr P's misplaced anger at the next session. A potentially reparative interaction may look something like the following:

Mr P: Toby's teacher tells me you have still not seen Toby since our last meeting. How is he going to get better if he does not receive a sufficient service? [Mr P's tone is aggressive and patronizing]

M: Mr Pemberton you seem very angry at the service Toby is receiving, and I'm wondering if you are finding it difficult to accept his diagnosis and what he needs to help him?

Mr P: We are all finding this difficult, I feel so out of control [Mr P holds his head in his hands]

At this point Mr P has accepted some of his own feelings of despair and Mary can offer additional support services to help Mr Pemberton and his wife cope with their situation. Had Mr P continued to project his anger, it would be sensible for Mary to offer a second opinion from a specialist speech-language therapist, perhaps handing over the case, or involving her manager to help her to resolve the conflict. When circumstances are difficult to resolve, another therapist could be assigned to work with this family. The significant management strategy in this case is that Mary does not handle Mr P's hostility in a single-handed manner; rather she should access support and work collaboratively to encourage Mr P to take responsibility for his personal feelings.

Case 3

"Carla" is a speech-language therapist with 14 years of clinical experience. She works both in the community and in a hospital on the acute wards with adult clients who have neurological disorders. She has been treating "Gerald" who has multiple sclerosis for the past year on a review basis in the community. Gerald was admitted to hospital 2 weeks ago and has just been diagnosed with pancreatic cancer. Carla has worked with progressive neurological disorders for 10 years and has had to become accustomed to her clients dying. She has attended numerous continued professional development events on managing loss and coping with bereavement; and thus prioritizes self-care in her work. Despite this, there have been occasions with certain clients where Carla has been prone to feeling a client's sadness, pain, helplessness, and grief. The following interaction takes place on the acute ward after Carla has assessed Gerald's swallowing:

C: I'm pleased to say that your swallowing has not deteriorated Gerald and you will be able to continue to have slightly thickened fluids and a soft fork mashable diet.

G: Thank goodness for that, where would I be without that thickener stuff! [Gerald has a glint in his eye and a sarcastic but playful tone of voice]

C: I know I'm sorry it doesn't taste better.

G: It's ok as long as they don't put too much in. Anyway, I doubt I'll need it much longer . . . I don't know if you've heard, but I have been given a new diagnosis.

C: Yes I've just read your notes. How are you doing? [A memory is evoked of Carla's own grief 3 years earlier when her uncle died of cancer]

G: I'm getting by. It's Eileen, the wife I worry about. I know how hard it is. [Gerald remains calm and collected, and appears largely unmoved by the knowledge of his new life-threatening medical condition]

When Carla returns to the department, she begins to weep, deep heartfelt tears. Once her tears subside, she is surprised at the extent of her reaction. In the last year, Carla has formed a deep attachment to Gerald. As well as sharing the odd joke, Gerald has spoken about his experience of having multiple sclerosis and of how he lost his mother to the same disease when he was 10 years old. Despite knowing and treating many clients in similar circumstances, Carla was deeply affected by Gerald and became tearful, while Gerald assumed a fairly calm and contained demeanor at the time. It is likely that a projective identification process was in operation in which Gerald was communicating his sadness unconsciously. The projection of the unmanageable feeling of sadness was successful in reaching Carla (particularly as she was reminded of her own sadness, following her uncle's death), and an emotional resonance was created with her experiencing the feeling at a visceral level. It is important to consider that counter-transference in end-of-life care settings is an ever present dynamic and that as clinicians we are vulnerable to intense feelings of sadness and grief since we are being confronted with our own mortality (Katz & Johnson, 2006, p. xxii).

How should Carla manage this case? Utilization of clinical supervision becomes vital for processing the projected feelings of transference in this case. Within clinical supervision, Carla will have the opportunity to process and analyze why this particular client is affecting her so deeply. Katz and Johnson (2006) emphasize the importance of processing counter-transferential material in order to prevent future blind spots and to highlight and prevent potential harmful statements or actions such as abrupt withdrawal from the case. Carla will also be able to discuss how she can best support Gerald and Eileen, with the potential for referring them for counseling via the palliative care service. More importantly, she can recognize the process that has occurred and use these reactions to inform her management, thus ensuring optimal assistance to her clients and their families. Through increased awareness, she may be able to moderate her involvement in the case, thereby allocating an appropriate level of energy to each of the individuals in her caseload.

THE POTENTIAL FOR CLINICIANS TRANSFERRING ONTO OTHERS

Since transference can arise in all relationships and is not a one-way process, it is important to consider the likelihood of a clinician working with individuals with communication disorders transferring his or her own internal and unresolved relationship issues onto patients, carers, and other professionals. "Transference applies to all of us in all our relationships. Everywhere we go, we are ceaselessly replaying some aspect or other of our early life" (Kahn, 1997, p. 28). Some authors such as Jones (2005), suggest that early life experiences and attachment styles can influence an individual's chosen health care occupation. Moreover, Vincent (1996), while studying the life histories of social work students, concluded that unmet childhood needs can result in attempting to meet those needs in adult life through work-related situations.

Accordingly, it is possible that a clinician who has experienced early life adversities, may re-enact them or compensate for unmet needs, within the context of their current care-giving situation. For example, Masterson (1993) describes a "rescue fantasy" in which therapists whose own self-development was deprived in childhood, transfer their problematic self-representations onto their clients; and then do for their clients what they always wanted to have done for themselves (Masterson, 1993, p. 220). This has significant implications for heightening our self-awareness as clinicians. Unlike counselors and psychotherapists, personal psychotherapy, is not a consideration within the training of speech-language therapists or audiologists. Therefore, access to clinical supervision is highly advantageous for clinicians to reflect on and to disentangle intense emotional reactions, thus ensuring safe and professional practice. This obviously has important implications for a more in-depth understanding of transference issues in the training of clinical supervisors.

Case 4

"Simon" is a speech-language therapist who has been working in the field of learning disabilities for 4 years. He runs a social skills group for clients aged 11–15 years. Prior to leaving for work he had an argument with his partner regarding their personal finances. Simon was reminded of his (unacceptable) feelings of inferiority, impotence, and lack of control as a child, when he was aware that his single mother was struggling to keep up with household bills. The following interaction takes place at the social skills group later that morning:

Simon: Right then. Let's start by looking at how we begin a conversation with someone. Remember last week we looked at greeting someone? Can anyone remember what we need to do?
Giles: Looking . . . we have to look.
Simon: That's right Giles we have to give eye contact.
Joe: [Laughing, then begins to laugh hysterically].
Simon: No that's not what we do [firm tone of voice].
Joe: [continues to laugh uncontrollably].
Simon: [sighs and stares at Joe angrily].
Joe: [stops laughing and begins to cry].

In this interaction, Simon has confronted Joe both verbally and nonverbally. In a situation where Simon would normally offer a compassionate response to his client, he is unnecessarily sharp. Simon is still holding anger from his earlier argument with his partner; and is transferring this anger onto his client. Joe the client has identified with Simon the therapist's inner child representation, which has evoked feelings of impotence and loss of control, and Joe has acted out this feeling by crying.

IMPORTANT TRANSFERENTIAL CONSIDERATIONS FOR CLINICIANS

Clinician transferences can impact on the professional decisions and management strategies we take in patient care and can induce counter-transferential responses in the client. Intense feelings in response to a person's transference or because of our own internal conflicts, can lead to divergence from our usual practice. It is therefore worth reflecting on the following potential reactions highlighted by Bernstein and Bernstein (1980, p. 48).

In my being overly protective with this client is there an underlying need in me for sympathy, protection and warmth?

Am I being cold and indifferent towards this client because I fear closeness so much?

Am I being superior to this client/colleague/carer in order to protect my own feelings of inferiority?

When a patient is rude or uncooperative is my anger emerging because of my intense need to be liked?

Am I being overly optimistic and reassuring because this client reminds me too much of my own problems that I am having difficulty dealing with?

Am I giving unsolicited advice unnecessarily so that I appear all-knowing?

Am I talking more than listening to a client because of my own need to impress them (and be idealised)?

If your answer is yes to any of the above questions, it will be of utmost importance to observe these needs, attenuate their intensity and take correct-ive action in order to preclude jeopardizing the needs of the client or abusing your power as a clinician. Thus, it is important for each clinician to consider their own motivations, to ensure that they are not having an obstructive impact on their client's progress.

CONCLUSION AND IMPLICATIONS FOR PRACTICE

The current practices of speech-language therapists and audiologists involve close relationships with all kinds of clients, carers, colleagues, managers, and other professionals. In such relationships, opportunities for the psycho-analytic processes of transference, counter-transference, and projective iden-tification arise in abundance. However, to date, training institutions have focussed on the conscious aspects of communication and communication dis-orders, distilling the necessary aspects of enhancing communication develop-ment and repairing and alleviating the burden of communication breakdown. What is less familiar and necessitates more attention, particularly in the light of the development of the clinical supervision process, is an understanding of the unconscious processes involved in interactions, and an awareness, by clinicians, of how to deal with them at a conscious level. While addressing all professional relationship conflicts in a therapeutic way is not suggested, there are significant implications for speech-language therapy practice. I suggest the following:

- flexible strategies for dealing with problems;
- extra time for the clinician to reflect on their feelings and consider the most appropriate courses of action;
- access to clinical supervision to offload feelings and consider management options;

- collaboration with colleagues or management to gain further support and potentially share the clinical case;
- a decision to discontinue working closely with certain individuals;
- self-scrutiny to ensure clinician transferences are not obstructing the client's progress.

In considering the above, clinicians will be further equipped to develop their professional skills in the management of relationships, with the net effect of protecting and assisting both the well-being of their clients and themselves as practitioners.

NOTE

1 Transactional analysis is a psychotherapeutic approach developed in the late 1950s by Eric Berne.

14 Self-reflection in clinical practice

Ellen-Marie Silverman
The Speech Source, Inc., USA

Know thyself

(Inscription, at the temple of Apollo, Delphi)

INTRODUCTION

Many considered Walter Cronkite the most trusted man in America during his tenure as evening news anchor. When he died, former colleagues spoke of his strength and comforting presence. They eulogized him saying, "What you saw was what he was." For us, too, the more transparent we become, the more trusted we may be. In fact, who we are may matter more than what we do (e.g. Kornfield, 2009). To be seen as who we are involves knowing who we are. Identifying our core beliefs about ourselves, others, and the world around us that govern our thoughts and actions leads to recognition of our genuine self.

SELF-KNOWLEDGE

Doing well and being happy

Religion, psychology, and philosophy all encourage us to seek self-knowledge to become authentic, or true to our highest potential (e.g. Chödrön, 2005; Palmer, 1999; von Franz, 1964). Religions apply a variety of self-reflective practices. For instance, Quakers apply personal queries (Bill, 2005). Jews engage in self-appraisal intensely during the weeks prior to the New Year. Muslims do so during the entire month of *Ramadan*. Buddhists, Taoists, and Native Americans practice meditation to obtain self-knowledge and to smooth integration of the self with the whole. Psychologies, too, utilize many tools, including dreams (e.g. Jung, 1964/2004) and script identification (e.g. Steiner, 1994) to deepen self-knowing. While the emphases of these two orientations differ, both value doing well and being happy. The ancient Greek philosopher Socrates expressed this goal in the extreme while defending himself during the trial conducted to determine whether he would live or die after his teachings displeased prominent citizens of Athens. It was then and there he advised, "The unexamined life is not worth living" (cited in Brickhouse & Smith, 1994, p. 13).

Identifying personal core beliefs

Some view acquiring self-knowledge as taking inventory of personal traits, abilities, and short-comings to maximize success at work and in relationships (e.g. McCaulley, 1990). Trait identification may lead to the selection of a compatible career, but knowing what we believe can lead to longevity in its practice. What we deeply believe about ourselves, others, and the world fashions what we think, experience, feel, do, and say (e.g. Berne, 1996). Since the purpose for and methods of attaining the first form of self-knowledge are relatively well known, especially by guidance and vocational counselors and psychologists, this chapter concentrates on the second, a more useful self-knowledge for clinicians, who already may have undergone personal trait analyses leading to the choice of this work but may not have been guided to consider the relationship of personal and collective beliefs to the practice of it. Doing so may keep us afloat when buffeted by the inevitable and unexpected challenges clinical relationships can present (e.g. Silverman, 2009b).

Our beliefs exert potent influences on our lives. No one demonstrated this more eloquently than Viktor Frankl, a German prisoner during World War II. Even when confined within the debasing conditions of the Theresienstadt, Auschwitz, and Türkheim Nazi concentration camps, this eminent Viennese psychiatrist and eventual founder of logotherapy believed life was worth living. He attributed his very survival during those challenging times to holding to that singular belief (Frankl, 1959/2006).

Albert Einstein urged each of us to make the most important decision we will ever make for ourselves, namely, whether we believe we live in a friendly world that supplies our needs or in a hostile one that requires us to struggle. This is because Einstein insisted that belief and action are closely related (Hoffman & Dukas, 1981). In 2005, cell biologist Bruce Lipton presented research findings supportive of Einstein's belief. They suggested to him that our mind regulates our health and well-being at the cellular level, where, he concluded, belief resides, an interpretation consistent with brain–computer interface research (Santhanam, Ryu, Yu, Afshar, & Shenoy, 2006).

Our beliefs about academic issues, professional matters, and clinical technique guide our work with clients and caregivers, but the beliefs we hold about ourselves, others, and the world we share may exert an even more fundamental influence on their lives. These personal beliefs focus our interactions, filter our intake of information, and guide our application of it. Some such beliefs are, "I can't trust anyone," "Getting close hurts," and "No one is going to tell me what to do." We form these beliefs early in life. We do so based on our interpretation of experience as shaped by the historical, societal, cultural, and family *milieu* into which we were born, our individual nature and psyche (e.g. Jung, 1964/2004; Steiner, 1994), and the language we learn, especially the first (Casasanto & Boroditsky, 2008). And, like the self-fulfilling prophecies they can be, they grow strong as they fashion our day-to-day experience and our response to it (e.g. Woollams & Brown, 1979).

Unlike professed beliefs, or *credos*, which Frankl's (1959/2006) and Einstein's (Hoffman & Dukas, 1981) represent, personal core beliefs elude ready verbal expression and defy casual attempts at detection because, by age 6 or so, they have taken up residence in our subconscious (Steiner, 1994). It is from that aspect of mind, remote from immediate conscious awareness, that they direct our thoughts and actions leading us to feel satisfaction, elation, triumph, conflict, bitterness, angst, and so forth. Some of these happenstances we savor. Others, we dislike. But all such reactions can distort our decision-making and lead to conclusions that may not only be unwarranted but unhelpful because they represent, in effect, conditioned, mindless responses (Kabat-Zinn, 2005; Langer, 1990) to what is (Tolle, 2006).

Visualizations

Comprehending the influence of core beliefs on our behavior by reading about them is like learning to drive a car by reading a *rules of the road* pamphlet. Only direct, personal experience can reveal their function and power. The following two visualizations provide such an opportunity. They highlight the influence personal beliefs can exert on thought, emotions, bodily sensations, and behavior in the context of daily life, as they do in our work (e.g. Silverman, 2009b).

If you choose to participate, then please first observe the following preliminaries: Locate a quiet place as free as possible of external distractions. Sit. Make yourself comfortable. Relax. Breathe in slowly and out slowly several times. Settle. If you are uncomfortable for any reason with the thought of performing them, then, please, do not do so. You might feel like doing so another time, or you might not. That is all right. Trust your feelings. If you choose to perform the visualizations, you might find listening to a tape recording of the directions or to the voice of someone reading them aloud will enable you to experience a fuller response than responding as you read.

Imagine, if you will, your body conspicuously different from most. Perhaps, you have a face disfigured by Bell's palsy, a prosthetic arm, or albinism. Or, if you currently experience an actual physical difference, imagine yourself with another sort of obvious challenge, such as Tourette's syndrome, an overt stuttering problem, or morbid obesity. Now, in whatever way you envision your body as markedly different, picture yourself at home planning a trip to a nearby mall to purchase a necessary pair of shoes. Attend to your thoughts, emotions, and bodily sensations as you contemplate the journey. See yourself traveling to the mall, making your way to the shoe store. Envision yourself encountering shoppers, relating to salespeople, making the purchase, then returning home safely. Pay particular attention to what you think, the emotions you feel, and the sensations in your body as you experience each phase of the journey. End the visualization. Return your attention to your immediate physical surroundings. Slowly breathe in and out several times. Settle. When your mind becomes still, imagine yourself no better or no worse than anyone else and easily able to perform any activity you desire. Now, once again, imagine yourself at home planning a trip to the mall to buy the needed pair of shoes. Once again attend to your thoughts, emotions, and bodily sensations as you contemplate the journey. See yourself traveling to the mall, making your way to the shoe store, encountering shoppers, relating to salespeople, making the purchase, then returning home safely. As before, note what you think, the emotions you feel, and the bodily sensations you experience as you experience each phase of the journey. End the visualization. Return your consciousness to your immediate physical surroundings. Slowly breathe in and out several times.

Compare your experience during the second visualization to that of the first. You probably noted differences in what you thought, the emotions you felt, and the bodily sensations you observed as well as the particular events you imagined, even though the shopping task you were instructed to perform was the same. As you contemplate why, you may recognize what you believed about yourself and others in each circumstance created your imagined experience. For instance, perhaps, visualizing yourself as different may have led to difficulty attending to sensations throughout your body because you were so busy worrying about being accepted. You also may have had difficulty noting your thoughts and emotions if you believe being different means being rejected. A heightened anxiety level associated with the possibility would have impeded your perception. Maybe you did feel your body and notice that in some areas or throughout, it felt constricted, heavy, even cool or cold. That may have been quite different from when you visualized yourself as ordinary, or adequate. Then, you may have noticed areas that felt warm, light, at ease, even spacious. And your thoughts and emotions may have tilted from uncertainty and apprehension toward confidence and enthusiasm.

Even though you may not have been fully or partially aware of the basic belief that difference can lead to rejection as you followed the instructions, it possessed the power to generate thoughts and related emotions and sensations as well as the experiences you chose to encounter. Such is the power of core beliefs. Until we bring them into conscious awareness to evaluate their accuracy and appropriateness based on our present knowledge and experience, we will repeatedly experience work-related challenges that mystify, possibly immobilize, us. By accessing and evaluating our certainties, we can modify or eliminate those that lead to dissatisfying outcomes and adopt ones more likely to fashion satisfying clinical experience.

As particle physics (e.g. Bohm, Hiley, & Peat, 1987; Stapp, 2007), social neuroscience (e.g. Goleman, 2006), Jungian psychology (e.g. Jung, 1964/ 2004), and Buddhist psychology (e.g. H.H. the Dalai Lama, 2005; Hanh, 1995; Kornfield, 2009) make explicit, we have no reason *to* believe that, in our work, our personal beliefs fail to count. According to specialists in those disciplines, we share inextricable bonds with clients, caregivers, and colleagues. As Zen Master Thich Nhat Hanh (1995) has explained, all phenomena arise and exist together within a matrix of cause and effect. What we deeply believe affects others and vice versa (Orloff, 2005), since, apparently, we are hard-wired to be empathic (e.g. Goleman, 2006). That implicates our very presence, which encapsulates our core beliefs, as a factor in our work at least as influential as our knowledge of communication disorders theory and practice (e.g. Goleman, 2006; Hanh, 1995; Kabat-Zinn, 2005; Kornfield, 2009; Silverman, 2009b).

While we may prefer to draw a solid line of demarcation between our personal beliefs and our professional conduct, we inevitably recognize this is impossible. Physicist David Bohm (Bohm et al., 1987) reported that merely observing an electron alters its momentum. How, then, we might ask, do our implicit interactions with clients, caregivers, colleagues, and students affect their momentum? The aware answer must be: more than we know. Disparate evidence suggests personal beliefs translate into thoughts and behavior that have a decided effect on others (e.g. Dossey, 2003) and our environment (e.g. Emoto, 2005). Posture and bearing, facial expression and grooming, ease and discomfort, movement and stillness, and verbal messaging through tone of voice, loudness, and pacing all signal, at least as strongly as the words we use, how we intend to relate, i.e. whether as partner (e.g. Charon, 2006; Silverman, 2009b) or rescuer (e.g. Berne, 1996; Woollams & Brown, 1979).

Our primary tool is relationship (Silverman, 2003a, 2007, 2009b). As we become more self-aware, we can more readily distinguish clients' and caregivers' complaints, conditions, and lives from projections of our own. And, paradoxically, by recognizing others as the unique individuals they are, we become increasingly able to recognize the common bond we share. This awareness readies us to adopt beliefs to empower, encourage, and, otherwise, facilitate healing (Charon, 2006; Silverman, 2003b, 2009b; Spillers, 2007), our clients' and our own. Conversely, when we hold beliefs that distance us from clients and our innate selves, we fail to be as helpful as we might. My one session with "Sister Edna" when I worked as an on call therapist in an inpatient rehabilitation department reminded me this is so (Silverman, 2003b, 2009b). The speech pathology notes identified her as *globally aphasic*. During co-treatment with an occupational therapist, I found myself pitying newly hemiplegic Sister Edna, so frail, so exposed, using her nondominant hand to wash her upper body with a cloth. Apparently aware of my silent but intense reaction, she turned toward me, looked me hard in the eye, and said scornfully, "I need empathy, not sympathy!" A completely grammatical, basically appropriate, high-order statement articulated with sparkling precision. Later that morning, I found her seated at a table in the patient lounge looking longingly at a cup of orange juice placed in front of her but beyond her reach. I asked her if she wanted the juice. Without hesitating, she said, "Yes." Global aphasic? Hardly!

How could such a glaring misdiagnosis be made? In this hospital, and in other facilities in which I worked, therapists saw patients, but they did not really *see* them. They concentrated on filling out forms. That, to them, seemed to be their work. If they had been but present for the patients, how much more helpful they might have been and how much more joyful (Hanh, 1995). How tragic they were not, not just for the patients but for them as well. Relating so heartlessly ultimately leads to job dissatisfaction and burnout (e.g. Felton, 1998; also see Chapter 16).

Although we may believe our professional relationships exist solely to facilitate change for clients, we may be surprised when we discover the alchemical tool of relationship can and will kindle desirable change in us, too, if we allow it (e.g. Jung, 1964/2004; Siegel and Lowe, 1992; Silverman, 2006). This kind of collateral gift was evocatively represented in the 2003 film, *Seabiscuit*, where, in the closing scene, Red Pollard, jockey of Seabiscuit, the legendary superstar racehorse, speculated on the improbable success shared by the undersized, mistreated thoroughbred and the trio of troubled souls who handled him. Played by Tobey Maguire, Pollard voiced, "Everyone thinks we found a broken-down horse and fixed him, but he fixed us, every one of us." The unshakable bond forged by the renegade horse, grieving owner, has-been trainer, and alienated jockey exemplifies the adage that the whole is greater than the sum of its parts. And healing can come to us, too, in unexpected ways, through the relationships we develop with clients and caregivers, as I myself have experienced (Silverman, 2006).

Selecting an effective tool

Core beliefs, unlike other personal beliefs, such as professed beliefs, reside below conscious awareness rendering them relatively inaccessible to casual inquiry. For instance, if an interviewer asks you which political candidate for the presidency of the United States you believe better prepared to fill the position, you may have a ready opinion. If you disclosed it, and the interviewer followed-up with "Why?" you may not be able to express your reason or reasons as readily as your choice. You may need several more seconds to compose a sufficient reply. If, after you did, the intrepid inter-viewer once again responded with yet another "Why?" you might find, if you wished to share your reasoning, you needed even more time to answer this question than the previous two. To provide a sufficient answer at this level of inquiry requires sifting through relatively involved reasoning to uncover the precise belief or beliefs that led to your choice. And this reply, should you make it, ultimately would reveal essential beliefs you hold about yourself and your relationship with others (e.g. Berne, 1996).

Similarly, when surprised by an unforeseen bump or blow-up in a clinical relationship, we may discover why by identifying the reason we entered the relationship. A tool that helps is repeatedly asking "Why?" as did the interviewer. Then, if we honestly wish to know, we persist until we grasp the belief that has been limiting our awareness. Some beliefs that may surface are: "It's all up to me." "If others don't like me, I will die." And "It's me or them." I used the procedure to understand why I accepted a seemingly aphonic client for treatment who I was certain was malingering only to learn he was. A trial attorney in his mid-50s, he was suing the anesthesiologist who performed the laryngeal intubation he claimed destroyed his voice and his livelihood. Upon producing the voice he claimed to have lost, he fled treatment. After settling, I repeatedly asked myself "Why?" until I uncovered the belief, "I can't say 'No' to someone who asks for help because I don't want to hurt their feelings." Instantly, I knew, intellectually, emotionally, and physiologically, that was the root of my decision. Pruning away its twisted branches has since helped me be more discerning, self-respecting, and welcoming of intuition in decision making.

SELF-REFLECTION

A therapeutic procedure for us

Psychoanalysis pioneers Sigmund Freud and Carl Gustav Jung required their students to undergo psychoanalysis to intimately learn the methodology, a requirement that continues today for analysts in training. Many continue the process as professionals to deepen their self-knowledge. While personal analysis has not been an entry requirement to practice communication disorders, and never may be, deepening our self-knowledge may be instructive for us, too. It may help us, for instance, develop and refine a greater healing presence (e.g. Sipiora & Baumlin, 2002) and resist burnout (e.g. Felton, 1998; Gilbert, 2001; Nemes, 2004).

If, as a 21-year old clinician in the mid-1960s, I had sought to understand why I disliked, avoided, and competed with the mothers of the preschool autistic children who were my first clients, I may have begun healing from a deep-seated anger to be more of a healing presence (Silverman, 2009b). But there was no cause for me then to consider deeply the consequences of my untoward approach to those women. I was, after all, emulating my supervisors by assuming an attitude of superiority and a practice of judgment. They taught that we, not the clients nor the caregivers, knew what was best for them. Acting on that belief allowed me to self-righteously rationalize why this mother deserved my scorn and that mother my contempt, and so on. Doing so felt deeply satisfying while simultaneously disquieting. I recognized I was engaging them on a personal, rather than a professional, level to hurt them to satisfy my needs, which was quite contrary to my nature as I understood it.

Because more than a few arrived at the clinic crushed by guilt believing they caused their child's problem, since parental causation was a prevailing hypothesis (e.g. Bowlby, 1990), they did not demand better from me. They, in fact, seemed satisfied they had found a clinician who seemed committed to their children, and that I was. So, my harsh behavior toward the mothers, unchallenged by supervisors or by the women themselves and tolerated by me, increased without abating as did my sense of superiority and of wrong-doing. Years later, as a transactional analysis trainee, I reflected deeply on this situation that had haunted me for almost 20 years and discovered the deeply personal belief I formed at age 3 that was the source of my trouble-some behavior (Silverman, 2009b). I have largely forgiven myself for adding to those mothers' grief and the supervisors whose instruction unintentionally unleashed an aspect of my shadow (von Franz, 1964) I did not know how to effectively manage. Yet, I still carry enough remorse to feel obligated to write this chapter to echo Hippocrates' encompassing instruction, to abstain from doing harm.

Doing the work

Seeking personal change through reading articles and books or by attending conferences and workshops does not of itself bring change. The only way to change is to change (e.g. Chödrön, 2005; Kongtrül, 2006; Reynolds, 1980, 1976). We frequently explain this to clients and caregivers. Yet, when it comes to personal change, we occasionally act as though we have forgotten. In my experience, getting started obliges us to recognize and move past three critical obstacles:

1   exempting our interactional style from scrutiny when treatment stalls;
2   dreading discovering our faults; and
3   feeling stressed by the speediness of life and our busyness.

Facing and surmounting them demands courage, honesty, equanimity, and kindness to ourselves

That's not in my job description

Our role definition as speech-language pathologists in the United States resembles that of the long-time authoritarian posture assumed by physicians. As a matter of note, we even have adopted the medical title, pathologist, and it is well to remember that physicians who practice pathology study the causes, nature, and effects of diseases by examining organs, tissues, fluids, and dead bodies. They do not relate to living patients. Assuming the mantle of speech-language pathologist has led many of us to practice similarly.

We, too, attend to the client and not necessarily, or to the same degree, to the client–clinician relationship. We seem to view our work as more of a quantitative than a qualitative activity. And we are, in fact, more likely to graduate having taken a course in research design than in counseling.

Moreover, like many physicians, some of us choose to believe that in matters of clinical decision making we, not clients or caregivers, know what is best (e.g. Silverman, 2003a). This authoritarian posture creates a formidable stumbling block to self-reflection by suggesting that slow or no progress, erratic attendance, disinterest, failure to follow-through with assignments, untimely withdrawal from treatment, or other expressions of resistance arise without provocation from us. This leads us to look first to the client when such impasses occur. We review economic circumstances and current living conditions. We re-examine medical, psychological, and pharmacological data. We reconsider diagnoses. And, as necessary, we consult with school personnel regarding academic performance and social behavior. If we find no apparent cause for the disappointing performance, we may review our treatment plan to reassess goals and strategies and consult with colleagues about adopting alternate motivational techniques. When we have exhausted all means of finding the cause within the client and our treatment protocol, we consider temporary or final termination from treatment.

Before we arrive at this level of decision making, we may benefit from also looking deeply into ourselves for beliefs we may hold about relating that could precipitate or contribute to a client's disappointing response to treatment. But our role definition may obviate such inquiry. By embracing the belief *we know best*, we establish a circumstance where we subconsciously believe we have done no wrong if our knowledge and skills are up to date. We, thereby, exempt our authoritarian attitudes and behavior as factors. Yet it may be that the aura of superiority these broadcast may lead a client to feel less competent and, possibly, powerless, feelings which can encourage rebelliousness (e.g. Goulding & Goulding, 1978). If so, a belief designed and adopted to presumably increase our confidence may ultimately erode it, as we repeatedly experience client rebellion without knowing why. This portrait of practice suggests the process of reflection may benefit a profession collectively as well as its members individually. Like other viable institutions, such as governments, school systems, and universities, professions become more effective when they maintain an awareness of their core beliefs and their effect on the provision of service.

In contrast to the authoritarian model of practice is one adopted by physicians practicing the relatively new specialty of narrative medicine (e.g. Charon, 2006). Within this model, seemingly influenced by transactional analysis (e.g. Berne, 1996; Goulding & Goulding, 1978; Silverman, 2009b) and emphasizing mutuality, clinicians and clients collaborate as partners, and clinician self-reflection plays a clear role. Perhaps, more uniformly we, too, will find partnering competent clients more congenial to our aim of providing satisfying clinical service than rescuing them (e.g. Silverman, 2008a).

I'm afraid of what I might discover

In the West, we seem obsessed with personal fault finding (Silverman, 2009a), which the media encourages through commercials, gossip, and self-help products. To become a media-defined object of acceptance and admiration and to appear up-to-date requires expenditure of time or finances, or both. Our profession, too, through continuing education requirements, directs us to periodically redefine ourselves to fit the contemporary image of competency, which, while reasonable, increases the extent of our acceptance seeking. Yet such activity, while anxiety provoking, may be more tolerable than engaging in self-reflection, which can reintroduce us to elements of ourselves we may prefer to render invisible. We may resist, for example, discovering beliefs that allow us to act in an intolerant or hateful manner because we do not wish to feel even more personally discontent than we already may be (e.g. von Franz, 1964), especially if we are experiencing the self-deprecating after effects of abuse from parents or others.

But personal denigration is not the purpose of self-reflection (Kongtrül, 2006). Professional growth is. When we uncover core beliefs we formulated as young children that continue to direct our thoughts and behavior and help fashion our circumstances and relationships to recognize they do not represent our current knowledge and experience, we do not benefit from calling ourselves "bad," or "stupid," or "wicked." We can recognize that, as a young child, given our relatively limited experience and immature cognitive apparatus, we may have made appropriate decisions about life. But now we need to decide whether we need to modify or discard them. Then we move on. Self-reflection is not another name for a blame game. It is an opportunity to be more reality based in relationships. As diarist and writer Anaïs Nin (cited in Epstein, 1999, p. 834) wryly observed, "We do not see things as they really are. We see things as we are." Self-reflection, when practiced with kindness toward ourselves, increases the clarity of our sight.

I'm too busy

New information and tools to enhance our practice arrive in our email box and through the mail almost daily. Requirements for job site practice change continually, often demanding increased efficiency and productivity. Paperwork requirements mount. Meetings and consultations fill out our work days. Finding adequate time to calmly address patients can be daunting.

We try to meet our personal needs evenings and weekends, but scheduling time for solitude often seems an expendable luxury. We are physically fatigued and soul-tired (Norris, 2008). Under these circumstances, telling ourselves self-reflection does not seem compatible with our lifestyle can be convincing. But, when we recognize taking 30 minutes or so to self-reflect occasionally can eliminate untold hours of anxiety and frustration later, we may reconsider. Self-reflection saves time and energy and increases our enthusiasm as we discover we can find satisfying solutions to even our most vexing challenges by turning within.

SUMMARY AND CONCLUSIONS

While we commonly believe providing quality service derives from ample and updated knowledge and skills, our effectiveness actually may stem from self-awareness. What we believe about ourselves, others, and the world influences our clinical relationships at least as much as our knowledge of communication disorders. These core beliefs that we form early in life filter our intake, processing, and expression of information and focus our interactions. Residing below the level of conscious awareness they defy casual detection. Uncovering them, we can function more in accord with our current knowledge and experience to offer increasingly satisfying clinical service. Ongoing self-reflection, a process psychotherapists and psychoanalysts find basic to developing effective clinical relationships, can lead us to these beliefs. Repeatedly asking and answering "Why?" when we examine how we behaved in a manner that left us feeling angry, hurt, inadequate, or unsettled in some other way can help us reach the core belief behind the troublesome behavior. To enjoy a long-lived, useful career, we need foremost to know ourselves. Self-reflection offers that possibility.

15 Using oneself as a vehicle for change in relational and reflective practice

Elaine Geller
Long Island University, Brooklyn Campus

ONE CLINICAL STORY

"Nafi", a 3½-year-old youngster was brought to the university clinic by his parents, "Salah" and "Muslimah." Nafi was nonverbal and had profound developmental challenges across many domains including poor eye gaze and engagement, minimal affect, poor self-regulation, pre-symbolic play and limited joy in play, sensory integration challenges, and a profound impairment in language and communication. The family was from Lebanon and the mother was primarily Arabic-speaking and the father was Arabic- and English-speaking. Initially the parents reported deep concern that Nafi "didn't respond to his name nor use words and refused to repeat words." The first time the mother brought Nafi into the therapy room, she sat down on a small chair, wrapped her arms tightly around him (so he would not run) and told him to "sit, look and listen to Dr. Geller." When I suggested that Nafi could explore the room and the toys – the mother refused. Nafi had received early intervention services for the prior 2 years with a focus on getting him to attend to tasks, sit, look and listen, follow directions, point to, and label, objects.

From the start of the intervention, the goal was to implement relationship-based principles with the mother as the primary agent of change. I had to establish an alliance with Muslimah so that she became interested in participating in each session without feeling overwhelmed or uncomfortable. I carefully explained that the work would be dyadic and thus, the mother and child became the client. Although the father was very involved in the ongoing treatment, his work schedule limited his ability to be engaged in each session.

As the therapeutic alliance was being established, the language barrier between the mother and the speech-language pathologist was an early obstacle that was immediately addressed. Arabic was clearly the language of treatment since it was the verbal and emotional language between Nafi and his mother. Since Muslimah was the primary interactant during sessions, she could use Arabic in working with Nafi and thus, teach early language forms to her son and to myself. This was a new way of working for the mother since Nafi's two prior speech-language practitioners had emphatically told her that she should "never" use Arabic with her son. The mother already had two major disappointments; her son was hard to engage and when she tried to engage him, she could not use her native language. She reported that she often "slipped" and used Arabic. This led to strong feelings of guilt that she might be doing some harm. The language issue was quickly resolved by finding an Arabic-speaking speech-language pathologist who agreed to work with the client and family individually and also, collaboratively with myself. The Arabic-speaking practitioner became the means through which I came to understand the family's cultural beliefs and practices, values, hopes, and dreams for their child.

A fundamental principle of the intervention was to help each parent become more affectively or emotionally attuned to Nafi's intents, signals and emotional displays. This also meant that the parents and the clinician had to deepen their ability to interpret his nonverbal signals and actions. This approach was in direct contrast to the parents' rather directive and intrusive style (and previous behavioral interventions) which all focussed on decreasing Nafi's disruptive behaviors and getting him to comprehend directions and label objects. With ongoing guidance and support, the mother slowly learned how to interpret Nafi's nonverbal signals and be with him in new ways; that is, focussing on sustained back and forth engagement. The most challenging work for the mother was to learn to tolerate, and not immediately anticipate and meet, Nafi's needs. The most challenging work for the father was to meet Nafi at his developmental level rather at some arbitrary preconceived level based on his chronological age.

As the work progressed (albeit slowly), I was constantly reminded that I was considered a family member; that is, Muslimah's sister. Interestingly, neither parent could consider calling me by my first name. Muslimah was very gentle and soft-spoken and had experienced profound sadness and disappointment around her relationship with her son. The mother was highly sensitive and somewhat overreactive to me and constantly looked to me for approval. If I offered a suggestion, the mother would immediately become quite sad and even depressed, if she felt that I had disapproved of her actions. Other relational challenges evolved in this work. For example, Saleh (who worked near the university) would frequently drop into my office unannounced and expected me to immediately see him. He would be rather emphatic and demanding during these visits about how I should be working with Nafi. During these visits, he would hint that Muslimah was afraid to directly share her thoughts and feelings with me. I worked with this family for several years.

INTRODUCTION

One of the most valuable constructs in relational and reflective clinical practice is the professional *use of self*. The clinical story briefly outlined above will be used to highlight how I integrated constructs related to the professional *use of self* with current clinical practices in speech-language pathology. The professional use of self is a broad construct first discussed in the infancy and mental health literature in the early 1990s by Bertacchi and colleagues (Bertacchi & Coplon, 1992; Bertacchi & Stott, 1992). Bertacchi and Stott (1992) defined the use of self as "understanding oneself and using oneself as a vehicle for good practice" (p. 133). Eggbeer, Fenichel, Pawl, Shahmoon Shanok, and Williamson (1994, p. 54) expanded on this definition and added that the professional use of self involves "the examination of internal processes and reactions, the willingness to question and to struggle with uncertainty." More recently, Eggbeer, Mann, and Seibel (2007, p. 5) described the use of self as how professionals "understand, and use (our) thoughts, feelings, values, and behaviors" in clinical work with clients and families.

In a more extensive discussion, Heffron, Ivins, and Weston (2005) defined the use of self as "the process of being aware of one's own internal experience and how that experience influences behavior" (p. 324). Among other things, they stated that this includes "recognition of the judgments, wishes, intolerances, hot buttons, or fears that one brings or that become activated in clinical encounters" (p. 324). Broadly, the professional use of self involves the practitioner observing his/her own thoughts, feelings and behaviors as an important source of communication and information in a variety of clinical experiences (Eggbeer et al., 1994; Heffron et al., 2005). This is an active, dynamic and intersubjective process that implies that professionals pay attention to their own inner experiences, pay attention to the other person's inner experiences, and the interactions between them. This construct includes and expands upon traditional psychoanalytic concepts such as transference and counter-transference (see also Chapter 13 on transference, counter-transference and projective identification).

Most allied health disciplines focus on a substantive body of theoretical, analytical and technical knowledge about a particular field. In speech-language pathology, the focus of graduate study involves understanding normal and disordered speech, language and communication processes in order to ameliorate the client's communication struggles. Although discipline-specific expertise is imperative, clinical work is always embedded within relationships. Attention to the affective and intersubjective aspects of clinical relationships has been neglected in speech-language pathology. In order to understand the latent dimensions of relationships, practitioners need to become more relationally informed and psychologically minded (Foley & Hochman, 2006). As Eggbeer and her colleagues (2007) noted, "the most extensive disciplinary – and even interdisciplinary – knowledge and skill in the world, if applied in isolation, are not sufficient" (p. 5). That is, working with clients and families without knowledge of relational and reflective principles minimizes the potential for the most optimal clinical outcomes.

This chapter illustrates how the professional use of self can become an instrument, or means, through which information, knowledge, and support can be given to clients, families and other practitioners. I will tease apart the dynamic and varied components that underlie this construct and highlight how these components were infused into the work with Nafi and his parents. The goal is to illustrate how areas often "out of the practitioners' awareness" come into awareness in order to enhance growth and change. Heffron and her colleagues (2005) operationalized this construct by integrating ideas from various psychoanalytic perspectives. Their working model will be used as the framework for this discussion. Depending on one's discipline-specific expertise, these ideas may be used in slightly different ways. This discussion highlights how practitioners can deepen self-awareness, self-reflection, and self-regulation as they pay attention to the underlying dynamics of clinical relationships. This knowledge is beyond scientific, theoretical, analytical, and technical information that is emphasized in the discipline. Many of the principles inherent in the use of self have been traditionally viewed as out of the scope of practice, or purview, of the speech-language pathologist. In order to integrate and apply these principles into speech-language practices, systematic and formal training and supervision would be imperative (Geller & Foley, 2009a).

This chapter is organized in the following manner. Topics for discussion include:

1   a brief history of the concept of the professional use of self;
2   an explanation of key terms such as relationship-based learning and the therapeutic alliance, reflective practice, out of awareness (or latent) processes, and the management of one's feelings;
3   an exploration of skills that underlie the use of self such as mindsight and empathy, affective attunement, holding or containment, inquiry versus interrogation, and working from a strength-based perspective; and
4   one clinical case story that illustrates how an experienced speech-language pathologist (me) integrated these principles with contemporary clinical approaches.

A BRIEF HISTORY

The use of self is a construct that emerged early on in the infancy and mental health movement (Bertacchi & Coplon, 1992; Bertacchi & Stott, 1992; Eggbeer et al., 1994). Many of these fundamental principles evolved from the seminal work of Selma Fraiberg and her colleagues (Fraiberg, Adelson, & Shapiro, 1975) who worked with young mothers and their infants who lived in dire circumstances. They focussed attention on understanding the inner life of the baby and the mother and who the infant represented to the mother (that is, the infant as transference object). Among their many contributions they illustrated how the relationship between the practitioner and the parent served as an instrument for making positive and dynamic changes in the infant/toddler–parent relationship. What grew out of the early infancy and mental health movement was attention to the power of relationships and the importance of linking the present and the past in order to promote change and growth. Although Selma Fraiberg did not use the term reflective capacity, her work demonstrated how reflective functioning grew in the mothers and enabled them to see their infants' internal states and the connections between them (Slade, 2002).

Interestingly, Ward and Webster (1965) stated that understanding human dynamics and relationships "does not replace knowledge of the more traditional content of speech pathology and audiology; rather, this is conceived of as a basic context in which to build knowledge of content" (p. 105). However, graduate education and clinical practice have been made more concrete by focussing on analytical, theoretical, and technical knowledge in order to ameliorate client struggles. This makes sense since speech-language pathology evolved from medical, behavioral, and educational models (see Chapter 12 for further discussion). This concentration on science and application of theory to practice has minimized studying the basic context in which clinical work unfolds. For example, how individuals operate during moment-to-moment interpersonal and experiential situations (Geller, 2006; Geller & Foley, 2009a and 2009b) and how one's internal experiences and reactions to clients and families can support or hinder the ongoing clinical process. It is the linkage of cognitive, subjective, and affective material that needs to be embedded into clinical work.

Insights from mental health disciplines have been integrated into the practice of some speech-language pathologists. For example, in early intervention programs (Foley & Hochman, 2006), professionals have moved from working with young children in isolation from their family to working with the dyad; that is, the unit of intervention becomes the client and parent(s). This can be seen in the Hanen Centre programs where the family is seen as the client and is viewed as critical for the child's development (Girolametto & Weitzman, 2006). Similarly, in the DIR model (developmental, individual differences, relationship-based), the involvement of the parent(s) is seen as integral for successful intervention (Greenspan & Wieder, 2006). These programs highlight a shift in early intervention from the individual to the relationship (Kalmanson & Seligman, 2006). Of further note, this shift underscores the belief that parents (or significant others) become the primary agents of change rather than the sole practitioner.

Similar paradigm shifts have been seen in occupational therapy. In an overview of the evolution of the therapeutic use of self, Taylor (2008) described three distinct periods in how occupational therapists viewed their work. The first period involved focussing on clients' motivation and capacity to do the occupational therapy tasks/activities with the occupational therapist seen as the expert (or guide). Similar to speech-language pathology, the occupational therapist "orchestrated" the environment and generated goals and procedures. The second period involved focussing on the client's underlying

biomechanical and neuromuscular mechanisms that influenced body functioning. Similar to speech-language pathology, this era was rooted in application of medical models (attention to etiology and symptoms) to occupational
therapy. During both of these periods, the occupational therapist was viewed
as the expert and authority figure. In the most recent paradigm shift, occupational therapists focus on clinical goals (that is, occupational activities/
tasks) while paying equal attention to the therapeutic relationship. As Taylor
(2008) noted, there is increased attention towards a more collaborative, caring, and empathic relationship with clients with the goal of empowering them
to become more involved in deciding goals and outcomes.

A parallel process is emerging in speech-language pathology as clients
(from infancy through adulthood) and their families are encouraged to
become collaborative partners in the unfolding clinical process. As Holland
(2007) discussed, there is an expanded concept of who is the expert in the
discipline. Holland (2007, p. 6) stated that there are at least three experts –
"the person who lives *in* the disorder, those who live *with* the disorder –
the family and significant others" and the practitioner. Collaborative and
relational work can be applied to all clients and families across the life
span (Foley & Hochman, 2006; Greenspan & Wieder, 2006; Holland, 2007).
Traditional attitudes of the speech-language pathologist as an expert (who
prescribes solutions, makes clinical decisions, and maintains a professional
distance from clients) have shifted towards the speech-language pathologist
as a collaborative partner (joining with clients and families to problem
solve and make clinical decisions). This movement is evident across many
allied health disciplines where the focus has moved from a unidirectional (or
one-person psychology) to a bidirectional model. Geller and Foley (2009b)
described this change as moving away from "doing something to" clients and
families to "doing something with" clients and families.

Interestingly, when Taylor (2008) queried occupational therapists about
their understanding of the professional use of self, they reported that knowledge of this construct was essential to positive clinical outcomes; however,
they had received minimal (if any) formal training in this area. Similarly,
in speech-language pathology, these areas have rarely been integrated into
academic and clinical education (Geller & Foley, 2009a). Clearly, discipline-
specific training involves observing particular things – "all professionals
observe, but what is looked for is trained into – or out of – each discipline"
(Shahmoon-Shanok, Henderson, Grellong, & Foley, 2006, p. 399). What
has been neglected in speech-language pathology is an understanding of the
power of relationships and the transformational impact of practitioners on
clients and families (and vice versa). An understanding of these processes and
how to apply them to clinical work remains somewhat obscure.

KEY CONSTRUCTS IN THE USE OF SELF

Relationship-based learning

One of the key principles in the use of self is the formation of the *therapeutic alliance*. Relationships are viewed as the organizing construct around which clinical work unfolds. It is well known that relationships have two components: (1) an interactive component that is behavioral and observable in which patterns of actions and signals are understood between partners; and (2) an intersubjective component that is intrapsychic and involves internal affective states, intents, intuitions, and feelings shared between participants (Fivaz-Depeursinge, Corboz-Warnery, & Keren, 2004). The foundation of relationship-based work involves *intersubjectivity*; that is, the shared implicit relational knowledge that two people have concerning themselves and the other person, and how they are together. Each relationship is unique in and of itself because of shared subjective states (Geller & Foley, 2009b).

The underlying premise in relationship-based intervention is that developmental change is best facilitated within a positive, nurturing, secure, safe, trusting, and authentic relationship. The practitioner is invested in the client's development, has earned confidence and trust, and uses empathy to appreciate the other's emotional reality. The speech-language pathologist embraces families and clients without preconceived notions, judgments, or criticisms. Within this unfolding relationship, shared goals and problems can be addressed. It is the intersubjective aspects of relationships that have not been explored; however, when understood, they become the foundation for developmental change and growth.

The work with Nafi and Muslimah illustrates several key premises of relationship-based work. The relationship between the practitioner and each member of the family had to be nurtured in a safe, trusting, authentic and nonjudgmental environment. From the start of my relationship with this family, I felt enormous pressure. They appeared to be needy, demanding, extremely anxious and somewhat desperate for Nafi to talk. I had to derive a rudimentary sense of each parent's inner life; that is, I needed to know about their own relationships with their own parents and siblings, what their growing up was like in Lebanon, the reasons they moved to the United States, and what living in the United States meant to them. Of course, I needed to learn about their culture and beliefs and what they expected of each other, their children and the practitioner. Most importantly I had to explore each parent's internal representations of Nafi as well as their hopes, dreams, fantasies, and disappointments about his developmental struggles. Similarly, the mother's internal representations of the clinician were considered in supervision. I sensed that Muslimah was quite cautious, hesitant and perhaps, fearful, about expressing her feelings about the clinical work; her frustrations and disappointments; and her expectations of the speech-language pathologist.

I received weekly individual and group reflective supervision to explore these new areas of interest.

The quality of the alliance that emerges over time between the practitioner and parent mirrors the quality of the relationships between the parent and child. As Kalmanson and Seligman (2006) have observed, "parents' relationships with practitioners and their infants (children) have uncanny parallels" (p. 257) and insights in one relationship frequently offer insights about the other relationship. Interestingly, the same themes frequently emerge across relationships; however, they are approached and managed in different ways. As the intervention with Nafi moved forward, Muslimah became more affectively attuned to Nafi's signals, intents, and emotional displays and a parallel shift was seen in her interactions with her two older children. Similarly, Muslimah's interactions with me (positive and negative) seemed to parallel other relationships in her life.

Developing a reflective practice

Donald Schön's (1983, 1987) work on reflective functioning has become the basic framework for what is now called reflective practice. Reflective practice involves constantly "stepping back" from the immediate clinical situation and observing and conceptualizing and reconceptualizing what one is doing, thinking, intending, and feeling. Schön (1983, 1987) differentiated a two-fold learning process: (1) the development of substantive knowledge, or content, of the particular discipline (theories, goals, procedures, and facts); and (2) the development of reflective knowledge, applying theories, facts and goals to moment-to-moment experiences and interactions. Practitioners go beyond theories and devise new methods of reasoning, construct and test new categories of understanding, devise strategies of action, and new ways of framing (or reframing) problems (Schön, 1987, p. 39).

Schön (1983) differentiated the process of reflection-on-action versus reflection-in-action. Reflection-on-action is the opportunity to think back on prior clinical experiences and review and sort out multiple layers of meaning. This ongoing process of re-examining clinical material is done during supervision. Here the practitioner and supervisor explore feelings, intuitions, and impressions and these ideas germinate – often without immediate clarity or action. This enables the practitioner to return to the clinical relationship with increased awareness, and over time, with new insights and ways of approaching clinical obstacles. In contrast, reflection-in-action involves observing self and other (and the interaction of self and other) at the moment of the clinical encounter. This process occurs later in one's professional development (Geller & Foley, 2009a).

The goal in reflective practice is to interweave substantive knowledge with the implicit, affective, and intersubjective states of client and practitioner. Again, this shift in practice integrates content with the process underlying clinical activities, and includes the feelings evoked by content and process

(Heffron, 2005, p. 116). The objective of reflective supervision is to process and explore subjective material so that the practitioner returns to the work in a more open manner. At *all* times, the clinical work remains central to the process of reflective practice and supervision.

Engaging in supervision was necessary in order to work relationally and reflectively with Nafi and his parents. Practitioners need a reflective context (that is, supervision) to continually slow down and "step back" and pay detailed and nuanced attention to one's inner experiences. During moment-to-moment clinical encounters, I struggled with feelings and reactions towards the family. With guidance and support in supervision, I slowly learned that I could contain these feelings during the work with Nafi and Muslimah. The constant stepping back in supervision enabled me to become more conscious of my reflexive behaviors (or triggers) that were naturally evoked in this relationship. When I returned to subsequent sessions, I was more easily able to address earlier material that was missed or could have been handled more effectively. For example, if Muslimah appeared to be upset when I offered a hint, or some guidance about how to engage her son, then I learned to come back to this material in a more empathic way. Over time, I used myself to inform the work and this enabled me to broaden my perspective and to more clearly appreciate each parent's vantage point (see Chapter 13 for further discussion of reflective practice).

Out of awareness (or latent) processes

Dorothy Martyn (2007), a child psychotherapist, stated that "to address forces not visible to the naked eye, both in ourselves and in others, is indeed the essence of responsibility . . ." (p. xxii). Furthermore, "to believe that we can be 'accountable' on the strength of what we consciously can know and do by the action of the will, without a high respect for what may be operating in us outside our awareness, is sheer folly" (Martyn, 2007, p. xxii). In order to understand the latent or hidden dimensions of relationships, the principles of transference and counter-transference need to become part of the language of the speech-language pathologist.

Briefly, *transference* involves the process in which important figures from an individual's past get activated in the present clinical relationship. The parent/client filters interactions with the practitioner through the lenses of past experiences. Although this question has rarely been addressed, the speech-language pathologist explores who she/he might represent to each particular client and family member. *Counter-transference* involves the feelings, memories, conflicts, and impulses that may arise in the practitioner in the course of his/her work with the client and family, and these feelings are often in reaction to the client and the client's transference. Again, the clinician explores who the client (or family member) represents to him/her. What is important is that one's past history and subjective experiences impact on current relationships and realities. Although these processes are largely unconscious and out of awareness, they can be accessed through analysis, reflection, and supervision.

Norman-Murch (1996) stated that few speech-language pathologists, occupational therapists, physical therapists, early interventionists, or special educators have had training in issues related to transference and counter-transference in relationships and are "often quite unaware of how powerful these forces can be" (p. 20). All non-mental health practitioners need to pay attention to the array of emotions and reactions that get evoked in them as they work with clients, families, supervisors, agencies, etc. (Seligman, 1993). This is necessary since these emotions (both positive and negative) may impede or create impasses in the ongoing clinical relationship. Without understanding these processes practitioners may misinterpret someone's actions or reactions, minimize the impact of one's past history on the current relationship, or not manage one's own feelings during clinical encounters. In exploring affective and subjective material in supervision, there are no interpretations of one's past history or any pathologizing or labeling of internal states. The primary goal is to return to the clinical work without dispersing inappropriate or negative feelings.

There appears to be a long standing belief that being a professional involves maintaining some sense of objectivity, neutrality, and distance from clients and families. Furthermore, practitioners should ignore or deny their feelings, reactions, and/or deeply held cultural beliefs (Heffron et al., 2005). However, relationships evoke subjective feelings that are quite normal. With guided exploration, practitioners became less afraid to understand themselves and their reactions to others. This process leads to a broader perspective about the client and family and their unique experiences. Embracing emotions rather than minimizing them allows the clinician to enter the realm of feelings with clients. As Luterman (2006) stated, ". . . not to enter this realm limits our ability to help our clients" (p. 9). However, without specific training, speech-language and hearing professionals are (often) anxious and uncomfortable about how to approach clients and families. Further, "what clients need most is someone who will listen compassionately and deeply to their feelings and not prescribe solutions" (Luterman, 2006, p. 33).

The work with Nafi and his family clearly illustrates the powerful transference and counter-transference between the mother and myself. I was confronted with understanding who the mother represented to me since many strong feelings were evoked in the relationship. Furthermore, I had to work really hard to contain my own frustrations (and at times, annoyance and impatience) with the mother around the ongoing issue of waiting for Nafi to make some signal of his intent, or need. Muslimah would basically do anything that Nafi wanted. She knew his limited repertoire by heart and rarely hesitated to meet his immediate needs. I would have to concentrate on learning how to help the family relinquish their constant efforts to control Nafi.

Furthermore, the mother's representations of the speech-language pathologist's role in her family had to be understood. As stated previously, the mother repeatedly told me that I was "like a sister." While Muslimah wanted to incorporate me into their family, neither parent could call me by my first name. In supervision, I came to realize that only a family member might comment on or become part of something as intimate as each parent's relationship with her and his child (for further discussion see Shahmoon-Shanok & Geller, 2009). Muslimah's feelings led to many perceived pressures for my time and involvement in many aspects of the family's life. This exacerbated my anxiety and my desire to please and nurture the alliance while at the same time wishing for some detachment and distance. This led to many dialogues in supervision around maintaining appropriate *boundaries* with this family and the perceived demands that were transferred onto me. Issues of optimal boundaries (that is, being too close or too distant) were a continual theme in supervision (Foley, Hochman, & Miller, 1994).

Similarly, my counter-transferential reactions to the father required deeper understanding in order to nurture and form an alliance with him. I slowly came to understand that the father's intrusiveness (and what felt like "bossiness") was just a reflection of his profound feelings of being powerless in the presence of his son's developmental challenges. My early reactions to each parent were often misunderstandings of the impact of each person's past history and experiences on the current relationship and its realities. I learned to interpret the father's behaviors and actions in light of his ongoing attempts to make a difference in Nafi's life. An understanding of these counter-transferential reactions led to a shift in my ability to hear each parent's perspective and struggles without prescribing, offering a solution, or sharing some insight. I learned to pay simultaneous attention to many hidden dynamics in these relationships and the competing feelings that emerged in me such as the desire to meet Mulsimah's needs, my wish to rescue Nafi and the mother, and my need for boundaries.

Managing one's feelings – self-regulation

Affect regulation involves the capacity to modulate affective states with the goal of knowing the meaning of one's inner affective states (Fonagy, Gergely, Jurist, & Target, 2002, pp. 4–5). Affective regulation is integrally linked to reflective functioning. As practitioners learn to continually monitor their own feelings – reactions, triggers, fears, annoyances, biases, etc., they are able to work with clients and families without dispersing negative attitudes. The notion of negative capability is crucial to how speech-language pathologists learn to manage their feelings. It is defined as "the capacity to experience emotion, one's own and others', but also to contain it for the sake of the work and, by doing so, to learn from and to use emotion to inform our understanding of the work" (French, 2000, p. 1). The development of negative capability involves holding or containing uncomfortable states of mind such as ambiguity, ambivalence, conflict, internal impulses to react, doubt, uncertainty, and/

or "not knowing." This skill develops over time as a product of ongoing reflective practice and supervision.

Learning how to manage emotional reactions has not traditionally been part of the training in speech-language pathology. In fact, this way of working is somewhat divergent from conventional practice and is reminiscent of the speech-language pathologist as the expert who directs, informs and at times, prescribes. Although there are times in which these behaviors are valuable and appropriate, there are other times (especially in the presence of emotionally painful or highly volatile situations) when professionals may have a strong impulse to act without forethought. When practitioners cannot manage their feelings, they may inadvertently become defensive and disperse negative attitudes onto the client or family. Dispersal of feelings may take several different forms such as explanations, being impulsive or reactive, or engaging in some physical action or activity (French, 2000).

Without training and supervision, practitioners may display particular behavioral patterns in order to manage difficult clinical situations (Heffron, 1999). These may include:

1   finding a quick solution (or answer) to a given clinical problem;
2   minimizing hard to address (and painful) issues that may arise in the course of intervention;
3   acting as if everything will be better if one avoids the past; and
4   wanting to be admired by, or to please, the other person so that certain issues get avoided.

The belief that professionals should maintain a positive and neutral stance often leads to staying away from uncomfortable topics that may provoke negative reactions. With time and supervision, speech-language pathologists learn to balance their practice addressing emotional and/or uncomfortable material with being informative, insightful, and prescriptive (when appropriate to the clinical situation).

Returning to the work with Nafi and his parents, I had to develop and deepen my ability to manage my feelings and reactions with each family member. As previously discussed, Muslimah was often highly reactive and sensitive to any suggestions or comments made by me while engaging with Nafi. I had to learn to make comments or suggestions in ways that did not offend the mother – or lead to her feeling devalued or criticized. I had to carefully modulate my nonverbal behaviors, affect, tone of voice, body posture, etc. I often felt like I was "walking on egg shells" with the mother. Similarly, with Saleh, I had to maintain attention to my annoyance at times, and impatience, with his constant and often unexpected and unannounced, visits to my office. With time, I came to understand the prescribed roles of each parent in the family. For example, three people would try to constrain and hold Nafi in order to dress him during the winter months. At those moments, Saleh would sit and watch this struggle. Or, Nafi would run aimlessly through the clinic and hallways with Muslimah chasing after him as the father sat and watched these unfolding scenes. These events tested my developing skill at holding and containing my feelings and reactions. My own past history and cultural beliefs and practices were clearly challenged. (See Chapter 7 for further discussion of cross-cultural issues.)

DEVELOPING CAPACITIES FOR THE PROFESSIONAL USE OF SELF

Speech-language pathologists cannot make changes in outer skills without first making inner changes in how they understand themselves and how they use this understanding to deepen their work with clients and families (Bertacchi & Stott, 1992). Some of the basic skills that need to be integrated with discipline-specific expertise are outlined below. Although these capacities are discussed as separate entities, in reality they are all interwoven and overlapping.

Mindsight (or theory of mind) and empathy

Theory of mind is the capacity to understand behaviors in terms of underlying mental states and to attribute beliefs, feelings, attitudes, intentions, etc., to self and others. The capacity for reflective functioning is an inherent dimension of theory of mind (Fonagy, 2002). Mindsight is defined as the capacity to imagine the internal experience of another person and to make sense of that experience (Siegel & Hartzell, 2003). The ability to imagine clients' and families' internal experiences and affective states expands the practitioner's capacity for empathy. Siegel and Hartzell (2003) suggested that affective attunement or mirroring, contingent responding, and repairing communication breakdowns, are skills that are necessary for mindsight.

Affective or empathic attunement is the capacity to go beyond the explicit meaning of a message (or a behavior) to understand the underlying emotional meaning or content. Stern (1985) defined affect attunement as the "performance of behaviors that express the quality of feeling of a shared affect state without imitating the exact behavioral expression of the inner state" (p. 142). Attachment theorists such as John Bowlby (1988) hypothesized that parents who were emotionally attuned to their infant/child's internal states provided a sense of inner security and safety for their child and a sense that they were deeply understood. Children who experienced a secure attachment were more easily able to explore the world without fear and maintained a self-organized and self-regulated capacity (Siegel, 1999).

Mindsight involves a two-fold process. The speech-language pathologist first listens for the emotional content and then aligns to the client's feeling state by re-casting (not imitating) the affective state. The practitioner pays heightened attention to the nonverbal aspects of interactions as well as to his/her own bodily (or physiological) sensations. These areas give clues as to unconscious meanings or less observable feeling states. Early on, Reik (1948) talked about ways psychoanalysts discovered unconscious messages and emphasized that in order to understand others one needed to look into one-self and one's reaction to the material (p. 147). He described this process as "listening with the third ear" which appears to be an early reference to the professional use of self as a means to inform the work.

The feeling of being deeply understood reinforces a sense of connectedness between the practitioner and client/family (see also Chapter 3 on hearing the client's story). The aim is for the client (and family) to feel heard, and ultimately, to be respected for his/her unique perspective and past experiences. When communication breakdowns (naturally) occur they create new opportunities for reflection and repair in which differences in perspectives between the client and practitioner are clarified. With time, I developed a deeper understanding of Muslimah's and Saleh's perspectives about their struggles living in the United States, feelings of discrimination and prejudice, and coping with a child with profound developmental challenges in a new culture and community. One day (after many months of interactions), Saleh revealed that he was "saving his tears until Nafi turned five." Of course, this comment reflected a rather old belief that if children on the autistic spectrum did not start to talk by 5 years of age they would never learn to talk. This statement was a clear reflection of the emerging trust and alliance that had developed between Saleh and myself. This moment of intimacy deepened my capacity to be empathic and attuned with the father and revealed a pro-found shift in the relationship. I was able to feel as well as hear the depth of his suffering.

Holding or containing others

Professionals manage their own feelings and those of their clients and families, through containing or holding the gamut of emotional reactions, impulses, and feelings that often get triggered during clinical work. This construct evolved from the seminal work of Winnicott (1958, 1960) who highlighted the critical role that maternal sensitivity and emotional attune-ment played in early child development; that is, the caregiver protects the baby from impingements from the outside world that might be stressful or wounding. The caregiver is seen as a *container* and the infant experiences the feeling *of being held* in a safe and protective space (Geller & Foley, 2009b). Winnicott (1958) detailed the similarities between the client–analyst relation-ship and the mother–infant relationship in that the practitioner ". . . has to display all the patience and tolerance and reliability similar to the mother's devotion to her child . . ." (p. 202).

In a parallel process, a safe and protected space is created between the practitioner and the client (or family) so that feelings can be explored, pro-cessed, and reflected upon rather than minimized or avoided. If the anxiety of the client (or family) can be held by the practitioner then the clinical work moves forward in a more optimal manner. *Parallel process* operates across all relationships. That is, my supervisors contained and held my feelings and reactions around the work with this family. Similarly, I slowly learned to become the container for Muslimah and Saleh's feelings about the clinical intervention, their son's developmental struggles, his educational experiences, etc. This process had to occur so that Muslimah and Saleh (and myself) learned to tolerate the very slow change process that was becoming more and more evident over time. My ability to learn how to manage my internal states would not have developed without ongoing reflective supervision. In the context of supervision, these new constructs were not only discussed but modeled by the supervisors.

Inquiry versus interrogation

Siegel and Hartzell (2003) discussed two patterns of connectedness that practitioners can adopt when working with clients and families. They can collaborate with clients and families through exploration (not having pre-conceived ideas or agendas), understanding (listening and hearing the other person's perspective) and joining with the other person (co-constructing clinical goals, outcomes, and decisions). This involves mutual clarity about shared goals and desired outcomes. The second pattern involves interrogating the other person, making judgments, and the desire "to fix" the other person. This pathway often leads to disconnection. Interestingly, these patterns of behavior are somewhat familiar when practitioners take an expert stance and view themselves as educators, informers, and advisors; that is, doing something "to" rather than "with" their clients and families.

Heffron and her colleagues (2005) described the power of gentle inquiry in the supervision relationship that is parallel to the practitioner–client/family relationship. The goal is to provide a safe place in which a client (or other) can express their thoughts and feelings without being put on the spot or becoming defensive (p. 332). Gentle inquiry (rather than bombarding clients or families with questions, directives or information) leaves time and space for increased self-reflection and self-awareness. In the work with this family, I learned to approach the parents through gentle inquiry and open-ended questions without making them feel uncomfortable or defensive. I also encouraged the parents to join me in figuring out goals for Nafi and (whenever possible) engaged them in the process of problem solving and decision making. The goal in working relationally was for each parent to contribute their ideas about outcomes, to find their own answers, and to become more open to new possibilities with the ongoing guidance and support of the speech-language pathologist. This process enabled all participants to share their thoughts and feelings as well as tolerate "not knowing" and also "not acting" and allowing time for solutions and new possibilities to unfold.

Strength-based perspective and reframing

An inherent aspect of relationship-based intervention is offering hope and acknowledging the capacities of the client, family member, or significant other. Many practitioners have been trained within a medical model in which the client's symptoms are eloquently detailed. A natural consequence of this deficit-oriented model has been heightened attention to the other person's developmental deficits or challenges. In the shift to relational and reflective work, the belief is that optimal developmental change occurs in an environment in which both sides are recognized – one's strengths and one's vulnerabilities (Shahmoon-Shanok, 2006).

Reframing is a skill frequently used with parents in order to provide a more positive or developmentally appropriate meaning, or interpretation, of a child's behavior (Geller & Foley, 2009b; Heffron et al., 2005). Reframing is offering a different viewpoint, or idea, about another person's actions or attributes. Parents and others may make judgments about their children that may reflect (among many other things) transference, projection, or a lack of knowledge of child development. Speech-language pathologists can help parents broaden their perspectives and entertain other possibilities about how their child's behavior may be better understood. Reframing is always done in a manner that supports the capacities of the other person and offers (whenever possible) a more strength-based perspective.

In the work with this family, each parent needed a broader perspective in which to recognize Nafi's capacities in the presence of his serious developmental vulnerabilities. Muslimah and Saleh learned to appreciate some of Nafi's unique talents and competencies. These included how he teased adults, his subtle sense of humor, his playful ways of engaging others, his affectionate side, and his increasing ability to convey his intentions. Of equal importance, each parent learned to recognize their own competencies in how they engaged, understood, and supported their son's development.

In sum, after 2½ years of intensive work, the intervention was terminated. Significant changes were observed for all participants in this process. Nafi expanded his nonverbal system of communication and used gaze, affect, gestures (etc.) to communicate a limited range of intents. Nafi initiated social games with his mother and learned to say "mama" and other Arabic words (such as "habibi" meaning loved one). The mother learned to engage her son in more joyful and playful ways. The mother saw her own strengths in new ways of being, and relating, with her son. She appreciated Nafi's growth (albeit slow) and came to share with me her thoughts, feelings, pain, sadness and grief about his profound developmental struggles. The relationship between myself and the father evolved more slowly.

REFLECTIONS

Benefits and challenges in the professional use of self

Costa (2006) stated that "the feelings and beliefs that are engendered in the helper can serve as a guide for empathy, inquiry, and intervention with the family" (p. 132). That is, the professional's use of his/her internal experiences, subjective and affective states – the self – is critically important for informing and deepening the practitioner's understanding of the clinical process and the child–parent relationship (Costa, 2006). Muslimah and Saleh showed growth in their understanding and ability to engage and be with their son in new ways. Nafi also made significant developmental changes – albeit slowly. In a parallel manner, I was able to use myself to augment and enhance the relational work that evolved with this child and his parents. In using constructs traditionally associated with mental health disciplines, and with guidance and support in supervision, I became more informed about the power of relationships to optimize developmental change in this family. I deepened my understanding of how each parent's internal states and experiences impacted on their actions, behaviors, and interactions. Additionally, I became more responsible for the latent dimensions of these relationships and how they supported (or hindered) the ongoing clinical process.

In this clinical case study, each individual in the relationship was truly transformed. I deepened my self-awareness and learned how my past history influenced and informed my current clinical perspective. My experiences in reflective supervision helped integrate this new way of working. Once these ideas become embedded with discipline-specific knowledge, there was no turning back to more traditional ways of practice. The long standing practice in which parents are excluded from clinical work may lead to parents feeling inadequate in engaging, or being, with their child. This powerful dynamic often goes unaddressed in traditional clinical practice in that parents may feel displaced and this may lead to increased resistance to the work (Geller & Foley, 2009b). The shift to relational and reflective practice clearly highlights this latent dimension of traditional speech-language therapy.

There are challenges in interweaving mental health principles with discipline-specific knowledge. Practitioners need formal training and ongoing supervision. Going against conventional practices and beliefs may cause anxiety, resistance, and some fear. Speech-language professionals learn to shift roles from doing something "to" clients to doing something "with" clients and families. Moreover, speech-language pathologists learn to respect their affective and subjective feelings and use this material to understand and inform the work. Emotions are only managed for the sake of returning to the clinical relationship in a more reflective and empathic manner. Finally, there is always the risk of knowing too little and of course, feeling too much (Costa, 2006).

In sum, the capacity to deepen self-awareness, self-reflection and self-regulation is integral to the professional use of self. As Costa (2006) stated, there are many positive outcomes to recognizing ". . . the unexamined role that the interventionist's own life and subjective experiences in the work can play in influencing all aspects of the clinical relationship from engagement to interpretation, to process of the work, and even to termination . . ." (p. 134). These capacities and skills are inherent dimensions of the professional use of self and are not reserved or limited to only those practitioners in the mental health arena.

ACKNOWLEDGMENTS

I wish to express my deep appreciation to Rebecca Shahmoon-Shanok, LCSW, PhD and Gilbert Foley, EdD for their ongoing group and individual supervision around this client and the family. A detailed and more extensive discussion of this case study can be found in Shahmoon-Shanok and Geller (2009). I also wish to express my gratitude towards Barbara Greenstein, PhD, for her continued support in implementing a relational and reflective model in speech-language pathology.

16 Burnout and self-care in the practice of speech pathology and audiology

An ecological perspective

Eleanor Ross
University of Witwatersrand, South Africa

> Burnout. The word evokes images of a final flickering flame, of a charred and empty shell, of dying embers and cold grey ashes.
>
> (Maslach, 1986, p. 3)

INTRODUCTION

Stress and burnout have been found to contribute significantly to the poor job satisfaction and retention rates of speech-language pathologists (Harris, Prater, Dyches, & Heath, 2009; Tatham, Cough, & Maxwell, 2006). These findings have implications for the future of the profession, which relies on an established professional cohort that is responsible for mentoring new graduates, creating a research culture, and consolidating the position of the profession in the community to ensure that critical speech and language therapy services are available for the growing number of persons needing these services (Whitehouse, Hird, & Cocks, 2007). For these reasons it is critical for both students and qualified speech-language pathologists and their employers to be aware of the causes, signs, and symptoms of stress and burnout as well as the self-care and prevention strategies that can be adopted to enhance health, resilience, and well-being. The story of "Terry" illustrates many of the issues addressed in this chapter.

> Terry is a speech-language therapist who graduated from university 5 years earlier. Soon after graduating, she obtained employment at an inner-city school where many of the learners present with language learning difficulties. At the time of taking up this position, Terry was passionate about her career and felt that she was achieving her true purpose in life. However, with the passage of time, she has found that she is spending an inordinate amount of time on administrative paperwork, many of the learners seem unmotivated to engage with therapy interventions and they seem to show minimal progress. Consequently, Terry is beginning to experience feelings of dissatisfaction with her job and is

starting to question whether the profession of speech-language therapy is her true calling.

WHAT IS STRESS?

Stress is caused not only by external factors or stressors, but is also generated internally by people's hopes, fears, expectations, and beliefs. Consequently, what is stressful to one person may be regarded as a challenge to another, depending on the person's perceptions of their situation, as well as their perceptions of their ability to cope with that situation (Patel, 1989).

The individual's assessment that a stressful situation exists, whether or not it appears so to an outsider, plays a crucial role in initiating a stress response. In the absence of such an appraisal there is no stress in the person's psychological schema. Furthermore, even if a situation is perceived as demanding or threatening, it may not necessarily mobilize a stress response if the individual feels that they are able to cope adequately, either on their own or with the help of external resources or support from significant others in their lives. In general, the balance arising from the interaction of these four components – external demands, internal needs and values, personal coping resources, and external resources or support – determines whether or not a particular situation will be experienced as stressful.

Once a situation has been judged as demanding or frustrating, it is likely to engender a comprehensive physiological response that has mental, emotional, physical, and behavioral components. "Stress" is therefore defined as a specific response of the body to all nonspecific demands. When people perceive that the demand exceeds their resources, their body and mind are aroused and all systems are geared up to either fight the challenge or flee from the situation in order to avoid harm. This primitive stress response prepares us for fight or flight, and involves the following biological changes.

The liver releases sugar and fats into the bloodstream, which provide immediate energy. The respiration rate increases, thereby providing more oxygen. The red blood cell supply to the bloodstream increases, carrying more oxygen to the muscles of the limbs and the brain. The heart rate increases and the blood pressure rises, enabling sufficient blood to reach the necessary areas. Blood-clotting mechanisms are activated in anticipation of injury. Whereas this response was probably beneficial in the Stone Age when people were likely to confront a saber-toothed tiger, nowadays an increased clotting tendency may cause thrombosis, leading to a heart attack or stroke. The muscles become tense in preparation for strenuous action. For example, the shoulders may be braced and the fists and jaw clenched in anticipation of a fight. Saliva dries up and digestion ceases so that blood may be diverted to the muscles and brain where it is needed more urgently. Perspiration increases so that the body may cool down in readiness for a rise in temperature when fighting. The bowel and bladder muscles may become less firm. The pupils dilate, allowing more light to enter so that the person can see better in the dark. Finally, all senses are heightened, enabling the person to make immediate decisions and take swift action.

This physiological response is also associated with mental, emotional, and behavioral changes. Mental changes vary from increased alertness and ability to make rapid decisions, to memory lapses and rash judgment. Emotional changes can include irritability, anger, fear, hostility, and even rage and fury. In terms of behavioral change, the person may become aggressive.

A certain amount of stress occurs all the time. In fact, there is no life without some degree of stress. It is also important to note that not all stress is necessarily negative or harmful. Whereas too little stress can cause boredom and frustration, a moderate or optimum amount of stress can be stimulating and represent a challenge to the person's coping skills (Germain & Gitterman, 1995). However, excessive amounts of stress or stress experienced over extended periods of time, together with ineffective coping and personal vulnerability, can cause physical ill health, poor interpersonal relations, and impaired task performance. Negative emotions and stress can lead to abnormalities in heart rhythm, which in turn can lead to reduced ability to think clearly; reduced decision-making efficiency; reduced ability to communicate; impaired physical coordination and a higher risk of heart disease and blood pressure problems (Dolny, 2009). Other adverse effects of excessive stress include a decline in productivity, absenteeism, poor industrial relations, high staff turnover, job dissatisfaction, accidents, post-traumatic stress disorders, and burnout. Hans Selye (1975), the father of stress research, described these four stages as understress, eustress, overstress, and distress respectively.

WHAT IS BURNOUT?

Burnout is conceptualized by Rushton (1987, p. 177) as "the last stage of stress," and is defined by Maslach (2003) as a syndrome of emotional exhaustion, depersonalization, and reduced personal accomplishment that can occur among individuals who work with people. According to Lubinski (2001), the four factors that tend to make the helping professions inherently stressful include: (1) the complexity of clients and their needs; (2) the difficulty in evaluating "success"; (3) poor perceptions of helping relationships by others; and (4) the decision-making process inherent in many helping relationship agencies. The phenomenon of burnout is sometimes referred to as compassion fatigue because of the emotional costs of caring for people (Figley, 2002). According to the ecological metaphor, burnout or compassion fatigue is viewed as a form of ecological dysfunction or misfit between people and their ecosystems, representing the imbalance or misfit between environmental demands and stress–coping resources (Ross, 1997).

The development of burnout

What is unique about burnout is that the stress experienced is a response to the chronic emotional strain of working extensively with people, particularly when they are experiencing problems. The person becomes emotionally overinvolved, overextends him- or herself and feels overwhelmed by the emotional demands imposed by other people. The response to this situation (and thus one dimension of burnout) is *emotional exhaustion*. Occupational demands in the form of interpersonal conflict, work overload, and role conflict also contribute to emotional exhaustion. Once people feel emotionally exhausted or depleted, they are usually unable to give of themselves to others. They may take on the role of "petty bureaucrat," doing everything according to the rules, detaching themselves psychologically, and emotionally distancing themselves from others.

With increasing detachment the person may develop an attitude of cold indifference to the needs of other people and a callous disregard for their feelings. The emergence of this detached, callous, dehumanized response heralds the appearance of the second dimension of the burnout syndrome, namely *depersonalization*. The person tends to develop a cynical opinion of other people, expecting the worst of them and even disliking them. Feeling negatively about others can progress until the person begins to feel guilty about mistrusting others and starts disliking him- or herself.

At this juncture the third dimension of burnout emerges – a feeling of *reduced personal accomplishment*. Caregivers then develop a sense of failure and inadequacy regarding their inability to relate to clients. Self-esteem is adversely affected, depression may occur and some people may seek therapy for their personal problems. Others change jobs or seek alternative employment that does not involve stressful contact with people.

> Similarly, Terry is feeling emotionally exhausted. She has lost her sense of purpose, commitment and compassion for her work at the school. Secretly, she feels glad when parents or learners cancel appointments with her. Terry no longer has faith in the learners to grow and develop. At the same time, she is aware of this cynical attitude within herself, feels guilty about these feelings and is experiencing a deep sense of failure as a therapist.

Symptoms of burnout

The more common signs and symptoms associated with burnout can be divided into three categories: physical symptoms, affective–cognitive symptoms and behavioral symptoms.

- *Physical* symptoms include: chronic fatigue, increased susceptibility to illness and infections, frequent headaches, shortness of breath, backaches, stomach aches, gastrointestinal disturbances and insomnia.

- *Affective–cognitive* symptoms include the development of a negative self-concept, suspicion, rigidity, depersonalization, cynicism, emotional lability, meaninglessness and alienation, depression, lack of motivation, the feeling that work is drudgery, the belief that one is losing one's professional effectiveness, and a sense of emotional and spiritual depletion.
- *Behavioral* symptoms include displays of anger, impatience and irritation, gallows humor, overuse of food, tobacco, alcohol, tranquillizers or sleeping tablets, difficulty in finishing tasks, reluctance to get up in the morning for work, problematic interpersonal relations at home and at work, finding it increasingly difficult to empathize with clients, reluctance to socialize, impaired concentration and job performance, increased errors and accidents and absenteeism. Other behavioral symptoms include refusal to participate in staff development programs, failure to adapt to agency changes, avoidance of specific job tasks, the making of overly critical comments about the agency and staff, displays of boredom, refusal to share agency information with new workers, an increase in general inefficiency, coming late for meetings, low morale and job satisfaction, and giving the impression of seeking to retire on the job.

Terry presents with several of these symptoms.

Terry has noticed that she has been contracting influenza and experiencing headaches more frequently than in the past. She is finding it increasingly necessary to take a mild tranquillizer to help her sleep at night. Terry is also reluctant to get up in the mornings and looks forward to weekends when she does not have to go to work.

Effects of burnout

It can thus be seen that the emotional exhaustion, depersonalization and reduced sense of personal accomplishment that characterize the syndrome of burnout and distinguish it from other stress responses are often associated with a decline in physical and psychological well-being. Moreover, the harmful effects of burnout usually go beyond the individual person. Burnout can adversely affect the caregiver's family, who may experience increased friction in the home. It can negatively affect clients and patients who receive inferior service and are treated in an uncaring manner. This phenomenon can also impact on the employing organization, which is subject to its employees' poor work performance and low productivity, and has to deal with high rates of absenteeism and staff turnover. Furthermore, burnout can adversely affect the image of a helping profession as well as its commitment and accountability to consumers.

THE ECOLOGICAL APPROACH TO STRESS AND BURNOUT

The main criticism that can be leveled against many of the American and British models of stress and burnout formulated prior to the 1990s, was that they tended to focus on deficits within the individual worker, with minimal attention paid to family factors, the work environment, or the wider social context. These theories implied that stress stemmed primarily from negative personality traits or character defects of the individual worker and his or her inability to cope with the stresses of the work environment. Consequently, stress management practices evolving from this viewpoint have tended to adopt a medico-pathological paradigm. They place emphasis on treating individuals to make them "stress fit" and productive, rather than changing and improving other ecosystems in the environment that affect the individual's subjective experience of stress (Newton, Handy, & Fineman, 1995). According to Newton et al. (1995), the effect of such approaches was to depoliticize the problem of work stress and reduce organizational issues to a question of individual differences in stress appraisal and coping ability. Newton et al. (1995) maintain that stress researchers need to place the individual worker within a historical, social, and political context. In addition, stress management programs need to go beyond individual strategies and incorporate other ecosystem interventions as well.

The ecological paradigm, with its emphasis on the interdependencies and reciprocal transactions between people and their environments or social systems (Sheafor & Horejsi, 2006), would seem to take into account the criticisms leveled against the earlier theories of stress and burnout, and provides an alternative theoretical framework for analyzing the phenomena of stress and burnout among speech-language pathologists. From an ecological perspective, causes or correlates of stress and burnout may occur within the individual person, the family and the work environment, as well as the broader sociocultural milieu.

Individual or personal stressors

Individual factors and personality characteristics play a role in the burnout process. For example, some researchers report that men are more susceptible to developing callous feelings about the people they work with and hence are more likely to experience burnout, while other studies find very little difference between the two sexes in this respect (Swidler & Ross, 1993). With regard to age, research has shown that burnout is usually lower among older and more experienced workers, although a great deal depends not only on work experience but also on the person's level of maturity and stability. Research has also established a link between burnout and personality factors such as locus of control, hardiness, and type A behavior. Individuals with an external locus of control, low levels of hardiness, and type A behavior are generally more vulnerable to stress than those with an internal locus of control, high levels of hardiness, and type B behavior (Ross, 1997). Other individual sources of stress alluded to by David Luterman (Chapter 1) and Kirsty McDonald (Chapter 13) elsewhere in this volume, include unconscious and unresolved issues on the part of professionals such as the need to be needed, the need to control, the need to feel important, and the need to rescue people, repair damage or eradicate suffering, which tend to disempower and foster dependent relationships among clients. In contrast, resilient people have an optimistic outlook, the ability to deal with their emotions, and the capacity to bounce back from stress and adversity. In a similar vein, persons with high levels of emotional intelligence are less susceptible to stress because they have the ability to recognize, manage, and use their emotions in positive and constructive ways, and to understand and communicate with others in ways that allow them to connect to other people, overcome conflict, and repair wounded feelings.

Family stressors

Stress and burnout seldom, if ever, affect only individuals. Family and work are interdependent, and stress spills over from the family life to the work milieu and from the job setting to the worker's home life (Barling, 1994). Furthermore, because the family is a complex social system, stress in one family member is likely to impact on every other family member and affect the functioning of the family as a unit. On the one hand, stress in the family or marital system can potentially increase the vulnerability of individual members to physical and emotional distress. On the other hand, a family's support for its members can act as a social buffer against the stresses and strains of daily life and can have a positive effect on coping. Moreover, although stress and burnout affect both genders, within the female-dominated professions women are particularly vulnerable to the competing demands of balancing work and family life (Lubinski, 2001). Vulnerability or resistance to stress depends largely on the interplay of psychosocial attributes of family members, the dynamics of family interactions and communications, and the problem-solving strategies established by the family (Rice, 1992).

> The interdependence of work and family is highlighted in the case of Terry. Terry has started working until late and is taking work home. The school headmaster is pressurizing her to get certain reports in on a monthly basis and Terry feels that she is not coping. Ironically, she finds that the more she works, the less she can meet her deadlines. Her family is constantly nagging her to spend more time with them and her husband has told her that he does not want her to bring work home. Her children are also complaining that she is often irritable and impatient with them.

Ross (1997) conducted a postal survey of a national sample of 637 South African social workers, followed by in-depth interviews with 50 practitioners in the Gauteng area. She found that those with one or more children reported experiencing significantly lower levels of emotional exhaustion, depersonalization and personal accomplishment than those with no children. Factors within the family system perceived by respondents to contribute to occupational stress included family career conflicts, stresses related to discussing work concerns with family members, husbands' devaluation of wives' social work career and salary, postgraduate studies, and the negative aspects of living status, i.e. living alone or with another person or persons. Factors that reduced work stress included family support and cohesion, the opportunity to ventilate and discuss work concerns with family members, and the positive aspects of living status.

Work stressors

Among the general stressors that are likely to be experienced by persons working in any setting are unclear or poorly defined work boundaries between members of staff; time pressures and heavy, emotionally demanding workloads; role conflict, i.e. when two aspects of a job are incompatible; role ambiguity, i.e. when persons have inadequate or misleading information regarding how to perform their roles; inability to influence policy and decision making within the organization; lack of autonomy and the need to observe hierarchies of authority; and poor salary, fringe benefits, status, and promotion prospects. Other work stressors include lack of support from supervisors and colleagues; conflicts with superiors and/or co-workers; unpleasant and/or unsafe physical working environments; bureaucratic procedures and restrictions, paperwork and administration; underemployment and/or limited opportunities for variety or a challenge; and lack of feedback on performance. Moreover, there is also the nature of the clientele or problems; lack of resources and facilities; responsibility, pressure, and managerial stress; stressful organizational structures (e.g. in "tall" organizations power is vested in top-level managers, whereas in "flat" organizations there is democratic sharing of power and decision making among all employees) and climates (e.g. positive climates are characterized by high levels of motivation and commitment, while negative climates are characterized by high levels of competitiveness, fear of retrenchment, budget cuts, etc.); inadequate or unsupportive supervision; lack of work experience; the employing authority, e.g. government organizations versus private clinics or practices; and finally, inadequate job security and career development (Ross, 1997).

According to Whitehouse, Hird, and Cocks (2007), job dissatisfaction among speech-language clinicians has been attributed to a number of sources, including low pay, lack of respect from colleagues, bureaucracy, lack of career progression, a mismatch between career expectations and actual career experiences, and high levels of work-related stress. Harris, Prater, Dyches, and Heath (2009) identified caseload size and salary as contributing more stress than other items on the Speech-Language-Pathologist Stress Inventory administered to 97 school-based speech-language pathologists in Utah.

Sociocultural stressors

It is important not only to consider the individual speech and hearing clinician in relation to his or her work milieu and family environment, but also to take into account the broader historical, social, and political context. For example, during the present historical juncture many South African health care practitioners are reported to be working under highly stressful conditions, exposed to high levels of crime and violence, working with very heavy caseloads, frustrated by low salaries for meeting their own needs and by inadequate resources and facilities to meet the needs of communities racked by high rates of poverty, unemployment, housing shortages, and family breakdown. For example, the shortage of qualified speech-language pathologists and audiologists needed to cater for the vast number of persons with communication disorders suggests that many of these therapists are probably working with excessively high caseloads. Internationally, the global economic recession with its accompanying retrenchments and budget cuts, is likely to impact on the stress levels of speech-language clinicians in many parts of the world.

BURNOUT IN SPEECH-LANGUAGE PATHOLOGY AND AUDIOLOGY

Burnout can occur in any occupation. However, certain professions have been identified as being especially vulnerable to burnout, for example lawyers (Maslach & Jackson, 1978), police (Maslach & Jackson, 1979), teachers (Fimian & Blanton, 1987), nurses (Fimian, Fastenau, & Thomas, 1988), social workers (Arches, 1991) and speech-language pathologists (Fimian, Lieberman, & Fastenau, 1991).

Among the earliest studies of burnout among speech-language pathologists was a survey conducted by Miller and Potter in 1982. As many as 43% of participants considered themselves to have experienced moderately severe burnout. Statistically significant correlations were found relating degree of burnout to the effect of job status on personal life, job satisfaction, job effectiveness, and the lack of availability of management and support services for coping. It is of interest that burnout was not related to setting, years of employment, caseload, client severity level, paperwork demands, or collegial relationships.

In 1993, Swidler and Ross conducted a postal survey of burnout among a national sample of 202 South African dual-qualified speech and hearing therapists. The main finding was that, as a group, speech-language pathologists and audiologists were experiencing moderate levels of emotional exhaustion and low levels of depersonalization as well as high levels of personal accomplishment. These findings suggest that despite feeling emotionally exhausted, therapists could still derive a sense of accomplishment from the work and did not necessarily experience negative attitudes towards clients. Those most susceptible to burnout were therapists working in hospitals, mainly treating peripheral hearing disorders, working either as audiologists only or as speech therapists and audiologists, with heavy caseloads and extensive paperwork, and perceiving themselves to be under large amounts of work pressure (Swidler & Ross, 1993).

Common work stressors included the writing of detailed reports; bureaucratic rules; inspections; poor progress made with clients using the groupwork method in schools; poor cooperation with teachers, parents and therapists; pressure to achieve rapid results; working in isolation in private practices; financial handling of private practice; lack of training in certain areas of treatment; culturally inappropriate test materials; insufficient knowledge and understanding of the profession on the part of the public and other disciplines; time pressures; and feeling ill-equipped to provide counseling to clients and family members with emotional difficulties – particularly severely impaired patients who showed little improvement (Swidler & Ross, 1993).

Sociocultural stressors included poor progress made by children from disadvantaged socioeconomic backgrounds, irregular attendance by clients at therapy, not being able to treat patients who could not afford to pay clinic fees, reduction of available posts in the public sector, low salaries, riots and political unrest, lack of reliable transport to and from the townships, political differences among co-workers, difficulties in working with clients from different cultural and language groups, language barriers between teachers and therapists, difficulties in obtaining medical histories from grandparents who functioned as primary caregivers, and frustration with parents who only brought their children for assessment at a late age (Swidler & Ross, 1993).

More recently, Poche, Tassin, Oliver, and Fellows (2004) studied 120 licensed speech-language pathologists working in public schools in Louisiana and found that the top five stressors were: too much paperwork; inadequate salary; no time to relax; easily overcommitted; and no time to get things done. They explain that speech-language pathologists are responsible for screenings, evaluations, individual education plans, daily progress notes, Medicaid forms, lesson plans, 6-week progress reports, teacher–parent consults, and classroom modifications. "When these demands are multiplied by 50-plus students, the paperwork becomes overwhelming. Therefore, speech-language pathologists often are not able to prepare adequately and have time for personal priorities and to relax, which can lead to job stress and burn-out" (p. 16).

In 2006 Tatham et al. surveyed a group of speech therapists within one regional health authority in the UK and found that they reported high levels of stress. Although large numbers were happy in their jobs, a significant number wished to leave.

In a review of the literature, Whitehouse et al. (2007) noted that former speech and language clinicians emphasized professional dissatisfaction stemming from poor pay, lack of career progression, lack of respect from colleagues, increasing bureaucracy, a mismatch between career expectations and actual career experiences, and high levels of work stress.

STRATEGIES FOR MANAGING STRESS AND PREVENTING BURNOUT

Whereas earlier writers suggested very poor prognoses for persons suffering from burnout, more recent researchers maintain that such an episode can be the beginning of an important learning experience in that it can be a stimulus for becoming aware of other problems, for assessing these problems, for developing new coping strategies and for being transfigured in the process. However, it is imperative that both management and employees implement strategies for reducing stress and burnout.

Because stress and burnout affect all areas of life, the ecological approach to stress management adopts a multidimensional program that incorporates interventions at the level of the individual or personal system, the family system, the work system, and the broader societal system in order to enhance the "fit" between people and their ecological environments (Ross, 1997). It has been suggested that health care practitioners keep a stress diary and do a stress audit whereby they take stock of their lives, assess their strengths and weaknesses, and determine in what life domains they experience stress. They need to assess the level and intensity of stress, evaluate the extent to which they themselves are responsible for increasing their stress levels, and prioritize the stressors that need attention. Thereafter they need to formulate a creative self-care and stress management plan that incorporates any or all of the different systems or life domains including individual, family, work, and societal interventions (Ross & Deverell, 2004).

Individual interventions

Individual interventions can be subdivided further into the cognitive, emotional, social, spiritual-philosophical and physical dimensions.

The cognitive dimension

It is important for clinicians to be knowledgeable regarding what constitutes burnout, its signs and symptoms, how it develops, and how it can be prevented. Intellectual or mental strategies that can be utilized by therapists for managing stress include cognitive restructuring, systematic desensitization, thought-stopping, reframing, problem solving, reading, studying, and attending seminars and workshops.

The emotional dimension

The provision of opportunities for ventilation of feelings, support from team members and the development of coping capacities can reduce the emotional strain of working in the area of health care. Staff may then be able to treat clients competently and with commitment and compassion. In order to promote self-awareness and regulate counter-transference responses, practitioners need to have access to skilled individual supervision, consultation, workshops, seminars and support groups where participants can ventilate and examine feelings, increase knowledge, work through concerns, and derive emotional support and a sense of connectedness with other health care practitioners. Kirsty McDonald in Chapter 13 on transference, also underscores the need for self-awareness to moderate involvement with individual clients and their families.

Furthermore, by helping practitioners to set realistic expectations for treatment goals, by varying caseloads – if this is at all feasible – so that staff are not overloaded with end-stage patients with very poor prognoses for growth and improvement, and by including challenging cases, supervisors can help reduce the emotional strain of working with terminally ill, severely disabled, or emotionally demanding persons.

It can also be helpful to engage in "timeout" work-related activities, away from direct clinical service, such as committee work, lunchtime discussions, continuing education programs, and special projects to give staff some respite from highly stressful, emotionally depleting work. Other stress-management strategies include problem solving, goal setting, time management, lifestyle assessment, decision making and conflict resolution. Humor can also be very effective in relieving tension.

The social dimension

Ongoing social support is a critical factor in helping therapists to avoid burnout and maintain mental health. It has been noted in the literature that health care professionals who experience a sense of isolation, minimal contact with others who are exposed to similar problems, and who lack opportunities to express emotionally charged feelings, are more likely to develop burnout. In contrast, the availability of support from co-workers, spouses and significant others is often associated with low levels of stress and burnout. It is therefore imperative that supervisors and directors of employing organizations incorporate staff support groups into the routine work week and encourage all employees to attend group sessions. Networking and training in assertiveness and interpersonal skills can also help alleviate stresses inherent in this type of work.

Morale-building activities such as staff retreats, award dinners and family events can also help to meet the social needs of professionals. In addition, participation in social and cultural activities and pastimes and the availability of supportive social networks can help caregivers achieve a balance between work, and home and leisure-time activities.

The spiritual-philosophical dimension

According to Hammer and Marting (1988), the spiritual-philosophical dimension refers to values derived from religious, familial, or cultural tradition or from personal philosophy. Such values may serve to define the meaning of potentially stressful events and provide strategies for responding to these.

Working with patients who are severely impaired, terminally ill or who have poor prognoses for change and development, tends to challenge professionals to think about illness, death, and mortality. Skilled supervision, group support, debriefing, meditation and prayer can potentially help clinicians explore "some of the most profound questions of human existence pertaining to the value of life and relationships, and how one chooses to live" (Shernoff, 1990, p. 7). Meditation and time alone can also promote a sense of renewal. The spiritual dimension is elaborated upon in Chapter 17.

The physical dimension

Physical well-being, stamina and fitness can potentially decrease the level of negative response to stress and facilitate more rapid recovery. Physical strategies for managing stress include regular exercise, timeout, sleep and rest, a nutritionally balanced diet, a hot bath, jacuzzi or sauna, massage, progressive relaxation, autogenic training, meditation, yoga, visualization and imagery, and biofeedback.

Family interventions

Maslach (1986, p. 106) maintains that family, friends and acquaintances are important allies in the battle against burnout. Although tension and conflict are normal occurrences in any human relationship, family and friends are also a potential source of help and comfort, of recognition and rewards, of good feelings and pleasurable experiences, and provide informal opportunities to talk through difficulties. A recurrent finding in the research literature is the importance of a good marriage or intimate relationship in handling burnout, as the emotional support provided by such a relationship may counterbalance the emotional stresses emanating from the job. For this reason, it is important to build supportive family relationships to help cope with stress and prevent burnout.

In view of the deleterious effect that work stresses and strains can have on family relationships, Maslach (2003) suggests that people should regard their work and home as two different environments and endeavor to make a transition from one domain to the other. She uses the analogy of a diver who needs to make a gradual transition from a high-pressure environment and decompress before resurfacing from a deep descent. She also recommends establishing clear boundaries between job and home, not bringing work home and not allowing oneself to be continually "on call."

Work interventions

Stress-coping interventions at the work-environment level should ideally focus on changing or improving the individual's skills in coping with occupational stress, as well as changes in the work environment itself. Planning ahead and goal setting can help to minimize the stress of the unknown. Effective time management can help one find harmony or balance in the use of time, which can enhance personal productivity on the job and also provide one with more time for exercise, recreation, hobbies, and other leisure-time pursuits. Rice (1992, p. 359) advises any time management program to start with a personal inventory of how time is being used or (mis)managed. Some of the most common forms of time mismanagement are lack of clarity about one's goals, and failing to make decisions that need to be made, trying to do more than is necessary or possible, procrastinating, avoiding unpleasant duties and striving for perfectionism.

Rice (1992) recommends listing objectives that need to be accomplished in long-term, intermediate and short-term periods, and thereafter arranging them from most to least important. More time should be invested in the most important or top priority items, and assertiveness skills used to refuse additional requests. Larger jobs can be broken up into smaller, more manageable tasks. Distractions can be reduced by contracting with oneself to work on a certain task for a set period or until one has achieved a certain objective, and avoiding the use of open-door policies that allow for constant interruptions. It can also be helpful to keep a "to do" list and mark off each item as it is completed. Other time management strategies include delegating tasks to others, scanning material instead of reading through everything in great detail, and keeping a diary so that one can keep track of commitments.

Within the work environment, other important avenues for stress management are high-quality supervision and consultation (emphasized by Kirsty McDonald in Chapter 13 on transference), both formal and informal colleague support, ongoing training, keeping the work varied and stimulating and, if possible, reducing the workload. In addition, it can be helpful to take regular breaks from technology in the form of emails, one's cell phone and laptop.

Societal interventions

Some of the more common societal stress-coping strategies include managing change, and community involvement. For example, there is general consensus that change in organizations should be planned, and that supervisors and managers need to provide support for staff and show empathy for the difficulties that change generates for them (Weinbach, 1994). Community involvement can be a potential source of support for many professional persons. For example, Quick, Nelson, and Quick (1990) studied a group of executives and found that volunteer and civic work is often a source of joy and pride, and offers timeout from job stress.

It can thus be seen that interventions at the personal, family, work, and societal levels can potentially help reduce stress and prevent burnout among health care professionals.

Swidler and Ross (1993) investigated the stress-coping strategies of their sample of South African speech-language pathologists and audiologists. Common techniques utilized involved regular exercise, time away from work, religious practices, as well as careful planning and organization of work schedules and demands. Some negative strategies such as smoking, overeating, and drinking large quantities of coffee were also reported.

THE VALUE OF STRESS MANAGEMENT IN PROMOTING HEALTH

Patel (1989, p. xi) highlights the following potential benefits of stress management:

- reduced level of anxiety;
- lowered blood pressure;
- a decrease in the intensity and frequency of headaches;
- better quality of sleep;
- reduced risk of heart attacks;
- better relationships with people at work;
- improved general health;
- greater enjoyment of life;
- enhanced personal and family relationships;
- greater physical energy;
- better sex life;
- improved concentration and performance at work;
- enhanced sense of well-being;
- better social life.

Dolny (2009, p. 41) adds the following benefits of effective stress management:

- improved creativity and problem solving;
- better decision making;
- greater flexibility in the way we think;
- improved memory; and
- enhanced immunity to disease.

CONCLUSION

In essence, the management of stress and the prevention of burnout are encapsulated in the following poem by an unknown author.

Take time to work. It is the price of success.
Take time to think. It is the source of power.
Take time to play. It is the secret of perennial youth.
Take time to read. It is the road to wisdom.
Take time to be friendly. It is the road to happiness.
Take time to dream. It is hitching your wagon to a star.
Take time to love and be loved. It is the privilege of the gods.
Take time to look around. It is too short a day to be selfish.
Take time to laugh. It is the music of the soul.
Take time to live!

17 Spiritual dimensions of the clinical relationship

Cindy S. Spillers
University of Minnesota Duluth

INTRODUCTION

The word "spirituality" has not yet entered the formal lexicon of speech-language pathologists and audiologists in North America. Within the past 10 years two articles in mainstream American Speech-Language-Hearing Association (ASHA) journals have broached this topic. Silverman's guest editorial in the *ASHA Leader* (2003a) offered speech and hearing professionals a debut invitation to consider the spiritual dimensions of their work. My (2007) article in the *American Journal of Speech-Language Pathology* (*AJSLP*) used existential and grief theories to describe some of the spiritual dimensions of clients' experiences with their communication disorders. Both authors invited speech-language pathologists and audiologists to look beyond the obvious and measurable, and to recognize other dimensions at work in the clinical relationship.

Spirituality is amorphous and messy, with no defined boundaries. Its resistance to measurement and quantification unsettles many clinicians due to the profession's heavy emphasis on all things objective and empirical. The emphasis on the objective and measurable is certainly necessary for designing and executing efficacious assessment and treatment procedures (see Chapter 11). However, when any profession trains its eyes only on that which it knows how to see, it risks being like the person looking under the street lamp for her/his wallet, even though s/he lost it in the dark alley around the corner. Albert Einstein is credited with saying that not everything that matters can be measured. Such a statement from a Nobel Laureate can give science-based disciplines permission to look beyond what they already know how to measure in order to make the acquaintance of elements they do not yet know. Spirituality is one such element whose acquaintance can open up new vistas in clinical practice for this profession. This chapter introduces professionals to some of the spiritual elements befogged in the clinical relationship. It offers only an introduction with no assumptions about completeness or definitiveness. The theme of journeys runs through the chapter, culminating in an introduction to a common metaphor for the spiritual journey. The story of "Alonso" a 22-year-old male who stutters, illustrates many issues addressed in the chapter.

WHY SPIRITUALITY?

The Western health care system is in the midst of a renaissance involving a return to the body–mind–spirit model of health and healing. Disciplines such as medicine, nursing, palliative care, occupational therapy, psychology, and social work have focussed increasing attention on the role of a person's spiritual experiences in her/his recovery from disease and disability (Handzo & Koenig, 2004; Hilsman, 1997; Perez, 2004; Remen, 1996). Western medicine's penchant for separating the body from the mind and spirit may actually conflict with the natural healing processes of humans (Perez, 2004). Several authors (e.g. Hilsman, 1997; Perez, 2004; Spillers, 2007) independently argued that a client's unaddressed spiritual needs may interfere with long-term positive treatment outcomes. Further, Schulz (2005) suggested that people with disabilities want their spirituality addressed by the professionals from whom they receive services, particularly those closely involved with their rehabilitation.

As a critical dimension of our humanness, spirituality weaves itself into our daily experiences, both the mundane and the cataclysmic. Traumatic life events, such as a stroke or head injury, often invoke a crisis in meaning and initiate a grief response (Luboshitzky, 2008; Spillers, 2007). Difficult life circumstances, such as living with stuttering or hearing impairment, may also engender a crisis in meaning (Luboshitzky, 2008; Spillers, 2007), with or without accompanying grief. People sometimes struggle to answer questions of why they have a disability and what their future holds (Luboshitzky, 2008; Schulz, 2005). One's spiritual beliefs and experiences help them answer these questions and influence the answers at which they arrive. Such questions can arise in the normal course of assessment and treatment with clients (Spillers, 2007). Therefore, it behooves speech-language pathologists and audiologists to visit these questions with their clients in order to understand the totality of the client's experience and to offer comprehensive, effective services.

Yet many practitioners show reluctance, even fear, at the prospect of talking about such issues with clients. Kirsh, Dawson, Antolikova, and Reynolds (2001) found that most occupational therapists and occupational therapy students believed spirituality to be an important dimension in clients' therapeutic experiences, but gave it less attention than mental, physical, and sociocultural dimensions of clients. Although the vast majority of occupational therapists surveyed believed that illness and disability can affect an individual's spirituality, only about half of those surveyed believed that addressing clients' spiritual issues was within their scope of practice. Kirsh et al.'s (2001) review of research in occupational therapy uncovered four common reasons for occupational therapists' reluctance to broach the spirituality conundrum with clients:

1   lack of academic preparation;
2   lack of time or opportunity to address such issues during treatment sessions;

3   outside of their scope of practice;
4   difficulty thinking about and expressing one's own spirituality makes it even more difficult to address such issues with another person.

Many speech-language pathologists and audiologists probably share these sentiments. In addition, we can add a fifth reason for the reluctance of professionals to broach spirituality with clients: lack of concreteness and objectivity. Spirituality's amorphous nature makes it difficult to name and quantify with currently acceptable measuring tools.

DEFINING TERMS

Burkhardt and Nagai-Jacobson (2002) likened defining spirituality to trying to lasso the wind: neither has tangible substance that boundaries can contain, yet both exert unmistakable influence on the world around them. Defining spirituality takes on added dimensions of difficulty in Western Judeo-Christian cultures because of the religious overtones that suffuse it. Many people view spirituality and religion as one and the same. Although a person's spirituality and religion may intertwine and inform each other, they are not the same and require differentiation.

Differentiating between spirituality and religion

Spirituality has two central dimensions: *meaningfulness* and *relationship*. The search for meaningfulness includes the way in which we fulfill what we believe to be our life's purpose (D'Souza, 2007; Frankl, 1959/2006; Luboshitzky, 2008). Meaningfulness is the fundamental way in which we relate to our lives and find meaning in life events and circumstances. Relationship, as a dimension of spirituality, includes our relationship to a higher power, to nature, to others, and to ourselves (Pesut, 2002). Part of our purpose in life lies in the quality and nature of these relationships. Spirituality helps us deal with the invisible elements of life that we can neither see nor control. It can provide the means for stepping beyond the immediate, personal experiences and relationships of life to see the universal and transcendent meaning in those experiences and relationships (Young-Eisendrath, 1996). Finding meaning in experiences, particularly experiences of change and suffering, is one of the most salient contributions of spirituality to the therapeutic relationship.

Most theologians and philosophers view spirituality as an innate and fundamental characteristic of the individual. Religion, on the other hand, is usually seen as a human construct arising out of the human imagination. Religions involve formal, human-constructed, institutionalized beliefs, rituals, practices, and doctrines (Delaney, 2005; Hodge, 2001; Koenig, 2004; Winslow & Wehtje-Winslow, 2007). Burkhardt and Nagai-Jacobson (2002) suggest that religion often serves as an expression of spirituality but is not part of our essential nature. Many people describe themselves as spiritual but not religious, demonstrating their innate need to understand their purpose in life without ascribing to a religious doctrine to find that meaning. Religion, then, manifests as external and social; spirituality, as internal and private.

Soul

Soul is another enigmatic facet of our humanness that evades definition. Poets through the ages have written about the numinous and mysterious nature of the soul. The thirteenth-century poet, Rumi, tells us that "soul cannot be / contained by the sky" (1999a, p. 79). In the early fourteenth century, Meister Eckhart (2002) described the soul as an oasis: "An oasis / for all life the soul becomes / when it is unveiled" (p. 104). St. John of the Cross's sixteenth-century poem, *Dig Here the Angel Said*, beautifully describes the freedom released by mining the fearfulness and worry that overlay the treasures of our souls: "Finding our soul's beauty does that – gives us / tremendous freedom/ from worry./ 'Dig here,' the angel said – / 'in your soul, / in your/ soul.' " (2002, pp. 326–327). More recently, Mary Oliver's poem, *Some Questions You Might Ask* (1992, p. 65), is an ode to the complexity and confusion wrought by examining our modern-day assumptions about what the soul is and who has one:

> Who has it, and who doesn't?
> I keep looking around me.
> The face of the moose is as sad
> as the face of Jesus.

Soul makes itself known through images, metaphors, stories, and impressions (Moore, 1992; Palmer, 2004) not easily recognized under the analytical and logical microscope of the mind. Yet we intuitively know when something has soul (Moore, 1992). We speak of a musician playing with soul or of a person speaking from the depth of her/his soul. The Irish attune to the soul of the landscape (O'Donohue, 1997). To describe something as soulful brings to mind genuineness, authenticity, and depth. When something comes from the soul it arises from that deep interior, that hidden and protected space of the heart.

Hafiz (2002) uses the metaphor of a rose to describe soul in his poem *How Did the Rose* (p. 161), asking how the rose finds the courage to reveal its hidden beauty to the world. Courage comes from feeling gentleness and acceptance "Otherwise we all remain too/frightened" (Hafiz, 2002, p. 161). Palmer uses the metaphor of a wild animal reminding us that wild animals are savvy and resilient, yet also exceedingly shy and wary (Palmer, 2004). To catch a glimpse, however brief and partial, one must steal quietly and slowly into the animal's habitat and wait (Palmer, 2004). So it is with soul. For soul to reveal itself, we must create spaces in which it feels invited, safe, and respected (O'Donohue, 1997). Even then, the rose may not open or the animal may appear as an indistinct shadow for the briefest of moments.

Palmer (2004) cautions that we have become quite adept at creating spaces inviting to the intellect, the emotions, and the ego, but not the soul. His statement probably describes most of the clinical relationships sculpted by speech and hearing professionals. Rarely does the speech pathologist or audiologist create a place for soul to appear in the relationship with a client. Even if soul does reveal itself for a moment, clinicians may not recognize it as such and may be inclined to respond intellectually or emotionally. In the case of Alonso (see below), for example, soul may have tried to emerge from hiding in the picture that he drew of his stuttering and in talking about his deep dislike of his stuttering. Viewing his fear and dislike of his stuttering as something to fix through systematic and rigorous desensitization may send his soul back into hiding. Such an approach might disallow Alonso an opportunity to face the shadow that chases him and discover the oasis hidden behind its veil – the oasis that can offer him freedom from his fear and worry.

CASE STUDY OF ALONSO

"Alonso" is the fictitious name of a person who stutters, created from the stories of several people who stutter. Alonso is a 22-year-old male, journalism student, who stutters. He said that he chose journalism because he enjoys writing; however, he did not realize that interviewing people was such an integral part of a journalist's job. Alonso's stuttering would be considered interiorized because he demonstrates very few outward stuttering behaviors. He reported and demonstrated his avoidance strategies of pausing, using fillers, circumlocutions, and changing words. Initially Alonso reported that his stuttering did not bother him very much. He enrolled in therapy to learn how to control the few outward stuttering behaviors that he does have so that he "doesn't embarrass himself" while interviewing people as a journalist. Alonso's family had immigrated to the United States from Brazil when he was about 12 years old. He reported that he stutters more in Portuguese than he does in English because "English has so many words that mean the same thing. It's much easier to change words." He scored very high on assessments of fear and avoidance. As therapy got underway, the strength of his fear, embarrassment, and shame became increasingly evident. Commonly with interiorized stuttering, the person perceives the penalty of stuttering to be so high that s/he dares not risk showing the stuttering outwardly. In talking about his stuttering, Alonso rarely used the word "stuttering," and referred to it with the indefinite pronoun, "It," with a capital "I," as if it had its own identity. When asked to draw a picture of his stuttering, he drew a picture of himself running, with a large, dark shadow chasing him (see Figure 17.1). As he talked more about his stuttering, Alonso reported that he hated his

Figure 17.1 Alonso's picture of his stuttering.
Note: This picture is a recreation drawn by Shelley Norden.

stuttering so much that he could not bear to acknowledge it. He continued explaining that if he were to let his stuttering out in the open, people would not like him and would reject him. Alonso reported that nobody else in his family stutters. His family never talked about it, except to pray that God would take it away. When he was in about the second grade, Alonso said that he asked a priest what to do about his stuttering, and the priest told him to pray the rosary every night, asking God to take it away. Alonso did this until he was in about fourth grade, and reported giving up the idea that God would take his stuttering away. By the time he and his family immigrated, Alonso said he no longer believed in God. He remembered hearing his grandmother remark that God had chosen him for some reason, but it seemed to Alonso that he was not chosen for positive, benefi-cent reasons.

SPIRITUAL DIMENSIONS OF THE PERSON

Differentiation, interiority, communion

The cosmologist Brian Swimme suggested that three primal principles of the universe surface in all things, characterizing everything from planets to trees to humans: *differentiation, interiority,* and *communion* (*An Amazing Journey,* 2004a, 2004b, 2004c; Conlon, 2004). These three patterns work in concert, present and evident at all times; one cannot work without the other two.

Differentiation

According to Swimme (2004a), the first activity of the universe was differentiation: each element in the universe and each species differentiated itself from every other element and species. Within each category of elements and species, each member becomes a separate and different entity from every other member (Swimme, 2004a). Differentiation means that neither two snowflakes nor two clients are exactly alike. We readily intellectualize this principle, numbing us to its truth. Since the mind appreciates organization and patterns, humans tend to look for similarities that allow us to group people and things together, make predictions, and respond accordingly. Bureaucratic systems in which we work encourage the minimizing of differentiation by focussing on labels and illness, overlooking the human experience of suffering (see Chapter 2).

Differentiation requires us to acknowledge our separateness from others and recognize our existential aloneness (Spillers, 2007; Tillich, 1980; Yalom, 1980). As a unique entity, separate and apart from all other entities, an unbridgeable gap exists between us and the rest of the world (Yalom, 1980). To be differentiated and solitary does not mean to be isolated, however. Palmer (2004) defines solitude as never living apart from *ourselves*, rather than as living apart from others. In our solitude we can be fully present to ourselves, whether or not we are with other people.

For Alonso, although his stuttering may superficially resemble the stuttering of other people who stutter, he has his own unique experience with it and his own unique story. Some of his discomfort with his stuttering may stem from his perception of how it separates him from others, leading to a feeling of isolation. By interiorizing his stuttering, Alonso may be living apart from himself, hiding that part from himself and from the world. The estrangement from self may actually cause deeper distress than the isolation from others that he feels (Chapter 2).

Interiority

Swimme suggests that the second task of the universe was to develop interiority wherein each differentiated entity must discover and then become its whole, true self (Surette, 2004; Swimme, 2004b). Interiority describes the notion that each separate and differentiated thing has an internal dimension that is not apparent from the outside. Palmer (2004) uses Thomas Merton's notion of "hidden wholeness," suggesting that only a small fraction of a person or thing can be known to the outside world. Hafiz's poem speaks of the interiority of the rose; its deepest beauty lies hidden unless it opens itself to the world (Hafiz, 2002).

Discovering our interiority means discovering our true self, rather than the ego-ideals whom we think we should be (Bausch, 1999; Moore, 1992). The true self cradles our shadow of brokenness and woundedness that we try to hide from ourselves. In order to welcome the true self with all of its imperfection and brokenness, we may need to let go of those ideals that we hold out for ourselves. The letting go of ideal images represents a symbolic death of the selves whom we never were and will not become (Yalom, 1980).

The wild animal of soul dwells in the deep recesses of this hidden true self, making the discovery of our hidden wholeness a soul-making journey. Because of our differentiation, this journey of discovering our true self is ours alone to make, thus invoking our existential aloneness and responsibility (Morena, 2001; Myss, 1997; Spillers, 2007; Yalom, 1980). The work of this journey can lead to finding meaning (Yalom, 1980), because mining our interiority and discovering our wholeness help us to recognize our purpose in life. Our greatest gift to ourselves and to the world may be the unfolding of this hidden whole self and bringing it forward in our daily lives (Moore, 1992; Palmer, 2004; Surette, 2004; Swimme, 2004b).

Interiority reminds us of the hidden mystery within each client and within ourselves. Clinicians can see only the client's outer presence, often dominated by the presenting communication problem. Single-minded focus on fixing the external communication problem can create an environment inviting to intellect yet hostile to the delicate rose of soul. Such external focus may circumvent clients' attempts to mine their deep interiors and emerge with a new sense of wholeness. Had Alonso's clinician focussed her attention exclusively on the purpose and logistics of desensitizing his communication fears, she might have denied Alonso an opportunity to step beyond his immediate experience of stuttering to find transcendent meaning. Transcendent meaning might include gifts and virtues available through stuttering and through the clinical relationship. And she, herself may never glimpse the beauty of the man gazing out from behind that stuttering.

Communion

Communion allows each separated being to share its hidden wholeness with others. Even as solitary individuals, we cannot live in total isolation because we share an interconnection with each other and with the rest of the universe (Swimme, 2004c). Rumi pondered the seeming contradiction between differentiation and communion: "I wonder myself / How can I be separated and yet in union?" (1999b, p. 62).

In Hafiz's poem, communion occurs with the rose's opening to share its beauty with the world. The belonging that communion offers can shelter us from the vastness of the differentiated universe as well as the vastness of our own deep interiors (O'Dononhue, 1999). Through our relationships with others we can experience our aloneness without feeling an accompanying emotional loneliness.

The therapeutic relationship can be an act of communion, giving clients and clinicians a sense of belonging and well-being. The relationship does not inherently nourish the need to belong, however, and sometimes contributes to clients' feelings of alienation and isolation (Fourie, 2009). To offer belonging, Alonso's relationship with his clinician must allow him to explore his interior self and touch the wounding that accompanies his communication disorder. The relationship must honor the "grace of broken places" (Bausch, 1999, p. 15) surrounding his stuttering.

Relationship between spirituality and disability

The spiritual dimension of well-being allows us to negotiate the limitations and unknowns of life, opening the door for finding meaning in those elements of life that we cannot control (Hilsman, 1997). Our spirituality compels us to ask substantive questions about our purpose and the order of things. Events and circumstances in our lives impinge upon our spiritual nature as much as they impinge upon our physical and emotional natures. Traumatic life events are often accompanied by a crisis in meaning in which major life questions loom large before us (Luboshitzky, 2008; Spillers, 2007). What happened here? Why? Who am I now? How am I supposed to live my life now? These are the types of questions one asks before embarking on a spiritual journey. Making our way through these questions can take us on that journey to the soul, giving us the opportunity to recognize our differentiation from others, to explore our vast interiors, and to feel acutely our interconnectedness with others. This soul-making journey also affords us the opportunity to transcend our own pain and suffering, finding compassion and renewal (Young-Eisendrath, 1996).

Schulz pursued the question of spirituality in relation to disability (Schulz, 2005). She interviewed 12 adults with disabilities, 6 with childhood-onset disabilities and 6 with adult onset. For both groups spirituality seemed to hold a significant place in relation to their disability, with notable differences between the groups. For most of the people in the childhood-onset group, their disability served as an avenue for connecting to a higher power. This group also reported finding a sense of purpose and meaning in their disabilities early in their lives (Schulz, 2005).

The individuals with adult-onset disabilities saw their conditions as a call to awakening (Schulz, 2005). They reported grappling with questions of "why" and "what now" (differentiation) leading them to self-reflection (interiority) and connection, or re-connection, to self, others, and a higher power (communion). All participants viewed their disabilities positively (Schulz, 2005). They spoke readily of how their disabilities helped shape their lives, gave their lives meaning, and provided opportunities to learn and grow.

The subjects in Schulz's study evidenced signs of resilience (Bonanno, 2004; Young-Eisendrath, 1996). Bonanno posits a variety of pathways to resilience, one of which he calls "hardiness" (Bonanno, 2004). He attributes three dimensions to hardiness: (1) commitment to finding meaningful purpose in life; (2) belief that one can influence one's surroundings and the outcomes of events; and (3) belief that one can learn and grow from positive and negative experiences in life. These dimensions of meaning, self-direction, and growth may arise from one's spiritual center. Schulz's participants spoke frequently about finding meaning and growing from their experiences (2005). They evidenced self-direction as they spoke about assuming responsibility for how they respond to their disabilities and about being pro-active and advocating for themselves.

Grieving

Many people with disabilities find themselves engaged in grieving at some point. As a normal human response to loss, grief allows a person to separate from the loss and make sense out of it (Moses, 1989; Schneider, 1984; Spillers, 2007). In disability, grief represents the individual's struggle to confront a symbolic death and loss of a future dream (Luterman, 2001; Moses, 1989). The parents of the child with autism may need to grieve the lost dream of the perfect whole child so that they can recognize the uniqueness and value of the child they have (Crowe, 1997; Luterman, 2001; Moses, 1989). Alonso may need to accept the symbolic death of his fluent self and reconcile with the self who stutters.

The work of change is embedded in the grief response and change often initiates a dance with loneliness. Change and grief can feel like very lonely places for two reasons. First, they require us to relinquish what feels safe and familiar in exchange for something unfamiliar and foreign. Second, change and grief hold the mirror that reflects our differentiation and individuation back to us. No one can make the changes for us; change is our work to do and we bear the responsibility for doing that work. Remen (1996) found loneliness to be a common experience among people with cancer. Many of her patients had commented to her that their experiences with illness had made them aware of a life-long disconnection from others. Through the isolating experience of their illnesses, many had begun the slow healing of their own loneliness, rediscovering their pervasive interconnectedness with others. Their experiences suggest that change and grief offer us opportunities for communion.

The work of change and loneliness can manifest in feelings of anxiety, fear, and depression associated with grieving (Moses, 1989; Spillers, 2007). In Moses' model of grieving, anxiety allows individuals to gather their stores of energy, fear beckons them to take the journey inward where they will do the difficult work of change, and depression allows them to touch that deep inner emptiness and begin the work (Moses, 1989; Spillers, 2007). The work of the grieving state of depression involves recreating one's understanding of self and one's role in the world (see Chapter 11).

The states of grieving share names with common emotions such as denial, depression, anxiety, fear, and anger. Consequently, if clinicians see grieving only as an emotional course they may miss its fundamental spiritual nature. Grieving offers a path to the soul, and the work of redefining the self and creating a meaningful life is soul work. Moses (1989) suggests that grieving must be done with a significant other person. This other person becomes the antidote to the isolation of grief by offering the interconnectedness of communion and by being the vessel to contain the grieving person's story. To offer belonging and to become that vessel, professionals must learn to create spaces inviting to the soul.

SUFFERING, DISABILITY, AND SPIRITUALITY

Grief, loss, meaning, resilience, and transcendence, all coalesce in the alchemical crucible of suffering. Through pain, grief, and suffering, we can transmute loss into insight, compassion, wisdom, and intimacy – what Young-Eisendrath (1996) calls the "gifts of suffering." Perhaps no experiences bring us closer to our separateness (differentiation) and aloneness (individuation) than experiences of suffering (O'Donohue, 1999; Younger, 1995). And perhaps no experiences hold the possibility of intimacy (communion) through compassion, growth, and transfiguration as much as suffering (O'Donohue, 1999; Young-Eisendrath, 1996; Younger, 1995). Many poets through the ages have written of suffering as well as of soul. It is the soul that suffers in times of difficulty and need. In his poem, *Undressing*, Rumi recognizes the alchemy of suffering and its invitation to transformation when he tells readers: ". . . the moment you accept what/troubles you've been given, the door/will open. Welcome difficulty . . ." (Rumi, 1999c, p. 65).

Western culture tends to see suffering as a negative anomaly, something harmful, and assiduously work to remove it as soon as possible (Luboshitzky, 2008; Moore, 1992). With its focus on curing disease and restoring function, our Western allopathic health care system seems to invest a great deal of money and effort into reducing and eliminating people's suffering. The ethic of our health care system may reinforce our disdain for and shame about any pain or suffering that comes our way (Luboshitzky, 2008; Moore, 1992; Remen, 1996; Young-Eisendrath, 1996). The Western view of suffering is sometimes compounded by a common Judeo-Christian belief that holds that humans experience pain, illness, and suffering because of sin and evil (Bausch, 1999; Borg, 2002; Faiver, Ingersoll, O'Brien, & McNally, 2001; Kushner, 1981).

In our campaign to eradicate suffering from our lives, we often believe that we need to abolish the thing that causes the suffering. Alonso's turning his stuttering inward may represent an attempt to rid himself of it by driving it further underground. Other people who stutter often approach therapy with the fervent desire to make the stuttering go away. Understandably, Alonso and others who stutter see their stuttering as the source of much pain and suffering in their lives. Their desire to end their suffering leads them back to its perceived source: the stuttering itself.

Although we yearn for freedom from suffering, we really cannot be totally free of it. Suffering is part of our human condition and a universal experience of being alive (Chödrön, 2005; Kushner, 1981; Moore, 1992; Remen, 1996; Young-Eisendrath, 1996). Trying to eradicate suffering from our lives may ignore the human condition (Moore, 1992) and reinforce the belief that it is unnatural, perhaps even a symptom of sin and evil (Bausch, 1999; Borg, 2002).

The beast that brought our suffering is also the angel that bears a precious gift for us (Moore, 1992). Young-Eisendrath (1996) identifies the gifts of suffering as compassion, insight, and renewal. She goes so far as to say no suffering, no compassion, for the descent into the dark night of suffering allows compassion to arise. Situations of illness, disease, and disability – the beasts that bring the suffering – can provide unparalleled opportunities for personal growth and transmutation – the angels bearing gifts (Luboshitzky, 2008; Moore, 1992; Young-Eisendrath, 1996). To transfigure our suffering and find the grace of our brokenness, we must find meaning in it; suffering benefits us only if we find a purpose in it (Frankl, 1959/2006; Remen, 1996; Younger, 1995).

Speech and hearing professionals may unconsciously share the dominant culture's belief in the need to eradicate suffering. Such a belief can manifest in myriad ways, including focussing on fixing the external problem or rushing to assuage hints of grief, without allowing clients full expression of their emotions. When professionals rush to help clients eliminate their suffering and the conditions that may cause it, they may inadvertently thwart clients' needs to find some meaning in their experience. Professionals may unknowingly circumvent the inner journey to transfiguration of the loss and discovery of wholeness.

THE SPIRITUAL WORK OF CLIENTS

Journey language

People commonly use metaphoric language to describe liminal experiences not easily expressed with concrete, factual language. Travel and journey metaphors, such as feeling lost or finding one's self in a foreign land, offer favorite choices for describing experiences of suffering and change. Spillers (2007) proposed the notion that many clients travel two parallel journeys through their experiences with communication disorders. On the surface, they work through the steps of diagnosis and remediation of the communication problem while below the surface they may find themselves on a spiritual journey to their souls, engaged with their suffering and re-examining their identities and purposes (Spillers, 2007).

The richly metaphoric language of mythology offers a dialect with which to describe the spiritual journey work of clients. Although not literally true, myths have profound truth in that their symbolism describes common experiences of the human condition (Borg, 2002; Campbell, 1968; Segal, 1987). A metaphorical reading of a story emphasizes seeing the light of the metaphor rather than believing in the actual truth of the events (Borg, 2002). Part of the beauty of metaphors lies in the layers of nuanced meaning allowing us to interpret the symbols in a variety of ways; i.e. myths have no singularly right interpretations. The *hero's quest* offers a useful mythical story for describing clients' inner journey work. Joseph Campbell (1968) recognized that all cultures have hero myths that describe, in metaphorical language, common human transformational experiences (Campbell, 1968). The heroes represent all who seek wholeness and an authentic life (Morena, 2001; Segal, 1987).

One type of hero's quest, the *search for paradise*, is frequently used as a metaphor to convey the spiritual journey. In paradise myths, the hero seeks a perfect, paradisal place believed to be unsullied by the lesser angels and travails of humanity – greed, violence, restless passions and desires, fear, and suffering (Strainchamps, 2006; Wood, 2005). Wisdom, peace, wholeness, and joy await those who make the arduous journey to this most perfect and beautiful land (Morena, 2001; Strainchamps, 2006; Wood, 2005). The land is not really a physical place at all but an inner dimension of completion and wholeness where we find our own stores of the essences that we have sought outside of ourselves (Morena, 2001; Strainchamps, 2006). Common metaphors for this mythical place include home, the Garden of Eden, the Promised Land, Shangrai-La, Utopia, and the Emerald City in The *Wizard of Oz*. The *Wizard of Oz* (Baum, 1900/1987) is often interpreted as a modern-day spiritual quest (Bausch, 1999; Dhaliwal, 2004; Morena, 2001), and it has useful symbolism for understanding the therapeutic journey work of clients.

The search for paradise as a hero's quest

The journey begins with a call to adventure (Campbell, 1968; Estes, 2004; Morena, 2001; Segal, 1987). More often than not, the call comes in a chance encounter or an unavoidable event that launches the unsuspecting hero into an epic journey to a foreign and phantasmagorical place (Campbell, 1968; Estes, 2004). Although the call comes unexpectedly, the journey will not unfold unless the hero willingly participates (Campbell, 1968; Morena, 2001). In *The Wizard of Oz*, Dorothy's journey began when a cyclone inhaled her house from the Kansas farm and exhaled it in the Land of Oz, a land inhabited by Munchkins, witches, talking trees, and flying monkeys (Baum, 1900/1987). Her fervent desire to return home motivated her to undertake her journey. Since heroes begin their journeys by happenstance, they have made no preparations and have no provisions with them. Although unprepared, they are not left wanting because they receive help along the way and they discover that they have all that they really need within themselves (Campbell, 1968; Estes, 2004; Morena, 2001; Segal, 1987). Some of the allies encountered along the way are supernatural, such as Glinda the Good Witch; some are local residents who know the ways of the land, such as the Munchkins; and some are other pilgrims on their own quests, such as the Scarecrow, Tin Man, and Lion. Many of the companions encountered along the way represent wounded aspects of the hero (Morena, 2001).

The journey is fraught with unimaginable perils to endure, riddles to solve, and tests to pass (e.g. the haunted forest, flying monkeys, poppies of forgetfulness, imprisonment in the witch's castle, retrieving the witch's broom). The adventures and perils encountered usually represent the emotional and psychic battles that we all encounter in our inner worlds (Segal, 1987). With the help of allies, the hero eventually defeats the last beast, solves the impossible riddle, and reaches the Promised Land – the Emerald City (Campbell, 1968; Morena, 2001). But the journey does not end there because the hero must return to her/his homeland. The return journey has challenges of its own, including the challenge of reintegrating into the society that the hero had left behind (Campbell, 1969; Morena, 2001; Segal, 1987). Dorothy needed to return to the Kansas farm and describe her adventures to an unbelieving farm clan who readily dismissed it as a bad dream.

A spiritual teacher or guru often appears as a guide for the traveler (Dhaliwal, 2004; Paulson, 2006; Strainchamps, 2006; Wood, 2005), and the Wizard of Oz was such a guru. We want the guide to take us to paradise the easy way, just as Dorothy wanted the Wizard to take her back to Kansas. The Wizard could not bestow upon Dorothy or her companions the desires of their hearts, however; each had to find their dream within themselves through the testing and the purifying of the arduous journey. The pain and suffering of the journey gives the hero an opportunity to discover her/his true wisdom and inner strength (Campbell, 1968; Estes, 2004; Segal, 1987), and without the suffering, the discoveries would not occur (Young-Eisendrath, 1996). Consequently, had Glinda told Dorothy at the outset that she had the power to take herself home, Dorothy would not have reaped the bounty of her arduous journey. She would have left Oz impoverished, with no more wisdom, nor compassion, nor courage than when she had arrived.

Implications for the therapeutic relationship

The onset of a communication disorder can sound the call to adventure for clients and their family members (Spillers, 2007). The communication disorder is rarely expected and virtually never sought after. It almost always ushers the individual and family into unknown territory for which they have neither map, nor compass, nor provisions. Clients' journeys to their own promised lands take them through their own foreign and phantasmagorical interiors where they will encounter and do battle with their own inner demons; i.e. they will suffer. Each battle fought and demon vanquished brings them closer to discovering the gifts and strengths that lie safely protected within – wisdom, self-awareness, and wholeness. But the discoveries will not occur if the individual does not willingly choose to make the journey.

Coming home to one's self and feeling whole is a common theme in human existence and may constitute a deeper yearning of clients than professionals realize (see Chapter 2). When temporarily unable to recognize our own wholeness, we benefit greatly from another's illumination of it, reminding us that we can be whole once again. Dass and Gorman (1996) recounted the story of a person 12 years post stroke in which the individual expressed gratitude and respect toward the therapists, and lamented what was missing: "But . . . I have never, ever met someone who sees me as whole" (p. 27). The individual continued, recognizing that no one can give wholeness to her/him, yet yearning for someone to help her/his rediscover it: "What really hurts . . . that's it: that feeling of not being seen as whole" (Dass & Gorman, 1996, pp. 27–28). Similarly, in a keynote address to the National Stuttering Association, Alan Rabinowitz expressed how he felt broken inside, as if he were half of a person because of his stuttering (Rabinowitz, 2005). None of the people in his life, including the speech-language pathologists with whom he worked, helped him to see his wholeness.

For Alonso, finding wholeness probably means wandering through the dark night of his vast interior. Instead of running from the haunting shadow, he may need to face it, possibly befriending it. In doing so, he has an opportunity to transmute his suffering and understand what the poet Rabia (2002, p. 327) meant when she wrote: "I was born when all I once feared – I could / love."

Although professionals cannot bestow wholeness onto clients, they can recognize their clients' wholeness in many ways. Practitioners can honor clients' differentiation, encourage clients' exploration of their own interiority, and offer them opportunities for communion and the sharing of their hidden, whole selves. In a space inviting to soul, loss and brokenness can be transfigured into the discovery of wholeness.

References

Agar, M. (1986). *Speaking of ethnography*. Newbury Park, CA: Sage.

Alonzo, A. A., & Reynolds, N. R. (1995). Stigma, HIV, and AIDs: An exploration and elaboration of a stigma trajectory. *Social Science Medicine, 41(3)*, 303–315.

Alston, M., Sherratt, S., Ferguson, A., & Vajak, J. (2006, July). *Outcomes in a chronic aphasia group: Measures and results*. Paper presented at the Stroke: It's time – 2nd Australasian Nursing and Allied Health Stroke Conference, Sydney.

American Speech-Language-Hearing Association (2009a). *Demographic profile of American Speech-Language-Hearing Association*. Washington, DC: ASHA.

American Speech-Language-Hearing Association (2009b). *Honors of the American Speech-Language-Hearing Association*. Washington, DC: ASHA.

Anderson, T. P. (1977). An alternative frame of reference for rehabilitation: The helping process versus the medical model. In R. P. Marinelli & A. E. Dell Orto (Eds.), *The psychological and social impact of physical disability*. New York: Springer.

Antaki, C. (1994) *Explaining and arguing: The social organization*. London: Sage.

Arches, J. (1991). Social structure, burnout, and job satisfaction. *Social Work, 36(3)*, 202–206.

Armstrong, E. (2005). Language disorder: A functional linguistic perspective. *Clinical Linguistics & Phonetics, 19(3)*, 137–153.

Arokiasamy, C. V., Strohmer, D. C., Guice, S., Angelocci, R., & Hoppe, M. (1994). The effects of politically correct language and counselor skill level on perceptions of counselor credibility. *Rehabilitation Counseling Bulletin, 37(4)*, 204–314.

Atkinson, R. (1998). *The life story interview*. Thousand Oaks, CA: Sage Publications.

Aveline, M. (1996). The training and supervision of individual therapists. In W. Dryden (Ed.), *Handbook of individual therapy* (pp. 19–39). London: Sage.

Bakhtin, M. M. (1986). *Speech genres and other late essays*. Austin, TX: University of Texas Press.

Banja J. D. (1996). Ethics, values, and world culture: The impact on rehabilitation. *Disability & Rehabilitation, 18(6)*, 279–284.

Barling, J. (1994). Work and family: In search of more effective workplace interventions. In C. L. Cooper & D. M. Rousseau (Eds.), *Trends in organizational behavior* (pp. 63–73). Chichester, UK: Wiley.

Barrick, B. (1988). The willingness of nursing personnel to care for patients with acquired immune deficiency syndrome. *Journal of Professional Nursing, 4(5)*, 366–371.

Barrow, A. R. (2004). *Narratives of stroke and aphasia: An ethnographic investigation*. Unpublished PhD Thesis, Trinity College, Dublin.

Barrow, R. (2000). Hearing the story: A narrative perspective on aphasia therapy. *Bulletin of the Royal College of Speech & Language Therapists, 576(April)*, 8–10.

Barrow, R. (2008). Listening to the voice of living life with aphasia: Anne's story. *International Journal of Language and Communication Disorders, 43(S1)*, 30–46.

Bateman, A. (2004). Psychoanalysis and psychiatry: Is there a future? *Acta Psychiatrica Scandinavica 130*, 201–210.

Bateman, A., Brown, D., & Pedder, J. (2000). *Introduction to psychotherapy*. London: Brunner-Routledge.

Battle, D. (Ed.). (2002). Communication disorders in multicultural populations (3rd ed.). Woburn, MA: Butterworth-Heinemann.

Baum, L. F. (1987). *The wonderful wizard of Oz*. San Francisco: HarperCollins. (Original work published 1900)

Baumann, A. E. (2007). Stigmatization, social distance and exclusion because of mental illness: The individual with mental illness as a "stranger." *International Review of Psychiatry, 19(2)*, 131–135.

Bausch, W. J. (1999). *The yellow brick road: A storyteller's guide to the spiritual journey*. Mystic, CT: Twenty-Third Publications.

Baynton, D. C. (1996). *Forbidden signs: American culture and the campaign against sign language*. Chicago: University of Chicago Press.

Beck, M. (1999). *Expecting Adam: A true story of birth, transformation and unconditional love*. London: Piatkus.

Becker, G., & Kaufman, S. (1995). Managing an uncertain illness trajectory in old age: Patients' and physicians' views of stroke. *Medical Anthropology Quarterly, 9(2)*, 165–187.

Becker, L., & Silverstein, J. (1984). Clinician–child discourse: A replication study. *Journal of Speech and Hearing Research, 49*, 104–105.

Benner, P. (1984). *From novice to expert: Excellence and power in clinical nursing practice*. London: Addison-Wesley Publishing.

Berne, E. (1996). *Games people play*. New York: Ballantine.

Bernstein, L., & Bernstein, R. S. (1980). *Interviewing: A guide for health professionals*. New York: Appleton-Century-Crofts.

Bertacchi, J., & Coplon, J. (1992). The professional use of self in prevention. In E. Fenichel (Ed.), *Learning through supervision and mentorship to support the development of infants, toddlers and their families: A source book* (pp. 84–90). Washington, DC: Zero to Three.

Bertacchi, J., & Stott, F. M. (1992). A seminar for supervisors in infant/family programs: Growing versus paying more for staying the same. In E. Fenichel (Ed.), *Learning through supervision and mentorship to support the development of infants, toddlers and their families: A source book* (pp. 132–140). Washington, DC: Zero to Three.

Bill, J. B. (2005). *Holy silence. The gift of Quaker spirituality*. Orleans, MA: Paraclete Press.

Bishop, R., & Berryman, M. (2006). *Culture speaks: Cultural relationships and classroom learning*. Wellington: Huia.

Blood, G. W., Blood, I. M., & Danhauer, J. L. (1977). The hearing aid effect. *Hearing Instruments, 28*, 12.

Bobkoff, K., & Panagos, J. (1986). The "point" of language intervention lessons. *Child Language Teaching and Therapy, 2(1)*, 50–62.

Bohm, D., Hiley, B., & Peat, F. (1987). *Quantum implications: Essays in honor of David Bohm*. New York: Routledge & Kegan Paul Books.

Bonanno, G. A. (2004). Loss, trauma, and human resilience. *American Psychologist*, *59(1)*, 20–28.

Boone, D. R., & Prescott, T. E. (1972). Content and sequence analyses of speech and hearing therapy. *ASHA*, *14*, 58–62.

Borg, M. (2002). *Reading the Bible again for the first time*. San Francisco: HarperCollins.

Bouillaud, J. (1825). Recherches cliniques propres a demontrer que la perte de la parole correspond a la lesion des lobules anterieurs du cerveau, et a confirmer l'opinion de M. Gall, sur le siege de l'organe du language articule. *Archives Generales de Medecine*, *8*, 25–45.

Bowlby, J. (1988). A *secure base: Parent–child attachment and healthy human development*. New York: Basic Books.

Bowlby, J. (1990). A *secure base: Parent–child attachment and healthy human development*. London: Routledge.

Bramley, N., & Eatough, V. (2005). The experience of living with Parkinson's disease: An interpretive phenomenological analysis case study. *Psychology & Health*, *20*, 223–236.

Brickhouse, T. C., & Smith, N. D. (1994). *Plato's Socrates*. Oxford, UK: Oxford University Press.

Brisenden, S. (1986). Independent living and the medical model of disability. *Disability, Handicap & Society*, *1(2)*, 173–178.

Brock, A. J. (1929). Rufus of Ephesus, on the interrogation of the patient. In *Greek medicine*. New York: Dutton.

Brookshire, R. (1997). *Introduction to neurogenic communication disorders* (5th ed.). St Louis, MO: Mosby.

Brookshire, R., Nicholas, L., Krueger, K., & Redmond, K. (1978). The clinical interaction analysis system: A system for observational recording of aphasia treatment. *Journal of Speech and Hearing Disorders*, *43*, 437–447.

Brown, P., & Levinson, S. (1987). *Politeness: Some universals in language usage* (2nd ed.). Cambridge, UK: Cambridge University Press.

Brumfitt, S. (1985). The use of repertory grids with aphasic people. In N. Beail (Ed.), *Repertory grid technique and personal constructs* (pp. 89–107). London: Croom Helm.

Brumfitt, S., & Barton, J. (2006). Evaluating well being in people with aphasia using speech therapy and clinical psychology. *International Journal of Therapy and Rehabilitation*, *13(7)*, 305–309.

Brumfitt, S. T., & Clarke, S. (1982). An application of psychotherapeutic techniques to the management of aphasia. In C. Code & D. J. Muller (Eds.), *Aphasia therapy* (2nd ed., pp. 89–100). San Diego, CA: Singular Publishing.

Bryce, S. (2002). Improving adherence to chronic disease treatments – Lessons from East Arnhem Land. *Australian Family Physician*, *13(7)*, 617–621.

Buck, A. H. (1917). *The growth of medicine from the earliest times to about 1800*. New Haven, CT: Yale University Press.

Bunning, K. (2004). *Speech and language therapy interventions: Frameworks and processes*. London: Whurr.

Burkhardt, M. A., & Nagai-Jacobson, M. G. (2002). *Spirituality: Living our connectedness*. Albany, NY: Delmar Thomas Learning.

Burns, K. (2005). *Focus on solutions: A health professional's guide*. London: Whurr Publishers.

Butler, R. (2009). Coming to terms with personal construct theory. In R. J. Butler (Ed.), *Reflections in personal construct theory* (pp. 3–20). Oxford, UK: Wiley-Blackwell.

Byng, S., & Black, M. (1995). What makes a therapy? Some parameters of therapeutic intervention in aphasia. *European Journal of Disorders of Communication, 30*, 303–316.

Cameron, G. (1930). *A treatise on the Canon of medicine of Avicenna incorporating a translation of the first book*. London: Luzak & Co.

Campbell, J. (1968). *The hero with a thousand faces* (Commemorative ed.). Princeton, NJ: Princeton University Press.

Cappella, J. N. (1983). Conversational involvement: Approaching and avoiding others. In J. M. Wiemann & R. P. Harrison (Eds.), *Nonverbal interaction* (Vol. 11, pp. 113–148). London: Sage Publications.

Carradice, A., Shankland, M., & Beail, N. (2002). A qualitative study of theoretical models used by UK mental health nurses to guide their assessments with family caregivers of people with dementia. *International Journal of Nursing Studies, 39*, 17–26.

Casasanto, D., & Boroditsky, L. (2008). Time in the mind: Using space to think about time. *Cognition, 106(2)*, 579–593.

Casement, P. (1985). *On learning from the patient*. London: Tavistock.

Cashdan, S. (1988). *Object relations therapy*. London: Norton & Co.

Cazden, C. B. (1988). *Classroom discourse: The language of teaching and learning*. Portsmouth, NH: Heinemann.

Charmaz, K. (1983). Loss of self: A fundamental form of suffering in the chronically ill. *Sociology of Health and Illness, 5*, 168–195.

Charon, R. (2006). *Narrative medicine: Honoring the stories of illness*. New York: Oxford University Press.

Chödrön, P. (2005). *The places that scare you: A guide to fearlessness in difficult times*. Boston: Shambhala.

Christensen, A. (2004). *Patient adherence to medical treatment regimens: Bridging the gap between behavioral science and biomedicine*. New Haven, CT: Yale University Press.

Cicourel, A. (1992). The interpenetration of communicative contexts: Examples from medical encounters. In A. Duranti & C. Goodwin (Eds.), *Rethinking content: Language as an interactive phenomenon* (pp. 291–310). Cambridge, UK: Cambridge University Press.

Clarke, H. (2003). Doing less, being more. In S. Parr, J. Duchan, & C. Pound (Eds.), *Aphasia inside out* (pp. 80–90). Maidenhead, UK: Open University Press.

Clarke, P., & Smith, N. (1992). Initial steps towards critical practice in primary schools. In N. Fairclough (Ed.), *Critical language awareness* (pp. 238–255). London: Longman.

Clarkson, P. (2003). *The therapeutic relationship* (2nd ed.). London: Whurr Publishers.

Coates, J. (1996). *Women talk*. Oxford, UK: Blackwell.

Cohen, P. A., & Tedesco, L. A. (2009). Willing, ready, and able? How we must exercise leadership for needed change in dental education. *Journal of Dental Education, 73*, 3–11.

Cole, K., & Dale, P. (1986). Direct language instruction and interactive language instruction with language delayed preschool children. *Journal of Speech and Hearing Research, 29*, 206–217.

Coleman, L. M. (1997). Stigma: An enigma demystified. In J. L. Davis (Ed.). *The disability studies reader*. New York: Routledge.

Collins English dictionary (2007). London: HarperCollins Publishers.

Concise Oxford dictionary (1985). London: Oxford University Press.

Conlon, J. (2004). The role of story. In *An amazing journey* (Session I, 4–6). St. Paul, MN: Global Education Associates Upper Midwest.

Cortazzi, M., & Jin, L. (2004). Reflections on speech-language therapists' talk: Implications for clinical practice and education. *International Journal of Language and Communication, 39(4)*, 477–480.

Costa, G. (2006). Mental health principles, practices, strategies, and dynamics pertinent to early intervention practitioners. In G. M. Foley & J. D Hochman (Eds.), *Mental health in early intervention: Achieving unity in principles and practice* (pp. 113–138). Baltimore: Brookes Publishing Co.

Cott, C. (2004). Client-centred rehabilitation: Client perspectives. *Disability & Rehabilitation, 26(24)*, 1411–1422.

Coupland, J. (2000). Introduction: Sociolinguistics perspectives on small talk. In J. Coupland (Ed.), *Small talk* (pp. 1–25). London: Longman.

Coupland, J., Coupland, N., & Robinson, J. D. (1992). "How are you?" Negotiating phatic communion. *Language in Society, 21*, 207–230.

Coupland, N., Coupland, J., Giles, H., & Henwood, K. (1988). Accommodating and the elderly: Invoking and extending a theory. *Language in Society, 17*, 1–41.

Croteau, C., Le Dorze, G., & Morin, C. (2008). The influence of aphasia severity on how both members of a couple participate in an interview situation. *Aphasiology, 22*, 802–812.

Crowe, T. (Ed.). (1997). *Applications of counseling in speech-language pathology and audiology*. Baltimore: Williams & Wilkins.

Cunningham, J. A., Sobell, L. C., and Chow, V. M. C. (1993). What's in a label? The effects of substance types and labels on treatment considerations and stigma. *Journal of Studies in Alcohol, 54*, 693–699.

Cyr-Stafford, C. (1993). The dynamics of speech therapy in aphasia. In D. Lafond, Y. Joanette, J. Ponzio, R. Degiovani, & M. T. Sarno (Eds.), *Living with aphasia: Psychosocial issues* (pp. 103–116). San Diego, CA: Singular.

Dalai Lama (2005). *The universe in a single atom. The convergence of science and spirituality*. New York: Morgan Books.

Damico, J. S., & Damico, S. K. (1997). The establishment of a dominant interpretive framework in language intervention. *Language, Speech, and Hearing Services in Schools, 28*, 288–296.

Damico, J. S., Oelschlaeger, M., & Simmons-Mackie, N. (1999). Qualitative methods in aphasia research: Conversation analysis. *Aphasiology, 13(9–11)*, 667–680.

Damico, J. S., Simmons-Mackie, N., & Hawley, H. (2005). Language and power. In M. Ball (Ed.), *Clinical sociolinguistics* (pp. 63–73). Malden, MA: Blackwell.

Damico, J. S., Simmons-Mackie, N., Oelschlaeger, M., & Tetnowski, J. (2000, June). *An investigation of therapeutic control in aphasia therapy*. Poster presented at the Clinical Aphasiology Conference, Waikaloa, HI.

Danhauer, J. L., Blood, G. W., Blood, I. M., & Gomez, N. (1980). Professionals and lay observers impressions of preschoolers wearing hearing aids. *Journal of Speech and Hearing Disorders, 45(3)*, 64–71.

Daniels, D. (2007). *Recounting the school experiences of adults who stutter*. Dissertation Abstracts International: The Sciences and Engineering, 68/5, (3004), 0419–4217.

Danziger-Klein, S. (1978). The uses of expertise in doctor–patient encounters during pregnancy. *Social Science and Medicine, 12*, 359–367.

Danziger-Klein, S. (1980). The medical model in doctor–patient interaction: The case of pregnancy care. In J. Roth (Ed.), *Research in the sociology of health care* (pp. 263–305). Greenwich, CT: JAI Press.

Dass, R., & Gorman, P. (1996). *How can I help?* New York: Alfred A. Knopf.

Davies, J. (2003). Expressions of gender: An analysis of pupils' gendered styles in small group classroom discussions. *Discourse and Society 14(2)*, 115–132.

Davis, G. A. (1983). A *survey of adult aphasia*. Englewood Cliffs, NJ: Prentice Hall.

Davis, G. A. (2000). *Aphasiology: Disorders and Clinical Practice*. London: Allyn & Bacon.

Deacon, H., & Boulle, A. (2006). Commentary: Factors affecting HIV/AIDS-related stigma and discrimination by medical professionals. *International Journal of Epidemiology, 35*, 185–186.

Delaney, C. (2005). The spirituality scale: Development and psychometric testing of a holistic instrument to assess the human spiritual dimension. *Journal of Holistic Nursing, 23*, 145–167.

Dhaliwal, H. (2004). The wizard of Om. *Ascent Magazine, 23*, Fall. Retrieved June 2, 2010, http://www.ascentmagazine.com/articles.aspx?articleID=39&issueID=2

DiLollo, A., Manning, W. H., & Neimeyer, R. A. (2003). Cognitive anxiety as a function of speaker role for fluent speakers and persons who stutter. *Journal of Fluency Disorders, 28*, 167–186.

DiLollo, A., Neimeyer, R. A., & Manning, W. H. (2002). A personal construct psychology view of relapse: Indications for a narrative therapy component to stuttering treatment. *Journal of Fluency Disorders, 27*, 19–42.

DiLollo, L. D., DiLollo, A., Mendel, L., English, K., & McCarthy, P. (2008). Facilitating ownership of acquired hearing loss: A narrative therapy approach. *Journal of the Academy of Rehabilitative Audiology, 39*, 49–67.

Dirschel, K. M. (1998). Nursing care of the stroke patient: The essence of healing. In W. Sife (Ed.), *After stroke: Enhancing quality of life* (pp. 71–78). New York: Haworth Press.

Dolny, H. (2009, September 4). Breathe in, breathe out. *Mail & Guardian Online*, p. 41.

Dossey, L. (2003). *Healing beyond the body: Medicine and the infinite reach of the mind*. Boston: Shambhala Publications.

Downs, D., Schmidt, B., & Stephens, T. (2005). Auditory behaviors of children and adolescents with pervasive developmental disorders. *Seminars in Hearing, 24(4)*, 226–240.

Drew, P., & Heritage, J. (Eds.). (1982). *Talk at work: Interaction in institutional settings*. Cambridge, UK: Cambridge University Press.

D'Souza, R. (2007). The importance of spirituality in medicine and its application to clinical practice. *Medical Journal of Australia, 186(10)*, S57–59.

Duchan, J. (1983). Autistic children are noninteractive: Or so we say. *Seminars in Speech and Language, 4*, 53–61.

Duchan, J. (1993). Clinician–child interaction: Its nature and potential. *Seminars in Speech and Language, 14(4)*, 325–333.

Duchan, J. (1999). Reports written by speech-language pathologists: The role of agenda in constructing client competence. In D. Kovarsky, J. Duchan, & M. Maxwell (Eds.), *Constructing (in)competence: Disabling evaluations in clinical and social interaction* (pp. 223–244). Mahwah, NJ: Lawrence Erlbaum Associates, Inc.

Duchan, J. (2001). Impairment and social views of speech-language pathology: Clinical practices re-examined. *Advances in Speech-Language Pathology, 3(1)*, 37–45.

Duchan, J. (2009). Engagement: A concept and some possible uses. *Seminars in Speech and Language, 30(1)*, 11–17.

Dunbar, R. (1996). *Grooming, gossip, and the evolution of language.* Cambridge, MA: Harvard University Press.

Eckhart, M. (2002). So fragile as we grow. *Love poems from God* (D. Ladinsky, Trans., p. 104). New York: Penguin Press.

Edwards, D., & Mercer, D. (1987). *Common knowledge: The development of understanding in the classroom.* London: Routledge.

Edwards, M. L. (1997). Deaf and dumb in ancient Greece. In J. L. Davis (Ed.). *The disability studies reader.* New York: Routledge.

Eggbeer, L., Fenichel, E., Pawl, J. H., Shahmoon Shanok, R., & Williamson, G. G. (1994). Training the trainers: Innovative strategies for teaching relationship concepts and skills to infant/family professionals. *Infants and Young Children, 7(2)*, 53–61.

Eggbeer, L., Mann, T. G., & Seibel, N. L. (2007). Reflective supervision: Past, present and future. *Zero to Three, 28(2)*, 5–9.

Eggins, S., & Slade, D. (1997). *Analysing casual conversation.* London: Cassell.

Elman, R. (2004). Group treatment and jazz: Some lessons learned (Ch.8). In J. Duchan & S. Byng (Eds.), *Challenging aphasia therapies: Broadening the discourse and extending the boundaries* (pp. 130–133). Hove, UK: Psychology Press.

Elman, R. (2005). Social and life participation approaches to aphasia intervention. In L. LaPointe (Ed.), *Aphasia and related neurogenic language disorders* (pp. 39–50). New York: Thieme.

Elman, R. (2007). Introduction to group treatment of neurogenic communication disorders (Ch.1). In R. Elman (Ed.), *Group treatment of neurogenic communication disorders* (2nd ed., pp. 1–10). San Diego, CA: Plural Publishing.

Emerick, L., & Haynes, O. (1973). *Diagnosis and evaluation in speech pathology.* Englewood Cliffs, NJ: Prentice Hall.

Emerson, J., & Enderby, P. (1996). Prevalence of speech and language disorders in a mental illness unit. *European Journal of Disorders of Communication, 31*, 221–236.

Emerson, J., & Enderby, P. (2000). Concerns of speech impaired people and those communicating with them. *Health & Social Care in the Community, 8(3)*, 172–179.

Emmons, S., Geiser, C., Kaplan, K. J., & Harrow, M. (1997). *Living with schizophrenia.* London: Taylor & Francis.

Emoto, M. (2005). *The hidden messages in water.* New York: Atria Books.

English, R. W. (1977a). Combating stigma toward physically disabled persons. In R. P. Marinelli & A. E. Dell Orto (Eds.), *The psychological and social impact of physical disability.* New York: Springer.

English, R. W. (1977b). Correlates of stigma toward physically disabled persons. In R. P. Marinelli & A. E. Dell Orto (Eds.), *The psychological and social impact of physical disability.* New York: Springer.

Epstein, R. M. (1999). Mindful practice. *Journal of the American Medical Association, 282(9)*, 833–839.

Epston, D., & White, M. (1999). Termination as a right of passage: Questioning strategies for a therapy of inclusion. In R. A. Neimeyer & R. J. Mahoney (Eds.),

Constructivism in psychotherapy. Washington, DC: American Psychological Association.

Erikson, E. H. (1982). *The life cycle completed: A review*. New York: W. W. Norton.

Erskine, R. (1998). Attunement and involvement: Therapeutic responses to relational needs. *International Journal of Psychotherapy, 3(3)*, 235–244.

Estes, C. P. (2004). What does the soul want? In J. Campbell (Ed.), *The hero with a thousand faces* (pp. xxiii–xv). Princeton, NJ: Princeton University Press.

Evans, A. M. (2007). Transference in the nurse–patient relationship. *Journal of Psychiatric and Mental Health Nursing, 14*, 189–195.

Evans, D. (2003). *Placebo: The belief effect*. London: HarperCollins.

Faber, A., & Mazlish, E. (1995). *How to talk so kids can learn at home and in school*. London: Picadilly Press.

Faircloth, C., Rittman, M., Boylstein, C., Young, M., & Van Puymbroeck, M. (2004). Energizing the ordinary: Biographical work and the future in stroke recovery narratives. *Journal of Aging Studies, 18*, 399–413.

Fairclough, N. (2001). *Language and power* (2nd ed.). London: Longman.

Faiver, C., Ingersoll, R. E., O'Brien, E., & McNally, C. (2001). *Explorations in counseling and spirituality*. Belmont, CA: Wadsworth/Thomson Learning.

Farnell, R. (1921). *Greek hero cults and ideas of immortality*. Oxford, UK: Clarendon.

Faugier, J., & Sargeant, M. (1997). Stigma: Its impact on professional responses to the needs of marginalized groups. *Nursing Times Research, 2*, 220–229.

Felton, J. (1998). Burn-out as a clinical entity – its importance in health care workers. *Occupational Medicine, 48(4)*, 237–250.

Ferguson, A. (1993). *Conversational repair in aphasic and normal interaction*. Unpublished PhD thesis, Macquarie University, Sydney.

Ferguson, A. (1998). Analysis of learning interactions. In K. Hird (Ed.), *Expanding horizons: Proceedings of the conference of The Speech Pathology Association of Australia, Fremantle, 11–15 May* (pp. 11–24). Perth: School of Speech and Hearing Science, Curtin University of Technology.

Ferguson, A. (2008). *Expert practice: A critical discourse*. San Diego, CA: Plural Publishing.

Ferguson, A. (2009). The discourse of speech-language pathology. *International Journal of Speech-Language Pathology, 11(2)*, 104–112.

Ferguson, A., & Armstrong, E. (2004). Reflections on speech-language therapists' talk: Implications for clinical practice and education. *International Journal of Language and Communication Disorders, 39(4)*, 469–507.

Ferguson, A., & Elliot, N. (2001). Analyzing aphasia treatment sessions. *Clinical Linguistics & Phonetics, 15*, 229–243.

Ferguson, A., & Harper, A. (2009, July). *"Speaking for" individuals with aphasia in multiparty interactions*. Paper presented at the 11th International Pragmatics Conference, Melbourne.

Ferrara, K. (1999). The social construction of language incompetence and social identity in psychotherapy. In D. Kovarksy, J. Duchan, & M. Maxwell (Eds.), *Constructing (in)competence: Disabling evaluations in clinical and social interaction*. (pp. 343–361). Hove, UK: Lawrence Erlbaum Associates Ltd.

Fey, M. (1986). *Language intervention with young children*. San Diego, CA: College-Hill Press.

Figley, C.R. (Ed.). (2000). *Treating compassion fatigue*. New York: Routledge.

Fimian, M., & Blanton, L. (1987). Stress, burnout, and role problems among teacher trainees and first year teachers. *Journal of Occupational Behavior, 8,* 157–165.

Fimian, M., Fastenau, P., & Thomas, J. (1988). Stress in nursing and intentions of leaving the profession. *Psychological Reports, 62,* 499–506.

Fimian, M. J., Lieberman, R. J., & Fastenau, P. S. (1991). Development and validation of an instrument to measure occupational stress in speech-language pathologists. *Journal of Speech and Hearing Research, 34(2),* 439.

Fisher, S. (1986). *In the patient's best interests.* New Brunswick, NJ: Rutgers University Press.

Fisher, S., & Groce, S. (1990). Accounting practices in medical interviews. *Language in Society 19,* 225–250.

Fisher, S., & Todd, A. D. (1986). Introduction: Communication in institutional contexts: Social interaction and social structure. In S. Fisher & A. D. Todd (Eds.), *Discourse and institutional authority: Medicine, education and law* (pp. ix–xviii). Norwood, NJ: Ablex.

Fivaz-Depeursinge, E., Corboz-Warnery, A., & Keren, M. (2004). The primary triangle: Treating infants in their families. In A. J. Sameroff, S. C. McDonough, & K. L. Rosenblum (Eds.), *Treating parent–infant relationship problems: Strategies for intervention* (pp. 123–151). New York: Guilford Press.

Foley, G. M., & Hochman, J. D. (2006). Moving toward an integrated model of infant mental health and early intervention. In G. M. Foley & J. D. Hochman (Eds.), *Mental health in early intervention: Achieving unity in principles and practice* (pp. 3–32). Baltimore: Paul H. Brookes Publishing Co.

Foley, G. M., Hochman, J. D., & Miller, S. (1994). Parent–professional relationships: Finding an optimal distance. *Zero to Three, 14(4),* 19–22.

Fonagy, P. (2002). Understanding of mental states, mother–infant interaction, and the development of the self. In J. M. Maldonado-Duran (Ed.), *Infant and toddler mental health: Models of clinical intervention with infants and their families* (pp. 57–76). Washington, DC: American Psychiatric Publishing, Inc.

Fonagy, P., Gergely, G., Jurist, E. L., & Target, M. (2002). Introduction. In P. Fonagy, G. Gergely, E. L. Jurist and M. Target (Eds.), *Affect regulation, mentalization, and the development of the self* (pp. 1–20). New York: Other Press.

Foucault, M. (1975). *The birth of the clinic: An archaeology of medical perception.* New York: Vintage Books.

Fourie, R. (2009). A qualitative study of the therapeutic relationship in speech-language therapy: Perspectives of adults with acquired communication and swallowing disorders. *International Journal of Language and Communication Disorders, 44(6),* 979–999.

Fraiberg, S., Adelson, E., & Shapiro, V. (1975). Ghosts in the nursery: A psycho-analytic approach to the problems of impaired infant–mother relationships. *Journal of American Academy of Child Psychiatry, 14(3),* 387–421.

Frank, A. W. (1995). *The wounded storyteller: Body, illness and ethics.* Chicago: University of Chicago Press.

Frank, J. D., & Frank, J. (1991). *Persuasion and healing: A comparative study of psychotherapy* (3rd ed.). Baltimore: John Hopkins University Press.

Frankl, V. (2006). *Man's search for meaning.* Boston: Beacon Press. (Original work published 1959)

Fransella, F. (1972). *Personal change and reconstruction: Research on a treatment of stuttering.* New York: Academic Press.

French, R. (2000). "Negative capability", "dispersal" and the containment of emotion. *Bristol Business School Teaching and Research Review, 3*, 1–19. Retrieved July 17, 2009, www.ispso.org/Symposia/London/20000French.htm

Frith, C. (1979). Consciousness, information processing and schizophrenia. *British Journal of Psychiatry, 134*, 333–340.

Garfinkel, H. (1967). *Studies in ethnomethodology*. Englewood Cliffs, NJ: Prentice Hall.

Garstecki, D. C., & Erler, S. R. (1998). Hearing loss, control, and demographic factors influencing hearing aid use among older adults. *Journal of Speech and Hearing, 41*, 527–537.

Gee, J. P. (2005). *An introduction to discourse analysis: Theory and method* (2nd ed.). London: Routledge.

Geekie, P., Cambourne, B., & Fitzsimmons, P. (1999). *Understanding literacy development*. Stoke on Trent, UK: Trentham Books.

Geller, E. (2006). *Broadening the ports of entry for speech-language pathologists: A relational and reflective model of practice and supervision.* Unpublished manuscript submitted in partial fulfillment of the certificate requirements for the Infant–Parent Study Center, Institute for Infants, Children and Families, Jewish Board of Family and Children's Services.

Geller, E., & Foley, G. M. (2009a). Broadening the "ports of entry" for speech-language pathologists: A relational and reflective model for clinical supervision. *American Journal of Speech-Language Pathology, 18*, 22–41.

Geller, E., & Foley, G. M. (2009b). Expanding the "ports of entry" for speech-language pathologists: A relational and reflective model for clinical practice. *American Journal of Speech-Language Pathology, 18*, 4–21.

Gergen, K. J. (1994a). *Realities and relationships: Soundings in social constructionism.* Cambridge, MA: Harvard University Press.

Gergen, K. J. (1994b). Self-narration in social life. In K. J. Gergen (Ed.), *Realities and relationships: Soundings in social construction* (pp. 185–209). Cambridge, MA: Harvard University Press.

Germain, C. B., & Gitterman, A. (1995). *Ecological perspective. The encyclopedia of social work* (19th ed., pp. 816–824). Silver Spring, MD: National Association of Social Workers.

Gilbert, P. (2000). The relationship of shame, social anxiety and depression: The role of evaluation of social rank. *Clinical Psychology & Psychotherapy, 7*, 174–189.

Gilbert, P. (2009). *An introduction to the theory and practice of compassion focused therapy for shame based difficulties.* Unpublished workshop notes.

Gilbert, T. (2001). Reflective practice and clinical supervision: Meticulous rituals of the confessional. *Journal of Advanced Nursing, 36(2)*, 199–205.

Gilmore, N., & Somerville, M. A. (1994). Stigmatization, scapegoating and discrimination in sexually transmitted diseases: overcoming "Them" and "Us." *Social Science Medicine, 39(9)*, 1339–1358.

Giorgi, A. (Ed.). (1985). *Phenomenology and psychological research*. Pittsburgh, PA: Duquesne University Press.

Girolametto, L., & Weitzman, E. (2006). It takes two to talk – the Hanen program for parents: Early language intervention through caregiver training. In R. J. McCauley & M. E. Fey (Eds.), *Treatment of language disorders in children* (pp. 77–104). Baltimore: Paul H. Brookes Publishing Co.

Glenn, P. (2003). *Laughter in interaction*. Cambridge, UK: Cambridge University Press.

Glozman, J. (1985). Personality changes in aphasia. *Defektologiya, 6*, 23–28.

Goffman, E. (1968). *Stigma: Notes on the management of spoiled identity*. London: Penguin. (First published 1963, Englewood Cliffs, NJ: Prentice Hall)

Goffman, E. (1974). *Frame analysis: An essay of the organization of experience*. New York: Harper Colophon.

Goldberg, S. A. (1997). *Clinical skills for speech-language pathologists*. London: Singular Publishing.

Goleman, D. (2006). *Social intelligence. The new science of human relationships*. New York: Bantam.

Gordon, N. (1991) The relationship between language and behavior. *Developmental Medicine & Child Neurology, 33(1)*, 86–89.

Goulding, R., & Goulding, M. (1978). The power is in the patient. A TA/Gestalt approach to psychotherapy. San Francisco: Trans Publishing.

Greenspan, S., & Wieder, S. (2006). *Infant and early childhood mental health: A comprehensive and developmental approach to assessment and intervention*. Washington, DC: American Psychiatric Publishing, Inc.

Grypdonck, M. (2006). Qualitative health research in the era of evidence-based practice. *Qualitative Health Research, 16(10)*, 1371–1385.

Gwyn, R. (2002). *Communicating health and illness*. London: Sage Publications.

Hafiz (2002). How did the rose. In *Love poems from God* (D. Ladinsky, Trans., p. 161). New York: Penguin Press.

Hagstrom, F. (2004). Including identity in clinical practices. *Topics in Language Disorders, 24(5)*, 225–258.

Halliday, M. A. K., & Matthiessen, C. M. I. M. (2004). *An introduction to functional grammar* (3rd ed.). London: Arnold.

Hamayan, E., & Damico, J. (1991). *Limiting bias in the assessment of bilingual students*. Austin, TX: Pro-Ed.

Hammer, A., & Marting, M. (1988). *Manual for the coping resources inventory*. Palo Alto, CA: Consulting Psychologists Press.

Handzo, G., & Koenig, H. G. (2004). Spiritual care: Whose job is it anyway? *Southern Medical Journal, 97(12)*, 1242–1245.

Hanh, T. N. (1995). *Mindfulness and psychotherapy*. Boulder, CO: Sounds True.

Haque, A. (2004). Psychology from an Islamic perspective: Contributions of early Muslim scholars and challenges to contemporary Muslim psychologists, *Journal of Religion and Health, 43(4)*, 357–377.

Harper, A. (2008). *Speaking for another person in interactions involving individuals with aphasia*. Unpublished Honours thesis Speech Pathology discipline, School of Humanities & Social Sciences, University of Newcastle, Australia.

Harris, M. J., Milich, R., Corbitt, E. M., Hoover, D. W., & Brady, M. (1992). Self-fulfilling effects of stigmatizing information on children's social interaction. *Journal of Personality and Social Psychology, 63(1)*, 41–50.

Harris, S. F., Prater, M. A., Dyches, T. T., & Heath, M. A. (2009). Job stress of school-based speech-language pathologists. *Communication Disorders Quarterly, 30(2)*, 103–111.

Haynes, W., & Oratio, A. (1978). A study of clients' perceptions of therapeutic effectiveness. *Journal of Speech and Hearing Disorders, 43*, 21–33.

Heffron, M. C. (1999). Balance in jeopardy: Reflexive reactions versus reflective responses in infant/family practice. *Zero to Three, August/September*, 15–17.

Heffron, M. C. (2005). Reflective supervision in infant, toddler, and preschool work.

In K. M. Finello (Ed.), *Handbook of training and practice in infant and preschool mental health* (pp. 114–136). San Francisco: Jossey-Bass.

Heffron, M., Ivins, B., & Weston, D. R. (2005). Finding an authentic voice: Use of self: Essential learning processes for relationship-based work. *Infants and Young Children, 18(4)*, 323–336.

Hegde, M., & Davis, D. (1999). *Clinical methods and practicum in speech-language pathology*. San Diego, CA: Singular Publishing Group.

Heifetz, R. A., Grashow, A., & Linsky, M. (2009). *The practice of adaptive leadership*. Boston: Harvard Business Press.

Heifetz, R. A., & Laurie, D. L. (1997). The work of leadership. *Harvard Business Review, 75*, 124–134.

Heifetz, R. A., & Linsky, M. (2002). *Leadership on the line*. Boston: Harvard Business.

Hengst, J., & Duff, M. (2007). Clinicians as communication partners: Developing a mediated discourse elicitation protocol. *Topics in Language Disorders, 27(1)*, 37–49.

Hengst, J., Duff, M., & Prior, P. (2008). Multiple voices in clinical discourse and as clinical intervention. *International Journal of Language & Communication Disorders, 43, Supplement 1*, 58–68.

Heritage, J., & Maynard, D. (Eds.). (2006). *Communication in medical care: Interaction between primary care physicians and patients*. Cambridge, UK: Cambridge University Press.

Herodotus. (1862). *Herodotus, the history* (G. Rawlinson, Trans.). New York: Dutton & Co. Retrieved July 4, 2009 from http://www.fordham.edu/halsall/ancient/greek-babylon.html

Hersh, D. (2001). Experiences of ending aphasia therapy. *International Journal of Language and Communication Disorders, 36 (suppl.)*, 80–85.

Hetu, R. (1996). The stigma attached to hearing impairment. *Scandinavian Audiology, 25*, 12–24.

Higgins, P. C. (1980). *Outsiders in a hearing world*. Beverly Hills, CA: Sage.

Hilsman, G. J. (1997). The place of spirituality in managed care. *Health Progress, 78(1)*, 43–46.

Hinckley, J. (2008). *Narrative-based practice in speech-language pathology*. San Diego, CA: Plural Publishing.

Hippocrates. (1946). *Genuine works of Hippocrates*. Baltimore: Williams & Wilkins Company.

Hippocrates. (2009). *Aphorisms* (F. Adams, Trans.) Retrieved August 2, 2009 from http://classics.mit.edu/Hippocrates/aphorisms.1.i.html

Hodge, A. (1986). *Cross-cultural communication; an ABC of cultural awareness*. Sydney: Janus Resources, Multicultural Centre, The University of Sydney.

Hodge, D. R. (2001). Spiritual assessment: A review of major qualitative methods and a new framework for assessing spirituality. *Social Work, 46(3)*, 203–214.

Hoffman, B. and Dukas, H. (1981). *Albert Einstein, the human side*. Princeton, NJ: Princeton University Press.

Holland, A. (1998). Why can't clinicians talk to aphasic adults? Comments on supported conversation for adults with aphasia: Methods and resources for training conversational partners. *Aphasiology, 12(9)*, 844–847.

Holland, A. (2007). *Counseling in communication disorders: A wellness perspective*. San Diego, CA: Plural Publishing.

Holmes, J. (1992). Women's talk in public contexts. *Discourse and Society, 3(2)*, 131–150.

Holmes, J., & Stubbe, M. (2003). *Power and politeness in the workplace: A sociolinguistic analysis of talk at work.* Harlow, UK: Longman.

Holowchak, A. (2001). Interpreting dreams for corrective regimen: Diagnostic dreams in Greco-Roman medicine. *Journal of the History of Medicine and Allied Sciences, 56(4)*, 382–399.

Horton, S. (2003). *A study of therapy for language impairment in aphasia: Description and analsyis of sessions in day-to-day practice.* Unpublished doctoral dissertation, City University, London.

Horton, S. (2006). A framework for description and analysis of therapy for language impairment in aphasia. *Aphasiology, 20(6)*, 528–564.

Horton, S. (2007). Topic generation in aphasia language therapy sessions: Issues of identity. *Aphasiology, 21(3–4)*, 283–298.

Horton, S., & Byng, S. (2000). Examining interactions in language therapy. *International Journal of Language and Communication Disorders, 35(3)*, 355–375.

Horton, S., Byng, S., Bunning, K., & Pring, T. (2004). Teaching and learning speech and language therapy skills: The effectiveness of classroom as clinic in speech and language therapy student education. *International Journal of Language & Communication Disorders, 39(3)*, 365–390.

Houston, M. (2008, January 8). A doctor's best attributes. *Irish Times (Health Supplement)*. Retrieved June 2, 2010, from http://www.irishtimes.com/newspaper/health/2008/0108/1199313601225.html

Hymes, D. (1966). Introduction: Toward ethnographies of communication. *American Anthropologist, 66*, 12–25.

Hyun, J., & Fowler, S. (1995). Respect, cultural sensitivity and communication. *Teaching Exceptional Children, 28(1)*, 25–28.

Iler, K., Danhauer, J., & Mulac, A. (1982). Peer perceptions of geriatrics wearing hearing aids. *Journal of Speech and Hearing Disorders, 47*, 433–438.

Inscriptiones Graecae. (2009). In *Encyclopædia Britannica*. Retrieved August 12, 2009, from http://www.britannica.com/EBchecked/topic/288995/Inscriptiones-Graecae

Isaac, K. (2002). *Speech pathology in cultural and linguistic diversity.* London: Whurr.

Jacyna, L. S. (2000). *Lost words: Narratives of language and the brain, 1825–1926.* Princeton, NJ: Princeton University Press.

Jeffers, S. (1987). *Feel the fear and do it anyway.* London: Arrow.

Jefferson, G. (1985). On the interactional unpackaging of a gloss. *Language in Society, 14*, 435–466.

Joanette, Y., Lafond, D., & Lecours, A. (1993). The person with aphasia. In D. Lafond, Y. Joanette, J. Ponzio, R. Degiovani, & M. T. Sarno (Eds.), *Living with aphasia: Psychosocial issues* (pp. 9–36). San Diego, CA: Singular.

Jones, A. C. (2004). Transference and countertransference. *Perspectives in Psychiatric Care, 40*, 13–19.

Jones, A. C. (2005). Transference, counter-transference and repetition: Some implications for nursing practice. *Journal of Nursing, 14*, 1177–1184.

Jung, C. G. (2004). Approaching the unconscious. In C. G. Jung (Ed.), *Man and his symbols* (pp. 18–103). New York: Doubleday. (Original work published 1964)

Kabat-Zinn, J. (2005). *Coming to our senses. Healing ourselves and the world through mindfulness.* New York: Hyperion.

Kagan, A. (1995). Revealing the competence of aphasic adults through conversation: A challenge to health professionals. *Topics in Stroke Rehabilitation, 2,* 15–28.

Kagan, A. (1998). Supported conversation for adults with aphasia: Methods and resources for training conversation partners. *Aphasiology, 12(9),* 816–830.

Kahn, M. (1997). *Between therapist and client. The new relationship: An integrated approach.* London: Tavistock.

Kalmanson, B., & Seligman, S. (2006). Process in an integrated model of infant mental health and early intervention practice. In G. M. Foley & J. D. Hochman (Eds.), *Mental health in early intervention: Achieving unity in principles and practice* (pp. 245–266). Baltimore: Brookes Publishing Co.

Katz, R., & Johnson, T. (2006). *When professionals weep.* New York: Routledge.

Kelly, G. A. (1955). *The psychology of personal constructs* (Vol. 1). New York: Norton.

King, J. (1954). Plato's concepts of medicine. *Journal of the History of Medicine and Allied Sciences, 9,* 38–48.

King, M. (2000). *Wrestling with the angel: A life of Janet Frame.* London: Picador.

Kirsh, B., Dawson, D., Antolikova, S., & Reynolds, L. (2001). Developing awareness of spirituality in occupational therapy students: Are our curricula up to the task? *Occupational Therapy International, 8(2),* 119–125.

Klein, M. (1946). Notes on some schizoid mechanisms. *International Journal of Psycho-Analysis, 27,* 99–110.

Klevans, D. R., Volz, H. B., & Friedman, R. M. (1981). A comparison of experiential and observational approaches for enhancing the interpersonal communication skills of speech pathology students. *Journal of Speech & Hearing Disorders, 46,* 208–213.

Klippi, A. (2003). Collaborating in aphasic group conversation: Striving for mutual understanding. In C. Goodwin (Ed.), *Conversation and brain damage* (pp. 117–143). Oxford, UK: Oxford University Press.

Klompas, M., & Ross, E. (2004). Life experiences of people who stutter, and the perceived impact of stuttering on quality of life. *Journal of Fluency Disorders, 29(4),* 275–305.

Koenig, H. G. (2004). Religion, spirituality, and medicine: Research findings and implications for clinical practice. *Southern Medical Journal, 97(12),* 1194–1200.

Kongtrül, D. (2006). *It's up to you: The practice of self-reflection on the Buddhist path.* Boston: Shambhala Publications.

Kop, W. J., & Gottdiener, J. S. (2005). The role of immune system parameters in the relationship between depression and coronary artery disease. *Psychosomatic Medicine, 67,* S37–S41.

Kornfield, J. (2009). *The wise heart: A guide to the universal teachings of Buddhist psychology.* New York: Bantam.

Korzybski, A. (1990). *Collected writings 1920–1950* (Collected and Arranged by M. Kendig). Englewood Cliffs, NJ: Institute of General Semantics.

Kovarsky, D. (1990). Discourse markers in adult-controlled therapy: Implications for child centered intervention. *Journal of Childhood Communication Disorders, 13(1),* 29–41.

Kovarsky, D. (2008). Representing voices from the life-world in evidence-based practice. *International Journal of Language and Communication Disorders, 43,* 47–57.

Kovarsky, D., & Curran, M. (2007). A missing voice in the discourse of evidence-based practice. *Topics in Language Disorders, 27(1),* 50–61.

Kovarsky, D., Curran, M., & Zobel Nichols, N. (2009). Laughter and communicative engagement in interaction. *Seminars in Speech and Language*, *30(1)*, 27–36.

Kovarsky, D., & Duchan, J. (1997). The interactional dimensions of language therapy. *Language, Speech and Hearing Services in Schools*, *28*, 297–307.

Kovarsky, D., Duchan, J., & Maxwell, M. (1999). *Constructing (in)competence: Disabling evaluations in clinical and social interaction.* Mahwah, NJ: Lawrence Erlbaum Associates, Inc.

Kovarsky, D., Kimbarow, M., & Kastner, D. (1999). The construction of incompetence during group therapy with traumatically brain injured adults. In D. Kovarsky, J. F. Duchan, & M. Maxwell (Eds.), *Constructing (in)competence: Disabling evaluations in clinical and social interaction* (pp. 291–312). Mahwah, NJ: Lawrence Erlbaum Associates, Inc.

Kovarsky, D., & Maxwell, M. M. (1992). Ethnography and the clinical setting: Communicative expectancies in clinical discourse. *Topics in Language Disorders*, *12(3)*, 76–84.

Kovarsky, D., Shaw, A., & Adingono-Smith, M. (2007). The construction of identity during group therapy among adults with traumatic brain injury. *Communication & Medicine*, *4(1)*, 111–115.

Kummerer, S., Lopez-Reyna, N., & Hughes, M. (2007). Mexican immigrant mothers' perceptions of their children's communication disabilities, emergent literacy development, and speech-language therapy program. *American Journal of Speech-Language Pathology*, *16(3)*, 271–282.

Kushner, H. S. (1981). *When bad things happen to good people.* New York: Schoken Books.

Landfield, A. W., & Leitner, L. M. (1980). Personal construct psychology. In A. W. Landfield & L. M. Leitner (Eds.), *Personal construct psychology.* New York: John Wiley & Sons.

Lane, H. (1999). *The mask of benevolence: Disabling the deaf community.* New York: Dawn Sign Press.

Langer, E. (1990). *Mindfulness.* New York: Da Capo Press.

Laplanche, J., & Pontalis, J. (1973). *The language of psycho-analysis.* London: Hogarth Press.

Lavretsky, H. (2008). History of schizophrenia as a psychiatric disorder. In K. T. Mueser & D. V. Jester (Eds.), *Clinical handbook of schizophrenia* (pp. 3–13). New York: Guilford Press.

Leahy, M. M. (2004). Therapy talk: Analyzing therapeutic discourse. *Language, Speech, and Hearing Services in Schools*, *35*, 70–81.

Leahy, M., & Walsh, I. (2008). Talk in interaction in the speech-language pathology clinic: Bringing theory to practice through discourse. *Topics in Language Disorders*, *28(3)*, 229–241.

Leahy, M., & Warren, A. (2006, July). *Making stuttering manageable: The use of narrative therapy. Research, treatment and self-help in fluency disorders* (pp. 320–324). Presentation at the Fifth World Congress on Fluency Disorders, Dublin, Ireland.

Legg, C., Young, L., & Bryer, A. (2005). Training sixth-year medical students in obtaining case-history information from adults with aphasia. *Aphasiology*, *19(6)*, 559–575.

Lendering, J. (2009). *Livius: Articles in ancient history.* Retrieved on September 15, 2009, from http://www.livius.org/he-hg/herodotus/herodotus01.htm

Levine, J., & Levine, I. S. (2009). *Schizophrenia for dummies*. Hoboken, NJ: Wiley.

Lipton, B. (2005). *The biology of belief. Unleashing the power of consciousness, matter, and miracles*. Santa Rosa, CA: Mountain of Love.

Lofland, J., & Lofland, L. H. (1995). *Analyzing social settings: A guide to qualitative observation and analysis* (3rd ed.). Belmont, CA: Wadsworth.

Lordat, J. (1843). Analyse de la parole pour servir a la theorie de divers cas d'Alalie et de Paralalie (de mutisme et d'imprefection du parler) que les nosologistes ont mal connu. *Journal de la Societe de Medecine Pratique de Montpellier, 7*, 333–353; 417–433.

Lorentzen, J. (2008). "I know my own body": Power and resistance in women's experiences of medical interactions. *Body & Society 14(3)*, 49–79.

Lubinski, R. (2001). Stress and burnout. In R. Lubinski & C. M. Frattali (Eds.), *Professional issues in speech-language pathology and audiology* (2nd ed., pp. 183–199). New York: Singular/Thomson Learning.

Luboshitzky, D. (2008). Exploring the spiritual meaning of suffering: A strategy of self-help, recovery, and hope. *Occupational Therapy and Health Care, 22(1)*, 21–38.

Luterman, D. M. (2001). *Counseling persons with communication disorders and their families* (4th ed.). Austin, TX: Pro-Ed.

Luterman, D. M. (2006). The counseling relationship. *The ASHA Leader, 11(4)*, 8–9, 33.

MacDonald, M., & Murray, M. (2007). The appropriateness of appropriate: Smuggling values into clinical practice. *Canadian Journal of Nursing Research, 39(4)*, 59–73.

Mackay, R. (2003). "Tell Them Who I Was": The social construction of aphasia. *Disability & Society, 18(6)*, 811–826.

Madden, M. L., Oelschlaeger, M., & Damico, J. S. (2002). The conversational value of laughter for a person with aphasia. *Aphasiology, 16*, 1199–1212.

Manning, W. H., (2001). *Clinical decision making in fluency disorders* (2nd ed.). San Diego, CA: Singular.

Markova, I. (1991). Asymmetries in group conversations between a tutor and peple with learning disabilities. In I. Markova & K. Foppa (Eds.), *Asymmetries in dialogue* (pp. 221–240). Savage, MD: Barnes & Noble Books.

Martin, D. (2009). *Language disabilities in cultural and linguistic diversity*. Bristol, UK: Multilingual Matters.

Martin, J. R., & Rose, D. (2003). *Working with discourse*. London: Continuum.

Martyn, D. (2007). *Beyond deserving: Children, parents, and responsibility revisited*. Grand Rapids, MI: William B. Eerdmans Publishing Co.

Marvell, A. (2003). *Marvell: The poems of Andrew Marvell* (N. Smith Ed.). Harlow, UK: Pearson Education.

Marx, K. (1978). *The Marx–Engels reader* (2nd ed.) (R. C. Tucker Ed.). New York: W. W. Norton.

Maslach, C. (1986) *Burnout: The cost of caring*. New York: Prentice Hall.

Maslach, C. (2003). *Burnout: The cost of caring* (reprint). Cambridge, MA: Malor Books.

Maslach, C., & Jackson, S. (1978). Lawyer burn-out. *Barrister, 5*, 52–54.

Maslach, C., & Jackson, S. (1979). Burned-out cops and their families. *Psychology Today, 12*, 59–62.

Masterson, J. (1993). *The emerging self*. New York: Brunner/Mazel.

Mattingly, C. (1994). The concept of therapeutic "emplotment" ... clinician and patient in the creation and negotiation of a plot structure within clinical time. *Social Science & Medicine, 38(6)*, 811–822.

McAllister, S., Lincoln, M., Ferguson, A., & McAllister, L. (2006). *COMPASS(R) (competency assessment in speech pathology) assessment and resource manual.* Melbourne: Speech Pathology Australia.

McCabe, R., Heath, C., Burns, T., & Priebe, S. (2002). Engagement of patients with psychosis in the consultation: Conversation analytic study. *British Medical Journal, 325*, 1148–1151.

McCarthy, P., Hall, D., & Peach, R. (1985). *Peer perceptions of first-grade and kindergarten hearing aid wearers.* Paper presented at the annual convention of the American Speech-Language-Hearing Association, Washington, DC.

McCaulley, M. (1990). The Myers-Briggs type indicator: A measure for individuals and groups. *Measurement and Evaluation in Counseling and Development, 22(4)*, 181–195.

McDougall, D., Hawkins, J., Brady, M., & Jenkins, A. (2006). Recent innovations in the changing criterion design: Implications for research and practice in special education. *The Journal of Special Education, 40*, 2–15.

Menz, F., & Al-Roubaie, A. (2008). Interruptions, status, and gender in medical interviews: The harder you brake, the longer it takes. *Discourse & Society 19(5)*, 645–666.

Miller, M., & Potter, R. (1982). Professional burnout among speech-language pathologists. *ASHA, 24(3)*, 177–181.

Mills, S. (2003). *Gender and politeness.* Cambridge, UK: Cambridge University Press.

Mishler, E. (1984). *The discourse of medicine: Dialectics of medical interviews.* Norwood, NJ: Ablex.

Mishler, E. (1986). *Research interviewing: Context and narrative.* Cambridge, MA: Harvard University Press.

Moes, M. (2000). *Plato's dialogue form and the care of the soul.* New York: Peter Lang.

Moes, M. (2001). Plato's conception of the relations between moral philosophy and medicine. *Perspectives in Biology and Medicine, 44(3)*, 353–367.

Moore, M. S., & Levitan, L. (2003). *For hearing people only* (3rd ed.). New York: Deaf Life Press.

Moore, R. (2008). *Clinical linguistic skills required by speech pathologists.* Unpublished honours thesis, University of Newcastle, Australia.

Moore, R., & Ferguson, A. (2009, May). *Talking the talk: Perceptions of clinical linguistic skills needed for speech pathology practice.* Poster presentation Speech Pathology Australia National Conference, Adelaide.

Moore, T. (1992). *Care of the soul.* New York: Harper Collins.

Morena, G. D. (2001). *The wisdom of Oz.* Berkeley, CA: Frog.

Morgan, A. (2000). *What is narrative therapy? An easy to read introduction.* Adelaide: Dulwich Center.

Moses, K. (1989). *Fundamentals of grieving: Relating to parents of the disabled.* Evanston, IL: Resource Networks.

Myss, C. (1997). *Why people don't heal and how they can.* New York: Three Rivers Press.

Neimeyer, R. A. (1995). Constructivist psychotherapies: Features, foundations, and future directions. In R. Neimeyer & M. J. Mahoney (Eds.), *Constructivism in psychotherapy* (pp. 11–38). Washington, DC: American Psychological Association.

Neimeyer, R. A. (2004). Constructivist therapy. In G. R. VandenBos, J. F. McNeil, &

S. Reynolds (Executive Producers), *American Psychological Association series: Systems of psychotherapy*. University Park, IL: Governors State University Communications Services.

Nelson, H. L. (2001). *Damaged identities, narrative repair*. London: Cornell University Press.

Nemes, J. (2004). Professional burn-out: How to stop it from happening to you. *The Hearing Journal, 57(1)*, 21–26.

Nettleton, S. (1995). *The sociology of health and illness*. Cambridge, UK: Polity Press.

Newton, T., Handy, J., & Fineman, S. (1995). *"Managing" stress: Emotion and power at work*. London: Sage.

Nofsinger, R. E. (1991). *Everyday conversation*. London: Sage.

Norman-Murch, T. (1996). Reflective supervision as a vehicle for individual and organizational development. *Zero to Three, October/November*, 16–20.

Norris, J., & Hoffman, P. (1990). Comparison of adult-initiated vs. child-initiated interaction styles with handicapped prelanguage children. *Language, Speech and Hearing Services in Schools, 21*, 28–36.

Norris, K. (2008). *Acedia and me*. New York: Riverhead Books.

Norris, M. R., & Drummond, S. S. (1998). Communicative functions of laughter in aphasia. *Journal of Neurolinguistics, 11*, 391–402

North, M. (2002). *Hippocratic Oath*. National Library of Medicine. Retrieved on June 2, 2010 from http://www.nlm.nih.gov/hmd/greek/greek_oath.html

Nystrom, M. (2006). Aphasia – an existential loneliness: A study on the loss of the world of symbols. *International Journal of Qualitative Studies on Health and Well-being, 1*, 38–49.

O'Donohue, J. (1997). *Anam cara: A book of Celtic wisdom*. New York: Cliff Street Books.

O'Donohue, J. (1999). *Eternal echoes: Celtic reflections on our yearning to belong*. New York: Cliff Street Books.

O'Hagan, M. (1996). Two accounts of mental distress. In J. Read & J. Reynolds (Eds.), *Speaking our minds: An anthology* (pp. 44–50). Basingstoke, UK: Palgrave Macmillan.

Oliver, M. (1992). *Some questions you might ask. New and selected poems* (p. 65). Boston: Beacon Press.

Oliver, M. (1996). *Understanding disability: From theory to practice*. Basingstoke, UK: Macmillan Press.

Ollman, B. (1976). *Alienation*. Cambridge, UK: Cambridge University Press.

O'Malley, E. (2009). The competencies for civic leadership. *The Journal of Kansas Civic Leadership Development, 1*, 7–15.

O'Malley, M. P. (2005). Silence as a means of preserving the status quo: The case of ante-natal care in Ireland. *Multilingua, 24*, 39–54.

Onslow, M., Packman, A., & Harrison, E. (Eds.). (2003). *The Lidcombe program of early stuttering intervention: A clinician's guide*. Austin, TX: Pro-Ed.

Orbach, S. (1999). *The impossibility of sex*. London: Penguin

Orloff, J. (2005). *Positive energy: 10 extraordinary prescriptions for transforming fatigue, stress, and fear into vibrance, strength, and love*. New York: Three Rivers Press.

Osvaldsson, K. (2004). On laughter and disagreement in multiparty assessment talk. *Text, 24(4)*, 517–545.

Palmer, P. (1999). *Letting your life speak: Listening for the voice of vocation*. Hoboken, NJ: Jossey-Bass.

Palmer, P. (2004). *A hidden wholeness: The journey toward an undivided life*. San Francisco: Jossey-Bass.

Panagos, J. (1996). Speech therapy discourse: The input to learning. In M. Smith & J. S. Damico (Eds.), *Childhood language disorders* (pp. 41–63). New York: Thieme.

Parker Hall, S. (2009). *Anger, rage, and relationship*. Hove, UK: Routledge.

Parr, S., Byng, S., Gilpin, S., & Ireland, C. (1997). *Talking about aphasia*. Buckingham, UK: Open University Press.

Patel, C. (1989). *The complete guide to stress management*. London: Vermilion

Paulson, M., Danielson, E., & Sodeberg, S. (2002). Struggling for a tolerable existence: The meaning of men's lived experiences of living with pain of fybromyalgia type. *Qualitative Health Research, 12*, 238–249.

Paulson, S. (Producer). (2006, May 14). Buddha's biography: Interview with Karen Armstrong. *To the best of our knowledge*. Wisconsin Public Radio: 06–05–14B.

Pauwels, A. (1995). *Cross-cultural communication in the health sciences*. Melbourne: Macmillan Educational Australia.

Payne, M. (2006). *Narrative therapy: An introduction for counselors* (2nd ed.). Thousand Oaks, CA: Sage Publications.

Penman, T., & deMare, T. (2003). Changing places: Reflections of therapists and group members on the power and potential of groups. In S. Parr, J. Duchan, & C. Pound (Eds.), *Aphasia inside out* (pp. 91–102). Maidenhead, UK: Open University Press.

Perez, J. C. (2004). Healing presence. *Care Management Journals, 5(1)*, 41–46.

Perkins, R. E., & Repper, J. M. (1996). *Working alongside people with long term mental health problems*. Cheltenham, UK: Nelson Thornes.

Pesut, B. (2002). The development of nursing students' spirituality and spiritual caregiving. *Nurse Education Today, 22*, 128–135.

Poche, L., Tassin, M. S., Oliver, P., & Fellows, J. A. (2004). Job stress in school-based speech-language pathologists. *Advance, 14*, 16.

Porter, R. (1997). *The greatest benefit to mankind: A medical history of humanity*. New York: Norton.

Pound, C. (2004). Dare to be different: The person and the practice. In J. Duchan & S. Byng (Eds.), *Challenging aphasia therapies: Broadening the discourse and extending the boundaries* (pp. 32–53). Hove, UK: Psychology Press.

Pound, C., Parr, S., Lindsay, J., & Woolf, C. (2000). *Beyond aphasia: Therapies for living with communication disability*. Bicester, UK: Speechmark.

Prutting, C. A., Bagshaw, N., Goldstein, H., Juskowitz, S., & Umen, I. (1978). Clinician–child discourse: Some preliminary questions. *Journal of Speech and Hearing Disorders, 43*, 123–139.

Quick, J. C., Nelson, D. L., & Quick, J. D. (1990). *Stress and change at the top: The parameter of the successful executive*. Chichester, UK: John Wiley.

Rabia (2002). Die before you die. *Love poems from God* (D. Ladinsky, Trans.) (pp. 326–327). New York: Penguin Press.

Rabinowitz, A. (2005). *Keynote address to annual conference of the Stuttering Foundation*. Available from The Stuttering Foundation, 3100 Walnut Grove Rd., Suite 603, P.O. Box 11749, Memphis, TN 38111–0749

Rahman, F. (1952). *Avicenna's psychology*. London: Oxford University Press.

Rampton, B. (2001). Language crossing, cross talk and cross-disciplinarity. In N. Coupland, S. Sarangi, & C. Candlin (Eds.), *Sociolinguistics and social theory* (pp. 261–296). London: Longman.

Raskin, J. D., & Lewandowski, A. M. (2000). The construction of disorder as human enterprise. In R. A. Neimeyer & J. D. Raskin (Eds.), *Constructions of disorder: Meaning-making frameworks for psychotherapy*. Washington, DC: American Psychological Association.

Reik, T. (1948). *Listening with the third ear: The inner experience of a psychoanalyst*. New York: The Noonday Press.

Reitzes, P. (2007). Teaching graduate and undergraduate students to model stuttering behaviors. *Journal of Stuttering, Advocacy & Research, 2*, 26–31.

Remen, R. N. (1996). *Kitchen table wisdom*. New York: Riverhead Books.

Reynolds, D. (1976). *Morita psychotherapy*. Berkeley, CA: University of California.

Reynolds, D. (1980). *The quiet therapies: Japanese pathways to personal growth*. Honolulu: University Press of Hawaii.

Reynolds, F., & Prior, S. (2003). Sticking jewels in your life: Exploring women's strategies for negotiating an acceptable quality of life with multiple sclerosis. *Qualitative Health Research, 13*, 1225–1251.

Rice, R. L. (1992). *Stress and health* (2nd ed.). Pacific Grove, CA: Brookes-Cole.

Riensche, L., Peterson, K., & Linden, S. (1990). Young children's attitudes toward peer hearing aid wears. *Hearing Journal, 43(10)*, 19–20.

Riessman, C. (1993). *Narrative analysis: Qualitative research methods series* (No. 30). Newbury Park, CA: Sage.

Ripich, D., Hambrecht, G., Panagos, J., & Prelock, P. (1984). An analysis of articulation and language discourse patterns. *Journal of Childhood Communication Disorders, 7(2)*, 17–26.

Ripich, D., & Panagos, J. (1985). Accessing children's knowledge of sociolinguistic rules for speech therapy lessons. *Journal of Speech and Hearing Disorders, 50*, 335–346.

Roberts, C., Davies, E., & Jupp, T. (1992). *Language and discrimination*. London: Longman.

Robillard, A. (1999). *Meaning of a disability: The lived experience of paralysis*. Philadelphia: Temple University Press.

Rogers, C. R. (1961). *On becoming a person: A therapist's view of psychotherapy*. Boston: Houghton Mifflin.

Ross, E. (1997). *Ecology of stress and burnout among South African social workers*. Unpublished doctoral thesis. Johannesburg: University of the Witwatersrand.

Ross, E., & Deverell, A. (2004). *Psychosocial approaches to health, illness and disability: A reader for health care professionals*. Pretoria: Van Schaik.

Rowan, J., & Jacobs, M. (2002). *The therapist's use of self*. Buckingham, UK: Open University Press.

Rumi (1999a). Fastened to a pole. *Rumi: The glance: Songs of soul meeting* (C. Barks, Trans.) (p. 79). New York: Penguin Press.

Rumi (1999b). Raw, well-cooked, burnt. *Rumi: The glance: Songs of soul meeting* (C. Barks, Trans.) (p. 62). New York: Penguin Press.

Rumi (1999c.) Undressing. Rumi: *The glance: Songs of soul meeting* (C. Barks, Trans.) (p. 65). New York: Penguin Press.

Rushton, A. (1987). Stress among social workers. In R. Payne & J. Firth-Cozens (Eds.), *Stress in health professionals*. Chichester, UK: John Wiley.

Sacks, H., Schegloff, S., & Jefferson, G. (1974). A simplest systematics for the organization of turn taking in conversation. *Language, 50*, 696–735.

Sadow, D., Ryder, M., & Webster, D. (2002). Is education of health professionals encouraging stigma towards the mentally ill? *Journal of Mental Health, 11(6)*, 657–665.

Safran, D. G., Taira, D. A., Rogers, W. H., Kosinski, M., Ware, J. E., & Tarlov, A. R. (1998). Linking primary care performance to outcomes of care. *Journal of Family Practice, 47*, 213–220.

Santhanam, G., Ryu, S., Yu, B., Afshar, A., & Shenoy, K. (2006). A high-performance brain–computer interface. *Nature, 442*, 195–198.

Sarangi, S., & Roberts, C. (Eds.). (1999). *Talk, work and institutional order*. New York: Mouton de Gruyter.

Sarno, M. T. (1993). Aphasia rehabilitation: Psychosocial and ethical considerations. *Aphasiology, 7(4)*, 321–334.

Sarno, M. T. (2004). Aphasia therapies: Historical perspectives and moral imperatives. In J. Duchan & S. Byng (Eds.), *Challenging aphasia therapies* (pp. 17–31). Hove, UK: Psychology Press.

Scheetz, N. (2001). *Orientation to deafness* (2nd ed.). Boston: Allyn & Bacon.

Schegloff, E. A. (2000). When "others" initiate repair. *Applied Linguistics, 21(2)*, 205–243.

Schegloff, E. A. (2003). Conversation analysis and communication disorders. In C. Goodwin (Ed.), *Conversation and brain damage* (pp. 21–55). Oxford, UK: Oxford University Press.

Schegloff, E. A., Jefferson, G., & Sacks, H. (1977). The preference for self-correction in the organization of repair in conversation. *Language, 53*, 361–382.

Schildknecht, C. (1996). Knowledge that the mind seeks: The epistemic impact of Plato's form of discourse. *Philosophy and Rhetoric, 29(3)*, 225–243.

Schleidt, W. M. (1999). Apes, wolves and the trek to humanity: Did wolves show us the way? *Discovering Archaeology, 1*, 8–10.

Schneider, J. (1984). *Stress, loss, and grief*. Baltimore: University Park Press.

Schön, D. A. (1983). *The reflective practitioner: How professionals think in action*. New York: Basic Books.

Schön, D. A. (1987). *Educating the reflective practitioner: Toward a new design*. San Francisco: Jossey-Bass.

Schulz, E. K. (2005). The meaning of spirituality for individuals with disabilities. *Disability and Rehabilitation, 27(21)*, 1283–1295.

Schulze, B. (2007). Stigma and mental health professionals: A review of the evidence on an intricate relationship. *International Review of Psychiatry, 19(2)*, 137–155.

Schum, R. L. (1986). *Counseling in speech and hearing practice*. Rockville, MD: National Student Speech-Language-Hearing Association.

Scollon, R., & Scollon, S. (2001). *Intercultural communication* (2nd ed.). Oxford, UK: Blackwell.

Seeman. M. (1959). On the meaning of alienation. *American Sociological Review, 24*, 783–791.

Segal, R. A. (1987). *Joseph Campbell: An introduction*. New York: Garland Publishing.

Seligman, L. (2009). *Fundamental skills for mental health professionals*. Upper Saddle River, NJ: Pearson.

Seligman, S. (1993). Why how you feel matters: Countertransference reactions in intervention relationships. *WAIMH News, 1(2)*, 1–6.

Selye, H. (1975). *The stress of life*. New York: McGraw-Hill.

Shadden, B. (2005). Aphasia as identity theft: Theory and practice. *Aphasiology, 19(3/4/5)*, 211–223.

Shadden, B., & Agan, J. (2004). Renegotiation of Identity: The social context of aphasia support groups. *Topics in Language Disorders, 24(3)*, 174–186.

Shadden B. B., Hagstrom, F., & Koski, P. R. (2008). *Neurogenic communication disorders: Life stories and the narrative self.* San Diego, CA: Plural Publishing.

Shah, Mazhar H. (1966). *The general principles of Avicenna's canon of medicine.* Karachi: Naveed Clinic.

Shahmoon-Shanok, R. (2006). Reflective supervision for an integrated model: What, why, and how? In G. M. Foley & J. D. Hochman (Eds.), *Mental health in early intervention: Achieving unity in principles and practice* (pp. 343–381). Baltimore: Brookes Publishing Co.

Shahmoon-Shanok, R., & Geller, E. (2009). Embracing complexity across disciplines: Reflective supervision and post-degree training integrate mental health concepts with speech-language therapy and graduate education. *Infant Mental Health Journal (Special Issue), 30(6)*, 591–620.

Shahmoon-Shanok, R., Henderson, D., Grellong, B., & Foley, G. M. (2006). Preparation for practice in an integrated model: The magic is in the mix. In G. M. Foley & J. D. Hochman (Eds.), *Mental health in early intervention: Achieving unity in principles and practice* (pp. 383–422). Baltimore: Brookes Publishing Co.

Sheafor, B. W., & Horejsi, C. R. (2006). *Techniques and guidelines for social work practice* (7th ed.). Boston: Pearson.

Shernoff, M. (1990). Why every social worker should be challenged by Aids. *Social Work, 35(2)*, 5–8.

Sherratt, S. (2007, July). *Humour in aphasia therapy: Why and how.* Paper presented at the 5th Asia Pacific Conference on Speech, Language and Hearing, Brisbane.

Sherratt, S., Alston, M., & Ferguson, A. (2007, September). *"This good business": Preliminary outcomes of social group therapy for aphasia.* Paper presented at the Living Successfully with Aphasia: Intervention, Evaluation and Evidence Conference, Toronto.

Shipley, K. G., & McAfee, J. G. (2009). *Assessment in speech-language pathology* (4th ed.). Clifton Park, NY: Delmar Cengage Learning

Shi-xu. (2005). *A cultural approach to discourse.* New York: Palgrave Macmillan.

Siegel, D. J. (1999). The *developing mind: How relationships and the brain interact to shape who we are.* New York: Guilford Press.

Siegel, D., & Hartzell, M. (2003). *Parenting from the inside out: How a deeper self-understanding can help you raise children who thrive.* New York: Penguin.

Siegel, S., & Lowe, E. (1992). *The patient who cured his therapist and other tales of therapy.* New York: Dutton.

Silvast, M. (1991). Aphasia therapy dialogues. *Aphasiology, 5*, 383–390.

Silverman, D. (2006) *Interpreting qualitative data* (3rd ed., p. 398). Thousand Oaks, CA: Sage.

Silverman, E.-M. (2003a). A clinical profession? *The ASHA Leader, 8(1)*, 23.

Silverman, E.-M. (2003b). Shared connections – Spirituality in clinical practice. *The ASHA Leader, 8(17)*, 40.

Silverman, E.-M. (2006). A personal choice. *The ASHA Leader, 11(16)*, 47.

Silverman, E.-M. (2007, October). *Creating conditions for change.* Paper presented at the 10th Annual International Stuttering Awareness Day Online Conference.

Silverman, E.-M. (2008a). Applying narrative techniques. *The ASHA Leader, 13(2)*, 46.

Silverman, E.-M. (2008b). Ongoing self-reflection. *American Journal of Speech-Language Pathology, 17(1)*, 92.

Silverman, E.-M. (2009a, October). *Doing the work.* Presented at the 12th Annual Online Conference.

Silverman, E.-M. (2009b). *Mind matters: Setting the stage for satisfying clinical service. A personal essay.* Charleston, SC: BookSurge Publishing.

Simmons-Mackie, N. (1999). *Constructing aphasia: Assessing our own language.* Presentation at the British Aphasiology Society, London.

Simmons-Mackie, N. (2000). Social approaches to the management of aphasia. In L. Worrall & C. Frattali (Eds.), *Neurogenic communication disorders: A functional approach.* New York: Thieme.

Simmons-Mackie, N. (2001). Social approaches to aphasia intervention. In R. Chapey (Ed.), *Language intervention strategies in adult aphasia* (4th ed., pp. 246–268). Baltimore: Williams & Wilkins.

Simmons-Mackie, N. (2004). Just kidding! Humour and therapy for aphasia. In J. F. Duchan & S. Byng (Eds.), *Challenging aphasia therapies: Broadening the discourse and extending the boundaries* (pp. 101–117). Hove, UK: Psychology Press.

Simmons-Mackie, N., & Damico, J. S. (1999a). Qualitative methods in aphasia research: Ethnography. *Aphasiology, 13(9–11)*, 681–687.

Simmons-Mackie, N., & Damico, J. S. (1999b). Social role negotiation in aphasia therapy: Competence, incompetence and conflict. In D. Kovarsky, J. Duchan, & M. Maxwell (Eds.), *Constructing (in)competence: Disabling evaluations in clinical and social interaction* (pp. 313–341). Hillsdale, NJ: Lawrence Erlbaum Associates, Inc.

Simmons-Mackie, N., & Damico, J. S. (2008). Exposed and embedded corrections in therapy for aphasia. *International Journal of Language and Communication Disorders, 43*, 1–12.

Simmons-Mackie, N., & Damico, J. S. (2009). Engagement in group therapy for aphasia. *Seminars in Speech and Language, 30(1)*, 18–26.

Simmons-Mackie, N., Damico, J., & Damico, H. (1999). A qualitative study of feedback in aphasia therapy. *American Journal of Speech-Language Pathology, 8*, 218–230.

Simmons-Mackie, N., & Elman, R. J. (in press). Negotiation of identity in group therapy for aphasia. *Aphasiology.*

Simmons-Mackie, N., Elman, R., Holland, A., & Damico, J. S. (2007). Management of discourse in group therapy for aphasia. *Topics in Language Disorders, 27(1)*, 5–23.

Simmons-Mackie, N., & Schultz, M. (2003). The role of humor in therapy for aphasia. *Aphasiology, 17*, 751–766.

Sinclair, J., & Coulthard, R. (1975). *Towards an analysis of discourse: The English used by teachers and pupils.* Oxford, UK: Oxford University Press.

Sipiora, P., & Baumlin, J. (2002). *Rhetoric and Kairos: Essays in theory, history, and praxis.* New York: State University of New York Press.

Slade, A. (2002). Keeping the baby in mind: A critical factor in perinatal mental health. *Zero to Three, 6*, 10–16.

Smart, J. (2001). *Disability, society, and the individual.* Gaithersburg, MD: Aspen.

Smith, D. L. (1996). Psychodynamic therapy: The Freudian approach. In W. Dryden (Ed.), *Handbook of individual therapy* (pp. 19–39). London: Sage

Smith, J. A., & Osborn, M. (2007). Pain as an assault on self: An interpretive phenomenological analysis of the psychological impact of chronic benign low back pain. *Psychology & Health, 22,* 517–534.

Smith, N. (2008). *I think there's something wrong with me.* London: Black Swan.

Sontag, S. (1991). *Illness as metaphor. Aids and its metaphor.* London: Penguin Books.

Spillers, C. S. (2007). An existential framework for understanding the counseling needs of clients. *American Journal of Speech-Language Pathology, 16,* 191–197.

St. John of the Cross (2002). Dig here the angel said. *Love poems from God* (D. Ladinsky, Trans., pp. 326–327). New York: Penguin Press.

Stapp, H. (2007). *Mindful universe: Quantum mechanics and the participating observer.* New York: Springer.

Stein, R., Gill, K., & Gans, D. (2000). Adolescents' attitudes toward their peers with hearing impairment. *Journal of Educational Audiology, 8,* 1–6.

Steiner, C. (1994). *Scripts people live: Transactional analysis of life scripts.* New York: Grove Press.

Stern, D. N. (1985). *The interpersonal world of the infant: A view from psychoanalysis and developmental psychology.* New York: Basic Books.

Stewart, I., & Joines, V. (1993). *TA today: A new introduction to transactional analysis.* Nottingham: Lifespace Publishing.

Stewart, M., Brown, J. B., Donner, A., McWhinney, I. R., Oates, J., Weston, W. W., & Jordan, J. (2000). The impact of patient-centered care on outcomes. *Journal of Family Practice, 49,* 796–804.

Stewart, T., & Birdsall, M. (2001). A review of the contribution of personal construct psychology to stammering therapy. *Journal of Constructivist Psychology, 14,* 215–226.

Strainchamps, A. (Producer). (2006, November 5). *Searching for Shangri-La: Interview with Caitlin Mathews. To the Best of Our Knowledge.* Wisconsin Public Radio.

Street, R., Gordon, H., & Haidet, P. (2007). Physicians' communication and perceptions of patients: Is it how they look, how they talk, or is it just the doctor? *Social Science & Medicine, 65(3),* 586–598.

Strong, P.M. (1979). *The ceremonial order of the clinic.* London: Routledge & Kegan Paul.

Surette, J. (2004). The within of things. In *An amazing journey* (Session III) (pp. 7–8). St. Paul, MN: Global Education Associates Upper Midwest.

Swain, J., Clark, J., Parry, K., French, S., & Reynolds, F. (2004a). *Enabling relationships in health and social care: A guide for therapists.* Oxford, UK: Butterworth-Heinemann.

Swain, J., French, S., Barnes, C., & Thomas, C. (2004b). *Disabling barriers – Enabling environments* (2nd ed.). London: Sage Publications.

Swidler, M., & Ross, E. (1993). Burnout: A smouldering problem among South African speech-language pathologists and audiologists? *South African Journal of Communication Disorders, 40,* 71–84.

Swimme, B. (2004a). Differentiation. In *An amazing journey.* Session III (p. 4). St. Paul, MN: Global Education Associates Upper Midwest.

Swimme, B. (2004b). Subjectivity. In *An amazing journey.* Session III (p. 6). St. Paul, MN: Global Education Associates Upper Midwest.

Swimme, B. (2004c). Communion. In *An amazing journey.* Session III (p. 8). St. Paul, MN: Global Education Associates Upper Midwest.

Tandon, R., Keshavan, M. S., & Nasrallah, H. A. (2008). Schizophrenia, "just the facts": What we know in 2008. 2. Epidemiology and etiology. *Schizophrenia Research, 102,* 1–18.

Tannen, D. (1989). *Talking voices: Repetition, dialogue and imagery in conversational discourse*. Cambridge, UK: Cambridge University Press.

Tannen, D. (1990). *You just don't understand*. New York: Morrow.

Tannen, D. (Ed.). (1993). *Framing in discourse*. Oxford, UK: Oxford University Press.

Tannen, D., & Wallat, C. (1993). Interactive frames and knowledge schemas in interactions: Examples from a medical examination/interview. In D. Tannen, (Ed.), *Framing in discourse* (pp. 57–76). Oxford, UK: Oxford University Press.

Tantum, D. (2002). *Psychotherapy and counselling in practice. A narrative framework*. Cambridge, UK: Cambridge University Press.

Tatham, A., Cough, B., & Maxwell, V. (2006). Research report: Stress in speech therapy. *Stress Medicine, 5(4)*, 259–264.

Taylor, R. R. (2008). The changing landscape of therapeutic use of self in occupational therapy: Historical overview (pp. 3–18). In R. R. Taylor (Ed.), *The intentional relationship: Occupational therapy and use of self*. Philadelphia: F. A. Davis Company.

Terrell, B., & Terrell, F. (1993). Non-biased clinical management. In D. Battle (Ed.), *Communication disorders in multicultural populations*. Boston: Andover Medical Publishers.

Thomas, C. (1999). *Female forms: Experiencing and understanding disability*. Buckingham, UK: Open University Press.

Thomas, C. (2007). *Sociologies of disability and illness*. New York: Palgrave Macmillan.

Threats, T. (2006). Towards an international framework for communication disorders: Use of the ICF. *Journal of Communication Disorders, 39*, 251–265.

Tillich, P. (1980). Loneliness and solitude. In J. Hartog, J. R. Audy, & Y. A. Cohen (Eds.), *The anatomy of loneliness* (pp. 547–553). New York: International Universities Press.

Togher, L. (2003). Do I have green hair? "Conversations" in aphasia therapy. In S. Parr, J. Duchan, & C. Pound (Eds.), *Aphasia inside out* (pp. 65–79). Maidenhead, UK: Open University Press.

Tolle, E., (2006). *A new earth. Awakening to your life's purpose*. New York: Penguin Books.

Twining, J. E. (1980). Alienation as a social process. *The Sociological Quarterly, 21(3)*, 417–428.

van der Gaag, A., & Anderson, C. (2005). The geography of professional practice: Swamps and icebergs. In C. Anderson & A. van der Gaag (Eds.), *Speech and language therapy: Issues in professional practice* (pp. 1–9). London: Whurr Publishers.

van Dijk, T. A. (1992). Discourse and the denial of racism. *Discourse and Society, 3*, 87–118.

Van Riper, C. (1973). *The treatment of stuttering* (2nd ed.). Englewood Cliffs, NJ: Prentice Hall.

Van Riper, C., & Erickson, R. L. (1996). *Speech correction: An introduction to speech pathology and audiology* (9th ed.). London: Allyn & Bacon.

Van Tellingen, C. (2007). About hearsay – or reappraisal of the role of the anamnesis as an instrument of meaningful communication. *Netherlands Heart Journal, 15(10)*, 359–362.

Vincent, J. (1996). Why ever do we do it? Unconscious motivation in choosing social work as a career. *Journal of Social Work Practice, 10*, 63–69.

von Franz, M. L. (1964). The process of individuation. In C. G. Jung (Ed.). *Man and his symbols* (pp. 158–230). New York: Doubleday.

Walker, M. L. (1995). Rehabilitation counseling. In A. E. Dell Orton & R. P. Marinelli (Eds.), *Encyclopedia of disability and rehabilitation* (pp. 618–623). Farmington Hills, MI: Cengage Gale.

Wallach Bologh, R. (1981) Grounding the alienation of self and body. A critical, phenomenological analysis of the patient in Western medicine. *Sociology of Health & Illness, 3(2)*, 188–206.

Walsh, I. P. (2002). Revealing ability amidst perceived disability in clinical inter- actions: A nice idea or a clinical imperative? *Journal of Clinical Speech & Language Studies, 12/13*, 118–146.

Walsh, I. P. (2004, July). *Power-sharing in conversations with people with schizophrenia; Redressing the asymmetry of healthcare discourse.* Paper presented at The Royal College of Psychiatrists Annual Meeting, Harrogate.

Walsh, I. P. (2007). Small talk is "big talk" in clinical discourse. *Topics in Language Disorders, 27(1)*, 24–36.

Walsh, I. P. (2008). Whose voice is it anyway? Hushing and hearing "voices" in speech and language therapy interactions with people with chronic schizophrenia. *Inter- national Journal of Language & Communication Disorders, 43(1)*, 81–95.

Walsh, I. P., & Leahy, M. M. (2009). "Cajoling" as a means of engagement in the dysphagia clinic. *Seminars in Speech and Language, 30(1)*, 37–47.

Walsh, I. P., Regan, J., Sowman, R., Parsons, B., & McKay, A. P. (2007). A needs analysis for the provision of speech and language therapy service to adults with mental health disorders. *Irish Journal of Psychological Medicine, 24(3)*, 89–93.

Walsh-Brennan, I. P. (2002). *"Speak to me . . . speak to me please" . . . Conversational sociability: An emergent ability amidst perceived disability in chronic schizophrenia.* Unpublished PhD Thesis, Trinity College Dublin, Ireland.

Wang, J. (2006). Questions and the exercise of power. *Journal of Pragmatics, 17(4)*, 529–548.

Ward, L. M., & Webster E. J. (1965). The training of clinical personnel II: A concept of clinical preparation. *ASHA, 7*, 103–106.

Warner, J., Byers-Brown, B., & McCartney, E. (1984). *Speech therapy: A clinical companion.* Manchester, UK: Manchester University Press.

Watkins, P. (2001). *Mental health nursing: The art of compassionate care.* Oxford, UK: Butterworth Heinemann.

Weinbach, R. W. (1994). *The social worker as manager: Theory and practice* (2nd ed.). Boston: Allyn & Bacon.

West, C. (1998). When the doctor is a lady: Power, status, and gender in physician– patient encounters. In J. Coates (Ed.), *Language and gender: A reader* (pp. 127–138). Oxford, UK: Blackwell.

White, M. (1989). *Selected papers.* Adelaide: Dulwich Center.

White, M. (1995). *Re-authoring lives: Interviews and essays.* Adelaide: Dulwich Center.

White, M. (2007). *Maps of narrative practice.* New York: W. W. Norton & Company.

White, M., & Epston, D. (1990). *Narrative means to therapeutic ends.* New York: W. W. Norton and Company.

Whitehorn, J. C., & Betz, B. J. (1954). A study of psychotherapeutic relationships between physicians and schizophrenic patients. *American Journal of Psychiatry, 111*, 321–331.

Whitehouse, A. J. O., Hird, K., & Cocks, N. (2007). Recruitment and retention of speech and language therapists: What do university students find important? *Journal of Allied Health, Fall*, 1–2.

Whitman, W. (1860) *Leaves of grass*. Boston: Thayer & Eldridge. Retrieved May 23, 2010 from www.whitmanarchive.org/published/LG/1860/whole

Wierzbicka, A. (1991). *Cross-cultural pragmatics: The semantics of human interaction*. Berlin: Mouton de Gruyter.

Wilcox, J., & Davis, G. A. (1977). Speech act analysis of aphasic communication in individual and group settings. In R. H. Brookshire (Ed.), *Clinical aphasiology conference proceedings* (pp. 166–174). Minneapolis, MN: BRK.

Wilkinson, R. (1999). Introduction. *Aphasiology, 4(5)*, 251–258.

Wilson, J. (1993). The supervisory relationship on family therapy training: Constructing a fit between trainee and trainer. *Human Systems, 4*, 73–187.

Wilson, J. (1998). *Child-focused practice: A collaborative systemic approach*. London: Karnac.

Wilson, J. (2007). *The performance of practice*. London: Karnac.

Wilson, M. (1996). Arabic speakers: Language and culture, here and abroad. *Topics in Language Disorders, 16(4)*, 65–80.

Winnicott, D. W. (1958). Hate in the countertransference. In *Collected papers: Through pediatrics to psycho-analysis* (pp. 194–203). New York: Basic Books.

Winnicott, D. W. (1960). The theory of the parent–infant relationship. *International Journal of Psychoanalysis, 41*, 585–595.

Winslade, J., & Monk, G. (1999). *Narrative counseling in schools: Powerful and brief*. Thousand Oaks, CA: Corwin Press.

Winslade, J., & Smith, L. (1997). Countering alcoholic narratives. In G. Monk, J. Winslade, K. Crocket, & D. Epston (Eds.), *Narrative therapy in practice: The archaeology of hope*. San Francisco: Jossey-Bass Publishers.

Winslow, G. R., & Wehtje-Winslow, B. J. (2007). Ethical boundaries of spiritual care. *Medical Journal of Australia, 186(10)*, S63–S66.

Wodak, R. (1996). *Disorders of discourse*. London: Longman.

Wolter, J. A., DiLollo, A., & Apel, K. (2006). A narrative therapy approach to counseling: A model for working with adolescents and adults with language-literacy deficits. *Language, Speech, and Hearing Services in Schools, 37(3)*, 168–177.

Wood, M. (2005). *In search of myths and heroes*. Berkeley, CA: University of California Press.

Woollams, S., & Brown, M. (1979). *TA: The total handbook of transactional analysis*. Englewood Cliffs, NJ: Prentice Hall.

World Health Organization (2001). *International classification of functioning, disability and health (ICF)*. Geneva: WHO.

Worrall, L. (2000). The influence of professional values on the functional communicaiton approach in aphasia. In L. Worrall & C. Frattali (Eds.), *Neurogenic communication disorders: A functional approach*. New York: Thieme.

Worrall, L., Davidson, B., Ferguson, A., Hersh, D., Howe, T., & Sherratt, S. (2007). What people with aphasia want: Goal-setting in aphasia rehabilitation. Paper Presented at the Annual Speech-Language-Hearing Association Conference, Boston.

Wulf, H. H. (1979). *Aphasia, my world alone*. Detroit, MI: Wayne State University Press.

Wyatt, T. (2002). Assessing the communicative abilities of clients from diverse cultural and language backgrounds. In D. Battle (Ed.), *Communication disorders in multi-cultural populations* (3rd ed., pp. 415–460). Woburn, MA: Butterworth-Heinemann.

Yalom, I. (1980). *Existential psychotherapy*. New York: Basic Books.

Yalom, I. D. (2002). *The gift of therapy. Reflections on being a therapist*. London: Judy Piatkus Ltd.

Yardley, L. (2000). Dilemmas in qualitative health research. *Psychology & Health, 15,* 215–228.

Young-Eisendrath, P. (1996). *The gifts of suffering*. Reading, MN: Addison-Wesley.

Younger, J. B. (1995). The alienation of the sufferer. *Advanced Nursing Science, 17(4),* 53–57.

Appendix

TRANSCRIPTION CONVENTIONS

Eggins and Slade, 1997 (p. 5) transcription conventions

.	certainty, completion (typically falling tone)
no end of turn punctuation	implies non-termination (no final intonation)
‚	parcelling of talk; breathing time
?	uncertainty (rising tone or wh- interrogative)
!	"surprised" intonation (rising falling tone)
WORDS IN CAPITALS	emphatic stress and/or increased volume
" "	change in voice quality in reported speech
( )	untranscribable talk
(words within parentheses)	transcriber's guess
[words in square brackets]	non-verbal information
= =	overlap (contiguity, simultaniety)
. . .	short hesitation within a turn (less than 3 seconds)
[4 secs]	indication of inter-turn pause length
dash – then talk	false start/restart

D. Silverman, 2006 (p. 398) transcription conventions

:::	a colon or series of colons represents an audible lengthening of the preceding sound proportional to the number of colons
[	Left-side brackets indicate where overlapping talk begins
]	Right-side brackets indicate where overlapping talk ends, or marks alignments within a continuing stream of overlapping talk
___	Underlining indicates stress or emphasis
((points))	Words in double parentheses indicate transcriber's comments, not transcriptions

=	Equal signs (ordinarily at the end of one line and the start of an ensuing one) indicate a "latched" relationship – no silence at all between them.
(0.8)	Numbers in parentheses indicate period of silence, in tenths of a second
(.)	A dot inside parentheses indicates a pause of less than 0.2 seconds

Author index

Adelson, E. 198
Adingono-Smith, M. 38, 45
Afshar, A. 184
Agan, J. 47
Agar, M. 37
Alonzo, A. A. 106, 108
Al-Roubaie, A. 95
Alston, M. 74
American Speech-Language Hearing Association 120
Anderson, C. 24
Anderson, T. P. 111
Angelocci, R. 116
Antaki, C. 90–1
Antolikova, S. 230
Apel, K. 140
Arches, J. 221
Armstrong, E. 37–8, 68
Arokiasamy, C. V. 116
Atkinson, R. 22, 28
Aveline, M. 172–3

Bagshaw, N. 38–9
Bakhtin, M. M. 41
Banja, J. D. 23
Barling, J. 219
Barnes, C. 23, 30
Barrick, B. 108
Barrow, A. R. 23, 30
Barrow, R. 22–3, 27, 30
Barton, J. 173
Bateman, A. 171
Battle, D. 79–80, 83
Baum, L. F. 241
Baumann, A. E. 106, 108
Baumlin, J. 189

Bausch, W. J. 235, 237, 239–41
Baynton, D. C. 108, 111
Beail, N. 47
Beck, M. 99
Becker, G. 31
Becker, L. 38
Benner, P. 124, 130–1
Berne, E. 182, 184, 187, 189, 191
Bernstein, L. 180
Bernstein, R. S. 180
Berryman, M. 92
Bertacchi, J. 197–8, 207
Betz, B. J. 18
Bill, J. B. 183
Birdsall, M. 140
Bishop, R. 92
Black, M. 36
Blanton, L. 221
Blood, G. W. 117
Blood, I. M. 117
Bobkoff, K. 38, 40–1
Bohm, D. 187
Bonanno, G. A. 237
Boone, D. R. 77
Borg, M. 239–41
Boroditsky, L. 185
Bouillaud, J. 161
Boulle, A. 108
Bowlby, J. 190, 207
Boylstein, C. 24, 30
Brady, M. 116
Bramley, N. 45
Brickhouse, T. C. 184
Brisenden, S. 23
Brock, A. J. 157–8
Brookshire, R. 36, 57
Brown, D. 171

Brown, J. B. 46
Brown, M. 185, 187
Brown, P. 81, 101, 103, 129, 135
Brumfitt, S. 140, 173
Brumfitt, S. T. 9
Bryce, S. 80, 92
Bryer, A. 71
Buck, A. H. 155
Bunning, K. 14, 60–1, 77
Burkhardt, M. A. 231
Burns, K. 28
Burns, T. 131
Butler, R. 145–6
Byers-Brown, B. 54–5
Byng, S. 9, 36–8, 46–7, 77

Cambourne, B. 40
Cameron, G. 159
Campbell, J. 241–2
Cappella, J. N. 41
Carradice, A. 47
Casasanto, D. 185
Casement, P. 172–3
Cashdan, S. 172
Cazden, C. B. 39
Charmaz, K. 13
Charon, R. 22–6, 28, 31–2, 187, 191
Chödrön, P. 183, 190, 240
Chow, V. M. C. 116
Christensen, A. 46
Cicourel, A. 40–1
Clark, J. 22, 28, 31, 33
Clarke, H. 35
Clarke, P. 90–1
Clarke, S. 9
Clarkson, P. 14
Coates, J. 103

Cocks, N. 213, 220, 223
Cohen, P. A. 148
Cole, K. 38, 40–1
Coleman, L. M. 110, 115, 120
Collins English Dictionary 53
Concise Oxford Dictionary 53
Conlon, J. 234
Coplon, J. 197–8
Corbitt, E. M. 116
Corboz-Warnery, A. 201
Cortazzi, M. 61
Costa, G. 211–12
Cott, C. 33
Cough, B. 213, 222
Coulthard, R. 39, 61
Coupland, J. 57–8, 90, 134–5
Coupland, N. 58, 134–5
Croteau, C. 71
Crowe, T. 238
Cunningham, J. A. 116
Curran, M. 42, 126–7
Cyr-Stafford, C. 55

D'Souza, R. 231
Dalai Lama 187
Dale, P. 38, 40–1
Damico, H. 38–9, 41, 47
Damico, J. 38–9, 41, 47, 80
Damico, J. S. 37–42, 45–7, 50, 57, 63, 74, 127, 153
Damico, S. K. 38, 41, 46, 50
Danhauer, J. 117
Danhauer, J. L. 117
Daniels, D. 173
Danielson, E. 45
Danziger-Klein, S. 93–4
Dass, R. 243
Davidson, B. 47
Davies, E. 80–1, 91
Davies, J. 103
Davis, D. 54
Davis, G. A. 55, 57–8, 76
Dawson, D. 230
Deacon, H. 108
Delaney, C. 231
deMare, T. 48
Deverell, A. 223
Dhaliwal, H. 241–2

DiLollo, A. 140–1, 143, 146
DiLollo, L. D. 140
Dirschel, K. M. 131
Dolny, H. 215, 227
Donner, A. 46
Dossey, L. 187
Downs, D. 117
Drew, P. 80
Drummond, S. S. 74
Duchan, J. 38–42, 46, 50, 57–8, 61, 91, 153
Duff, M. 37, 49
Dukas, H. 184–5
Dunbar, R. 10
Dyches, T. T. 213, 220

Eatough, V. 45
Eckhart, M. 232
Edwards, D. 40
Edwards, M. L. 121
Eggbeer, L. 197–8
Eggins, S. 123, 273
Elliot, N. 37, 56
Elman, R. 40, 50, 57, 63, 73–5
Elman, R. J. 47, 49
Emerick, L. 56
Emerson, J. 13, 124
Emmons, S. 126
Emoto, M. 187
Enderby, P. 13, 124
English, K. 140
English, R. W. 106, 108
Epstein, R. M. 192
Epston, D. 26, 28, 31, 33, 140–3
Erickson, R. L. 12
Erikson, E. H. 17
Erler, S. R. 108
Erskine, R. 176
Estes, C. P. 241–2
Evans, A. M. 170
Evans, D. 12

Faber, A. 96
Faircloth, C. 24, 30
Fairclough, N. 80, 94, 99, 101
Faiver, C. 239
Farnell, R. 155
Fastenau, P. 221
Fastenau, P. S. 221
Faugier, J. 108, 116

Fellows, J. A. 222
Felton, J. 188–9
Fenichel, E. 197–8
Ferguson, A. 37–8, 42, 47, 49, 56, 68–9, 71–2, 74, 77, 82, 91
Ferrara, K. 123
Fey, M. 38, 40–1, 50
Figley, C. R. 215
Fimian, M. 221
Fimian, M. J. 221
Fineman, S. 218
Fisher, S. 61, 93, 95
Fitzsimmons, P. 40
Fivaz-Depeursinge, E. 201
Foley, G. M. 197–202, 205, 208, 210–11
Fonagy, P. 205, 207
Foucault, M. 155
Fourie, R. 15–17, 19, 33, 55, 237
Fowler, S. 80
Fraiberg, S. 198
Frank, A. W. 26, 43
Frank, J. 15, 20
Frank, J. D. 15, 20
Frankl, V. 184–5, 231, 240
Fransella, F. 140, 145
French, R. 205–6
French, S. 22–2, 28, 30–1, 33
Friedman, R. M. 77
Frith, C. 131

Gans, D. 117
Garfinkel, H. 40
Garstecki, D. C. 108
Gee, J. P. 79–80
Geekie, P. 40
Geiser, C. 126
Geller, E. 198–202, 205, 208, 210–11
Gergely, G. 205
Gergen, K. J. 146
Germain, C. B. 215
Gilbert, P. 47, 177
Gilbert, T. 189
Giles, H. 134
Gill, K. 117
Gilmore, N. 106, 108
Gilpin, S. 9, 37, 47
Giorgi, A. 37
Girolametto, L. 199
Gitterman, A. 215

Glenn, P. 101, 136
Glozman, J. 173
Goffman, E. 40, 106, 108, 120
Goffman, I. 105
Goldberg, S. A. 54–5, 57, 60
Goldstein, H. 38–9
Goleman, D. 187
Gomez, N. 117
Gordon, H. 50
Gordon, N. 173
Gorman, P. 243
Gottdiener, J. S. 12
Goulding, M. 191
Goulding, R. 191
Grashow, A. 147–8, 150–1
Greenspan, S. 199–200
Grellong, B. 200
Groce, S. 95
Grypdonck, M. 23
Guice, S. 116
Gwyn, R. 22, 31

Hafiz 232, 235–6
Hagstrom, F. 22–3, 28, 30, 49
Haidet, P. 50
Hall, D. 117
Halliday, M. A. K. 80
Hamayan, E. 80
Hambrecht, G. 38
Hammer, A. 83, 225
Handy, J. 218
Handzo, G. 230
Hanh, T. N. 187–8
Haque, A. 159–60
Harper, A. 71
Harris, M. J. 116
Harris, S. F. 213, 220
Harrison, E. 77
Harrow, M. 126
Hartzell, M. 207, 209
Hawley, H. 40
Haynes, O. 56
Haynes, W. 55
Heath, C. 131
Heath, M. A. 213, 221
Heffron, M. 197–8, 204, 209–10
Heffron, M. C. 203, 206
Hegde, M. 54
Heifetz, R. A. 147–8, 150–1

Henderson, D. 200
Hengst, J. 37, 49
Henwood, K. 134
Heritage, J. 80, 93
Herodotus 154
Hersh, D. 42, 47
Hetu, R. 117
Higgins, P. C. 115
Hiley, B. 187
Hilsman, G. J. 230, 237
Hinckley, J. 36, 46, 50
Hippocrates 56, 156–7
Hird, K. 213, 220, 223
Hochman, J. D. 197, 199–200, 205
Hodge, A. 80–1
Hodge, D. R. 231
Hoffman, B. 184–5
Hoffman, P. 38, 40–1
Holland, A. 40, 44, 48–50, 57, 63, 71, 74, 99, 200
Holmes, J. 80, 95
Holowchak, A. 155
Hoover, D. W. 116
Hoppe, M. 116
Horejsi, C. R. 218
Horton, S. 37–9, 45–7, 77
Houston, M. 21
Howe, T. 47
Hughes, M. 46
Hymes, D. 37
Hyun, J. 80

Iler, K. 117
Ingersoll, R. E. 239
Inscriptiones Graecae 155
Ireland, C. 9, 37, 47
Isaac, K. 79–80
Ivins, B. 197–8, 204, 209–10

Jackson, S. 221
Jacobs, M. 17
Jacyna, L. S. 161–2
Jeffers, S. 31
Jefferson, G. 39, 58, 72, 95, 135
Jin, L. 61
Joanette, Y. 54
Johnson, T. 179
Joines, V. 171
Jones, A. C. 170–2, 179
Jordan, J. 46

Jung, C. G. 183, 185, 187–8
Jupp, T. 80–1, 91
Jurist, E. L. 205
Juskowitz, S. 38–9

Kabat-Zinn, J. 185, 187
Kagan, A. 33
Kahn, M. 179
Kalmanson, B. 199, 202
Kaplan, K. J. 126
Kastner, D. 38–9, 76 153
Katz, R. 179
Kaufman, S. 31
Kelly, G. A. 140, 145
Keren, M. 201
Keshavan, M. S. 124
Kimbarow, M. 38–9, 76 153
King, J. 157
King, M. 125
Kirsh, B. 230
Klein, M. 172
Klevans, D. R. 77
Klippi, A. 75
Klompas, M. 173
Koenig, H. G. 230–1
Kongtrül, D. 190, 192
Kop, W. J. 12
Kornfield, J. 183, 187
Korzybski, A. 24
Kosinski, M. 46
Koski, P. R. 22–3, 28, 30
Kovarsky, D. 37–42, 45–6, 50, 76, 91, 101, 126–7, 153
Krueger, K. 36
Kummerer, S. 46
Kushner, H. S. 239–40

Lafond, D. 54
Landfield, A. W. 145
Lane, H. 111, 113
Langer, E. 185
Laplanche, J. 170
Laurie, D. L. 148, 150
Lavretsky, H. 124
Le Dorze, G. 71
Leahy, M. 57, 61–2, 100, 103
Leahy, M. M. 37–8, 40, 48, 57, 68, 127
Lecours, A. 54
Legg, C. 71

Leitner, L. M. 145
Lendering, J. 154
Levine, I. S. 124
Levine, J. 124
Levinson, S. 81, 101, 103, 129, 135
Levitan, L. 108, 111
Lewandowski, A. M. 146
Lieberman, R. J. 221
Lincoln, M. 77
Linden, S. 117
Lindsay, J. 49
Linsky, M. 147–8, 150–1
Lipton, B. 184
Lofland, J. 40
Lofland, L. H. 40
Lopez-Reyna, N. 46
Lordat, J. 161–2
Lorentzen, J. 95, 98
Lowe, E. 188
Lubinski, R. 215, 219
Luboshitzky, D. 230–1, 237, 239–40
Luterman, D. M. 8, 112–13, 204, 238

MacDonald, M. 41
MacKay, R. 47
Madden, M. L. 74
Mann, T. G. 197
Manning, W. H. 140–1, 143, 146
Markova, I. 39
Martin, D. 79
Martin, J. R. 71, 80
Marting, M. 83, 225
Martyn, D. 203
Marvell, A. 169
Marx, K. 11
Maslach, C. 213, 215, 221, 225
Masterson, J. 172, 179
Matthiessen, C. M. I. M. 80
Mattingly, C. 36
Maxwell, M. 91
Maxwell, M. M. 37
Maxwell, V. 213, 222
Maynard, D. 93
Mazlish, E. 96
McAfee, J. G. 141
McAllister, L. 77
McAllister, S. 77
McCabe, R. 131

McCarthy, P. 117, 140
McCartney, E. 54–5
McCaulley, M. 184
McKay, A. P. 124
McNally, C. 239
McWhinney, I. R. 46
Mendel, L. 140
Menz, F. 95
Mercer, D. 40
Milich, R. 116
Miller, M. 221
Miller, S. 205
Mills, S. 103
Mishler, E. 37, 93–4, 160
Moes, M. 157
Monk, G. 142, 146
Moore, M. S. 108, 111
Moore, R. 68, 73–4, 76
Moore, T. 232, 235–6, 239–40
Morena, G. D. 236, 241–2
Morgan, A. 140, 142
Morin, C. 71
Moses, K. 238–9
Mulac, A. 117
Murray, M. 41
Myss, C. 236

Nagai-Jacobson, M. G. 231
Nasrallah, H. A. 124
Neimeyer, R. A. 140–1, 143, 146–7
Nelson, D. L. 227
Nelson, H. L. 23, 30
Nemes, J. 189
Nettleton, S. 23
Newton, T. 218
Nicholas, L. 36
Nofsinger, R. E. 133
Norman-Murch, T. 204
Norris, J. 38, 40–1
Norris, K. 192
Norris, M. R. 74
North, M. 156
Nystrom, M. 10, 16–17

O'Brien, E. 239
O'Donohue, J. 232–3, 236, 239
O'Hagan, M. 126
O'Malley, E. 148, 152
O'Malley, M. P. 94, 96
Oates, J. 46

Oelschlaeger, M. 37–8, 74
Oliver, M. 23, 30, 232
Oliver, P. 222
Ollman, B. 11, 16
Onslow, M. 77
Oratio, A. 55
Orbach, S. 173
Orloff, J. 187
Osborn, M. 45
Osvaldsson, K. 68

Packman, A. 77
Palmer, P. 183, 232–3, 235–6
Panagos, J. 38–41
Parker Hall, S. 170
Parr, S. 9, 37, 47, 49
Parry, K. 22, 28, 31, 33
Parsons, B. 124
Patel, C. 214, 227
Paulson, M. 45
Paulson, S. 242
Pauwels, A. 81
Pawl, J. H. 197–8
Payne, M. 140, 143, 150
Peach, R. 117
Peat, F. 187
Pedder, J. 171
Penman, T. 48
Perez, J. C. 230
Perkins, R. E. 124, 128, 130
Pesut, B. 231
Peterson, K. 117
Poche, L. 222
Pontalis, J. 170
Porter, R. 156
Potter, R. 221
Pound, C. 32–3, 49
Prater, M. A. 213, 220
Prelock, P. 38
Prescott, T. E. 77
Priebe, S. 131
Pring, T. 77
Prior, P. 49
Prior, S. 45
Prutting, C. A. 38–9

Quick, J. C. 227
Quick, J. D. 227

Rabia 243
Rabinowitz, A. 243
Rahman, F. 160

Rampton, B. 90–1
Raskin, J. D. 146
Redmond, K. 36
Regan, J. 124
Reik, T. 208
Reitzes, P. 54
Remen, R. N. 230, 238–40
Repper, J. M. 124, 128, 130
Reynolds, D. 190
Reynolds, F 22, 28, 31, 33, 45
Reynolds, L. 230
Reynolds, N. R. 106, 108
Rice, R. L. 219, 226
Riensche, L. 117
Riessman, C. 37
Ripich, D. 38–9
Rittman, M. 24, 30
Roberts, C. 61, 80–1, 91
Robillard, A. 17, 93, 96–8
Robinson, J. D. 58, 135
Rogers, C. R. 18, 55
Rogers, W. H. 46
Rose, D. 71, 80
Ross, E. 173, 215, 218–23, 227
Rowan, J. 17
Rumi 232, 236, 239
Rushton, A. 215
Ryder, M. 120
Ryu, S. 184

Sacks, H. 39, 72, 95
Sadow, D. 120
Safran, D. G. 46
St. John of the Cross 232
Santhanam, G. 184
Sarangi, S. 61
Sargeant, M. 108, 116
Sarno, M. T. 44
Scheetz, N. 111, 115
Schegloff, E. A. 39, 68, 71–2
Schegloff, S. 95
Schildknecht, C. 157
Schleidt, W. M. 10
Schmidt, B. 117
Schneider, J. 238
Schön, D. A. 24, 202
Schultz, M. 38–9
Schulz, E. K. 230, 237–8
Schulze, B. 108
Schum, R. L. 54, 59–60

Scollon, R. 81, 86
Scollon, S. 81, 86
Seeman, M. 12, 15
Segal, R. A. 241–2
Seibel, N. L. 197
Seligman, L. 128–30
Seligman, S. 199, 202, 204
Selye, H. 215
Shadden, B. 47
Shadden, B. B. 22–3, 28, 30
Shah Mazhar, H. 160
Shahmoon-Shanok, R. 197–8, 200, 205, 210
Shankland, M. 47
Shapiro, V. 198
Shaw, A. 38, 45
Sheafor, B. W. 218
Shenoy, K. 184
Shernoff, M. 225
Sherratt, S. 47, 74
Shipley, K. G. 141
Shi-xu 79, 92
Siegel, D. 207, 209
Siegel, D. J. 207
Siegel, S. 188
Silvast, M. 38
Silverman, D. 43, 45, 57, 100, 273
Silverman, E.-M. 184–5, 187–92, 229
Silverstein, J. 38
Simmons-Mackie, N. 37–9, 40–47, 49–50, 57, 63, 74, 127, 153
Sinclair, J. 39, 61
Sipiora, P. 189
Slade, A. 199
Slade, D. 123, 273
Smart, J. 106–7, 111–13, 115–18, 120
Smith, D. L. 170–2, 177
Smith, J. A. 45
Smith, N. 90–1, 97–9
Smith, N. D. 184
Sobell, L. C. 116
Sodeberg, S. 45
Somerville, M. A. 106, 108
Sontag, S. 24
Sowman, R. 124
Spillers, C. S. 10, 15, 17, 20, 187, 229–30, 235–8, 240, 242

Stapp, H. 187
Stein, R. 117
Steiner, C. 183, 185
Stephens, T. 117
Stern, D. N. 207
Stewart, I. 171
Stewart, M. 46
Stewart, T. 140
Stott, F. M. 197–8, 207
Strainchamps, A. 241–2
Street, R. 50
Strohmer, D. C. 116
Strong, P. M. 40
Stubbe, M. 80
Surette, J. 235–6
Swain, J. 22–3, 28, 30–1, 33
Swidler, M. 218, 221–2, 227
Swimme, B. 234–6

Taira, D. A. 46
Tandon, R. 124
Tannen, D. 93, 95, 101, 126–8
Tantum, D. 170
Target, M. 205
Tarlov, A. R. 46
Tassin, M. S. 222
Tatham, A. 213, 222
Taylor, R. R. 199–200
Tedesco, L. A. 148
Terrell, B. 80
Terrell, F. 80
Tetnowski, J. 38
Thomas, C. 23, 26, 30
Thomas, J. 221
Threats, T. 99
Tillich, P. 235
Todd, A. D. 61
Togher, L. 37–8, 40, 46
Tolle, E. 185
Twining, J. E. 14, 16

Umen, I. 38–9

Vajak, J. 74
Van der Gaag, A. 24
van Dijk, T. A. 91
Van Puymbroeck, M. 24, 30
Van Riper, C. 12, 54
Van Tellingen, C. 158
Vincent, J. 179

Volz, H. B. 77
von Franz, M. L. 183, 190, 192

Walker, M. L. 60
Wallach Bologh, R. 12
Wallat, C. 93
Walsh, I. 57, 61–2, 100, 103
Walsh, I. P. 44, 57–8, 61, 63, 101, 124, 127, 131, 134
Walsh-Brennan, I. P. 61
Wang, J. 94
Ward, L. M. 199
Ware, J. E. 46
Warner, J. 54–5
Warren, A. 100
Watkins, P. 125, 131, 136
Webster, D. 120
Webster, E. J. 199
Wehtje-Winslow, B. J. 231

Weinbach, R. W. 227
Weitzman, E. 199
West, C. 95
Weston, D. R. 197–8, 204, 209–10
Weston, W. W. 46
White, M. 23–4, 26–8, 31, 33, 140–3, 147, 150
Whitehorn, J. C. 18
Whitehouse, A. J. O. 213, 220, 223
Whitman, W. 9–10
Wieder, S. 199–200
Wierzbicka, A. 81
Wilcox, J. 76
Wilkinson, R. 37
Williamson, G. G. 197–8
Wilson, J. 134, 136
Wilson, M. 80
Winnicott, D. W. 208
Winslade, J. 142, 146
Winslow, G. R. 231

Wodak, R. 102
Wolter, J. A. 140
Wood, M. 241–2
Woolf, C. 49
Woollams, S. 185, 187
World Health Organization 18, 97
Worrall, L. 40, 47
Wulf, H. H. 60
Wyatt, T. 80

Yalom, I. 9, 235–6
Yalom, I. D. 170
Yardley, L. 23
Young, L. 71
Young, M. 24, 30
Young-Eisendrath, P. 231, 237, 239–40, 242
Younger, J. B. 13–14, 16–17, 239–40
Yu, B. 184

Zobel Nichols, N. 126–7

Subject index

Note: Page numbers in *italics* refer to figures; those in **bold** to tables.

abstraction, the alienated individual as an 11–12, 18
adaptive challenges 148–9, 152
adults, case history interviews 71–2
Aesculius 159
affect
 attunement 207
 regulation of 205
affirmations 7
age 103
alienation 9–20
 definition of 16
alphabet board 96
American Sign Language 112
American Speech-Language Hearing Association (ASHA) 229
 Honors of 120–1
Americans with Disabilities Act (ADA) 119
anamnesis 157
anxiety
 constructivist view of 145
 disorder 124
 holding (allaying) of 175
aphasia 13–14, 21, 23, 27
 and assisted communication 71–2
 and engagement 127
 group therapy for 74–6
 session plan for 57
aphonia, inner 17
Aristophanes 121
Aristotle 121
Asclepiuos 155, 156, 163–4
audiologists
 combating stigma by 105–21

ignorance about professional stigmatization 109
paternalism by 111
audiology, burnout and self-care in practice 213–28
audists 113
paternalism of 111
autism 116, 175–7, 238
autoethnography 97
Avicenna 57–8, 159–60, 163–5
awareness, processes out of 203–5

beliefs
 importance of 184
 professed 185
 see also core beliefs
Bell, Alexander Graham 111
Berne, Eric 182
bipolar disorder 124–5
Bouillaud, Jean Baptiste 160–1, 163–4
boundaries, maintenance of 205
brief therapy, solution-focussed 28
burnout 8, 188
 definition of 215–17
 development of 216
 ecological approach to 218–21
 effects of 217
 and gender 219
 in the practice of speech pathology and audiology 213–28
 prevention of 223–7
 stressors in
  family 219–20
  individual and personal 218–19
  sociocultural 221
  work 220–1
 symptoms of 216–17

cancer, pancreatic 178
careers, loss of 45
case histories
    diagnosing beyond the 141–2
    multiparty interviews in 69–73
case studies
    Adam 99
    AH 41
    Alfred 14
    Alfred (and wife Wilma) 71–3
    Alonso 233–4, *234*, 235–9, 243
    aphasia therapy group 74–6
    aphasic priest 161–2
    Brad (and parent Mary) 69–70
    CD 54
    Clare (partner of Jeremy) 174–5
    David 27
    DM 47–8
    Eleanor 29
    Gerald 178–9
    Giles and Joe 180
    Ian 15
    Jack 14
    Maeve 29–30
    Maureen 13
    mute man 161
    mute woman 161
    Nafi 195–6, 201–2, 204–11
    Pat 21, 33–4
    Peg 45
    Priscilla 14–15
    Richard 27
    Robbie 61
    Sister Edna 187–8
    Terry 213–14, 216–17, 219
    Toby's parents 175–7
    Veronica 11–13, 15, 19–20
challenges, adaptive 148–9, 152
change 238
    tracking of 30–1
childhood pattern *see* infantile prototype
children
    case histories of 69–71
    modification of wording for 71
civil rights, and stigmatization 106
clients
    attending to stories of 21–34
    and balance of institutional
        encounters 95–9
    and balance of power 98–9
    constructivist framework for
        counseling of 140–7
    as experts 141
    focussing on 1–165

hearing the stories of 25–8
    power and institutional control of
        93–5
    rapport with clinicians 53–65
    spiritual work of 240–3
    see also patients
clinical burnout *see* burnout
clinical encounters, lived experience of
        communication in 96–9
clinical interaction 35–6
    analysis of 37–46
    awareness of power in 49
    as context 40–3
    depictions of rapport during 53–65,
        101–2
    and discourse 43–4
    and evidence 46–7
    gender in 93–104
    multiparty 67–77
    narrative-based approach to 46–54
    and negotiation of identity 44–6
    power balance in 61–2, 93–104
    social construction of relationships in
        153–65
    styles of 38–40
clinical linguistic proficiency 67–77
clinical practice
    50-year perspective on 3–8
    cross-cultural contexts in 79–81
    implication of transference for 181–2
    models of 23, 99, 111, 153
    narrative-based 36–7
    self-reflection in 183–93
    see also practice
clinical relationships
    managing transference in 173–9
    spiritual dimension of 225, 229–43
clinicians
    client-centered 146, 148
    cultural incompetence of 84–5
    focussing on 167–243
    learning to be professional 100–3
    overcoming barriers to counseling
        139–52
    potential for transference by 179–80
    rapport with clients 53–65
    therapeutic procedure for 189–90
    transferential considerations for 180–1
    using the self as vehicle for change
        195–212
    see also therapists
clues, to unique outcomes 143
co-construction 146–7
collaboration, in service delivery 6–7

color blindness 90–1
communication
 breakdowns in 208
 disinhibition in 62
 lived experience of 96–9
 loss of 9
 problems in 96
  "not now" 96–7
  "out of context" 97
communication accommodation 68
communication disorder
 quantification of 18
 simulation exercises 115–16
 and stigma 105–21
communion 236–7, 239
compassion fatigue *see* burnout
competence, and client identity 45
connection, loss of 10
construct system 145
constructivism
 and adaptive leadership 139–52
 definition of 141
construing, alternative ways of 142–3
consumption 154–5
containing 208–9
content, culturally informed reading of
  90–1
context
 clinical interaction as 40–3
 cross-cultural 79–92
control, institutional 93–5
conversation
 analysis 68–9
 externalizing *29–30*
 facilitation of 74
core beliefs
 personal identification of 184–5
 tool for accessing 188–9
counseling
 adaptive leadership as model for
  enacting 150–1
 constructivist framework for 140–7,
  149
 goal of 5
 for hearing loss 4
 ignorance of aspects requiring 152
 lack of knowledge of techniques 151–2
 overcoming barriers to 139–52
 timing and scheduling of 152
counter-transference 171–2, 197, 203–5,
  224
country of origin 86–7
courtesy stigma *see* stigma-by-
  association

credos 185
Cronkite, Walter 183
cross-cultural context 79–92
cross-cultural discourse 82–9
cross-cultural training 115
cultural diversity, and speech-language
  therapy 79
culture
 awareness 90
 issues of 82–3, **83**
curious questioning 141–2, 152

Darwin, Charles 171
data collection 150–1
delusions 131, 160
demoralization 15–16
 hypothesis of 15
dependency 112–13
depersonalization 11, 216
developmental, individual differences,
  relationship-based (DIR) model
  199
diagnosis
 beyond case histories 141–2
 rejection of 35
dialogue
 and common purpose 17–19
 loss of 16–17
 therapeutic 9–20
difference
 and discrimination 80, 91
 and power 80
differentiation 235, 237, 239
dignity, battle for 99
disability 239–40
 and degrees of stigmatization 107
 and grief 3
 models of 23, 99, 111, 153
 and spirituality 237–8
disconnection 16–17
discourse 35–52
 and clinical interaction 43–4
 cross-cultural 82–9
 lay versus expert 88–9
 manifestation of power in 101
 markers of context in 40–1
 markers of 101–2
 roles in 81–2
 utilitarian 86
discourse analysis 91, 100
discourse attuning 134
discrimination, and difference 80, 91
disempowerment 41
documentation 30–1

dominance 91
dominant culture 92
Down syndrome 99
dress, as marker of context 41
dysarthria 14, 169
dysphagia 15
    and engagement 127

Einstein, Albert 184–5, 229
embarrassment 12–15
emotional exhaustion 216
emotional state, perils of ignoring 4
empathic genuineness 55
empathy 54, 207–8
engagement 126–8
epilepsy 160
evidence
    and clinical interaction 46–7
    measurable and documentable 31
expectations, unfounded 42
experience-near definition, negotiation
        of 27
experimenting 151
    with alternative interpretations
        144–5
exploration 151
extended repair sequences 39
externalizing 143–4

families
    as client 199
    constructivist framework for
        counseling of 140–7
    involvement in service delivery 6–7
fear, constructivist view of 145
feelings
    dispersal of 206
    management of 205–7
Frame, Janet 125
frameworks, social and medical 23, 99,
        111, 153
framing 101
Frankl, Viktor 184–5
Freud, Sigmund 123, 170, 189

gender 103
    and burnout 219
    in clinical encounters 93–104
    and stress 219
genuineness 55
getting on the balcony 150–1
gladdening influences (of Avicenna) 58,
        159–60
goals, clinical 200

grief
    not a pathology 3
    response 230
grieving 238–9
group interaction *see* multiparty
        interactions
group therapy 73–6, 97–8
guilt, constructivist view of 145–6

hallucinations 131–3
Hanen Center 199
happiness, and doing well 183–4
hardiness 237
healing interactions 154
    in ancient times 154–9, 163
    in medieval times 159–60, 163
    in the nineteenth century 160–3
    social construction of relationships in
        153–65
health practices, Babylonian 154
hearing aid effect 117
hearing loss, counseling for 4
helplessness, and over-helping 5–6
Herodotus 121, 154, 163
hidden wholeness 235–6
Hippocrates of Cos 156–8, 163, 190
HIV/AIDS, and stigmatization 106, 108,
        120
holding 208–9
hostility, constructivist view of 146
humor 224
    and engagement 134–6
    in therapy 36–7, 39
    use in group therapy 74

Ibn Sina *see* Avicenna
idealization, positive 174–5
identity
    acknowledgement and
        accommodation of 49–50
    destruction of 49
    loss of 12–15
    negative 45
    negotiation of 44–6
illness
    focus on 11
    mapping the territory of 24
    social meaning of 22–3
immune system 12
inadequacy, feelings of 6
incompetence, and client identity 44
individuation 239
infantile prototype 170
infantilization 118–19

infants, as transference objects 198
inquiry, versus interrogation 209
institutional enculturation 42
institutional interactions, goal-
orientation of 94
interest, commonality of 60
interiority 235–7
International Classification of Function
(ICF) 18, 97
interpretation, alternative types of 142–3
interpretive competence 134
interrogation, versus inquiry 209
interruptions, supportive and
nonsupportive 95
intersubjectivity 201
intervention, relationship-based,
underlying premise of 201
invisibility, sense of 14
involvement strategies 127
iterative model of adaptive leadership
150

jargon, use by health professionals 41
job dissatisfaction 188
John F. Kennedy School of Government,
Harvard University 147
Jung, Carl Gustav 189

Keller, Helen 112–13
Klein, Melanie 172

labeling 116–17
language
issues of 82–3, **83**, 85–7
metaphoric journey 240
latent processes 203–5
leadership
adaptive 139–52, **149**
definition of 148
iterative model of *150*
as model for enacting counseling
150–1
and therapeutic processes 148–50
therapy as an act of 147–51
learning
relationship-based 201–2
two-fold process of 202
Lidcombe Program 77
listening
as clinical tool 5
deep 7
importance of 22, 51
interested 152
with the third ear 208

loneliness 17, 238
Lordat, Jaques 161–5
loss, recognition of 145–6

Maguire, Tobey 188
marginalization 113–14
master status 115
meaning, crisis of 230, 237
meaningfulness 231
melancholia 160
mental health disorders
and relationship building 125–6
and therapeutic relationships 124–5
working along with 123–37
mental illness, and stigmatization 108,
120
Merton, Thomas 235
mindfulness 25, 33
mindsight *see* theory of mind
Miracle Worker, The 112
mistakes, clinical 7
motor neuron disease 96
multiparty case-history interview 69–73
multiparty interactions 68–73
management of 67–77
multiple sclerosis 178
mutism, elective 155
mutuality 60
mythology 240–1

narrative 35–52
analyzing mismatches in 47–8
application of 24–31
medicine 191
public 23
therapy 100, 140
narratives, personal 142
National Stuttering Association 243
negative capability 205–6
neuroimmunology 12
next turn other repair 72
Nin, Anaïs 192
Norden, Shelley *234*

organists 160
otherness, cultural discourse of 79
out of awareness processes 203–5
outcomes, unique 27–8, 143

pain, nature of 158
paradise, the search for 241–2
Parkinson's disease 14
passing 117–18
paternalism 110–11

patience 55
patients
   battle for dignity of 99
   see also clients
pauses, inter-turn 133–4
people with communication disorders
      (PWCD) 109
   combating stigma in 110–21
personal accomplishment, reduced 216
personal change 190
personal construct theory (PCT) 140
personal core beliefs, identification of
      184–5
perspective, strength-based 210
phenomenology, disregard of 11
philosophy, personal 225
Plato 121, 157–9, 163–4
playfulness, and engagement 134–6
pluralis hospitalis 102
politeness 83
   forms of 81
   framework for 101
   theory 103
power
   in clinical encounters 93–104
   clinician-controlled 94
   and difference 80
   inherence of 94
practice
   evidence-based 4
   implication of transference for 181–2
   models of 23, 99, 111, 153
   narrative-based 23–4, 28
      strategies for achievement of 51
   oscillating processes in *25*
   relational and reflective 195–212
      see also reflective practice
   self-reflection in 183–93
   shaping of 21–34
   see also clinical practice
presencing 130–1
   via silence 130–4
problems
   externalization of 26–7
   ownership of 5
   technical 148–9, 152
process
   out of awareness or latent 203–5
   parallel 209
   rapport as 56–63
productive performance 134
professional, learning to "do" 100–3
professional growth 192
projective identification 172–3

pronunciation, issues of 84
psychotherapy 17

questions
   ability to ask 68
   standard case history 141
   yes/no 94

racism 90–1
rapport
   building 101–2
   co-construction of 58
   depictions of 53–65
   as process 56–63, **64**
   as product 54, **64**
reflection-in-action 202
reflection-on-action 202
reflective capacity 199
reflective functioning 202, 207
reflective practice, development of 202–3
reframing 210
rehabilitation counseling 60
relationship 231
relationship building
   and mental health disorders 125–6
   therapeutic processes in 126–36
relationships 35–52
   intersubjective aspects of 201
   latent or hidden dimensions of 197,
      203
   social construction of 153–65
   in speech-language therapy 123–37
religion, differentiation from spirituality
      231–2
repair trajectories 72
repetition, and engagement 127–8
request–response–evaluation (RRE)
      sequence 38–9
rescue fantasy 179
rescuing 112
resilience 237
Rufus of Ephesus 157–8, 163–4

sadness, projection of 178
safety, fear for 120
same turn other repair 72
scapegoating 114–15
schizophrenia 58–9, 124–7, 130–1
scrutinization 119
Seabiscuit 188
self
   professional use of 195–212
      benefits and challenges in 211–12
      a brief history 198–200

developing capacities for 207–10
  key constructs in 201–7
self-awareness 211–12
  cultural 92
self-care
  in clinical work 7–8
  in the practice of speech pathology
    and audiology 213–28
self-disclosure, and engagement 128–30
self-esteem, of clients 6
self-estrangement 14–15
self-identity, crisis of 9
self-initiated other repair 72
self-knowledge 183–9
self-narratives, alternate 142–3
self-reflection 189–93, 212
  in clinical practice 183–93
  finding time for 192–3
  and self-denigration 192
self-regulation 205–7, 212
serenity, of clinician 55
service delivery, family-centered model of
  6–7
service users, silencing of perspectives of
  94–5
shading 117–18
shared perspectives 60
silence, presencing via 130–4
small talk, use in therapy 44, 57
social control, and stigmatization 110–15
social receding 12–15
society, stigmatization by 105
Socrates 157, 165, 183
solution, technical 151
soul 232–3
speaking about 71
speaking for 71
speaking help 71
speech, as marker of context 41
speech pathology, burnout and self-care
  in practice 213–28
speech-language pathologists
  authoritarian practices of 190–1
  as collaborative partner 200
  ignorance about professional
    stigmatization 109
  paternalism by 111
  rescuing and dependency 112
speech-language pathology, burnout in
  221–3
speech-language therapists, combating
  stigma by 105–21
speech-language therapy
  clinical interaction in 35–52

and cultural diversity 79
educational programs in 92
establishing relationships in 123–37
goals of 16
information gathering in 100–2
the transference relationship in 169–82
spiritualists 160
spirituality 225, 229–43
  definition of 231–3
  differentiation from religion 231–2
  and disability 237–8
  personal dimensions of 234–9
  reasons for 230–1
stereotyping 115–16, 146
stigma
  and civil rights 106
  combating of 105–21
  definition of 101–8
  three components of 110
    affective 120–1
    behavioral 110–15
    cognitive 115–19
  various degrees of 107
stigma-by-association 120–1
stigmatization
  professional 108–9
  and social control 110
stories
  the benefits of really attending to *32*
  listening *for* 26, 31
stress 213
  audit 223
  definition of 214–15
  diary 223
  ecological approach to 218–21
  and gender 219
  management 218, 223–7
    family interventions 225–6
    individual interventions 223–5
    societal interventions 226–7
    value in health promotion 227
    work interventions 226
stressors
  family 219–20
  individual and personal 218–19
  sociocultural 221–2
  work 220–2
stroke 9, 13–14, 23, 27, 29, 161–2
  mild 35
stuttering 48, 54, 101–2, 144, 233, 235–6,
  238–9
  child 69
  relapse in 145–6
suffering 239–40

suicide, thoughts of 9
Sullivan, Annie 112–13
supervision 203
    reflective 209
support groups, as clinical vehicle 6
sympathy 53–4
systemic functional linguistics 68–9

talk
    gender variations in 103
    sociorelational frame of 101
test questions 39
theory of mind 207–8
therapeutic actions (TAs) 19
therapeutic alliance 201
therapeutic emplotment 36
therapeutic processes
    and adaptive leadership 148–50
    challenges to 79–92
    in relationship building 126–36
therapeutic qualities (TQs) 19
therapeutic relationships 19–20, 31, 200,
    242–3
    and mental health disorders 124–5
therapeutic stance 141
therapists
    and balance of power 98–9
    combating stigma by 105–21
    ideal characteristics of 55
    using the self as vehicle for change
        195–212
    see also clinicians
therapy 28–30
    as an act of leadership 147–51
    characteristics of 36–7
    client-centered 40
    clinician-centered 38–40
    as collaborative activity 36
    disengagement from 47

impairment-focussed 38
narrative-based 100, 140
relationship-centered 50–1
repair (correction) in 39
use of small talk in 44, 57, 101–2
threat, constructivist view of 145
time, importance in consultations 21–2
togetherness, being at home in 10
transactional analysis 170, 182, 190–1
transcendent meaning 236
transcription conventions 273–4
transference *171*, 197, 203–4
    by clinicians 179–80
        important considerations 180–1
    definition of 170
    managing in clinical relationships
        173–9
    positive idealization 174–5
    relationship 169–73
        in speech-language therapy
            169–82
traumatic brain injury, and engagement
    127
troubles-telling 58
trust 59–60

unconditional positive regard 55
unique outcomes 27–8, 143
universe, primal principles of 234–7
utilitarian discourse 86

values, commonality of 60
verbosity 169
visualizations 185–8

well-being, physical 225
Wizard of Oz 241–2

Yolngu Aboriginal group 81